SAVING
America?

SAVING

America?

Faith-Based Services

and the Future of

Civil Society

ROBERT WUTHNOW

PRINCETON UNIVERSITY PRESS

Princeton and Oxford

LIBRARY OF CONGRESS CATALOGING-IN-PUBLICATION DATA

Wuthnow, Robert.

Saving America? : faith-based services and the future of civil society / Robert Wuthnow.

p. cm.

Includes bibliographical references (p.) and index.

ISBN: 0-691-11926-0 (cloth : alk. paper)

1. Church charities—United States. 2. Church and social problems—United States. 3. Social service—United States—Religious aspects. 4. Church work with the poor—United States. 5. Civil society—United States. 6. Federal aid to human services—United States. I. Title.

HV530.W885 2004

361.7'5'0973—dc22 2003066360

British Library Cataloging-in-Publication Data is available

This book has been composed in Adobe Garamond and Helvetica

Printed on acid-free paper. ∞

www.pupress.princeton.edu

Printed in the United States of America

10 9 8 7 6 5 4 3 2 1

CONTENTS

TABLES

I have to confess that I decided to write this book because of exasperation with the lack of understanding about religion that is so frequently evident among policy makers and journalists. Public officials who make pronouncements about faith-based social services rarely show that they have the slightest understanding of how religious organizations actually function in our society, other than being able to recount a few anecdotes. They simply think religion is a good thing and thus should be supported, and they figure government is the way to support it. Others oppose such support on principle. They appear to know equally little about how religion works, except perhaps from limited personal experience, contending that if something goes under the name of religion then it surely must be kept out of the policy arena.

Policy analysts in academic institutions have seldom taken the time to acquaint themselves with the relevant facts, either. Trained in economics or used to dealing with operations management or environmental risk assessments, they approach religion as if it could be understood in the same way as census data or national income projections. They retreat in horror when the data are not conclusive, scratching their heads about why any serious scholar would dive into such murky waters in the first place. The few who do venture into these waters focus on the occasional case study or legal controversy and provide little insight into the larger picture.

All this is curious because much of social science in the past thirty years has been driven by policy interests. During the 1950s and early 1960s, the social sciences were deeply concerned with emulating the natural sciences and thus expended a great deal of energy proposing abstract theoretical models of human behavior and initiating research oriented toward theory-building. By the end of the 1960s, that positivistic paradigm was beginning

to be questioned. A younger generation of scholars was attracted to the social sciences because of such real-world concerns as the Vietnam war, cam-
pus unrest, the civil rights movement, and postcolonial movements for
independence and economic development in many parts of the developing
world. As the plausibility of the positivistic paradigm has waned, policy-
oriented research has become increasingly attractive. Indeed, even research
published in general disciplinary journals and oriented closely toward
scholarly debates is often driven by such practical concerns as formulating
income-maintenance policies, dealing with the incarcerated population, or
understanding the role of media in policy discussions. Despite all this, it is
nevertheless possible to hear serious scholars say that the study of religion
is so marginal to the social sciences that students really need to know little
about it or, if they are interested, can learn all they need to know in a few
afternoons from nonspecialists.

In reality, the situation is far different. Serious scholarly studies of reli-
gion in the social sciences date to the very beginning of these disciplines.
In sociology, for instance, Karl Marx, Max Weber, and Emile Durkheim all
wrote extensively about religion. Before their contributions became dominant in American sociology, other leading scholars, such as Robert Park,
William James, and H. Paul Douglass, also dealt extensively with religion.
After World War II, many of the discipline's leading contributors—Talcott
Parsons, Pitirim Sorokin, Gerhard Lenski, Peter Berger, and Robert Bellah,
among others—continued to be seriously interested in religion. More important, empirical studies in the social sciences increasingly focused on religion, often combining quantitative and qualitative research. By the 1990s,
more than five hundred sociologists alone listed their primary specialties as
sociology of religion, and in psychology, political science, and anthropol-
ogy growing numbers also focused on religion.

There is thus a well-established tradition of research on which to base
discussions of faith-based social services. This research provides vital background information about the nature of congregations, how they are
organized, what programs they sponsor, how they enlist and motivate
volunteers, and how they interact with other organizations in the community. It supplies concepts for thinking about the distinctive aspects of faith-
based organizations and why they may or may not be effective. Some of
this research is local and qualitative, but much of it is national and quantitative. As more specialized studies of the activities and controversies sur-

rounding specific faith-based service organizations are now emerging, this larger body of research needs to be reconsidered for the basic information it provides about the role of American religion in delivering social services.

I began studying the role of religion in the service sector in the late 1980s. At the time, there was growing interest in understanding how the so-called independent or nonprofit sector was functioning in relation to and sometimes against the activities of the market economy and the government sector. Religion was a huge part of the nonprofit sector, yet it had been almost totally ignored by specialists in nonprofit organizational studies. My edited volume *Between States and Markets: The Voluntary Sector in Comparative Perspective* and my book *Acts of Compassion: Caring for Others and Helping Ourselves* (both published in 1991) were among the first systematic attempts to examine the relationship between religion and service provision within the nonprofit sector. I followed these books with a book-length study of community service and volunteering among teenagers— *Learning to Care: Elementary Kindness in an Age of Indifference* (published in 1995)—which further examined religious and humanitarian motives for engaging in service activities. About the same time, the larger questions about civil society that had been posed in the nineteenth century by Alexis de Tocqueville, among others, were being revisited by a number of social scientists as a result of the new democracies coming into existence in Eastern Europe after the collapse of the Soviet Union and in conjunction with evidence of declining civic engagement in the United States. My books *Loose Connections: Joining Together in America's Fragmented Communities* (published in 1998) and *Christianity and Civil Society: The Contemporary Debate* (published in 1996) sought to systematically examine the relationships among religion, civic involvement, volunteering, trust, and concepts of citizenship in relation to these larger discussions of the changing character of civil society in the United States.

Saving America? Faith-Based Services and the Future of Civil Society brings additional evidence to bear on the contemporary discussion of faith-based service initiatives from three national studies I have conducted in the past few years and from an extensive study of the service agencies in one community. The national studies are the Civic Involvement Survey, which I conducted in 1997 among a representative sample of approximately 1,500 adults; the Small Groups Survey, which I conducted in 1999 among a representative sample of approximately 1,300 adults; and the Religion and

Politics Survey, which I conducted in 2000 among a representative sample of approximately 5,600 adults. The community study was conducted in the Lehigh Valley in northeastern Pennsylvania—a community that resembles many other smaller metropolitan areas throughout the United States—between 1995 and 2003. It involved a representative survey of more than two thousand households in low-income neighborhoods, in-depth qualitative interviews with more than one hundred clients of service agencies, in-depth qualitative interviews with more than one hundred volunteers at service agencies in the community, two waves of interviews with randomly selected clergy, and three waves of interviews with agency directors. I also provide newly analyzed results from a half-dozen other recently completed national surveys that were conducted by other social scientists. Although these data cannot possibly address questions such as how a specific church in East Los Angeles may be serving its community or how a prison ministry in Iowa may be responding to legal issues, the information provided by the studies I summarize in this volume tell us much more about the ways in which congregations actually help their members, what their strengths and limitations are, which ones are most actively engaged, how specialized faith-based service organizations differ from congregations, how faith is expressed in these organizations, the kinds of clients who seek assistance from different organizations, and how the recipients of services think about trust and the compassion they experience than any other source presently available.

The debate about faith-based social services has been highly partisan and highly politicized. Yet policy makers on both sides of the debate make assumptions about the extent of religious involvement in service provision, how this involvement is organized, and why it is or is not effective. Those are the questions I address in this book. I show that many of the common assumptions about faith-based service provision are wrong. For instance, I show that congregations, despite being more numerous, are less important than more specialized faith-based service organizations as service providers. I show that the most extensive ways in which congregations provide services do not occur through the formal programs on which most discussion has focused but through the informal activities—the fellowship circles, Bible studies, classes, and worship services—that constitute what congregations themselves refer to as the "caring community." I show that the special role of congregations in mobilizing volunteers probably lies less in sheer numbers than most observers have thought and more in the quality and scope of those volunteers' relationships with other community organizations. I show that the faith-based service organizations that are most effective *are* effective for reasons that probably disqualify them from receiving government funding, at least under prevailing understandings of the separation of church and state. I show that the perceptions of recipients are often quite different from those of agency directors and volunteers. And I show that faith-based services do contribute positively to the *cultural* norms undergirding civil society, especially by reinforcing trust, but that they communicate ideals of unconditional love far less often than might be supposed from thinking about these ideals only within the context of religious teachings.

None of these results suggests that faith-based initiatives emanating from Washington should be scrapped. But they do underscore the gap that often exists between political rhetoric and local realities. The faith-based organizations that politicians often point to as reasons for expanding government support are often the exception rather than the rule. What congregations do best generally cannot be replaced by or even reinforced through government support. Yet there is considerable evidence to suggest that specialized faith-based service agencies function *just as well* as nonsectarian agencies and, for this reason, should not be discriminated against in receiving government support.

The larger questions about civil society go well beyond the present policy discussions of faith-based service provision and will endure long after government officials and the media have moved on to other topics. Other studies have examined the contribution of religious organizations and religiously motivated people to voting and to other forms of political participation and to the development of civic skills. But our understanding of religion's role in civil society has been limited largely to studies of middle-class people or at least to activities that mainly serve the middle class. At the same time, we know that civil society must take serious account of inequality if it is to be strong, and we know that opportunities for civic engagement are often severely restricted for lower-income families. Examining the contribution of religion to faith-based services for the needy is thus a way to cast the discussion of civil society in a new light. We are able to see especially whether faith-based organizations build bridges between the privileged and the disadvantaged segments of society and, if so, how these bridges may be strengthened.

The research for this volume was supported by grants from The Pew Charitable Trusts, the Lilly Endowment, the Russell Sage Foundation, the Templeton Foundation, the Fetzer Institute, the Institute for Research on Unlimited Love, and the Aspen Institute. I wish to thank the staff at those foundations for their support of this research. The surveys were conducted by the Gallup Organization in Princeton and by Schulman, Ronca & Bucuvalas Inc. in New York. Natalie Searl and her staff at Academic Research Services conducted most of the in-depth qualitative interviews. Karen Myers also assisted with the interviewing and transcribing. Rebekah Peoples Massengill provided bibliographic assistance and helped connect the arguments more closely with the recent scholarly literature. Joan M. Cundey graciously shared her 2003 Princeton University senior thesis, "Religion and Politics Today: The Role of Faith-Based Organizations in America's Welfare System," which alerted me to several recent studies I would otherwise have missed. Conrad Hackett and Becky Yang Hsu assisted with the bibliography and with analyzing the quantitative data from the Lehigh Valley and are currently engaged in additional research based on those data. Joan Walling helped analyze the qualitative data on trust and perceptions of caregivers' motives, and her forthcoming dissertation will discuss these data in greater detail. I am also especially grateful to the many agency directors, clergy, and volunteers who gave of their time to help me better understand and write about the important frontline service work they do so faithfully and effectively in their communities.

SAVING
America?

Why "Faith-Based"? Why Now?

The question of faith-based social services emerged as a major policy debate in the waning months of the twentieth century. The debate started in the mid-1990s as part of the Clinton administration's efforts to reform the social welfare system. The resulting 1996 welfare reform legislation included a provision known as Charitable Choice. This provision made it possible for churches and other religiously oriented service organizations to receive government funds more easily. As a result of this provision, service agencies and government officials started paying more attention to the possible contribution that religious organizations could make to the needs of lower-income families and other disadvantaged or at-risk persons. During the 2000 presidential campaign, the discussion intensified. The Bush administration subsequently set in motion a number of initiatives to further highlight and support the role of religious organizations in social welfare provision.

The questions raised by the debate about faith-based social welfare provision focus chiefly on what faith-based organizations are doing, how well they are doing it, and whether their activities should be supported with government funds. Few solid answers have been given. The more researchers have tackled these questions, the more they have come to realize that important conceptual and empirical issues must be addressed before definitive answers will be forthcoming. We need to know more clearly what we mean when we talk about "faith-based" organizations. We need to know what the relevant comparison groups are. And we need to be clear about how we are assessing organizations' effectiveness in carrying out their programs.

The recent discussion about faith-based social services, though, is part of a larger debate about the future of civil society in the United States. That debate focuses on the quality of our life together as citizens. It concerns whether the American public is willing to do its part to help one another and it includes questions about the role of trust and compassion in public life. Above all, it is a debate about inequality: whether civil society only works well for the affluent middle class or whether it also works well for lower-income families. Religion is an important part of this debate. The United States has ten times as many houses of worship as it does post offices. Far more people participate in religious organizations each week than in any other civic association. Nearly all Americans attest to believing in the supernatural and at least five of every six Americans claim to have a religious preference. Religion is increasingly being looked to by public officials to help solve community problems. Possible remedies for poverty, crime, drug abuse, homelessness, and many other social concerns have been linked to faith communities. Yet we have few answers about what religion is actually doing or what it may be capable of doing.

In this volume I present new evidence from more than a half-dozen major research studies that I and others have conducted in recent years. This evidence addresses many of the questions that have remained unanswered about the role of religion in providing social services and in turn contributing to the well-being of civil society. How many local congregations have formal programs to assist needy families in their communities? What kind of programs are these? How much money is spent on them? How well do congregations take care of their own? Do members develop personal relationships that help them in times of trouble? Are they challenged to help others? When people *are* challenged, do they get involved in volunteer activities? What kind of volunteer activities are these? Who is served and what social ties are forged by volunteers? How many specialized faith-based service agencies are there? How are they organized? What role does faith play in them? Which ones are most effective? Do lower-income families have connections with religious organizations? Who seeks help from faith-based organizations? How do they feel about the help they receive? Are religious organizations helping to promote trust? Are they helping to spread messages about love and compassion?

The answers that emerge demonstrate that American religion *is* playing a positive role in addressing the needs of lower-income families and that it is, more broadly, contributing to the strength of civil society. Yet it would be an exaggeration to conclude that religion can save America from the problems it presently faces in providing social services to those who need them most. This is not because those responsibilities must also be shouldered by government and by corporations and by individual taxpayers. Nobody believes that religion alone could take the place of those institutions and efforts. It is rather that religion's role in civil society is very deeply influenced—facilitated but also constrained—by the cultural norms and broader social structures in which it is embedded. In a word, religion is institutionalized. Therein lies its strength. But therein also lie the routinized ways in which it conducts business, the guiding expectations of its clergy and members, and the invisible hand that governs its relations with other community organizations. The research I present here suggests that houses of worship are not organized to provide dramatically more social services than they presently do. Many congregations are so small that they struggle merely to stay in operation at all. Larger congregations seldom devote more than 5 percent of their annual budgets to the support of formal service programs. What congregations do best is provide support for their members and periodic encouragement for them to care for the needy in their communities. Volunteering has been on the rise and it is often more frequent among people of faith than among others; yet we need to be careful about overestimating the impact of this volunteering. Much of it is devoted to staffing the internal programs of congregations rather than connecting them to the wider community. Faith-based service agencies have emerged as the front line of organized religion's involvement in service delivery. Some of these agencies are large, well funded, and quite effective. Many are small and incapable of doing all they would like to do. As we shall see, most do not emphasize faith very much and, with a few exceptions, it is unclear whether emphasizing faith more would be beneficial. Lower-income families do seek help from these agencies and from their congregations. They would have a harder time finding assistance if these organizations did not exist. They especially appreciate their congregations, even though the help they receive there is modest. They do not believe faith-based service agencies are more effective or trustworthy than secular agencies. When religious organizations help people, trust is often one of the most positive results. Trust, however, is much more complex than we generally realize. Spreading messages about love and compassion, too, is one of the important roles of religion. Yet there are cultural understandings of love that bear little resemblance to the ideals of unconditional love found in religious texts, and we are much better as a society at rewarding people for being givers than we are at maintaining the dignity of those who have to depend on the help of others.

Evaluating the contribution of American religion to the well-being of our society is thus a matter of bringing hard facts to bear on a number of difficult questions. It is not enough to say that religion should do more and certainly not enough to say that religion *could* do more if only government larders were opened and fewer restrictions were placed on it. Asking what religious organizations actually do to assist needy families forces us to view religion in a new way. We have to move beyond the commonly reported statistics about how many people attend religious services or how many believe in God. We also have to look further than if we simply wanted to know if a particular prison program works well or if fewer people are on welfare this year than last. It is one thing to tell heart-warming anecdotes about the good programs a particular church or ministry is operating, quite another to gauge systematically what is happening in the larger community or in the nation as a whole. Even information of that kind, though, needs to be considered differently if we are to understand how civil society is being affected by churches and by faith-based service programs. Civil society is about social relationships. Its strength lies in the quality of those relationships: whether they are enduring and supportive, whether they bring diverse groups together, whether they provide assistance when assistance is needed, and whether they make it possible for people to mobilize to achieve their values. These are the larger questions that must be considered. They are far more difficult and, indeed, longer lasting than policy debates about whether particular faith-based initiatives should or should not be expanded. They are questions about the organization of American religion, about how congregations function, and about the activities of specialized agencies and the services they provide.

Answering these questions requires more than summarizing the results of a single research study, as has been customary in scholarly publishing. No single study can address all of these questions. We are fortunate to have several good studies that address some of the relevant questions. These include large national studies that offer generalizations about houses of worship and about the American public. Yet, when these studies are compared, they sometimes yield widely discrepant results. As a first step, therefore, we must pay closer attention to the methods employed in these studies, looking carefully at what was done and whether the results are credible. In addition, we need to make better use of relevant information in surveys and other data sets that have not yet been analyzed. Those sources of information need to be brought to bear on the debate about faith-based service provision.

Bringing Evidence to Bear

This volume presents new and newly analyzed information from a number of recent studies and integrates this information with results that have been published by other researchers. I have conducted three national surveys in recent years that provide a wealth of information about religion and social services. I have also directed a community study over the past decade that has gathered information from the full service delivery system in that community: agency directors, volunteers, clergy, community leaders, and recipients. This information provides insights from hundreds of in-depth qualitative interviews in which people talk in their own words about their experiences and perceptions as clients of service agencies or as volunteers or staff. In addition, I present new information drawn from several other major national surveys.

In considering this information, I am interested in answering questions not only about faith-based services, but also about the larger role of religion in American society. Few observers would deny that religion has a vital place in the United States. We know, for instance, that belief in God, churchgoing, church membership, and the proportion of people who claim religion is important in their lives are all quite high in the United States compared to levels in many other societies, especially in Western Europe.[1] Yet there are mixed views of whether the religious commitment of many Americans makes much difference in their lives and to the wider society. The mixed views about the results of personal faith are relevant to discussions about the role of religion in public life as well. It may be that religion contributes importantly to our society by serving the needy in many ways, both formal and informal. It may also be that religion's role, while valuable, is not as significant as may have been assumed.

The criteria by which researchers usually seek to evaluate American religion range from such simple measures as attendance at religious services to more complex indicators of variation in belief, devotional practice, institutional involvement, leadership, and service.[2] The inclusion of service among these criteria is based on the view that religious teachings generally attach some significance to helping the needy and caring for the disadvantaged. To study congregations' and individuals' service activities is thus a way to determine the extent to which these teachings are being put into practice.

Information about congregations' and individuals' service activities is a useful place to begin in trying to understand the role of faith-based social services in civil society. But it is only a start. Too often that information shows that, yes, congregations and individuals do things voluntarily and of a benevolent nature, but reveals little else. Questions remain about which congregations and individuals do more, why they do, and what exactly they do. The question about what they do is especially important. Much of the volunteering and charitable giving that congregations generate may be directed toward maintaining the congregation itself—paying the clergy and keeping the facilities in good repair. If that is the case, and especially if the congregation is composed of comfortable middle-class families who have few needs they cannot meet themselves, then it is difficult to say that congregations are truly benefitting all segments of civil society, including the most disadvantaged. Alternatively, it may be that congregations' principal form of service is to their members, including people with serious needs, and that this service is far more important than the few specialized programs congregations may help to sponsor. If that were the case, it would cast the present discussion of faith-based service programs in a different light. It would, for instance, suggest that government policies should focus on facilitating the work of congregations, but it would raise difficult questions about how best to do this without violating constitutional guarantees about the separation of church and state. Yet another possibility is that specialized faith-based service agencies are really the major vehicles through which religion contributes to civil society, with congregations playing a supportive role to these agencies behind the scenes. If that were so, government policy might be directed toward these programs, and it might raise fewer questions about separation of church and state, especially if these specialized agencies refrain from attempting to make religious converts. These are alternative possibilities that policy makers seldom take into account.

I shall argue that faith-based social services are a complex array of activities that sometimes work quite well, that often differ little from the activities of nonsectarian organizations, that on the whole contribute positively to the functioning of civil society, and yet that also play a relatively small role in relation to government and other service providers. Faith-based agencies must therefore be understood in terms of their linkages with the larger social networks of which civil society is composed. This is not an argument that can be easily encapsulated in a single phrase or expressed through a vivid anecdote. Faith-based services are like government or families in this respect. We might be titillated by slogans about government being too big or families being in decline, but if we are thoughtful observers of these institutions, we know that the realities are more complex. In the case of religion, congregations *are* a source of formal service programs, but the proportion of congregations that are capable of sponsoring such programs is certainly less than 100 percent and many of these programs exist only because of coalitions among congregations and connections with nonsectarian community agencies. Formal service programs, moreover, are ultimately not what congregations are about. As we shall see, the functioning of congregations is better described as providing a caring community, and congregations work best when people form long-lasting personal friendships and participate in small groups. These informal relationships play an important role in supporting people and in helping them through difficult times. It is hard to assign a dollar value to these ways of helping. At the same time, the relationships in congregations are often homogeneous and may not reach across social status lines very effectively. Intentional volunteering programs sponsored by churches do some of that. Volunteering has been the focus of so much idealistic public rhetoric, though, that we need to take a close look at it to see if people actually volunteer for those most in need of it and, if so, why people volunteer and what kinds of networks are produced by their volunteering. The specialized faith-based service agencies that have attracted so much interest in recent years need to be considered quite distinctly from congregations but also in relation to them. Whether they are large and national in scope, such as Catholic Charities and the Salvation Army, or small and more limited in scope, such as a local food pantry or homeless shelter, these specialized faith-based service agencies have functions different from those of churches, they are usually organized quite differently than churches are, and they are often separately incorporated. The line separating them from nonsectarian service organizations—in which faith is not officially present but may be there informally—is often thin. Yet some of these faith-based organizations are markedly different from the others, and we need to be careful in sorting them out and to exercise caution in generalizing from them.

The missing voices in most discussions of service organizations are the recipients and potential recipients of these organizations. It is easier to study volunteers or clergy or agency directors than it is to track down people in lower-income families and find out what they think, need, and want. There is of course a body of literature about welfare recipients, made possible by government-mandated data collection from welfare agencies.[3] But these studies seldom tell us much about needy families who are not on welfare and they rarely include any information about religion. Recipients are not always in the best position to say whether faith-based service agencies perform effectively, or even if their own long-term needs have been met. They can, however, tell whether they were satisfied with the help they got and whether they felt the caregivers they dealt with were trustworthy. From examining the characteristics of recipients and potential recipients, we can also draw informed conclusions about who seeks assistance from particular kinds of service agencies (faith-based or otherwise), and why they do. In addition, recipients provide an excellent reality check on the information supplied by agency directors and volunteers. Directors may think they do a lot to cultivate trust in clients; clients may see it differently. Similarly, volunteers may think themselves motivated by laudable altruistic values, and yet recipients may feel that strings are attached to the assistance they receive.

Questions about trust, altruism, and perceptions of motives point to the fact that civil society is not composed only of networks and social services. Civil society is importantly composed of culture. Congregations convey messages about caring and the reasons to be concerned for the needy. Volunteers and specialized service agencies convey these messages as well. Through the interaction among agency directors and between caregivers and recipients, relationships of trust are established—at least ideally. Trust and the ability to trust help smooth the way for interaction of other kinds, such as efforts to improve the community or to pass caregiving received along to others in need. And trust is not, as some economists would have us believe, simply a matter of calculating probabilities. Trust is cultural, a cultural construction of scripts and narratives that tell us whom we can trust, on what basis we can trust them, and how to make sense of it when our expectations are not met. Besides trust, the culture of civil society is also composed of messages about caregiving itself, about the giving and receiving of gifts, about compassion, and about love. These messages and the values on which they are based are often assumed in discussions of faith-based services but are seldom examined. We will want to pay special attention to these cultural dimensions, to the kinds of scripts and narratives that sociologists have come increasingly to emphasize in work known as cultural sociology.[4] These cultural dimensions, like the service activities themselves, are complex. They involve storytelling of a special kind, storytelling that weaves self-interested motives together with altruism, and narratives that understand care received both as a free gift and as one surrounded with expectations and responsibilities.

Beyond the Modernization Story

To understand why so many of the questions I have just described remain unanswered requires stepping back from the current discussions about faith-based social services and situating these discussions in the context of historic and more recent relationships between religion and social service. These relationships have a long history, too long to recount in any detail here, but one that must be understood in general contour if we are to see the importance of the present debate. This is a history about which the telling has been as interesting as the events themselves.

In nearly all accounts of how social services developed in the United States, there is at least brief acknowledgment of an early history or prehistory in which religion figured prominently. Poor relief in colonial America was heavily influenced by patterns of social service provision in Western Europe. In England and other Protestant countries these patterns owed much to the distinctive relations between church and state that developed during the Reformation. Relief was administered through tax-supported alms houses and hospitals, local programs, and voluntary benevolences collected by the churches. Relationships of patronage and clientage bound people in local communities together in a kind of moral economy that protected the weak from periodic famines and losses from illness and death and ensured that the strong would have a more reliable workforce. Gradually the modern state came to play a more important role in monitoring social needs and centrally administering public welfare.[5]

The development of social service provision is a story that can be told in a way that fits comfortably with the so-called modernization framework that became popular among social scientists during the middle half of the twentieth century. In this framework the institutions that perform basic societal functions, such as the economy, family, and government, become more specialized, autonomous, and clearly differentiated from one another as societies become more modern and complex. The process is much like the development of more specialized tissues and organs in biological evolution. Thus, religion gradually retreats into its own domain, serving purely spiritual aims, while other institutions become more secularized. In addition, the modernization story suggests that societies become more rational or at least are governed more clearly in their major decision-making processes by rational considerations as they become more modern. To be a modern society, therefore, is to devote more effort to planning and to the use of scientific information in planning, and to be more concerned about questions of effectiveness and efficiency in the pursuit of major societal goals.[6]

Like other stories, the plotline of modernization stories generally begins with an opening scene, called the traditional period, moves on to an intermediate scene, called the transitional phase, and culminates in a final scene, called the modern period. The modernization story about social service provision suggests that in the traditional period social services were largely performed by religious functionaries, especially by local priests, and that charity was usually part of a patronage system that maintained the feudal order, preventing it from caving in under its own weight. In the traditional period social services may have been relatively effective because societies were simple and the needs were presumably not as great as later on, but social services were also not very well differentiated from religion or family and as a result these services mostly helped people who were members of well-established communities and were ill suited to the changes that came when people started moving around. In the transitional phase, the modernization story suggests that there was a kind of seesaw motion between the forces of traditionalism, which usually included religion, and the forces of modernization, which included the emerging state and the enlightened bureaucrats associated with the state. Through a process that often looked in retrospect to have consisted of taking two steps forward and one step backward, societies gradually developed a more effective system of delivering social services. In the meantime there was much anguish and inefficiency. Religious leaders sometimes championed more effective service programs, but just as likely wanted to restrict these programs and maintain control of them. Or religious leaders developed new ideas about individual responsibility and thus turned a cold shoulder to the needy. Sometimes there was an abundance of private charity, with hundreds of organizations attempting to ameliorate social problems, but the very proliferation of these programs led modernization theorists to believe that they were not as rationally organized as they should have been. Eventually the modern state, with its more rational ways, stepped in, took charge of welfare programs, and solved many of the problems that had existed during the transitional phase. Modern welfare programs had the advantage of dealing with the total population's needs, rather than being restricted to members of particular religious groups. These modern programs were based on a modern conception of rights, which reflected new understandings of the worth and dignity of the individual person, and they were administered scientifically in ways that were fair, efficient, and effective.

Of course the modernization story never quite adequately depicted the facts. It missed the high degree of rationality that was present in many of the medieval social programs and the complex relationships that existed then among states and religious leaders and wealthy individual patrons. It underestimated the continuing significance of religious organizations in providing social services during the centuries of transition prior to the modern period and the innovativeness and effectiveness of new benevolence associations and mutual aid societies. As social scientists looked more carefully at the history of the welfare state, they found that the very organizational capacity that permitted governments to develop more expansive service functions was predicated on strong private associations within civil society, including religious ones.[7] They discovered that the religious individualism that had previously been regarded as a barrier to inclusive welfare programs was not a significant barrier after all.[8] And, most important, the rational and scientific programs of welfare administration became easy prey for critics as decades passed and the cost of social programs increased without as much in tangible results as had been expected.

Once the modernization story came to be seen as a poor caricature of past developments it became easier for critics of the public welfare system to imagine an alternative story. That story was one of tragic decline rather than of optimistic development. The tragedy lay in the modern state itself. As it took over more of the functions of private charity, the state introduced inefficiency and ineffectiveness. Rationality and scientific calculations were cold and impersonal compared to the warmth of private charity, and thus were destined to fail. In this story, religion had actually been providing social services quite well until government stepped in, tried to do what religion had always done better, and pushed religion into the corner. The more government tried to do, the more religiously motivated volunteers who would have otherwise played a role stayed on the sidelines. Moreover, welfare recipients had little incentive to work because they had a right to public assistance and they were in any case not receiving the personalized attention they would have in religious organizations. Professionalized social service providers were not so much offering skilled assistance as protecting their new monopoly over service delivery. Government either needed to pull back and let private charities do more or it needed to at least work more cooperatively with those agencies, since working without them had produced disappointing results.[9]

The Faith-Based Services Debate

During the last two decades of the twentieth century the debate between proponents of the competing versions of social service provision became increasingly animated. The debate was about much more than religion, although religion came to be one of its more contested aspects. The conservative religious movements that emerged in the late 1970s and early 1980s in opposition to abortion and in favor of programs such as prayer in public schools and school vouchers were also concerned about government spending on social service programs. In a national survey conducted in 1984 by the Gallup Organization, for example, Americans who defined themselves religiously as conservatives were almost twice as likely to say they opposed "more government spending on social programs" as people who defined themselves as religious liberals (see table 1.1). The differences were even more pronounced among college graduates, where more than two-thirds of religious conservatives opposed more spending on social programs, compared with only a quarter of religious liberals.[10] This group of college-educated religious conservatives, moreover, had been growing during the 1970s and thus stood to be an increasingly influential group in national politics. Opposition to government spending had also been a significant plank in the Republican party platform on which Ronald Reagan had become president in 1980. Republicans were decidedly more opposed to government spending on social programs than Democrats, whether they were religious conservatives, moderates, or liberals, while among Democrats, those who were religiously conservative provided another constituency in which there was considerable opposition to spending on social programs.

With religious conservatives increasingly aligned with the Republican party, and with the emphasis on rolling back government that become prominent during the so-called Reagan revolution, discussions about the possible role of religious organizations in providing social services became increasingly partisan. On the right, government willingness to channel public funds to religious organizations came to be seen as a right that the religious community deserved, just as school vouchers or prayers in public schools were.[11] On the left, leaders of religious organizations worried that

TABLE 1.1

Opposition to Welfare Spending
(Percentage in each category who oppose more government spending on social programs)

	Religious Conservatives	Religious Moderates	Religious Liberals
All	47	38	25
High school degree or less	40	33	24
Some college	58	46	29
College graduate	68	46	24
Republicans	62	54	43
Democrats	35	23	14
Number	(277)	(714)	(288)

Source: The Gallup Organization, Liberal-Conservative Survey, 1984; machine-readable data file.

conservatives merely wanted to scale back public programs that their own organizations had encouraged government to support ever since the New Deal and especially since Lyndon Johnson's Great Society programs in the 1960s.[12] As the cost of social programs steadily increased, though, there was widening public support for efforts to initiate reforms aimed at reducing welfare rolls and requiring welfare recipients to seek jobs.[13] Against some opposition within his own party, President Clinton signed the Personal Responsibility and Work Opportunity Reconciliation Act into law in August 1996. The measure set limits on how long welfare recipients could receive public support and set in motion a number of reforms including the Charitable Choice provision that eased restrictions on religiously oriented service agencies that wished to apply for government funds to support their programs. A strong economy, a declining proportion of people with incomes below the poverty line (as discussed in chapter 6), and an expanding number of jobs during the last half of the 1990s reduced some of the difficulties of requiring welfare recipients to seek jobs. The reforms were sufficiently popular that both of the leading candidates for president during the 2000 campaign endorsed further reforms. Both candidates also promised to encourage greater participation in social service provision by religious and other private service organizations, although George W. Bush was more vocal in his encouragement than Democrat candidate Al Gore.[14]

In January 2001, President Bush signed an executive order creating and defining the responsibilities of a new agency at the White House for Faith-Based and Community Initiatives. In an accompanying document titled "Rallying the Armies of Compassion," Bush observed that "federal policy should reject the failed formula of towering, distant bureaucracies that too often prize process over performance." In place of such bureaucracies, he argued, should be a partnership between government and private agencies staffed by "quiet heroes [who] lift people's lives in ways that are beyond government's know-how." These private charitable groups, including such "faith-based" organizations as those run by Methodists, Muslims, and Mormons, were in Bush's view capable of healing the nation's ills "one heart and one act of kindness at a time." The president insisted that the new thrust in government funding be results oriented. "We must be outcome-based, insisting on success and steering resources to the effective and to the inspired." He also acknowledged that the program should be consistent with such principles as "pluralism, nondiscrimination, evenhandedness and neutrality."[15]

The questions raised by the January 2001 executive order and by subsequent efforts to craft legislative bills to expand or clarify the relationship between government and faith-based service organizations fell largely into two broad categories. One set of questions focused on the complexities of implementing faith-based programs when government funding and regulations are involved. These questions ranged from considerations about the rights and fair treatment of clients to considerations about separation of church and state and accountability to the wider public.[16] These "fairness and rights" considerations are evident in Bush's language about pluralism and evenhandedness. They focus especially on questions about recipients' access to agencies capable of meeting their needs without respect to religious preferences, nondiscrimination in supplying services to all qualified applicants, religious tests in hiring agency staff, and the free exercise of religion. A second set of questions concerned the agenda-setting function of policy makers, clergy, and other public leaders. These questions included considerations such as how much of social welfare provision can be expected to be accomplished through faith-based organizations, whether there are reasons to believe these organizations are more effective than government-sponsored or nonsectarian organizations in delivering social services, and whether there are sufficient secondary benefits from involving faith-based organizations in service provision to warrant public leaders calling greater attention to the activities of these organizations. We might refer to these as questions about "scope and effectiveness."[17] The "fairness and rights" questions and the "scope and effectiveness" questions are interconnected, of course; for instance, if faith-based service provision is sizable and effective, then it may be more important to work out the technicalities of rendering it more accountable to the public than if it is small and inconsequential. The two sets of questions nevertheless call for different kinds of expertise. The "fairness and rights" questions have rightly been addressed by scholars with legislative and legal expertise, while the "scope and effectiveness" questions fall more squarely into the domain of social scientists. It is for this reason that social scientists are now beginning to examine questions about what churches and more specialized faith-based organizations are doing and how well they are doing it.

While the policy debates about faith-based services have focused public and scholarly attention on the role of religion, these discussions have also narrowed the questions toward which most of this attention has been directed. When elected officials champion faith-based services, it has been difficult for critics not to be skeptical about the possibility that some hidden agenda is behind their support. Are they, for instance, in favor of faith-based services because they want to cut back on government programs? Are they currying favor with religious conservatives or with some other religious group that stands to gain from government funding? Are their own religious convictions clouding their perceptions of complex social realities? Apart from these questions, it has also been necessary to focus on such legislative and judicial matters as how to protect the rights of clients who may not wish to seek help from faith-based organizations, whether to permit faith-based organizations to discriminate on religious grounds in hiring staff, and how to prevent monies intended for social services to be used in ways that further the sectarian mission of religious organizations. All of those are important considerations, and yet they risk losing sight of the distinctive features of religion and its larger place in American society.

The value of renewed interest over the past decade in civil society is that it reorients thinking away from the modernization story and criticisms of that story. Where modernization pointed to institutional differentiation, civil society emphasizes the interaction among institutions. Voluntary associations draw people from their families and workplaces into organizations that may look very similar to businesses even though they are not oriented toward profits, and their activities may link local concerns with national interests and generate a political response even though they are not part of the government. Civil society is quite often an arena in which rational discussion takes place about matters of common concern such as schools, transportation, and the environment; at the same time, civil society is composed of neighborhoods, ethnic associations, and religious congregations that seek to preserve traditions in symbolic and expressive ways that transcend rational discussion. The gravest concern about civil society is that it is declining, or, more accurately, that public participation in the activities on which civil society depends is declining. Thus, the role of religion in civil society may be considered afresh by scholars or by public leaders who once wrote it off as a remnant of the past that would be less and less relevant in the present world. The possible contribution of religion to the social networks, values, and trust on which civil society depends can be entertained without taking sides as to whether it has a special role to play.

As a long-time student of American religion, I am heartened by the possibilities these new perspectives on civil society and the place of religion in civil society have created. Religion has too often been viewed by its defenders as an unrivaled source of personal meaning and purpose for its adherents and too often regarded by its critics as an impossibly naïve yearning for a lost belief system that can never again be fully believable. Religion is of course about meaning and belief. But it is not only about that. Religion is fundamentally social, about the relationships among people and within communities and between individuals and organizations, and it is therefore contextual. Its meanings are contextual, given life and given reality through the concrete settings in which it is expressed. Its implications are always conditioned by the contexts in which it occurs. This is why it is as important to understand the limitations of religion and the ways in which its ideals go awry or are not fully realized as it is to examine it strengths. We know full well that religion is capable of tremendous evil as well as of good. We know too that public rhetoric about the good and the evil of religion is generally belied by the complexities of real religion in real places.

Religion as an Embedded Practice

The critique of older perspectives that emphasized modernization leads us to recognize more clearly the need to understand religion—indeed all institutions—in a new way. Religion is too often conceived of, even by social scientists who study it, as a kind of autonomous sphere that, to be sure, interacts with other institutions (such as family or politics) but that can largely be understood on its own terms; that is, as a collection of congregations, denominational structures, clergy, and members with particular loyalties and beliefs. This view has been encouraged by academic specialization that leads people to focus on one sphere, because there is so much to be understood about that sphere, and sometimes by foundations that sponsor research concerned with the distinctive problems and dynamics of churches without paying more attention to the larger contexts in which those organizations function. In the extreme, the view of religion as an autonomous sphere is conducive to an economistic approach to religion that treats it as if it were composed of rational actors making choices in terms of a kind of contract oriented toward maximizing their self-interest. Religion then becomes little more than a set of suppliers who compete with one another to attract and satisfy customers. The implication of this view for policies about faith-based organizations is that government can probably find ways to evaluate competing programs and reward those that compete best. In recent years, scholars have begun to recognize the inadequacy of looking at religion in this way. The very notion of faith-based organizations working in partnership with government to supply social services reveals that religion is hardly as autonomous as the supply-demand theorists would have us believe. More broadly, we are coming to greater awareness that religion has not retreated from the public sphere as much as modernization theorists predicted it would and has instead become "deprivatized," in José Casanova's memorable phrasing, to the point that its interactions with governments are increasingly dynamic and influential.[18] Similarly, we are learning that personal religious practices cannot be understood by only studying churches or by asking people in surveys about church attendance; these personal practices manifest themselves in the workplace, at volunteer centers, and in homes. Yet the older view of religion as a largely autonomous sphere is the one that has prevailed among policy makers and has thus been the underlying perspective in recent policy debates about faith-based social services. In that view, religion is something that can be *acted upon* by government. It exists as a potential of well-meaning service-oriented believers who would simply do more if government let them. Funneling government funding to their service programs would help them do more. So would passing legislation removing barriers on religiously oriented programs that may have been present because of concerns about separation of church and state. There is some truth in the argument that funding and legislation of these kinds would affect religion—were there not, it would be of little value to entertain such policies in the first place. What is missed in these discussions is that religion is embedded in the wider society. Just as market transactions and other economic activities are embedded in social networks and communities, so religion is structured by and exists in interaction with its social environment.[19] Religion is embedded in social norms, in cultural values and understandings, and in arrangements of resources and power that fundamentally shape it and cause it to be the way it is. Tinkering with faith-based programs in ways that do not take account of these larger arrangements is done at the risk of both unforeseen and negative outcomes.

The embedding of religion occurs in the first instance through the historic competition among religious bodies that has produced the distinctive configuration of congregations and faith communities that now characterize American religion. It is no accident that many congregations are too small to be significantly engaged in social service provision. Forecasters predict that small congregations will die and increasingly be replaced by larger ones, including so-called megachurches that attract thousands of members. For the time being, though, small congregations exist in large numbers because many were founded by people who lived in small towns and farming communities, because these congregations have been remarkably robust and even resistant to change in these communities, and because many other small congregations have been founded in cities and suburbs to meet the needs of distinctive ethnic groups and new immigrant populations.[20] Although there are competitive advantages for congregations that are larger (such as being able to attract new members by offering a larger variety of programs), small congregations also adapt well to the American landscape. Religious voluntarism, which is in turn a function of the separation of church and state, is one of the important reasons for these congregations. Clergy and lay leaders who become dissatisfied with existing congregations can start new ones. Entrepreneurialism is often rewarded. Existing congregations are often complicit as well in helping to cover the costs of new mission churches deemed necessary because of new communities and new population groups. It is thus not the case that small congregations can simply be understood as losers in some competitive economic game. They exist and continue to be an important part of American religion because of the resources and opportunities available to them. At the same time, competition among congregations encourages what has been termed organizational isomorphism to occur, resulting in greater similarity in programs despite different histories or theological orientations.[21] Church offices, support staff, Sunday school programs, small group ministries, and even architectural styles are all instances of organizational isomorphism. Social service programs are no exception. Congregations that can afford them generally include them, even though these programs may be small or understaffed.

The embedding of congregations and of congregation-based service programs also involves the growing number of secular nonprofit service organizations that are present in most communities. The reality, contrary to much of the public rhetoric about faith-based organizations, is not one of services being provided either by government welfare offices or by churches.[22] Secular service organizations and specialized faith-based service agencies also exist in abundance. They do for many reasons, including government funding and favorable legislation, but also including long-term growth in service professions during the twentieth century and the need for professionalized services and bureaucratic structures to administer the greatly expanding range of social services that were needed and provided.[23] The growth of nonprofit organizations developed in a context of market competition much like that of for-profit organizations.[24] Although not oriented toward earning profits for owners and shareholders, nonprofit organizations nevertheless competed to attract clients, to secure funding, and to demonstrate their effectiveness to board members, clients, and potential funders. Markets are always messy. The nonprofit sector was thus characterized by redundancy and by fluidity as new organizations emerged and older ones died. The so-called faith-based organizations that developed in this context grew from multiple sources and took many forms.[25] The term *faith-based* itself came into being through at least implicit recognition of this multiplicity. As specialized service organizations, they needed to be distinguished from congregations, and yet calling them faith-based provided enough vagueness that congregations could be subsumed if it were convenient to do so. To say that they were faith-based also left open the extent to which they might indeed be influenced by faith: possibilities ranged (as we will discuss in chapter 5) from merely having been initiated by people of faith to being completely under the control of clergy or religiously oriented boards. It is more problematic to understand why *faith* became the preferred term rather than *religion,* but one may reasonably speculate that the predominance of Christian and even evangelical churches and church leaders had something to do with this choice—*faith* being perhaps a friendlier term than the more academic and distanced term *religion.* The imprint of Christianity on the preference for *faith* is also evident in the fact that faith is certainly more central to the Christian tradition than it is to Judaism, Islam, Hinduism, or Buddhism. Thus, the need for inclusive language amidst an increasingly diverse array of religious communities was only partially met. What is more important than the language itself, though, is the fact that faith-based service organizations emerged, not only in competition with secular service agencies, but also in complex interaction with them. Service organizations are linked to one another through cooperative funding and staffing arrangements. Volunteers are important conduits of skills and information that connect various service organizations. Clients typically seek assistance from several organizations, rather than meeting their needs only at one. Congregations are linked to one another and to secular organizations through cooperative service programs. And professional associations, interest groups, and foundations also supply linkages. All of this makes it impossible to understand the role of religion in service provision, let alone in civil society more broadly, without paying attention to these social connections.

The embedding of American religion in its service functions occurs further through the shared cultural understandings that make up civil society in the United States. These understandings are fraught with contradictions. On the one hand, there is a long history of altruism in American culture, if it can be called that, or at least of voluntarism and service. Neighborliness at the local level and the many fraternal associations and civic clubs that were founded in the nineteenth century were manifestations of this spirit and, as we shall see, recent surveys indicate that caring for the needy and contributing time to help with community service projects is still a value to which most Americans subscribe. On the other hand, Americans are also intensely individualistic, wanting to be self-sufficient, skeptical of people who are not self sufficient, and driven by such self-interested motives as greed, materialism, and excessive consumerism. Religious programs are situated amidst these contradictory impulses. They often encourage people to think more compassionately about the poor, but they also channel this thinking in individualistic ways that may encourage charity more than public advocacy on behalf of the poor.[26] There are other contradictory impulses as well. Faith sometimes encourages people to evangelize those they are trying to help, but norms of civic tolerance and respect discourage people from being too explicit about those efforts. Faith commitments undergird the caring communities present among the members of most congregations; these same commitments, though, may tell people to serve the needy outside their congregations rather than caring only for people within their own group. In relationships with clients, service providers and volunteers may be motivated by personal religious convictions, but their behavior may be governed more by professional norms that discourage them from disclosing these convictions. Just how much or how little faith is actually present in faith-based service organizations is thus an empirical question. It may be that government restrictions have inhibited its full expression, but it is just as likely that cultural norms are the reason.

The sum of these considerations is that religion is embedded especially within what has been called civil society. Civil society is the sphere of social relations and institutions that exists between the sphere of government and the sphere of for-profit market-oriented organizations.[27] It is the realm of free association and of voluntary associations that has proven so vital to U.S. democracy during the course of its history. We normally think of civil society as being concerned with the public expression of collective values, more so than with the private time people spend alone or with their families. However, the distinction between public and private is difficult to sustain once we recognize how much of our personal lives—whether concerned with childrearing, sexual practices, birth control, or merely television watching—is also a matter of public debate and even of public policy. Religion, too, combines the private, in the form of intensely personal religious convictions, and the public, in the form of worship, through participation in service activities, and in public discussion about the appropriate role of religion in our communities. It is more helpful to think of civil society in terms of the complex social norms and networks that tie individuals and organizations together. These are the kinds of cultural understandings and linkages I have just described. They promote cooperation or reduce the likelihood of overt conflict, they form the basis for mobilizing political participation or of initiating community programs that can be done without the involvement of government, and in the best of circumstances they tie people together in bonds of mutual obligation.

A Civil Society?

Differences in social status—or, less euphemistically, inequalities among social classes—are the hidden reality in American religion, and indeed in American society more generally.[28] They are the hidden reality that seldom receives the attention they deserve. Alexis de Tocqueville's influential treatment of civil society in the United States during the early nineteenth century focused more on the problems of *equality* than on those associated with inequality. Everywhere he traveled, Tocqueville was impressed that Americans were all alike, sharing roughly the same incomes and occupational opportunities and, perhaps even more surprisingly, regarding themselves as one another's equals. The problem was thus, in his view, to prevent the undifferentiated masses from devolving into a kind of tasteless, formless amalgam over which the media would have too much influence and upon which demagogues could prey. There was plenty of inequality in the communities Tocqueville visited. But in comparing the United States with the entrenched aristocratically ruled societies he knew in Europe, he could not help being impressed by equality more than by inequality.[29]

This emphasis on equality has continued to be an implicit assumption in most discussions of civil society. We find, for instance, that treatments of civic engagement are more concerned with the proportion of all Americans who vote, join community organizations, or serve as volunteers than with whether or not civic engagement is as abundant or as helpful to people in lower-income communities as to those in middle-class neighborhoods.[30] Volunteering, one almost assumes from these treatments, is just as beneficial if it helps middle-class children in well-staffed suburban schools as if it involves staffing a shelter for the homeless or doing pro bono work for the poor.

Discussions of faith-based service organizations are especially valuable, therefore, because they require us to consider activities that cut across class lines and that are deliberately concerned with assisting the disadvantaged and marginalized. Some of these discussions, however, require us to look even more carefully at what is meant by service or assistance. For example, the caring that takes place in congregations may help the occasional family within the congregation who happens to fall on hard times, but may not include a systematic effort to reach from the middle-class congregation in one part of town to the lower-income neighborhood in another part of town. Similarly, the public face of faith-based social services is sometimes that of programs concerned with prison inmates, who are supposedly there as a result of their own actions and are a burden to society unless some effective means of rehabilitation are found, or with substance abusers, who may be viewed in the same way. Valuable as it is to know what benefits these special populations, the larger questions about civil society cannot be fully addressed without paying attention to the broader needs of the poor and of other disadvantaged groups.

Bringing questions about religion together with questions about service provision also means extending our view of civil society beyond that of how much or how little lower-income families are represented at the polls and whether or not they can mobilize more effectively to make claims on public policy. The disenfranchisement of the poor and of minority groups is certainly a serious social problem. The trouble with focusing only on enfranchisement and interest-formation is that the end in view is never anything but government policy. Little wonder, then, that the picture of how civil society actually works is always somewhat out of focus. People not only work in concert with government, but also pursue activities separate from it. Those who need assistance would often be better served if laws and tax dollars took greater account of their needs. And yet the job training, emergency food and shelter, transportation, and child care is often provided partly through private sources. This is even more the case for the emotional and social support people receive through their congregations.

Considering the changing and much contested role of religion in providing social services in our society is thus an opportunity to take a fresh look at American religion itself. Whether or not the debate that has engaged so many researchers and policy makers over the past decade continues, we can be sure that American religion itself will remain an important part of civil society. It will remain important but sufficiently complex that careful attention to its contours and contributions will be required.

2

Congregation-Based Social Services

During the debate about welfare reform and Charitable Choice in the 1990s, President Clinton suggested that organized religion would be able to make a significant contribution to eliminating the need for public welfare if each congregation in the United States simply hired an indigent person.[1] Other leaders argued that congregations could at least do more to feed the hungry and house the homeless. These leaders implicitly shared the view that faith-based social service is best provided by congregations.

It has made sense to public officials to think of congregations as a potentially valuable front line in the provision of social services. Almost half of American volunteers donate their time to a congregation, and one-quarter of all volunteering takes place within religious congregations alone.[2] Nearly all the money given to them stays at the local level. Most congregations have full-time staff who could devote some of their work week to organizing social programs. Most have space in which service activities can occur. But what do congregations actually do? How many of them sponsor formal service programs? Who do these programs serve and how are they organized?

Throughout most of American history, congregations were small, seldom numbering more than one hundred members, and they were rarely staffed by more than one person. This changed during the twentieth century. While many congregations in small towns and rural areas remained small, those in urban and suburban areas often grew to the point that they could organize and staff specialized ministries. Service programs, such as food pantries and day care centers, came to be an important part of these ministries. They were often called social or outreach ministries because they extended the care congregations provided among their own members to the wider community.

First Baptist Church in Wayne, Pennsylvania, illustrates the congregational approach to social ministry. Affiliated with the American Baptist Convention and theological liberal in self-definition, it was founded in 1896 when residents of Philadelphia started migrating farther from the center of the city along the old Lancaster Pike to form what has long been known as the "mainline" district. Although it is within a few blocks of several of the wealthiest neighborhoods in the area, its membership (now approximately 250) has always been drawn from the middle class. Its present style of social ministry can be traced to the early part of the twentieth century, when growing numbers of African Americans and Italian immigrants settled nearby. Several members of the church became concerned that Highland Avenue, only three blocks from the church, was becoming a cardboard shantytown. They decided to focus their attention on its needs. Through the church, they began offering tutoring, financial assistance, and help with household odd jobs such as carpentry and cleaning. Some of those who received assistance became active in the church.

Over the years, the congregation continued to draw in people with special needs. At the end of World War II, it took in refugees from Eastern Europe. About the same time, church women started a racially integrated sewing circle to become better acquainted with their African American neighbors. In more recent decades the church has championed racial justice in the community, organized a resource center for single mothers, and brought refugees from Central America who were seeking political asylum. Several years ago, the members initiated a hospitality program and purchased a building next door to be used as a "mission house" in which refugees and other needy families could be housed temporarily.

Although many of the members pursue social ministries individually through their work or in their spare time, there is a deliberate effort to keep the congregation central. Clergy and lay leaders alike emphasize the importance of *combining* service with worship, prayer, education, and fellowship. They believe needy people flourish when they are drawn into a faith community where they can grow spiritually by helping others as well as by being helped.

One person who has been helped in this way is Jim Washington, an African American man in his mid-fifties who has been part of the congregation for the past decade. Mr. Washington had lost his job and, with only a high school education, was worried about his future. He was also recently divorced and concerned that his son was being raised without religion. Although Mr. Washington had attended a Baptist church during his youth, he was now living in a different part of the city and knew little about the local churches. He was attracted by the diverse racial composition of First Baptist and by the congregation's interests in social ministry. The church has helped him by giving him part-time employment and by drawing him into its activities. "First Baptist," he says, "is a church that put their words into action. They have a lot of mission groups. They do so much. My experience in the black churches was mixed. There was a lot of Jesus praising and singing songs and all of that. But in terms of doing mission outreach, there's not too much of that there. I'm still high on Jesus and Jesus praising, but I'm not one to sit there on my hands and expect for God to answer all my problems any more. God is a very integral part of my life, but we work as a team."

The congregational model of service provision has worked well at First Baptist because service, while carried out through specialized programs, has come to be an important part of the church's identity. Members justifiably take pride in the fact that they occupy a niche in the community that sets them apart from friends and neighbors who do little to help others. Although the church espouses diversity and imposes few doctrinal standards, its members have a clear sense of themselves as a Christian community, and being part of the community implies playing an active role in maintaining it. "It does carry responsibilities," says its pastor. "A community needs your time and your leadership and your gifts and your energies, visions, and ideas. Somebody who doesn't want to give that to a community, who just wants to soak up and not return, is not being a responsible partner in that community."

How typical is First Baptist? Do most congregations provide social services as a regular part of their ministry? Which kinds of service activities are most common? Are they organized formally or do they occur informally? Why are some congregations more involved in social ministry than others? How much of the typical church's budget is spent supporting these activities? Do congregations contribute to the provision of social services in other ways, such as through coalitions and joint programs? Do they, as First Baptist does, preach about social needs? And do they forge friendships that bridge the gaps among different racial groups and social strata?

These are all questions that researchers have tried to address in recent years. Congregations are clearly the first place to look if we are to understand how American religion contributes to the provision of social services. Congregations are present in nearly all communities and are easily identified, and much information can be obtained about them, often by simply conducting studies among their leaders. Data from a number of major studies help to provide answers. Sometimes the answers diverge, requiring us to consider carefully the reasons for the varying conclusions. Let us begin by considering the question of whether or not most congregations do have programs concerned with service activities.

Formal Sponsorship of Service Programs

The "Belief to Commitment" Project

The first significant attempt to measure the extent of congregational involvement in social service provision was a project initiated by Independent Sector, a Washington-based nonprofit research organization concerned with promoting nonprofits, volunteering, and philanthropy in the United States. In cooperation with the Gallup Organization and a technical advisory committee of researchers and church leaders, the Independent Sector project drew a national sample of congregations and solicited information from clergy at these congregations through telephone interviews and a mailed questionnaire. Because there were no comprehensive directories of American churches, the sample was drawn by culling through Yellow Pages in eighteen randomly selected metropolitan and nonmetropolitan areas within nine census regions scattered across the United States. This procedure yielded a random sample of 4,205 local congregations. Mailed questionnaires were filled out and returned by the pastors at 1,353 of these congregations in 1988.[3]

The results suggested that congregations were nearly always involved in providing social services to their communities. In all, 87 percent of the congregations "provided support for or services" in activity areas that the researchers defined as being concerned with "human services and welfare." These activities included family counseling (79 percent); recreation, camping, or other youth programs (79 percent); meal services (38 percent); housing or shelter for the homeless (32 percent); day care (31 percent); after-school programs (30 percent); teenage pregnancy programs (29 percent); tutoring programs (26 percent); battered women programs (25 percent); and housing for senior citizens (19 percent). In all, 41 percent of congregations reported supporting five or more human service activities and 64 percent reported supporting at least three such activities.[4]

Several other activities, which the researchers classified differently, also suggested widespread community involvement by local congregations: 42 percent of congregations were involved with civil rights and social justice programs; 46 percent with community development; 35 percent with refugee-related programs; 44 percent with supporting hospitals, clinics, nursing homes, or hospice programs; and 35 percent with assisting mentally retarded and physically disabled persons or crisis counseling hotlines.[5]

The study showed, too, that congregations contribute to their communities indirectly. For instance, a majority (60 percent) reported that community groups outside of the congregation used their facilities for meetings at least one day a week. Sixty percent also reported that they provided in-kind support such as clothing, food, or housing to human service programs operated by religious or other community groups. In addition, the study estimated that approximately 7 percent of clergy time was devoted to human service activities, as was 9 percent of other paid employees, and 12 percent of congregations' volunteers.[6]

One of the more important contributions of the Independent Sector study was the evidence it provided on variations in social service programs among small, medium, and large congregations. As shown in table 2.1, congregations with four hundred or more members were substantially more likely to have each of the specific social service programs listed than congregations with memberships ranging from one hundred to four hundred, which in turn were more likely to have these programs than congregations with fewer than one hundred members.[7] These differences undoubtedly reflect the fact that large congregations have more members, more staff, larger budgets, and perhaps more extensive ties to other organizations in their communities, all of which may be necessary to initiate social ministries. The role of size as an influence on social service programs is also worth noting because different estimates of the extent of service programs in congregations derive (as we shall see) from studies including different proportions of small congregations.

The main conclusion from the Independent Sector project was that congregations were an important source of social services in the United

States. As Independent Sector's Brian O'Connell observed in the foreword to *From Belief to Commitment,* the report summarizing the project's findings: "A very large part of the nonprofit sector's service to society is performed by religious institutions . . . . dwarfing all funds contributed to and by other voluntary organizations for local human services."[8]

The Invisible Caring Hand

A second effort to determine the extent of congregational involvement in social service activity was a research project conducted by Ram A. Cnaan, a professor of social work at the University of Pennsylvania, which became the basis for his book *The Invisible Caring Hand.*[9] Cnaan's project began as a study of historic Philadelphia churches sponsored by an organization concerned with the preservation of historic sacred buildings. Like the Independent Sector study, Cnaan's research suggested that Philadelphia churches

TABLE 2.1

Social Service Activities by Size of Congregation as Reported in Independent Sector Study
(Percentage of congregations sponsoring each type of activity)

	Fewer than 100 Adult Members	100–399 Adult Members	400 or More Adult Members	All Congregations
Day care	18	27	42	31
Family counseling	74	79	82	79
Housing for senior citizens	13	17	23	19
Housing/shelter for homeless	22	32	39	32
Meal services	25	35	49	38
Recreation/camp/youth programs	68	81	82	79
Refugee-related programs	24	32	46	35
Civil rights and social justice	30	41	49	46
Community development	37	44	52	30
Number	(277)	(570)	(472)	(1,353)

Source: Hodgkinson, Weitzman, and Kirsch, *From Belief to Commitment,* 1988.

frequently made their facilities available to community groups and were generally involved in supporting service activities such as providing food and shelter to the needy. These initial results persuaded Cnaan of the value of conducting similar research on a wider scale.

Between 1996 and 1999 Cnaan and his research team collected information from a total of 297 congregations. Forty-six of the congregations were in Ontario, Canada, and were selected to provide a comparison with the 251 U.S. congregations. In the United States, the congregations were clustered in seven metropolitan areas: 21 congregations were in Chicago, 54 in Indianapolis, 40 in Mobile, 15 in New York City, 63 in Philadelphia, 27 in the San Francisco Bay area, and 24 in Houston; in addition, 7 congregations were selected in Council Grove, Kansas, in order to provide a glimpse of how service activities were organized in a small rural community. Of the metropolitan congregations, 111 were selected because they were housed in historic buildings and the remainder were added to give greater representation to newer congregations. Thus, the congregations studied were not a true sample or representative of any predefined population, but were geographically diverse. By sending researchers to each congregation to collect information in person, Cnaan was able to gain a more complete picture of their activities than that provided by the Independent Sector study. By sometimes selecting congregations located in close proximity to one another, he was also able to examine how their activities were coordinated to serve community needs within particular neighborhoods.[10]

Cnaan found even greater congregational involvement in social service activities than the Independent Sector study did. Of the 251 U.S. congregations Cnaan studied, 92 percent reported being involved in sponsoring or supporting at least one social program. Nearly six in ten (59 percent) reported having programs in five or more program areas and 86 percent had programs in at least three areas. The most common programs included recreational, educational, and camping activities for children and youth, programs for the elderly and disabled, and programs for homeless and poor people.[11]

The study also explored the extent to which congregations provided social services or assisted people in need through informal means. As frequent as formal programs were, informal assistance was even more common. For instance, 78 percent of clergy at the churches studied said they had provided informal family counseling during the period year, compared with only 17 percent of congregations actually having formal family counseling programs. Similarly, 75 percent of the congregations studied had some mechanism for assisting the poor financially, often informally through an interview with the pastor, compared with only 30 percent that sponsored a formal cash-assistance program.[12]

Like the Independent Sector study, Cnaan's research suggested that congregations frequently perform community service simply by providing space for use by various community programs and groups. Among the most common of these groups were scouting programs (32 percent of congregations housed a scout troop), day care centers (housed by 30 percent of congregations), twelve-step or addiction groups (at 27 percent of congregations), and nursery schools (at 18 percent of congregations).[13]

Cnaan invited readers to consider the overall scope of congregational social services by imagining what the nation would be like if there were no congregations. Without congregations, he suggested, one-third of the children currently in day care centers would have no place to go. In addition, a majority of scout troops and twelve-step groups would probably have to find other places to meet. And "many food cupboards, soup kitchens, and homeless shelters would disappear," not to mention the hospital visits and care of elderly Americans that would diminish. In short, Cnaan concluded that a "significant social void" would be present without the community services provided by congregations.[14]

The National Congregations Study

The principal weakness of the Independent Sector and Cnaan studies was their lack of national representativeness. Although the Independent Sector study was designed to provide a comprehensive portrait of the nation's congregations, it fell short in at least two respects. First, by relying on telephone directories, it excluded small churches and other congregations that did not have telephones. Second, by obtaining completed questionnaires from only 32 percent of the congregations in the initial sample, it ran the danger of reporting information less characteristic of congregations at large than of congregations that happened to have clergy (or other staff) interested enough to fill out the questionnaires. Cnaan's study was even harder to draw generalizations from. Its congregations were mostly located in large cities, and within each city the congregations were not selected at random or necessarily to be representative of all congregations in that city. The methodological limitations of these studies, moreover, had serious implications for the conclusions that could be drawn from them about social service provision. Service programs might be less common in small congregations than in larger ones and might also be less common outside of major metropolitan areas; indeed, *From Belief to Commitment* showed both to be the case.[15] If pastors who had more to report were more likely to participate in the studies, this too would be a source of bias. All of these concerns suggested that social service provision might not be as abundant as these studies suggested. It still seemed likely that congregations were an important source of service provision, but perhaps not quite as important as the researchers concluded.

The National Congregations Study sought to overcome these weaknesses. Designed by University of Arizona sociologist Mark Chaves, the National Congregations Survey was conducted in conjunction with the 1998 General Social Survey, a national survey of individuals conducted by the National Opinion Research Center at the University of Chicago. Each individual in the survey who attended religious services at least once a year was asked to report the name and location of his or her congregation. Interviewers then tracked down these congregations and conducted a lengthy telephone interview with the pastor (or some other leader) about the congregation's social characteristics and activities, including a question about its social ministries. In all, information was collected from 1,236 congregations.[16]

The National Congregations Study suggested that social service involvement was considerably less common than the other studies had shown. Only 57 percent of congregation leaders reported that their congregations "participated in or supported social service, community development, or neighborhood organizing projects of any sort within the past 12 months." The most commonly mentioned of these projects focused on food, housing or shelter, and programs concerned with children or students. Like the Independent Sector survey, the study also showed that these projects were considerably less common at small congregations than at larger congregations (table 2.2).[17] Moreover, small congregations were much more common in this study than in the one that had been conducted by Independent

Sector. For instance, 71 percent of Chaves's congregations had fewer than one hundred regular adult participants, compared to only 20 percent in the Independent Sector survey.[18]

Chaves's research found other indications that congregation-based social service was less extensive than previously imagined. For instance, the median number of service programs per congregation was only one, and even among congregations that had any service programs, the median number was only two. Furthermore, only 12 percent of the congregations that sponsored a social service program had a staff member who devoted at least 25 percent of his or her time to social service projects.[19]

From these and other results in the study, Chaves drew a more cautious assessment of the role of congregations in social service delivery than Cnaan or the authors of *From Belief to Commitment* did. Social service programs,

TABLE 2.2
Social Service Activities by Size of Congregation as Reported in
National Congregations Survey (Percentage of congregations)

	Fewer than 100 Adults	*100–199 Adults*	*200 or More Adults*	*All Congregations*
Participated in or supported any social service, community development, or neighborhood organizing project within the past 12 months	50	69	80	57
Project mentioned:				
Feeding the hungry	26	45	53	32
Home building or repair	12	30	37	18
Programs focused on children	12	24	30	16
Clothing or blankets	8	15	19	11
Homelessness	5	15	16	8
Number	(883)	(188)	(165)	(1,236)

Source: National Congregations Survey, 1998.
Note: All relationships with size are statistically significant at or beyond the .001 level; numbers refer to "regular participating adults."

Chaves argued, are minor and peripheral to the lives of most congregations. Certainly these programs are not as common as the rudimentary religious activities of congregations, such as worship services and children's religious education classes. The average pastor does not spend as much time on them and the average member doesn't, either. In some congregations, cultural activities may be the focus of more congregational energy than social service. For instance, if 32 percent of congregations have programs providing food to the hungry, this is smaller than the proportion that have a group that puts on musical or theatrical performances (38 percent). Chaves also suggested that congregations' service activities probably focused on short-term or episodic needs, such as emergency food and shelter, which involve minimal contact between congregation members and the needy, rather than more holistic, transformational, or long-term contact—a conclusion that has important implications, as we will see in later chapters, for understanding whether faith is really a significant factor in faith-based service programs. The services that congregations do provide, moreover, typically require collaboration with other community agencies, rather than being performed solely by the congregation.

We shall want to revisit some of these arguments after considering evidence provided by other studies. For now, suffice it to say that Chaves is *not* suggesting that congregation-based social service is unimportant. Whatever congregations are doing to feed the hungry and shelter the homeless is better than nothing. His research simply invites us to be careful about attributing more to congregations than is warranted.

Because the data from the National Congregations Study were made public soon after the survey was completed, the study also provides a way to examine in greater detail why some congregations sponsor service programs and others do not. Table 2.3 compares congregations that do or do not sponsor service programs. The characteristics shown in the table include ones that Chaves finds significant as predictors of service involvement through multivariate analysis, but to make it easier to interpret the substance of these differences, I present the figures in tabular form. Here, we can see clearly why many congregations are without formal social service programs. The mean number of regularly participating adults at the congregations with no formal service programs is only 65 and the median number is only 29. These numbers are smaller by half than the comparable figures for congregations with service programs. There are other striking differences as well: in total number of regular participants, in having a pastor with a graduate degree, and in having a pastor who is full-time. The congregations without service programs, on average, appear too small to have very much in the way of formal programming of any kind. For instance, the median number of committees at these congregations is one, compared to five at the congregations with social programs. The congrega-

TABLE 2.3

Characteristics of Congregations with and without Social Service Programs

	Congregations with Social Service Programs	Congregations without Social Service Programs
Mean number of regularly participating adults	147	65
Median number of regularly participating adults	60	29
Mean number of all regular participants	226	99
Median number of all regular participants	95	47
% having a pastor with a graduate degree	55	26
% having a full-time paid pastor on staff	69	47
% with at least one committee	95	76
Median number of committees	5	1
% with group meetings of any kind	84	59
% with 5 or more group meetings	25	11
% with a choir	71	53
Median number of religious education classes	5	2
% with no denominational affiliation	11	30
% in neighborhoods with high education levels	24	13
Median % of congregation described as poor	32	45
% living in the southeastern United States	11	31
Number	(700)	(536)

Source: National Congregations Survey, 1998.

tions with no service programs also have fewer group meetings and fewer religious education classes, are less likely to have a choir, are more likely to have no denominational affiliation, are less likely to be located in neighborhoods with high education levels, and are more likely to include members who are poor. Interestingly, they are also approximately three times more likely than congregations with service programs to be located in the Southeast.

Faith Communities Today

At approximately the same time that the National Congregations Study was being conducted, another major research project on American congregations was initiated at the Hartford Institute for Religion under the supervision of researchers Carl Dudley and David Roozen. This was a collaborative project involving forty-one denominations and faith groups, including most of the major Protestant denominations, Roman Catholics, Jews, and Muslims. Like the Independent Sector study, this project was based on lists of congregations, but unlike the earlier study, greater care was taken to identify all congregations—small or large and whether they had telephones or not—and a considerably higher response rate (50 percent) was achieved as well. Information was collected through written questionnaires that included more than two hundred questions covering topics such as worship and identity, location and facilities, programs, leadership, organizational dynamics, and finances. In all, information was collected from 14,301 congregations, which the researchers believed to be representative of approximately 80 percent of all congregations in the United States.

The value of this study (apart from the large number of congregations) was that it permitted comparisons to be made between the relative frequency of community service programs and other kinds of congregational activities. According to *Faith Communities Today,* which summarized the study's main findings, 85 percent of congregations in the study included community service among their activities. Other than Sunday school classes, scripture study, and programs for youth, this was the highest percentage for any of the activities included in the study. In comparison, fewer congregations (77 percent) had choirs, even fewer (61 percent) had performing arts activities, fewer still (48 percent) had self-help or personal growth groups, and only 40 percent had book or issue discussion groups.[20]

Reconciling the Estimates

No study is capable of providing 100 percent accuracy in estimating the proportion of congregations that sponsor service activities. It matters, though, if the estimates are as widely discrepant as those generated in the four studies just considered. Should we conclude that nearly all congregations engage in social service activities? Or that only about half do? The former estimate, while leaving open the question of *how much* congregations do, at least gives the sense that most congregations recognize the importance of being involved in service delivery. The more cautious estimate suggests that a large number of congregations either do not value social service or have too few resources to be involved in providing it.

As we have seen, the estimates generated by the Independent Sector study and the Cnaan research are limited because of probable biases in the kinds of congregations that were included in these studies. The Hartford survey had a larger total number of congregations and a better response rate, but is still limited by the fact that nondenominational congregations were largely excluded and by some denominations not participating at all and others having a relatively low response rate. The National Congregations Study, therefore, may reasonably be considered the gold standard as far as current research is considered.

If we take the estimates provided by the National Congregations Study most seriously, we nevertheless need to be aware of several potential limitations of this study, and possibly adjust our conclusions accordingly. One aspect of the study (which may or may not be a limitation) should at least be recognized. The congregations from which information was collected include *two* kinds of nonresponse bias: individuals who did not respond to the General Social Survey in the first place, and then congregational leaders who did not participate in the follow-up study. The response rate in the 1998 General Social Survey was 76 percent. Among these respondents, 1,948 attended religious services at least once a year and thus were eligible to nominate their congregation. But information was collected from only 1,236 congregations, or 63 percent of the 1,948.[21] Multiplying the two percentages gives a response rate of 48 percent. Some of the missing congregations were excluded on purpose (because they were nominated by more than one person), but we need to be aware that generating congregations in this manner, although perhaps better than from directories, also introduces potential bias.

We also need to consider the possibility that the National Congregations Study may overestimate the number of small congregations in the United States and thus the proportion of congregations that do not sponsor service programs. The reason for thinking this becomes evident if we use the NCS figures to estimate the total number of churchgoers in the United States. Multiplying the mean number of regularly participating adults per congregation (112) by the generally accepted figure of 350,000 congregations yields a total of 39.2 million churchgoers. This is out of an adult population of approximately 209 million, or 18.8 percent. But that figure is low compared to almost any other way of estimating religious participation. For instance, the comparable figure from the 1998 General Social Survey of people who said they attend nearly every week is 25.4 percent, or 53.1 million. And, if those who attend at least once a month are included, the figure rises to 41 percent or 85.7 million.

It may be, too, that the National Congregations Study underestimates the extent of congregational involvement in social services because of the question used to elicit this information. As mentioned previously, only one question was included, a question that asked leaders to report if their congregation had "participated in or supported social service, community development, or neighborhood organizing projects of any sort within the past 12 months." Cnaan has criticized this method on grounds that more extensive in-person interaction with clergy in his study often prompted comments about programs that would have been missed by asking a single question. We can estimate how serious this problem may have been by considering only those congregations in the National Congregations Study that resembled those in the *Faith Communities Today* study. For instance, if we focus on congregations that had a denominational affiliation and that had a full-time staff person (on grounds that full-time staff would have been more likely to respond to the *Faith Communities Today* study), then the proportion of congregations that have service programs rises from 57 percent to 70 percent. But this figure is still well below the 85 percent obtained in the *Faith Communities Today* study. Some of that difference may be attributable to response bias in the Hartford study, but we might guess that as much as half of it is a result of clergy having more ample opportunity to think about their congregations' service activities through the list presented in the Hartford study than through the single question asked in the National Congregations Study.[22]

The possibility that clergy would actually answer differently if they had more time to think or if they were asked about specific programs rather than only being asked a single question can also be illustrated with the results of in-depth qualitative interviews in which we experimented deliberately to see what would happen. In interviews with fifty randomly selected clergy, my research assistants and I first asked exactly the same question used in the National Congregations Study. We obtained similar results: about half said their congregation had "participated in or supported social service, community development, or neighborhood organizing projects of any sort within the past 12 months," and about half said their congregation had not done this. As in the National Congregations Study, we observed that smaller congregations were less likely to have done this than larger congregations. But we also noticed that the questions preceding the one about social service projects may have established a negative response pattern among some of the clergy. These questions asked if the congregation had an elementary or high school and if the congregation gave any money to a college, university, or seminary. Clergy at small congregations usually said no to these questions and they sometimes quickly said no to the question about social service projects as well, only to backtrack when the interviewer paused to let them reflect on the question. More significant, the clergy who said their congregations did have service projects usually mentioned only one or two, but in subsequent questions remembered more, and those who denied having any service projects often mentioned something later on as well. A specific example will show what I mean. This is a pastor at a relatively small church with about 120 regularly participating adults in a semirural community. He says yes when asked about service projects and describes an annual canned food drive in which the church participates along with other members of the county conference of churches. This is the only project he can think of, and this response is confirmed when he is asked specifically about helping to sponsor a soup kitchen, a homeless shelter, and a tutoring program. When he is asked if the church has a counseling program, though, he realizes that he had not thought about that before as a service project and mentions one in which the congregation participates. He also mentions several informal programs that in his mind do not qualify as formal service projects but nevertheless involve helping needy people in the community. One of these informal programs involved providing almost total support for three refugee families for more than a year. There is also a fund for cash assistance, an informal program to provide clothing, and a visitation program for people in the hospital. In short, his congregation was doing quite a bit more than a quick response to one survey question would have revealed.

I want to say clearly that these comments are not meant to undermine the credibility of the National Congregations Study. It is, in my view, the most innovative approach to generating data from a national sample of congregations, and the information it provides about social services should be taken seriously. For the reasons I have suggested, that information may underestimate the proportion of congregations that formally sponsor service programs. How much is hard to say, but a reasonable guess would probably be about 10 percent. Thus, if we were to estimate how many congregations formally sponsor service programs, it might be better to say that about two-thirds do, rather than either a bare majority or nearly all.

We shall consider how congregations' social ministries are organized later in the chapter. One thing we should underscore now, though, is that "sponsoring" a social service program can mean many different things. In surveys, it may appear that congregations are bustling centers of service activity. In more extended personal conversations with pastors, these service programs often turn out to be rather minimally connected to the regular life of the congregation. Sponsorship means contributing some money once a year to the support of a service program or it can even mean only that an individual member of the congregation happens to be involved with that program. In our interviews, we found that clergy were honest in stating the limitations of their church's involvement when given a chance to describe it. They regretted that they were not able to do more and sometimes acknowledged that the programs they helped sponsor were ineffective. The pastor of a mainline Protestant church with about four hundred members and a regular attendance of half that provides a typical example. When asked about the church's service programs, he mentions a rescue mission, a homeless shelter, and a food bank. He adds quickly that the extent of the church's involvement in all three is minimal. It sends a small check to the rescue mission each year, it takes up a collection to buy underwear for the men at the homeless shelter, and it is connected to the food bank through a member who is on its board. The church also contributes to the support of some ministries for children and the elderly through its denomination, and there is a small core of a dozen or so members who regularly do volunteer work for service programs near the church. The community would be served less well were it not for the church. But the pastor is under no illusion that the congregation is playing more than a small role in meeting the community's needs.

Members' Awareness of Service Programs

The studies we have considered thus far reflect what clergy report about congregations' involvement in social ministries. These studies miss an important dimension of congregational life by not soliciting information from members. Members are often as knowledgeable about aspects of their congregations—especially those in which they are personally involved—as clergy. Members frequently serve on deacon boards, sessions, vestries, and other decision-making bodies. They participate in planning committees, and, if nothing else, read about congregational activities in church leaflets and newsletters and are periodically solicited to support these activities. It is important to know what members perceive their congregations to be doing to provide social services. Knowledgeable members are more likely than unknowledgeable members to tell others about these services, make use of them, or volunteer for them. A social program that nobody knows about truly fits the biblical image of a candle hidden under a basket.

In considering members' awareness of social programs, the place to begin is the vastly different picture of American religion that emerges when we focus on members and other lay participants than when we focus on congregations. This point has been emphasized by Mark Chaves in his research on congregations. He argues that it is meaningful to count the number of congregations, as we have done, to see how many are involved in sponsoring service programs. But he also encourages us to recognize that some congregations account for much more of the churchgoing public than others do. The difference is best illustrated in the fact that most congregations, as we have seen, are relatively small, yet most Americans *participate* in congregations that are medium in size or large. For instance, the mean number of regularly participating adults rises from 112 per congregation, if we calculate the average size among all congregations, to 711, if we compute the average size of congregation in which the typical congregant participates.[23] The reason the number rises so dramatically is that larger congregations account for a much larger share of the churchgoing public than smaller congregations do. As Chaves and his colleagues observe, "only 10 percent of American congregations have more than 350 regular participants, but those congregations contain almost half of the religious service attendees in the country."[24]

For our purposes, the fact that a majority of the churchgoing public is concentrated in medium or large churches means that religiously involved Americans are more likely to be exposed to congregation-based service programs than we may have assumed on the basis of the fact that so many congregations are small and that many of these congregations appear too small to sponsor formal service programs. This does not mean that the statistics on congregations are unimportant. For instance, if we were to take seriously Bill Clinton's idea of congregations each hiring someone who was on welfare, we would see that the number hired would probably be considerably fewer than 350,000. Many congregations are too small to hire anybody but their pastor. If we want to know, though, about the chances that members are exposed to service programs and to opportunities to participate in these programs through their congregations, then it makes more sense to look where the members are, rather than treating congregations as if they were interchangeable units.

In the National Congregations Study (NCS), an estimated 75 percent of regular adult participants are involved in congregations that sponsor a service program (even though only 57 percent of congregations, according to the NCS data, have such programs). We can, however, derive better estimates of the specific kinds of programs that church members know about from studies soliciting information directly from members. Several national studies of this kind have been done in recent years.

Table 2.4 shows the results from two national surveys in which respondents were asked if they were currently members of a religious congregation and then, if they were, were asked to say whether or not their congregation had helped to sponsor various service activities during the year preceding the survey. The results in the top part of the table are from the Religion and Politics Survey, which was conducted under my supervision in 2000, and those in the bottom are from the Civic Involvement Survey, which I designed and commissioned the Gallup Organization to conduct in 1997.

The former survey included fewer questions about service activities (and was done by telephone) but was conducted among a larger number of respondents, while the latter includes questions about a larger number of service activities and was done in person by going to respondents' residences. In both studies approximately 55 percent of the public claimed to be members of congregations and were able to estimate the approximate size of their congregation.

The results indicate that nearly all members of congregations belong to congregations that help to sponsor one or more kinds of service activities. Of the four activities asked about in the Religion and Politics Survey, 92 percent of church members said their congregation helped to sponsor at least one of them. In the Civic Involvement Survey, 92 percent again said their congregation helped to sponsor at least one of the activities listed. These figures, incidentally, are higher than the comparable figure of 75 percent obtained in the National Congregations Study (and thus underscore the probability that estimates in that study are low for reasons mentioned previously).

We again see that congregation size is a factor in the likelihood of members saying that their congregation sponsors these various activities. The third (or so) of members who attend the smallest congregations, though, are still likely to report that their congregations sponsor at least one service activity (87 percent and 90 percent in the two surveys, respectively).

Where these data are most illuminating is in showing the relative frequency of the various kinds of service activities. Unlike the National Congregations Study, which did not ask specifically about particular activities, or the Independent Sector and *Faith Communities Today* studies, which relied on pastors to fill out a lengthy questionnaire by themselves and return it by mail, these two surveys asked interviewees to respond directly to questions about specific service activities. In both surveys, food assistance or distribution was the most frequently mentioned activity (as was also the case in the open-ended responses from clergy in the National Congregations Study). Although the two surveys asked slightly different questions about food assistance, the responses were virtually identical. More than eight of ten members said his or her congregation helped to sponsor such a program, and the proportions ranged from about three-quarters in the smaller congregations to about nine-tenths in the largest ones. Counseling programs appear to be the next most common after food assistance, with

TABLE 2.4
Members' Reports of Service Activities by Size of Congregation
(Percentage of members who belong to congregations of each size who say their
congregation helped to sponsor each activity during the past year)

	Less than 300	300–999 Members	1,000 or More	All Members
Religion and Politics Survey				
A food pantry or soup kitchen	75	86	89	82
A shelter for the homeless	42	54	66	52
A day care center	36	52	60	48
A tutoring program	36	46	58	45
At least 1 of these	87	94	97	92
At least 2 of these	59	74	86	72
Mean	1.9	2.4	2.7	2.3
Number	(1227)	(1045)	(773)	(3045)
Civic Involvement Survey				
Distributing food to the poor	77	88	90	84
A counseling program	61	73	78	69
Day care or after-school program	33	48	52	42
An inner-city ministry	38	41	42	40
Shelter for the homeless	28	44	45	37
A tutoring program	26	36	44	34
Meetings for alcoholics	24	35	41	31
A ministry to prisoners	22	30	34	28
A program for job seekers	18	20	31	22
Low-income housing	16	22	29	21
An AIDS ministry	11	18	25	17
At least 1 of these	90	93	95	92
At least 2 of these	76	85	92	82
Mean	3.5	4.6	5.1	4.2
Number	(385)	(259)	(206)	(850)

Source: Religion and Politics Survey, 2000; Civic Involvement Survey, 1997.

Note: Congregation size is number who belong to congregation as reported by members.

about seven in ten members saying their congregations help to sponsor counseling programs. Day care centers, shelters for the homeless, and tutoring programs came next in frequency, although the two surveys differed in the responses given to these activities. Between one-third and one-half of church members report that their congregations sponsor these programs. Other activities, such as meetings for alcoholics, ministries to prisoners, programs for job seekers, low-income housing, and AIDS ministries are present among the service activities that congregations help to sponsor, according to one-sixth to one-third of all members.

I want to emphasize that these responses concern service activities that congregations *helped to sponsor.* I will say more about this later in the chapter, but, for now, we need to remember that congregations are unlikely to be operating such programs entirely on their own. To help sponsor a program may mean participating in a program operated by a coalition of congregations. Or, as I mentioned earlier, it may mean little more than sending an annual donation from the church budget or helping the program solicit volunteers through the congregation's newsletter.

There are two reasons not to discount these activities too quickly, though. One is that there is real and symbolic significance to *members* when their congregations help to sponsor service programs. Sponsorship makes these activities visible to members and renders them legitimate, thus raising the chances that members will contribute money or time to their support and encouraging members to think about the value of service. The other is that needy people being served by these programs also become aware of their existence. Clients and potential clients of service programs are often members of congregations, too. Knowing that their congregation helps to sponsor a program is a way of knowing that such a program may be there to serve their needs. (I will return to these points again when considering churches and volunteers in chapter 4 and churches and recipients of social services in chapter 6.)

Congregations' Financial Contribution

Sponsoring or helping to sponsor social service programs typically requires some investment of funds on the part of congregations. How much do congregations contribute financially to the support of service activities in their communities? The amount of money that religious organizations collect from members and other supporters makes up one of the largest shares of philanthropic giving in the United States, accounting for approximately half of all donations from individuals to charitable causes.[25] Is a significant amount of this giving passed on to needy individuals? Is it used to run programs that serve the wider community? Or is it mostly used to pay clergy salaries, maintain buildings, and cover the routine operating costs of congregations?

In official church publications these questions are often answered by reporting the amount spent on benevolences. Benevolence giving is defined as monies that congregations send outside of the congregation for mission and ministry.[26] Among the denominations (largely mainline Protestant) that define benevolence giving this way and that report financial statistics, the amount of total giving spent on benevolences has averaged approximately 12 percent in recent years. There is, however, significant variation in the figures reported by various denominations, reflecting differences in reporting practices as well as in the manner in which social ministries are categorized. For instance, the Southern Baptist Convention has reported approximately 1 percent of total contributions being allocated to benevolences in recent years while the United Methodist Church has reported approximately 20 percent.[27] Because benevolence giving includes monies spent on *any* activity other than the congregation itself, it is also difficult to know what proportion of this amount is devoted to service activities.

The National Congregations Study provides an alternative way of estimating the typical congregation's spending devoted specifically to social service programs. Of the 1,236 congregations studied, 772 (or 62 percent) provided information both about total annual spending and about the amount (if any) spent on social service programs. Table 2.5 shows the mean figures for total budget and expenditures on service programs for 772 congregations and for congregations falling into three categories of size according to the number of regularly participating adults reported. The mean figure for expenditures on social services for 772 congregations of $7,540 amounts to 5.6 percent of the mean figure for total expenditures of $134,162. Congregations with fewer than two hundred regularly participating adults spend much less, on average, in absolute amounts on social services than larger congregations, but the smallest congregations (fewer than one hundred adults) spend a larger percentage of their budget on social services than congregations with more members. We need to be cautious in drawing conclusions from these data because so many of the congregations (38 percent) did not report sufficient financial information.[28] These data also do not include an estimate of the cost of staff time or facilities that may have been spent on service programs.

Other estimates are available from sources that do not claim to represent congregations nationally, but which do help to make sense of congregations' financial contributions to service programs. One estimate is provided by the Presbyterian Church (USA), which annually collects financial data from member congregations and reports these data in a way that distinguishes the amount spent on "local mission" programs. The figures shown in table 2.6 give an indication of how Presbyterian giving is allocated. Of the nearly $3 billion spent in 2000, nearly two-thirds (62.96 percent) went for the maintenance of local congregations' internal programs, such as clergy and staff salaries, building maintenance, and utilities. Approximately 5 cents of every dollar was devoted to local mission activities. This is the category that includes most of the local service programs under consideration here, such as contributions to the support of a homeless shelter or tutoring program. Approximately 17 percent of total expenditures went for capital spending, such as new buildings, renovations, or mortgage payments on existing property. About 6 percent was invested, slightly more than 1 percent was sent to the denomination for the expenses of its national offices, almost 5 percent was spent on mission programs beyond the

TABLE 2.5

Financial Information Reported by Size of Congregation

	Fewer than 100 Adults	100–199 Adults	200 or More Adults	All Congregations
Total annual expenditures (mean)	$50,597	$157,584	$472,809	$134,162
Expenditures on social service programs (mean)	$3,498	$5,929	$27,228	$7,540
Services as % of total	6.9	3.8	5.8	5.6
Number	(514)	(141)	(117)	(772)

Source: National Congregations Survey, 1998.
Note: Numbers refer to "regular participating adults."

local community through the denomination's regional and national bodies, and about 2 percent was devoted to other mission activities.

These figures demonstrate several things about church giving. First, the amount spent on local service activities is a relatively small proportion of total giving, probably on the order of 5 percent, assuming that "local mission" does not include large expenditures for nonservice programs. Second, in dollars per member, the amount spent on local service activities is also quite small, amounting to less than $60 per year. Third, the total raised for service activities—nearly $150 million—by this one denomination points to the importance of congregations' involvement in service activities. And fourth, the fact that nearly the same amount is expended on mission programs beyond the local level, many of which are concerned with social needs (such as world hunger, sustainable agriculture, and international relief), suggests the importance of extending the discussion of congregations and social services beyond that of local communities.[29]

TABLE 2.6
Congregational Expenditures, Presbyterian Church (USA)

	Total (dollars)	Per Member (dollars)	Percentage of Total
Local program	1,838,731,521	728.12	62.96
Local mission	149,994,055	59.40	5.14
Capital expenditures	509,303,127	201.68	17.44
Investment expenditures	169,243,483	67.02	5.80
Per capita apportionment	40,029,941	15.85	1.37
Validated mission	141,761,451	56.16	4.86
Presbyterian General Mission	36,847,233	14.59	1.26
Synod General Mission	8,988,415	3.56	.31
General Assembly Mission	53,657,246	21.25	1.84
Other mission	71,257,581	28.22	2.44
Total expenditures	2,920,321,159	1,156.45	100.00

Source: Congregational Receipts and Expenditures, Presbyterian Church (USA), 2000; www.pcusa.org.

None of the estimates thus far take into account the fact that in many congregations clergy devote some of their time to social service activities. Other contributions that have financial value include the use of facilities, time volunteered by members of the congregation, or in-kind donations, such as meals, canned goods, and clothing. Ram Cnaan's study of 251 congregations in seven cities attempted to estimate the total value of these contributions. He estimated that on average congregations spent an equivalent of 22.6 percent of their annual operating budget on such expenditures for social services. Of this amount (which Cnaan estimated at approximately $51,000 per year), the largest share (41 percent) was accounted for by the estimated value of volunteer time (calculated at $11.58 per hour). Clergy and staff time allocated to service activities accounted for another 25 percent of congregations' total contribution. The cost of utilities and the value of space made up another 20 percent. And direct financial support amounted to 12 percent of the total.[30] These figures, then, shed light on congregations' financial contribution to social services in two ways. On the one hand, they point to the value of activities that have monetary value but that do not show up in standard church budgets. On the other hand, they suggest that the direct financial contribution of congregations to social services may be only about 3 percent of congregations' total budgets.

What does this money actually buy? Aggregate statistics such as this are not well suited to answer this question. The line-item budgets of local congregations are a better source for determining how congregations spend the money they list as being devoted to service programs. Although no congregation can be regarded as typical, figures obtained from one congregation are illustrative. Central Church is a large congregation that is theologically conservative but progressively involved in social ministries. Its total annual budget, which has been growing steadily in recent years, was approximately $1.4 million in 2002. For public purposes, the congregation's leadership allocates this amount to functional areas, rather than following the more traditional pattern of treating salaries, missions, investments, and the like, separately. It is thus possible to see how the congregation's leaders regard its contribution to social ministries. "Worship" makes up 15 percent of the total budget. This category includes an allocation of clergy and staff time to sermon preparation, the organization of worship services, and support for the church's adult and children's music ministries. Four percent, 6 percent, and 6 percent of the total budget are allocated respectively to youth, student, and children's ministries. These amounts cover staff salaries concerned with the junior and senior high youth programs, children's Sunday school classes, teacher training, and a pilot preschool program. Seven percent of the total budget is allocated to "congregational care and nurture." Most of this amount appears to be spent on paying clergy and staff for doing pastoral care, such as home visits or counseling, and the remainder covers costs associated with a lay counseling program and the adult Sunday school program. Fifteen percent of the budget pays for the maintenance of existing buildings, utilities, capital improvements, and interest on current debt. And 16 percent goes for the cost of otherwise unallocated activities, especially the church office staff and associated administrative costs. This leaves 31 percent of the budget for "missions."

A closer look at Central Church's $436,000 missions program reveals that 94 percent of this amount is spent helping support approximately seventy-five missionaries in the United States and in other countries. Six percent (approximately $26,000, or 1.9 percent of the total budget) is allocated to a "Social Action Committee" that ministers among the poor, needy, and oppressed. These ministries include a list of twenty specific programs that the church has officially chosen to help sponsor. Most of these are local and are directly involved in social service provision, but at least four are national or international programs to which the congregation contributes. The local programs include a food and clothing assistance center operated by a coalition of churches of which Central is a part, a crisis pregnancy center to which Central contributes an annual donation, the local chapter of Habitat for Humanity, an AIDS ministry, and a job training program.

Central Church's Social Action Committee expresses the congregation's commitment "to understand and proclaim Christ's compassion for all people, by awareness and involvement in social issues and through intentional outreach to the community." If Central Church had been included in one of the national surveys we have considered, it would fall among the larger congregations in terms of regular adult participation and its pastor would have been able to check a long list of social ministries it helps to support. A close look at the congregation's financial commitment to these ministries suggests that they represent a very small amount of the church's budget. Yet leaders from the congregation would argue that even this small expenditure on social ministries facilitated a much wider array of contributions. A nationally prominent speaker visited the church and helped persuade its members to be more concerned about the poor. The congregation's children decorated Christmas packages for AIDS patients, the youth group prepared a meal for men at one of the local homeless shelters, volunteers helped the Habitat Team construct five new houses, and small cash donations went directly to families referred to the church by the public welfare department. What stands out most clearly from this example is that congregations, even with large memberships and sizable budgets, work *with* other community organizations, rather than providing social services on their own. We will look more closely at how congregations organize these relationships with other agencies, but first we need to consider what research studies show about the variations in congregations' commitment to social service.

Which Congregations Do More?

There has been considerable interest among scholars and among church leaders in determining which congregations are more likely than others to be involved in social service activities and to understand the reasons for these differences. This interest is partly driven by a sense of pride, I suppose, as leaders of one kind of church compare programs with leaders of another, but it also provides clues about why church-based programs are as prevalent as they are or about what might be done to stimulate more. As we have seen, larger congregations are more likely than smaller congregations to help sponsor service programs and to be involved in a wider variety of such programs. Other factors matter as well. From the National Congregations Study, Chaves concludes that the social class composition of both the congregation and the neighborhood in which it is located influence the likelihood of churches sponsoring social programs. Having mostly middle-class members is more conducive to service activities than having large proportions of either poor or wealthy members, he suggests, and being located in a low-income neighborhood is also conducive to sponsoring service activities. Thus, the large downtown congregation composed of middle-class people but located near or in low-income neighborhoods is the church in which service activities are most likely to be found.

Congregations like this have the resources to help and are in the vicinity of neighborhoods in which social needs are most visible.[31]

The role of religious tradition in encouraging or inhibiting congregations' interest in service activities has not shown consistent results in previous research. Chaves found that congregations associated with evangelical denominations and congregations described by their leaders as theologically conservative were *less* likely to sponsor social service programs than other, presumably more liberal or progressive denominations. This pattern was also evident when Chaves examined specific kinds of social programs, such as food, shelter, and support for the sick, and when he took into account other differences, such as size, location, and racial composition. In contrast, Cnaan's research failed to find statistically significant differences between self-defined theologically conservative churches and other churches in either the number of social programs they sponsored or the percentage of annual budget devoted to these programs, controlling for various measures of congregation size, budget, age of congregation, and other reported characteristics of the congregation.[32] The differences between Chaves's and Cnaan's results may be attributable to different ways of measuring theological conservatism or to the way questions were asked or included in the analysis as control variables.[33]

Two of the surveys in which church members reported on their congregations' service activities provide an additional source for examining the influence of religious tradition on service activities. These data have the advantage of larger numbers of cases, more detailed questions about denominational affiliations, and the ability to take account of both congregational and individual characteristics. One permits a comparison of congregations associated with different religious traditions, while the other permits comparisons based on the perceived conservatism or liberalism of the congregation's theological orientation. The comparisons among denominational traditions are shown in table 2.7. The top part of the table shows the percentage of members of evangelical Protestant churches, mainline Protestant churches, historically black Protestant churches, Catholic parishes, and other religious traditions who said that their congregation helped to sponsor a food pantry, a day care program, a homeless shelter, and a tutoring program. The bottom part of the table presents the likelihood (expressed as odds ratios from logistic regression analysis) of each religious tradition sponsoring each of these programs in comparison with the likelihood of mainline Protestant churches sponsoring these programs, taking account of region, residence, congregation size, respondent's level of education, and respondent's frequency of attendance at religious services.[34]

In these comparisons, evangelicals are less likely than mainline Protes-

TABLE 2.7
Congregations' Service Activities by Religious Tradition

	Food Pantry or Kitchen	Day Care Program	Homeless Shelter	Tutoring Program
Percentage of members of each group who say their congregation sponsors the activity listed				
Evangelical Protestant	79	44	46	37
Mainline Protestant	87	56	58	38
Black Protestant	77	44	49	60
Roman Catholic	86	47	57	50
Other	74	45	50	51
Odds ratios from logistic regression equations (mainline Protestant as reference group)				
Evangelical Protestant	.591**	.711**	.594***	.932
Black Protestant	.557**	.659*	.674*	2.414***
Roman Catholic	.762	.515***	.767*	1.295*
Other	.435***	.692**	.720*	1.686***
Region (south)	.884	1.112	1.111	1.148
Residence (urban)	1.107	1.406**	1.123	1.483***
Residence (suburban)	1.515**	1.797***	1.452***	1.366**
Congregation size	1.000***	1.001***	1.000***	1.000***
Respondent's education	1.228***	1.062	1.121**	1.191***
Respondent's attendance	1.006**	.993***	1.006***	1.006***

Source: Religion and Politics Survey, 2000.
Note: Congregation members with denominational affiliations only; N = 2,967; * $p < .05$, ** $p < .01$, *** $p < .001$.

tants to say their churches sponsor three of the four service programs (tutoring is the exception). This is true both when the raw percentages are examined and when the odds ratios including controls are considered. Members of historically black congregations are less likely than mainline Protestants to say their churches sponsor food pantries, day care programs, or homeless shelters, but they are much more likely than mainline Protestants to say their congregations support tutoring programs. Catholics resemble mainline Protestants on the question about food pantries, are less likely than mainline Protestants to say their congregations support day care programs or homeless shelters, and are more likely to say their churches sponsor tutoring programs. Members of other faiths are more likely to say their congregations support tutoring programs, but are less likely to say their congregations sponsor the other three kinds of programs.

Comparisons of congregations in terms of members' *perceptions* of the congregation's theological orientation are shown in table 2.8. Here we have the ability to examine a larger number of service activities, but the numbers of respondents in the survey was smaller. Perceptions of theological orientation are subjective and thus may not accurately reflect reality, but they do provide an alternative to denominational affiliations (which can mask differences among congregations within denominational traditions). In these data, we are also able to control for congregations' size, whether the congregation is located in an inner city or suburb, and the frequency with which the respondent attends religious services.

On balance, the results are more consistent with Chaves's conclusion that theologically conservative congregations are less involved in social services than with Cnaan's conclusion that there are no differences. For instance, if we tally the number of respondents who said their congregation sponsored any *two* of the service programs on the list, we see that those in theologically conservative congregations are the least likely to say this, while those in theologically liberal congregations are the mostly likely. Looking at the specific programs in the table, the percentages of liberal congregations sponsoring them are higher than the percentages among conservative congregations in ten of the eleven comparisons. Yet the statistical analysis that takes into account the possible effects of other factors, such as congregation size and location, suggests that congregations' theological orientation is a significant influence on the likelihood of only some kinds of service programs. Inner-city ministries, counseling programs, meetings for alcoholics, and AIDS ministries are the specific programs significantly more likely to be sponsored by liberal congregations than by conservative ones. It is also worth noting that almost all of these service programs (the exceptions being food distribution and low-income housing) are more likely to be sponsored by congregations located in inner-city neighborhoods than by those in suburban areas or small towns.[35]

The best conclusion from these various pieces of evidence is that con-

TABLE 2.8

Congregations' Service Activities by Religious Orientation
(Percentage of congregations in each category that had helped to sponsor each service activity during the past year)

	Theologically Conservative	Theologically Moderate	Theologically Liberal	Odds Ratios
Ministry to prisoners	28	25	30	0.993
An inner-city ministry	37	40	56	1.320*
Counseling program	66	69	84	1.434**
Program for job seekers	20	23	22	1.077
Meetings for alcoholics	28	34	44	1.430**
Distributing food to the poor	82	87	86	1.366
Shelter for the homeless	36	36	48	1.157
AIDS ministry	14	15	38	1.726***
Low income housing	20	20	25	1.065
Tutoring program	31	33	39	1.157
Day care program	40	43	39	0.997
Any two of the above	79	87	92	2.191***
Number	(512)	(288)	(79)	(879)

Source: Civic Involvement Survey, 1997.

Note: Congregation's theological orientation as identified by members; N = 879; odds ratios for theological orientation from logistic regression equations, controlling for respondent's attendance, congregation size, and location of congregation; * p < .05, ** p < .01, *** p < .001.

gregations affiliated with mainline Protestant denominations and theologically liberal congregations probably are somewhat more inclined than other congregations to sponsor social service programs, but that there are also exceptions to this pattern. This means that generalizations about the relationship between religious tradition and service programs must be regarded with caution.[36] Indeed, other factors, such as congregation size and location, are probably more important than religious tradition.

How Service Programs Are Organized

I mentioned earlier that much of the information we have about congregation-based service programs includes activities in which congregations merely help as sponsors in addition to activities initiated and sponsored solely by the congregation. So how much do congregations do on their own and how much do they do in conjunction with other organizations? David Roozen, one of the authors of the *Faith Communities Today* study, sent me the following information. Among the white Protestant churches in his study, 86 percent claimed to have directly or in cooperation with another agency or congregation provided a food pantry or soup kitchen, but only 49 percent *directly* provided this service. Similarly, 64 percent had either directly or cooperatively helped to sponsor a thrift store, but only 34 percent had done this directly. Other programs followed the same pattern: the proportion that either directly or cooperatively sponsored affordable housing fell from 39 percent to 19 percent if only congregations directly providing affordable housing were considered; substance abuse programs, from 30 percent to 14 percent; community organizing, from 25 percent to 14 percent; health programs, from 26 percent to 14 percent, and so on.[37]

From these figures, we could conclude that there is a lot of double or triple counting going on in studies of congregation-based service programs, meaning that congregations are not doing nearly as much as these studies have suggested. However, there is a different conclusion that is also consistent with these figures. Congregation-based service programs are an important way in which civil society is glued together. They contribute to the larger society by promoting cooperation. Rather than each congregation starting its own programs (although plenty do), congregations work together with other congregations and with specialized service organizations. Information, volunteers, and clients flow back and forth through these channels of cooperation. People share ideas, talents, and resources. The civil society is stronger as a result, just as it is when individuals cooperate. But if this is the case, we need to look more closely at how congregation-based service programs are actually organized.

Some helpful quantitative information is available from an analysis of the social service networks of more than five hundred congregations conducted by Nancy Ammerman.[38] Ammerman found that 83 percent of the connections congregations had with other organizations involving human services were with local and regional organizations, while 17 percent were with national or international partners. She also found that among congregations with any connections there was little difference in the proportions involved in informal coalitions (62 percent), involved in cooperative relations with religious nonprofits (66 percent), or involved in cooperative relations with secular nonprofits (58 percent). These figures were considerably higher, though, than the proportion of congregations involved in service networks that included governmental units (29 percent). It is of course difficult to know exactly what these figures mean, but they at least suggest that congregations are fairly widely connected, not only with other churches, but also with more specialized nonprofit organizations and, although to a lesser extent, with government agencies.

To gain a clear sense of how congregations organize their formal service programs, it will be most helpful to focus on a few specific examples. In the case of First Baptist Church in Wayne, Pennsylvania, we saw earlier that its social ministries are sponsored directly by the congregation itself. Its housing for refugees, for instance, is adjacent to the church and operated almost entirely by volunteers and funding from the congregation. In this case, the congregation still relies to a small extent on partnerships, such as the resettlement agency of the denomination and, on occasion, through informal contacts with government agencies concerned with immigration and public welfare. Yet most of the service activity is administered by the congregation itself.

At First Baptist, the pastor played a large role in initiating the congregation's social ministries, but he received enthusiastic support for these efforts from an active group of lay members, and then the social outreach committee provides continuity, oversight, and coordination for the congregation's various service programs. This pattern is fairly typical. In all but the smallest congregations, a committee structure usually exists that divides responsibilities for such programs as worship, children's or adult education, visitation, stewardship, and social outreach. Ideas about new projects that should be initiated by the congregation or supported in some way are funneled to the committee, which in turn may recommend them to the pastor, congregation as a whole, or other leadership group (such as elders, vestry, or deacons). The outreach committee thus serves as a node in any number of overlapping networks involving other organizations in the community.

One kind of network is illustrated at St. Leo's Catholic Church. The network is called Congregations United for Community Assistance (CUCA). CUCA links the social outreach committees at a half-dozen or so churches in the same inner-city neighborhood. Collectively, the churches provide a part-time salary for a staff person and St. Leo's provides her an office in spare space formerly used by its parochial school. Mostly, CUCA ensures that the participating churches do not duplicate one another's efforts. If a new program is initiated, one of the participating churches formally becomes its sponsor and the rest informally become cosponsors, sometimes providing modest funding but more commonly helping to advertise the program and soliciting volunteers. Occasionally CUCA is able to exercise greater influence because of representing all the participating churches (for instance, in a program to monitor police violence in the neighborhood). The part-time staff person has also written grants to secure funding from the city or state.

It is not atypical for congregations to be involved in multiple networks. For instance, St. Leo's is also part of a network of congregations that works together to put on an annual health fair. Unlike CUCA, which meets regularly throughout the year, the health fair network meets periodically to develop publicity for the health fair and to provide physicians and nurses to staff the fair. Both networks involve multiple congregations and thus make it easier to organize events than if any single church worked alone. Another network in which St. Leo's participates illustrates a collaborative venture in which the church plays only a secondary role. This is an adult literacy program. Most of the work is done by a nonprofit organization in the community that specializes in adult literacy. The organization advertises for clients and volunteers at local churches. St. Leo's also supplies space for some of the classes.

The foregoing are examples of networks that have been formalized so that several congregations and other community agencies can work together. There are also numerous examples of informal networks. These usually consist of referrals, often by clergy of needy people whose needs require more assistance than the congregation can provide. The priest at St. Leo's, for instance, routinely receives requests from lower-income families for money to tide them over to the next paycheck or welfare check. But, he says, "we never give out cash here from the parish." The parish doesn't have the means, for one thing, and he doesn't want to start a practice that would result in more people coming for such help. "We are a parish community that tries to take care of its members as much as we can," he explains. "But for large problems, we try to redirect people to the agencies that can help work through those problems." Such referrals are facilitated by the fact that clergy often serve on the boards of other service agencies or know their directors through cooperative programs.

Unlike at St. Leo's, other congregations have in-house committees or funds that do provide direct assistance, including cash, to needy people in the community. These funds are sometimes administered by the same social outreach committee that oversees formal service programs and in other cases is a special department in charge of benevolence. At an independent African American church, for example, the benevolence committee evaluates the needs of every individual who seeks direct assistance from the church, and then sometimes provides help in the form of meals or lodging at a local hotel or refers the person to a shelter or rescue mission.

Congregations that directly sponsor a formal service organization with staff or volunteers of its own are usually ones with larger memberships or more ample budgets. The typical pattern is for these programs to emerge gradually through the interests of one or more members of the congregation, although sometimes a congregation may step in to administer a separate program that would otherwise be in danger of closing. With a modest financial commitment, the congregation may hire a part-time staff person to administer the program, or pay for a volunteer to receive training. Then the success or failure of the project falls largely on the staff person's ability to recruit volunteers and solicit additional funding. We will discuss these separate faith-based programs more fully in chapter 5.

Conclusions and Unanswered Questions

The evidence we have examined in this chapter suggests that congregations contribute in a number of ways to the provision of social services in the United States. Many—probably most—congregations help to provide formal service programs, either by organizing and administering such programs, by participating in coalitions that support such programs, or by contributing financial support. Most Americans who participate in religious congregations are aware of service projects and believe that their congregations support such projects.

Yet the evidence also suggests the limits of congregation-based service provision. Congregations are more likely, it appears, to help other organizations supply services than to invest heavily in organizing formal programs of their own. Few congregations devote more than a small proportion of their annual budget to supporting service ministries.

Making sense of such evidence requires stepping away from the various facts and figures and reflecting more broadly on the roles that congregations play in our society. We cannot understand the fact that congregations sponsor relatively few social ministries or devote relatively small shares of their budgets to these ministries, for instance, simply by accusing church leaders of being hypocritical—that is, of claiming to care for the needy but failing to follow through on their claims. We must rather inquire into the social and cultural influences—what I referred to in chapter 1 as institutional embeddedness—that encourage most congregations to be involved a *little* in social services, and not more.

A useful starting point is the fact that congregational *size* has such a notable impact on the likelihood of congregations having social ministries (or larger numbers of them), but seemingly little impact on the share of budgets devoted to these ministries or the likelihood of people feeling supported by their congregations. These patterns suggest that congregations generally recognize the importance of caregiving, but are constrained in the kinds of programs that they can sponsor formally.[39] Larger congregations have more members and larger budgets, and are thus able to contribute to a wider variety of social ministries. Few congregations, though, contribute very much to these ministries because other activities take priority. Salaries need to be paid, buildings must be maintained, and regular programs (such as worship and children's education) have to be provided if the congregation is going to attract and retain participants at all.

Congregations exist, just as businesses do, in a competitive environment.[40] If pastors' salaries are too low or if the building falls into disrepair, members can easily switch to a more attractive location. At the same time, if a congregation does nothing to help the needy, that too may be a strike against it, relative to the competition. In short, a kind of equilibrium develops that encourages congregations to be involved in service provision, but not too heavily involved. The exceptions are the occasional congregation (like First Baptist) that carves out a distinctive niche in the community by specializing in social ministries, just as other congregations may specialize in sponsoring exceptional choirs or youth programs.

The unanswered question is how congregational leaders decide to sponsor or contribute to the support of particular service programs. For instance, why does a congregation like Central Church contribute to such a diverse portfolio of social ministries, and why do more congregations support food programs than, say, ministries to people with AIDS? We would need more information from pastors and from closed-door administrative sessions than is currently available to answer these questions. But we can make some informed guesses.

Congregations are like other organizations in making decisions in terms of pressures from the marketplace and from particular constituencies. Support for service programs is probably governed by two considerations: how familiar the need is to members of the congregation, and the presence of special-purpose groups interested in particular programs. Familiarity accounts for the fact that food distribution is much more commonly supported by congregations than, say, AIDS programs or shelters for abused women. Food distribution not only has a long history of support in congregations but is a relatively well-publicized need. The presence of special-purpose groups accounts for the fact that many congregations adopt a portfolio of causes and ministries, rather than devoting their energies fully to any one cause or ministry. Contributing in small ways to many programs means being able to respond positively to particular interest groups. This pattern also suggests that the growing number of nonprofit organizations in the wider society has prompted congregations to diversify their ministries.

In the final analysis, congregations are the heart of American religion and thus play a central role in service provision, and yet they are neither the primary location of such provision, at least as far as formal programs are concerned, nor can service provision be understood solely in terms of congregational analysis. Congregations are more like the staging grounds for service provision than like actual service providers. They mobilize people, support them spiritually, remind them of their moral responsibilities, and reinforce their commitments by putting them in contact with like-minded believers. Through such mobilization, some service programs are supported directly. But much of the service activity that results from religious commitments takes place informally within the congregation itself, through the work of individual volunteers, and through special nonprofit organizations oriented specifically to the provision of social services. It is to these topics that we must now turn.

Congregations as Caring Communities

The ideal of a "caring community" that many clergy and church leaders try to encourage among their adherents is rather different from the service model we examined in the last chapter. In the service model, congregations devote resources to service programs that are formal, specific, and often somewhat separate from the rest of the congregation. But, as many clergy see it, a congregation should be different from a service organization. In a service organization, people with resources help people who lack resources. Resources consist of professional training, organizational skills, being able to raise and channel charitable donations or government funds to worthy causes, or having the time in one's job description or the funds in one's portfolio to be helpful to people in need. The service-organization model suggests that congregations should serve their communities, much like the welfare department or the Red Cross, by raising funds and recruiting volunteers, organizing programs to help the needy, and finding ways to advertise the availability of these programs to the wider community. As we have seen, congregations often do some of this. Part of their ministry is to initiate or contribute to the support of service programs, such as homeless shelters, food pantries, clinics, and day care programs. Yet this is not the only or even necessarily the most important way in which congregations contribute to the needy and to the benefit of civil society.

The service-organization model certainly does not adequately capture the ways in which clergy and lay leaders *think* about the caring that takes place—or that should take place—in their congregations. As caring communities, congregations usually try to emulate some understanding about the first-century followers of Christ who came to be known for their love and support of one another. Sociologists would say that caring communities differ from service organizations in at least three important ways.

First, social interaction in communities takes place more regularly, over a longer period of time, and across a wider variety of activities than social interaction in a service organization. Second, being part of a community necessarily implies a distinction between those who are "insiders" and those who are "outsiders," whereas a service organization tends to redefine these relationships in terms of "providers" and "recipients" or "professionals" and "clients." And third, communities are characterized by what is sometimes called a "thick" set of shared values, beliefs, understandings, traditions, and norms, whereas the relationships involving service organizations and clients are more likely to consist of "thin," arms-length, or contractual understandings.

In principal, congregations should function as caring communities in these ways. If they do, they may contribute to the "saving of America" in ways poorly captured by the service-organization model. Indeed, some of the controversy over government funding of faith-based organizations can be understood in terms of the differences between congregations as caring communities and congregations as service organizations. As caring communities, congregations may function best by encouraging participants to help other participants, rather than trying to help any and all who may need help in the wider community.[1] The caring community, moreover, may function best by encouraging deep friendships and long-term relationships, rather than by organizing formal programs. Such friendships may, however, involve deeply shared values and thus depend on like-mindedness rather than on an open spirit toward diverse beliefs and norms.

To examine whether or not congregations live up to the ideal of being caring communities, we need to examine some data on specific aspects of what it may mean to be a caring community. In this chapter I present evidence on the following questions: Are congregations places where the value of caring for the needy is emphasized, for example, through sermons or classes on this topic? Do congregations provide civic space in which meetings and other community activities can be held? Do congregations sponsor small support groups that actually encourage participants to care for one another? Are congregations places in which friendships develop? Do participants in congregations feel that they could depend on their congregations if they needed help? Through participation in congregations, do people develop friendships with people who are less privileged than themselves, that is, people who may need their help at some point? And do participants in congregations develop ties with people who have access to wealth and power—people who may have the kinds of resources that can be useful for helping those in their congregations with fewer advantages?

Emphasizing the Value of Caring

Congregations are above all places of worship. Participants meet regularly to pray, to offer praise in singing, to recite familiar creeds, to hear preaching, and to celebrate the sacraments. At the heart of the traditional worship service is the sermon. In the National Congregations Study, 95 percent of congregations included sermons as part of their regular weekly worship services.[2] Sermons remind participants of biblical teachings. Insofar as caring for the needy is an important aspect of these teachings, sermons become a vehicle for exhorting congregants to express concern for the needy in their personal lives and through their congregations. In short, congregations promote awareness of social needs and of the importance of addressing these needs.

At least congregations function *in principle* as sources of awareness about social needs. In practice, research suggests that they do in fact fulfill this function. Although studies of clergy behavior are not as common as one might suppose, the best research on clergy provides evidence on the topics they cover in their sermons. For instance, in a large-scale study of clergy in eight Protestant denominations, political scientist James L. Guth and several coauthors found that "hunger and poverty" were among the issues clergy said they most frequently addressed in their sermons. The percentages who said they addressed hunger and poverty "very often" or "often" ranged from 61 percent among Assemblies of God clergy to 90 percent among Disciples of Christ pastors. On average, the only social or moral issues that were addressed more commonly were "family issues" and "alcohol and drug abuse," while such issues as school prayer, civil rights, and the environment were addressed less frequently. Further analysis of the data showed that the frequency with which many of the issues asked about in the study were covered in sermons varied considerably by denomination and by pastors' theological orientation (for instance, abortion and pornography were preached about more often by theologically orthodox pastors in conservative denominations, while women's issues and Latin America were discussed less often by these pastors). Hunger and poverty, though, were topics that varied relatively little by theological orientation or denomination. These topics, it seemed, were considered important by most pastors, regardless of differences in theology, affiliation, or personal background.[3]

Of course pastors may emphasize different things when they preach about hunger and poverty. I have made it a point in my research over the years to ask pastors to tell me the themes of the sermons they preach having to do with the poor.[4] A common theme is that economic poverty is really a reflection of spiritual poverty. The Reverend John Marsh, who pastors the nondenominational New Covenant Life Church, illustrates this theme when he describes the "startling poverty" in his area as "a spiritual issue." He remembers helping at a homeless shelter and realizing that the trouble wasn't economic, but spiritual: "When people have rejected God, or perhaps when they have no truth that's ever been taught them about how to really relate to God through faith in the Lord Jesus and the power of the Holy Spirit, they're going to look to something else, and that something else could be drugs or it could be the occult or some other destructive thing that ruins relationships and can ruin health and basically makes havoc of the human person." The result, in this pastor's view, is alienation and emotional instability, which in turn lead to joblessness and homelessness. He therefore believes that poverty cannot be dealt with effectively unless people are drawn into the life-transforming experience of a faith community. A very different theme, one that is also common among pastors, emphasizes the ways in which society contributes to the problems of the poor. For instance, the Reverend Mitchell Stewart at Second Presbyterian Church says he reminds his listeners that many people in their community are suffering because of "insecurity in the job market" and "the downsizing of companies." He also worries about insufficient care facilities for the elderly and problems with drugs and alcohol among young people. These problems nevertheless have a spiritual dimension in that they are aggravated by the materialism, greed, and selfishness of middle-class Americans. It is thus helpful for people to become part of a caring faith community as a way of overcoming selfishness. Whichever theme is emphasized, clergy uniformly say that the appropriate response should be love and compassion, including concrete efforts to ameliorate suffering.

Whether churchgoers remember *hearing* sermons about caring was addressed in the 1997 survey of the public that I conducted about civic involvement. Table 3.1 shows how church members and nonmembers who attended religious services with varying frequency responded when asked if they had heard a sermon in the year prior to the survey about caring for the poor. In all, 42 percent of the public claimed to have heard a sermon on this topic. This proportion rose to 58 percent among church members and to 73 percent among church members who attended services every week. Further analysis of the data indicated that there were no significant differences, once frequency of attendance and congregation size were taken into account, in these responses among members of theologically conservative, moderate, or liberal congregations.[5] It would be interesting to know if church members who hear such sermons actually do more to help the poor than church members who do not hear these sermons—a question that to my knowledge has not been investigated. What we can conclude, at least, is that congregations do supply many Americans with occasional reminders about caring for the poor.

The Religion and Politics Survey, on which we have drawn previously, provides some additional information about the topics church members

TABLE 3.1

Sermons about Caring for the Poor
(Percentage who said they had heard a sermon about caring for the poor within the past year among those who attended religious services)

	Congregation Members	Nonmembers	All Respondents
Frequency of attendance			
Every week	73	a	72
Almost every week	56	a	57
Once or twice a month	54	43	51
A few times a year	35	26	30
Never	20	3	5
Total	58	17	42
Number	(915)	(599)	(1,528)

Source: Civic Involvement Survey, 1997.
Note: a = too few for stable percentages.

remember hearing discussed in their congregations. In this study, members who attended at least a few times a year were asked if they had heard a sermon, lecture, or group discussion in their congregation during the past year that dealt with various topics. None of the topics asked about in the survey concerned caring specifically, but three of the questions dealt with topics relevant to the broader issue of how congregations may raise awareness of the needs of the poor (see table 3.2). "The government's policies toward the poor" was a topic that 38 percent of church members claimed to have heard discussed at their congregations during the past year. Almost the same proportion (36 percent) said they had heard discussions of "the widening gap between rich people and poor people." And a larger proportion (58 percent) said they had heard discussions about "improving relations between blacks and whites." In each case, there were few differences among members who attended more than once a week, once a week, almost every week, or once or twice a month, but the figures for these members were higher than for those who said they attended only a few times a

TABLE 3.2
Sermons about Inequality
(Percentage of church members who had heard a sermon on each topic during the past year)

	Government Policies toward the Poor	The Gap between Rich and Poor People	Relations between Blacks and Whites
Frequency of attendance			
More than once a week	40	32	62
Once a week	40	38	60
Almost every week	40	40	61
Once or twice a month	38	38	60
A few times a year	29	28	44
Total	38	36	58

Source: Religion and Politics Survey, 2000.
Note: N = 3,184.

year. Further examination of the responses showed that African Americans were more likely than white Americans to have heard discussions of all three topics, and on the two about the poor, Catholics were more likely to have heard discussions than evangelical or mainline Protestants.[6]

The National Congregations Study also provides some evidence about the ways in which congregations may promote a culture of caring among regular participants. In an article about mainline Protestants from these data, Chaves and two coauthors report that six mainline members in ten were in congregations that had hosted a representative of a social service organization as a visiting speaker during the year preceding the survey and that an equal number were in congregations that held group meetings or classes to organize or encourage people to do volunteer work. The respective proportions who responded similarly to these two questions among other Protestants were 25 and 45 percent, and among Catholics, 46 and 79 percent. A majority of mainline Protestants and Catholics were also members of congregations in which there had been a meeting to plan or conduct an assessment of community needs.[7]

From these various sources, then, it seems evident that congregations often include some sermons or other discussions about community needs. Although the studies are not strictly comparable, it also seems likely that there is more discussion of caring for the poor than there is about government policies or inequality more broadly. Being caring, showing love, and helping others informally may be the more commonly accepted way of addressing needs than discussing public policies or launching formal service programs. This, at least, is a conclusion that critics sometimes draw from considering the emphasis churches seem to place on charity and volunteering in comparison with advocacy.[8]

Congregations as Civic Space

Another way in which congregations may facilitate a culture of caring is by making space available for community meetings. We saw in chapter 2 that Cnaan's research suggests the important role houses of worship play in providing meeting space for community groups (such as scouting troops). Chaves reports that a large proportion of churchgoers attend congregations that permit outside groups to use or rent space in their building: 85 percent of mainline Protestant members are in such congregations, as are

73 percent of Catholics and 55 percent of other Protestants.[9] Of course such uses would include opening the fellowship hall to a musical group for rehearsals and perhaps even renting the sanctuary for weddings. Church buildings are abundantly available in most communities and often have fewer restrictions than, say, public schools or hotels. We should not assume too readily, though, that these buildings are actually used as civic space.

The Civic Involvement Survey yields some helpful information for assessing the role of church buildings as civic space. The survey asked a nationally representative sample of adults if they had attended any meetings during the past year that dealt with community issues. About three people in ten (29 percent) said they had (see table 3.3). And because the question (and other questions preceding it) did not mention religion, there was nothing about the question itself that would have prompted people to interpret their churchgoing as attendance of this kind. What influenced the likelihood of having attended such meetings was, rather, the kind of community in which people lived. Those who lived in upper-income neighborhoods were the most likely to have attended such meetings, whereas those in lower-income neighborhoods were about half as likely to have attended such meetings, with persons from middle- or mixed-income neighborhoods falling in between. Respondents were then asked to say where the meetings they had attended had taken place (with the possibility of naming more than one location, since people may have attended more than one meeting). *Churches,* along with schools, headed the list. In each of the kinds of neighborhoods (upper-, mixed-, middle-, and lower-income) at least half of those who had attended meetings about community issues at all had attended a meeting that had been held at a church. This proportion was slightly higher than the percentage who had attended such meetings at town halls or government buildings or at neighborhood centers, and it was substantially higher than the percentage who had attended such meetings at their place of work, someone's house, a volunteer center, a restaurant or hotel, or a college or university.

It is important not to exaggerate the importance of these civic uses of church buildings. Because the proportion of adults who attend any meetings about community issues is low, relatively few people actually participate in such meetings at churches, and this is especially the case for residents of low-income neighborhoods (where only 11 percent would have been to a community-issues meeting at a church during the year). Those who do participate, though, may learn valuable civic skills; even those who simply play a role in conducting church business may also learn (and enhance) such skills and become involved in community matters through interactions with other church members.[10] Through leading meetings, speaking up for one's point of view, voting at congregational meetings, or helping to organize children's Sunday school programs, people develop the capacity to lead and the ability to understand how civic groups function. And churches may be more available to people in poor communities for these purposes than many other such locations; for instance, the 50 per-

TABLE 3.3
Churches as Locations for Community Meetings

	Upper Income	Mixed Income	Middle Income	Lower Income	All Respondents
Percentage who had attended any meetings during the past year that dealt with community issues	43	30	29	22	29
Among these, percentage who had attended meetings at each place					
Church	70	56	55	50	56
School	62	50	57	50	56
Town hall/gov't building	51	46	49	38	48
Neighborhood center	40	44	42	46	43
Place of work	46	22	32	29	32
Neighbor's house	51	32	30	17	31
Volunteer center	19	18	22	23	21
House outside neighborhood	32	12	22	12	20
Restaurant or hotel	24	16	22	8	20
College or university	22	22	20	10	19
Number	(86)	(165)	(1,046)	(217)	(1,522)

Source: Civic Involvement Survey, 1997.

cent of meeting attendees in low-income neighborhoods who attended a meeting at a church is not much lower than the 55 percent of residents of middle-income neighborhoods, whereas the likelihood of having met at a college or university, restaurant, hotel, or house outside the neighborhood is much smaller for residents of low-income communities than for those in middle-income communities. These results, then, lend further support to the important conclusion drawn by political scientist Sidney Verba and his coauthors in their major research project on political participation. Religious institutions, they write, "play an unusual role in the American participatory system by providing opportunities for the development of civic skills to those who would otherwise be resource-poor."[11]

We must also put the role of churches as civic space in perspective by acknowledging that churchgoers may not view their congregations as places for discussing social and political issues, especially if these issues are controversial. Despite the fact that congregations encourage people to think about such needs as caring for the poor, several features of congregations reduce the likelihood that members will actually talk about social issues with other members: even the most active members may not see one another more than once a week, their attention is more likely to be drawn to religious or spiritual concerns than to social issues, and they may feel it inappropriate to bring up topics about which there may be disagreement. For all these reasons, other networks and places may be more common as locations for discussions of social issues.

The figures in table 3.4 show the contexts in which people living in high-, mixed-, middle-, and low-income communities express themselves on social and political issues. Talking about such issues with other members of one's church or synagogue is not uncommon: between one-quarter and one-third of people in each kind of community said they did this. And this is about the same proportion as for talking with members of other community organizations. But the most common contexts are among family members and friends. Even neighborhoods and the workplace are more common locations for civic conversations than churches.

The value that congregations add as spaces for civic meetings and discussions, therefore, is twofold. Congregations facilitate meetings for discussing community needs and for planning programs to meet these needs if a physical place in which to hold such meetings is available. This is especially true if that place is familiar to community residents, can be used

TABLE 3.4
Contexts for Discussing Social Issues

	Upper Income	Mixed Income	Middle Income	Lower Income	All Respondents
Percentage who ever talk about social or political issues with					
Family members	92	71	81	77	80
Friends	95	68	80	76	79
Neighbors	63	44	51	48	50
People at work	64	37	48	43	47
Church/synagogue members	34	22	30	28	30
Members of other community					
organizations	38	20	30	21	28
Number	(86)	(165)	(1,046)	(217)	(1,522)

Source: Civic Involvement Survey, 1997.
Note: Income categories refer to respondent's description of his or her neighborhood.

free of charge, and is associated culturally with values such as caring and civic responsibility. In addition, congregations draw people out of their homes and put them in contact with a larger and perhaps more diverse group. Unlike the discussions of social and political issues that take place among family members and friends, those involving other members of one's congregation are in a sense more public. They may include people with whom one disagrees, but with whom one still chooses to interact, and they can sometimes result in programs or classes or find their way into sermons and formal gatherings.

Caring in Small Groups

Although congregations (at least small ones) may be like one big family in which everyone knows and cares for everyone else, the actual caring that takes place in congregations is generally facilitated by small groups that bring parts of the congregation together on a regular basis for study, prayer, fellowship, or some other activity. In the National Congregations Study, 73 percent of congregations had groups that met once a month or more often for various purposes, such as religious, social, and recreational activities (not counting ordinary administrative committees), and when congregations were weighted according to size, 87 percent of all members appeared to be in congregations with such groups. The most common groups included women's groups, Bible study groups, groups for children, groups for the elderly, and prayer groups. In the Civic Involvement Survey, 76 percent of church or synagogue members said their congregation helped to sponsor "small fellowship groups." Members of large and small congregations were about equally likely to give this response; for example, 76 percent of members in congregations with fewer than one hundred members said their congregation sponsored small fellowship groups, 78 percent did in congregations of three hundred to five hundred members, and 83 percent did in congregations of more than two thousand members.

Estimates of the number of Americans who actually participate in small groups vary depending on how survey questions are worded. In earlier research, I found that 40 percent of U.S. adults claimed to be involved in a "small group that meets regularly and provides caring and support for its members."[12] About two-thirds of these groups were associated with congregations, consisting mainly of Bible studies, prayer fellowships, Sunday school classes, and self-help groups, with the remainder mostly being book clubs, discussion groups, and recreational groups. In the Civic Involvement Survey, 24 percent of adults nationally said they currently "attended a Bible study or fellowship group," 19 percent said they "regularly attended an adult Sunday school class," and 9 percent said they participated in a "self-help group." In that study, 32 percent of Americans claimed to be participating in at least one of these three kinds of groups. In a national study I conducted in 1999 to examine the role of small groups in promoting forgiveness, I found that 35 percent of Americans said that they were involved in a "prayer group meeting or Bible study group" or in "any other small group, such as a self-help group, support group, men's or women's group, or Sunday school class."[13]

As is true of American congregations more generally, small groups attract a wide cross-section of people. The members of small groups are white, African American, or Hispanic in about the same proportions as in the population at large. They divide into age categories about the same way the public at large does: 43 percent are in their thirties or forties, 38 percent are in their fifties or older, and only 16 percent are between the ages of 18 and 30. Small group members do differ from the general public in terms of being better educated; for instance, 42 percent are college graduates, compared with 28 percent in the public at large. The most important way in which small-group members are different from the general public is in their level of religious involvement: 85 percent are church members, compared with 60 percent of U.S. adults, and 70 percent say they attend religious services weekly, compared with 28 percent of the general public.[14]

Critics of small groups argue that these groups attract people who are mostly interested in themselves, rather than people who care about others. Critics also argue that people either flit in and out of these groups, rather than staying long enough to establish genuine caring relationships, or become so engrossed in their own problems that the groups fail to link people to wider community concerns and institutions (the way Masonic lodges, social clubs, and churches presumably did in the past).[15] The data shown in table 3.5 suggest that most of these criticisms are unwarranted. A large majority of small groups have been in existence for at least five years, and large proportions of members have also been involved that long, so it is inaccurate to say that these groups are ephemeral. The level of commitment to these groups is high, judging from the regularity with which they meet, the length of meetings, and the personal importance members attach to their groups. The groups are indeed small, much smaller than the average congregation, for instance, and their size probably is conducive to the intimate relationships that develop in them; but they are not so small as to be merely cliques of a few friends who get together occasionally for coffee (the median size is between sixteen and twenty members). Although people may join these groups for self-interested reasons (such as wanting personal fulfillment or seeking friends), they apparently manage to care for one another enough to feel that these needs have been met. A very large majority say their groups have given them emotional support, and nearly two-thirds say their group helped them through an emotional crisis and helped them when they or someone in their family was sick. Nor do the groups' members perceive their caring to be focused exclusively within their groups. A majority say group discussions have focused a lot of attention on helping the needy and three-quarters say their group has done things for the community and that they personally have worked with the group to help people outside of the group. On all of these measures, the members of groups that are associated with churches or synagogues score higher than those who belong to other kinds of groups. And the fact that their groups are affiliated with congregations means that these groups are not as isolated as critics sometimes believe. The affiliation with congregations means that group members are part of a larger organization than the group itself, and through their congregations often have a connection with denominational agencies or other community organizations as well.

TABLE 3.5
Characteristics of Members of Small Groups
(Percentages having each characteristic)

	Church-Based Groups	Other Groups	All Groups
Group has been in existence 5 years or more	73	64	70
Involved in group at least 5 years	60	42	55
Attend group meetings about once a week	66	47	60
Group is very important personally	88	73	83
Group meetings last at least 1.5 hours	58	76	64
Group has at least 16 members	52	52	52
Nearly everyone comes to group meetings	77	62	72
Group provides emotional support	88	79	86
Group helped you through emotional crisis	67	55	64
Group helped you when someone was sick	68	48	62
Group provided physical care or support	47	37	44
Group does things for the community	85	63	78
A lot of attention to helping the needy	65	41	58
Worked with group to help people outside	83	62	77
Number	(972)	(407)	(1,379)

Source: Forgiveness Survey, 1999.

The role small groups play in facilitating forgiveness is particularly interesting. Although forgiveness has not often been included in discussions of caregiving and social services, there is a growing body of research that suggests its relevance.[16] The inability to forgive others has been associated at least anecdotally with community violence and domestic abuse. Victims of crime, abusive relationships, and even divorce attest to the need to forgive and experience forgiveness as part of the emotional healing process. Being able to forgive oneself for financial failures, broken relationships, and other perceived misdeeds also appears to be a component of overcoming addictions and other high-risk behavior.[17] By their own accounts at least, small group members claim that forgiveness is frequently emphasized in group discussions. In all, 86 percent said their group had paid at least some attention to "forgiving other people" in the past year, and 63 percent said their group had paid a lot of attention to this topic. Almost as many (75 percent) said their group had paid some attention to "forgiving oneself," and 50 percent said their group had paid a lot of attention to this aspect of forgiveness. Qualitative interviews with group leaders and members and observations of groups showed that forgiveness was emphasized in several ways: through books or study guides that explicitly focused on forgiveness, through confessional prayer, through sharing and discussing emotional concerns, and through discussing biblical principles or role models of forgiveness.

One example of how small groups promote forgiveness comes from a Catholic layman who was divorced ten years ago and has participated regularly since then in a spiritual direction group at his church. He says "there was a lot of resentment" that included not only anger but "low-grade depression" as a result of the divorce. Being in the group has helped him be more honest with himself, to seek professional help at one point, and to make peace with his children. Another example is a Presbyterian woman whose husband was a pastor and whose congregation decided to fire him. She was so angry that the incident almost destroyed her faith. She eventually started attending a small group at another church and has especially appreciated times when the group has prayed for her. She says she isn't quite ready to forgive but that the group is helping her move in that direction.

It is hard to know if group discussions of forgiveness actually alter behavior, especially over the long term. Follow-up interviews with some of the people in the Forgiveness Survey eighteen months later suggested that there *were* some effects in the short term. People who said in the survey that their group had helped them forgive others were more likely eighteen months later than people who did not give this response to say that they had apologized recently to someone for something they had done or said, had recently asked someone to forgive them, had worked at improving a broken relationship, and had thought more about forgiveness recently.

Of course forgiveness is merely one aspect of caring. The broader conclusion from research about small groups in congregations is that these are quite often settings in which opportunities to give and receive care become evident and the value of caring is reinforced. It may be that caring seems to be associated with participation in small groups because caring people join these groups in the first place. However, there does seem to be evidence that people who spend more time in small groups are more likely to have both received care and given it than those who have spent less time. For instance (see table 3.6), people who have been members of their groups over a longer period of years are more likely to say the group has helped them through an emotional crisis, and to say that the group did things for the community and that through the group they were able to serve people outside of the group. The first and third of these are also positively associated with how often members attend meetings of their groups, and the second (doing things for the community) with how long the group has been in existence. These relationships are statistically significant when the effects of members' education levels, gender, and age are taken into account. Size of the group is unrelated to these three measures of giving and receiving care—a finding that runs against the view that small groups may be too small to do any good in their communities. And, with all these other characteristics taken into account, being formally connected with churches continues to be positively associated with these measures of caring.

Congregations as Sources of Social Capital

Besides sponsoring service programs and reminding parishioners about the value of helping the needy or providing them with small groups, congregations may fulfill an important community function simply by facilitating the formation of friendships and other personal ties. Such ties, or "social capital," as it is increasingly termed, can become the means through which people in need receive care informally from others in their congregations. Social capital can also encourage those with resources to share these resources with others and to become involved in supporting social ministries.

In his widely discussed research on social capital, political scientist Robert Putnam has suggested distinguishing two kinds of social capital: that which consists of social *bonds* among relatively homogeneous groups, and that which builds *bridges* between or among heterogeneous groups.[18] In the present context, both kinds of social capital are relevant. *Bonding* is relevant insofar as congregations promote friendships within the congregation itself that become the basis for people feeling that they can depend on others in their congregations for help when they need it. *Bridging* is rel-

TABLE 3.6
Correlates of Group-Based Caring
(Logistic regression coefficients)

	Helped with Emotional Crisis	Did Things for the Community	Served People outside the Group
Duration of involvement in group	.120***	.109***	.108***
Frequency of attendance at meetings	.276***	−.101	.269***
Duration of group's existence	−.023	.123***	.040
Size of group	.003	−.009	−.008
Group is church-based	.245*	1.048***	.739***
Member's education level	−.216***	−.092	−.079
Member's gender (male)	−.391***	−.174	−.221
Member's age	−.007*	−.016***	−.013
Chi-square	117.241	184.722	92.744
Degrees of freedom	8	8	8
−2 Log likelihood	1685.113	1248.126	982.392
Nagelkerke R-square	.112	.194	.120

Source: Forgiveness Survey, 1999.
Note: N = 1379; * $p < .05$, ** $p < .01$, *** $p < .001$ (Wald Statistic).

evant to the extent that involvement in congregations increases the likelihood that people become acquainted with others of either lower status or higher status than themselves. Having lower-status friends, such as a friend who has been on welfare, means that participation in a congregation may expose a person to people in need and thus increase the likelihood of feeling a responsibility to help them. Having higher-status friends, such as someone with wealth or power, means potentially having access to the kinds of resources that may be useful in meeting one's own needs or in helping others who are in need.

Some evidence of the extent to which bonding takes place within congregations is shown in table 3.7. The data are from the Civic Involvement Survey. Respondents who said they were members of a congregation were asked how many close friends they had in the congregation. The number of friends mentioned can be taken as a rough indication of the extent to which members have bonded with others in their congregation. The table reports the results for all members and for members of congregations of various sizes.

TABLE 3.7
Friendships by Congregation Size
(Percentage who have close friends in congregation)

	Fewer than 200	200 to 999 Members	More than 1,000	All Members
Number of close friends in congregation				
Eleven or more	41	40	47	42
Six to ten	13	18	16	16
Three to five	26	21	18	22
One or two	13	14	11	13
None	6	6	8	7
Number	(259)	(385)	(206)	(850)

Source: Civic Involvement Survey, 1997.
Note: Pearson chi-square = 10.780, d.f. = 12; p > .5.

In all, 42 percent of members said they had more than ten close friends in their congregation. Another 38 percent claimed to have between three and ten close friends in their congregation. Thirteen percent said they had one or two close friends, and only 7 percent said they had no close friends in their congregation. In other words, nearly all church members claim to have at least one close friend in their congregation, and a large proportion have many friends in their congregation. The comparison among small, medium, and large congregations shows that approximately the same percentages of members in each had more than ten friends, six to ten friends, and so on. Unlike the information considered in the previous chapter on formal service programs, therefore, small congregations seem to be just as capable of generating and sustaining *informal* social bonds among members as large congregations; indeed, it is probably more notable that members of large congregations also make friends in these contexts, since the larger numbers might suggest greater difficulty in forming personal connections.

This information on friendships in congregations also makes it possible to examine other factors that influence the likelihood of such bonding taking place. Friendships within congregations are statistically more likely among older people than among younger people (perhaps because older people have been members of their congregations for a longer period), among women than among men, among members of congregations in small towns or inner-city neighborhoods than among members of congregations in suburbs, and among frequent churchgoers than among less frequent attendees. There are no significant differences between blacks and whites in the number of congregational friendships or between members who describe their congregations as theologically conservative, moderate, or liberal.[19] However, in another study that made comparisons among denominations possible, the median number of within-congregation friends mentioned by members of white evangelical Protestant churches and by members of historically black Protestant churches was higher than the median number mentioned by mainline Protestants and Catholics.[20] Although the number of congregational friends does not appear to be influenced by size of congregation, it is important to note that members of small congregations are likely to be friends with a significantly larger *proportion* of the whole congregation than are members of large congregations—certainly a relevant consideration in thinking about congregations as caring communities.[21]

The chances that people forge social bonds within their congregations thus appear to be influenced by some of the factors that shape friendships in general (such as gender and location). But bonding does go hand in hand with participation in congregations. Those who participate more frequently are more likely to make friends in their congregations, and having friends probably encourages people to participate more often and to feel better about being part of their congregation. We do know from another study, for instance, that the more friends a person has in his or her congregation the more likely that person is to express satisfaction about the congregation's fellowship, sermons, and music and to say that attending worship services has been important to his or her spiritual growth. People with more friends in their congregations are also more likely to say they have felt especially close to God while being with close friends and they are also more likely to do things with these friends outside the congregation, such as go with them to plays or concerts.[22] This kind of bonding is potentially an important means through which congregations can meet the needs of members, whether there are formally organized service programs or not. In other words, congregations do not serve simply as formal service providers, but as places where social ties develop that can help meet needs informally.

An indication of congregations' role in providing support through the informal ties that develop among members is available from a question about whom people feel they can count on if they need help. Respondents were given a hypothetical situation in which they or someone in their immediate family became ill, and were then asked which of various people or groups they thought they could count on for help in this situation. The results are shown in table 3.8.

Among all respondents, 40 percent said they could count on church members—a proportion that ranks lower than counting on close friends, relatives, or neighbors, but substantially higher than counting on people at work, volunteers, welfare agencies, nonprofit organizations, or members of a service club. Among church members, nearly six in ten (58 percent) felt they could count on church members for help, and even among nonmembers, 12 percent felt they could. Additional analysis of these data shows that feeling one can count on church members for help is greater among people who attend services more often, among members of congregations in small towns or inner-city neighborhoods than among members of congregations in suburbs, and among members who have more close friends

TABLE 3.8
Perceived Source of Assistance
(Percentage who said they could count on each for help if they
or someone in their family became ill)

Source of assistance	Congregation Members	Nonmembers	All Respondents
Close personal friends	67	64	66
Relatives outside your immediate family	54	53	54
Your neighbors	49	37	44
Church members	58	12	40
People at work	31	27	29
Volunteers in your community	17	12	15
Social welfare agencies	10	12	11
Nonprofit organizations	10	8	9
Members of a service club	8	6	7
Number	(915)	(599)	(1,528)

Source: Civic Involvement Survey, 1997.

in their congregations. Feeling that one can count on church members is not affected by age, race, gender, size of one's congregation, or the theological orientation of one's congregation.[23]

Gregariousness

The fact that people who participate actively in congregations have more friends than those who do not raises the possibility that it is not so much participation that matters as being gregarious. In other words, congregations may simply be places where gregarious people gather, and, if that is the case, then congregations may function well for those people, providing them with a caring community, but do less well at drawing in and serving people who are less gregarious. It is surprising that this possibility has seldom, if ever, been examined empirically, especially because so much attention has focused on measuring and explaining variation in church attendance. Fortunately, we have some data from a national survey that permit us to address this question.

In table 3.9 people who say they attend religious services every week are compared with those who say they attend services less than weekly (but at least a few times a year) and with those who say they never attend. The comparisons involve responses to three self-descriptions and an index that combines these responses. About two-thirds of the weekly churchgoers agree that "it energizes me to be around other people," whereas this proportion drops to half among those who never attend religious services. Relatively few Americans admit that "it drains me to be around other people," but this proportion rises from only one person in fourteen among weekly church attendees to almost one in five among nonattendees. Similar differences are evident in responses to the statement, "I prefer to have a lot of quiet time alone, rather than being around other people." I constructed the Gregariousness Index shown in the table by giving people in the survey one point for agreeing with the first statement and one point each for disagreeing with the second two statements. The index shows even somewhat more clearly than each of the individual statements how regular churchgoers differ from nonattendees. Almost half of weekly church attendees score high on the Gregariousness Index, compared with fewer than a third of the nonattendees. And, in contrast, nearly one-third of the nonattendees score low or medium low on the scale, compared with fewer than one-fifth of the weekly attendees. These results are statistically significant. They also hold up when other factors that affect church attendance, such as age, race, and gender, are taken into account.[24] In sum, it does appear that congregations attract gregarious people more than they attract people who find it harder or less rewarding to be around other people; at least those who enjoy being around other people participate in congregations more actively than those who do not.

But there is another interesting aspect to this issue of gregariousness that we must also consider. The fact that congregations are magnets for people who like people means that congregations are not as attractive to people who like to be alone; and yet congregations can still be places where loners find friends. In other words, those who do choose to participate may be drawn in and indeed discover that it is easy to make friends, perhaps by the very fact that congregations are made up of gregarious people. There is at least some evidence that suggests this possibility. For instance, if we restrict our attention to people who say they are members of a congregation and then ask how many friends they have in the congregation, we find that the differences between those who score low on the Gregariousness Index and those who score high are quite small. These differences *are* statistically significant; that is, gregarious church members have more friends than nongregarious members (taking account of differences in age, education, and gender). Yet the differences are quite small, and in absolute terms the nongregarious members report having a substantial number of close friends in their congregations.[25] Specifically, the average number of close friends in the congregation reported by people who score low, medium low, or medium high on the Gregariousness Index is about ten, whereas this number rises to about twelve among those who score high on the index.

TABLE 3.9
Gregariousness and Church Attendance

	Attend Weekly	Attend Less Often	Never Attend	All Respondents
Percent in each category of church attendance who say they mostly agree with each statement				
It energizes me to be around other people	64	53	50	56
It drains me to be around other people	7	9	19	10
I prefer to have a lot of quiet time alone, rather than being around other people	33	33	43	35
Gregariousness index				
High	46	37	31	39
Medium high	36	40	37	38
Medium low	14	19	21	18
Low	4	4	11	5
Number	(517)	(742)	(263)	(1,522)

Source: Arts and Religion Survey, 1999.
Note: Pearson chi-squares, respectively = 20.675, 25.196, 8.444, 23.876, d.f. = 2,2,2,4; p < .001, .001, .05, .001.

The data from which these results are obtained provide one additional way of examining the possible consequences of being involved in a congregation. If congregations function as caring communities, we should see this care being demonstrated when people experience sickness, bereavement, or other personal crises. Some literature suggests that there is a relationship between church attendance and psychological well-being, and that congregational ties engender helpful ways of coping with various problems.[26] Yet the literature remains ambiguous on the question of social capital: Is it the social capital a person generates through participating in a congregation that helps in times of trouble? Or is it something else—possibly, as what we have just considered may suggest, the fact that people in congregations are merely more gregarious to begin with? In the national survey we have been considering, respondents were asked first, "Has there ever been a time in your life when you were ill, lonely, troubled, or grieving the loss of a loved one?" Then those who said yes (86 percent) were asked to say how much or how little various things had proven helpful during that time. One of these was "talking with friends." Almost everybody said this had been helpful, but the responses varied, with 73 percent saying "very helpful," 19 percent saying "somewhat helpful," and 6 percent saying "not helpful." These friends, of course, could be anywhere, not necessarily from one's congregation. Thus, the critical question is whether being a frequent participant in a congregation would still increase the likelihood of saying that talking with one's friends had been helpful during a time of personal crisis.

The short answer is yes. But we need to look closely at the results to be sure that this conclusion is warranted (see table 3.10). Controlling for some of the other things that may confound the relationship (such as age, education, and gender), frequency of church attendance is positively associated with saying that talking with one's friends was very helpful during a time of personal crisis. Of the other factors, neither age nor education is significantly related to this response. But being female is—a finding that is consistent with other research suggesting that women rely more heavily on their friends for support than men do.[27] None of the relationships is very strong, but it is helpful to compare the effects of church attendance with those of gender: the difference between weekly and less regular attendees is about three-quarters as great as the difference between men and women, and the difference between weekly attendees and nonattendees is actually

TABLE 3.10
Church Attendance, Social Capital, and Receiving Support
(Ordinary least squares regression results for saying that "talking with friends" was very helpful, somewhat helpful, or not helpful)

	Standardized Regression Coefficients	Level of Significance	Standardized Regression Coefficients	Level of Significance
Church attendance	.074	.012	.058	.049
Age	−.015	.597	−.009	.753
Education	.014	.609	.011	.687
Female	.098	.001	.097	.001
Gregariousness index	—	—	.101	.001

Source: Arts and Religion Survey, 1999.

Note: N = 1,261; only respondents who said there had been a time in their life "when you were ill, lonely, troubled, or grieving the loss of a loved one."

greater than the difference between men and women. However, we also need to take account of the possibility that church attendees find talking with their friends more helpful simply because church attendees, as we have seen, are more gregarious. In the right-hand columns of the table, the Gregariousness Index is included and it is in fact positively associated with saying that one's friends were very helpful. Including the index also reduces the strength of the relationship between church attendance and saying that talking with one's friends was helpful. Judging from the size of the two coefficients (.074 and .058), it appears that about one-third of the effect of church attendance can be "explained away" by gregariousness.

These results nevertheless lend some support to the idea that being actively involved in a congregation generates the kind of social capital that actually becomes useful when a person is in need of support. This relationship is not merely a function of church people being more gregarious in the first place. Participation in a congregation apparently reinforces friendships and provides opportunities for fellow congregants to know about personal needs, so that when these needs arise, support can be given.

Congregations as Sources of Influential Friends

If congregations facilitate the kinds of interaction that produce bonding, do they also encourage bridging? There are of course many possible kinds of bridging, such as the links that are forged between congregations and service agencies (considered in chapter 2) and those created by members who take part in other community organizations (considered in chapter 4). But one of the more interesting kinds of bridging is the link that may exist between ordinary citizens and people in their community who have power, wealth, or other kinds of influence. This is surely a key factor in the larger health of civil society. When democracies work well, there are ways of bridging the chasm that often exists in more hierarchical societies between the haves and the have-nots. In terms of how congregations may help to provide for the needs of their members and others in their communities, therefore, the ability to bridge between these people and those who have influence is thus an important consideration.

At issue here is not the fact that influential people necessarily care about the needs of the poor, but the possibility that connections to these people may be a resource that can be used to secure favorable public policies or to gain access to jobs or simply provide a window into circles of knowledge or wealth. There is a long tradition of scholarship suggesting that congregations are relatively diverse in terms of the social statuses their members occupy. For instance, despite the fact that congregations attract people of similar social strata, it has often been the case that mill hands and mill owners attended the same churches, that farmers and bankers did, and that some families had the financial resources to pay for most of the congregation's bills while others contributed relatively little.[28] Insofar as people participate actively in their congregations, they may then have opportunities to rub shoulders with the few fellow members who are wealthy, hold public office, and the like.

Apart from whom they know in their congregations, regular attendees also have the opportunity to make acquaintances who, in turn, are friends of influential people in the community. As we have seen, regular participants generally have more friends in their congregation, and these friends may be an important link to making friends with influential people in the wider community. In addition, congregations sometimes invite public officials to speak at meetings, or sponsor committees that bring people of wealth or people with positions of corporate responsibility to the congregation. The question is whether or not these possibilities are actually a part of the typical member's experience.

Table 3.11 summarizes the results obtained from analyzing the effects of congregational membership and participation on having four kinds of influential people among one's friends: an elected official, a corporate executive, a scientist, and a wealthy person.[29] The results take account of a person's own social status (level of education and whether that person is employed in a professional or managerial occupation), since people are more likely to have influential friends if they themselves are in the higher echelons of society. The figures also take account of possible differences in friendship patterns on the basis of age, gender, race or ethnicity, and where a person lives. The results show that being a member of a congregation is positively associated with having three of the four kinds of influential friends listed (the exception is having a friend who is a scientist). However, frequency of attendance is not significantly related with having any of these kinds of friends. The kind of congregation a person belongs to doesn't matter much, either, except that Jews are more likely to have influential friends than members of any of the Christian groups, and members of small congregations are less likely to have three of the four kinds of friends than members of medium-sized or large congregations. What does matter is being a leader in one's congregation: leaders are significantly more likely to have influential friends in three of the four comparisons.

On balance, these results are not very encouraging as far as the possibility of congregations helping people bridge into circles of influence is concerned. The fact that membership is associated with having influential friends, but attendance is not, suggests that people who already have influential friends are the kind who join congregations, not that participating actively in a congregation becomes a way of making such friends. The fact that holding a leadership position in one's congregation is associated with having influential friends is subject to several different interpretations. It, too, could mean that people with more influential friends are simply the ones who get chosen for these leadership positions. Or it is possible that people in leadership positions have more opportunities to interact with other influential people in their congregations and in their communities. In either case, congregational leaders do appear to be a link between con-

TABLE 3.11
Religious Participation and Influential Friends
(Adjusted odds ratios from the logistic regression of friendship with elected officials,
corporate executives, scientists, and wealthy persons on selected independent variables)

	Elected Official	Corporate Executive	Scientist	Wealthy Person
Membership	1.450***	1.335***	1.033	1.309***
Attendance	.950	.946	.969	.911
Evangelical	1.067	.985	.952	.995
Black church	1.491†	1.028	.610†	.934
Catholic	.907	.929	.895	.996
Jewish	.473*	1.102	1.252	1.819**
Other religion	.963	1.269*	1.399*	1.134
Unaffiliated	.921	1.099	1.158	.959
Small congregation	.990	.742**	.743*	.730***
Large congregation	1.044	1.211*	1.083	1.063
Leadership role	1.542***	1.517***	1.424***	1.082
Age	1.432***	1.096*	.928	.876***
Male	1.340***	1.184**	1.251**	1.142*
Black	.988	.836**	.774**	.829**
Hispanic	.892	.693**	.888	.737**
Urban	.570***	.975	1.094	.997
Suburban	.690***	1.259**	1.213*	1.222**
South	1.117	1.176*	1.070	1.236***
Education	1.373***	1.475***	2.155***	1.388***
Professional-mgr.	1.249**	1.574***	1.274**	1.216**
−2 Log likelihood	5076	6563	4837	7277
Degrees of freedom	20	20	20	20
Nagelkerke R-square	.103	.143	.218	.094

Source: Religion and Politics Survey, 2000.
Note: N = 5,630; † p < .10, * p < .05, ** p < .01, *** p < .001.

gregations and wider circles of influence. So, for a person who otherwise has little contact with influential people, going to church and interacting with these congregational leaders may at least be an indirect way of accessing those people of power and wealth. Being in a small congregation probably means that its leaders are less likely to know influential people than being in a larger congregation. But this difference may be counterbalanced by the fact that the average member has a greater chance of being friends with a congregational leader in a small congregation than in a large one.

Overcoming Status Distinctions

Making friends with influential people may have no particular warrant in religious teachings. The same cannot be said for befriending the downtrodden, disadvantaged, and otherwise marginalized people in one's community. Christians have the example of Jesus set before them in the Bible—an example of someone who deliberately made friends with social outcasts and who saw no problem in violating caste divisions or the lines separating Jews and Gentiles. If church teachings matter, we should anticipate that active churchgoers would have more friends among the disadvantaged than those who attend less frequently. This might be the case because of churchgoers intentionally putting church teachings into practice. It might also result in less intentional ways, such as marginalized people being attracted to congregations and thus being in the midst of middle-class or mainstream people more so than might be the case in their own neighborhoods or families.

Table 3.12 shows results for the effects of weekly attendance at religious services on the likelihood of having a friend who is a manual worker, a person who has been on welfare, an African American, or a person who is Hispanic. The data are from Putnam's Social Capital Benchmark Survey, so the questions about other personal characteristics are not exactly the same as the ones shown in the previous table, but, as before, we are able to take account of the fact that these kinds of friendships are influenced by a person's gender, race or ethnicity, and social status (level of education and income).[30] The results also take account of differences attributable to some people simply having a larger number of friends than others, and the kind of congregation one attends and whether or not a person does volunteer work are also considered. Three main results are evident in this table. First,

Table 3.12

Religious Participation and Contacts with Marginalized Persons
(Adjusted odds ratios from the logistic regression of friendship with a manual worker,
person on welfare, African American, and Hispanic on selected independent variables)

	Manual Worker	Person on Welfare	African American	Hispanic Person
Weekly attendance	.953	.865***	.910***	.847***
Male	1.659***	.760***	1.087***	1.192***
Black	.753***	1.793***	10.248***	1.118***
Hispanic	.688***	1.012	.860**	8.600***
College	.667***	.784***	1.078*	1.151***
Grade school	.616***	.922*	.632***	.741***
Income > $50,000	1.227***	.962	1.340***	1.224***
Friends = 10+	1.482***	1.315***	1.514***	1.439***
Friends < 3	.643***	.882***	.668***	.737***
Evangelical	1.314***	1.428***	1.636***	1.184***
Other Protestant	1.219***	1.266***	1.317***	1.248***
Catholic	.980	1.107*	1.116**	1.443***
Other Christian	1.197***	1.804***	1.473***	1.828***
Jewish	.445***	.888	1.570***	1.429***
Other religion	.715***	1.459***	1.537***	1.679***
No preference	.862***	1.172***	1.291***	1.475***
Volunteer	1.788***	1.770***	1.871***	1.633***
-2 Log likelihood	33928	37683	35068	37682
Degrees of freedom	17	17	17	17
Pseudo R-square	.090	.061	.160	.121

Source: Social Capital Benchmark Survey, 2000.
Note: N = 29,233; * $p < .05$, ** $p < .01$, *** $p < .001$.

weekly attendance at religious services does *not* seem conducive to having friends among marginalized groups; in fact, the odds of having such friends are actually *lower* among those who attend regularly than among those who do not. Second, the likelihood of having friends among marginalized groups *is* influenced by the kind of congregation a person is affiliated with; for instance, evangelicals, other Protestants, Catholics, and other Christians are all more likely to have such friends than mainline Protestants or Jews. And third, having done volunteer work is one of the most significant factors in increasing the likelihood that a person will have a friend from a marginalized group.

If going to church raises members' consciousness about the needs of the poor or about the need to reach across racial, ethnic, and social class boundaries, then attending religious services regularly would presumably increase the chances that church members would have friends among marginalized groups. The fact that regular churchgoers actually are less likely to have such friends is thus an indication that churches may not be as effective in transmitting ideals of caring and compassion as they would like to be. What is more encouraging is the fact that volunteering does increase the chances of people making friendships that span class, race, and ethnicity. This result suggests that congregations may at least have an indirect role in overcoming status distinctions. To the extent that congregational involvement encourages people to become volunteers, this volunteering does bridge such distinctions. The fact that volunteering is positively associated with friendships among marginalized groups may also be an indication that volunteering forges stronger bonds than simply ones involving short-term, arms-length helping relationships.[31]

Summing Up

The evidence we have considered in this chapter gives substantial support to the idea that congregations play an important *social* role in the lives of most members. Congregations provide forums in which the value of caring for the needy is emphasized. They provide space for community meetings and opportunities for members to learn civic skills. Most congregations initiate and host small fellowship groups in which a large number of members participate, and these groups encourage participants to think about caring for the needy, encourage them to reflect on the value of forgiving others and healing broken relationships, and help people through emotional crises. Participants also report that these groups do things for the wider community and help them to be of assistance to people outside the group. Less formally, the average church member derives social capital from his or her participation—social capital in the form of close friends and reassurance that one can depend on these friends during times of illness, bereavement, or trouble. Unlike formal service programs, these informal sources of caring and support are not as likely to require being part of a large, well-financed congregation. They take place in congregations of all sizes. They *are* more characteristic of gregarious people than of people who prefer to spend time alone, but even loners appear to be drawn into social networks by virtue of the fact that congregations attract gregarious people.

The evidence on congregations' ability to generate social capital that forges relationships among *diverse* groups (bridging) is more mixed than the evidence about caring within the relatively homogeneous networks of close friends and small groups (bonding). On the one hand, the fact that sermons, classes, and small groups so frequently emphasize caring for the needy suggests that members are likely to do something to put these ideals into practice (about which we will say more in the next chapter). The fact that regular and extended participation in small groups is associated with doing things for the community or for people outside the group also suggests that small groups encourage some degree of bridging activity. On the other hand, the evidence seems less supportive of the idea that participating in congregations may increase the likelihood of ordinary people having contract with persons of wealth or other special resources. And the same is true about participating in congregations generating friendships between the average member and people who are needy or who have been marginalized by mainstream society. Insofar as these kinds of bridging relationships develop, they seem to occur indirectly, through contact with church leaders or through volunteering, rather than simply from being present at worship services.

It is not surprising, given the ways in which congregations create a caring, supportive environment for members, that participation in congregations appears to have beneficial results of various kinds for those who participate. This is not the place to review the literature on these benefits, but studies have found a number of *correlations* between measures of religion (including churchgoing) and other aspects of personal and community well-being.[32] These relationships suggest that participating in congregations may, among other things, be a source of meaning and belonging that keeps older people healthier, perhaps even adding to their longevity, and that the social norms reinforced by churches discourage teenagers from engaging in behavior such as using drugs or joining gangs that use drugs. Other research, although not always producing consistent results, has suggested beneficial effects of churchgoing such as lower rates of teen pregnancy, better grades in high school, fewer negative results on children from parents' divorcing, greater satisfaction with one's job, and a more general sense of personal well-being. On many of these topics, further research is needed to determine if religious participation is actually a causal factor and, if so, why it produces the observed effects.[33] Still, the research thus far does suggest that congregations serve for many people as caring communities.

If congregations do function in these ways, then the possibility that participation in congregations is eroding becomes a matter of broader social concern and not just a concern to religious leaders or to others who happen to care about religious beliefs. The possibility that religious participation is eroding is suggested mainly by comparisons of younger, middle-aged, and older Americans. Although the most reliable surveys in which questions about church attendance have been asked over the past three decades show modest declines at most, the low rate of attendance among younger Americans suggests that there may be significant declines in the next few decades. Some scholars in fact argue that these potential declines are especially evident when three cohorts are compared: the so-called Builders (those born before World War II), who seemed to be more religiously oriented and who took their civic responsibilities more seriously; the "Boomers" (born between 1946 and 1964), whose religious and civic loyalties were challenged by the turbulence of the 1960s counterculture; and the "Busters" (born after 1964), whose parents may have been Boomers and who, in any case, were reared in an environment of affluence and mass media that further discouraged religious participation.[34]

In view of the arguments about these three cohorts, it is useful to look briefly at the figures in table 3.13. Busters are less than half as likely as Builders to attend religious services weekly and more than twice as likely as Builders to say they never attend. Boomers fall approximately in the middle. When only members are considered, Busters are also more likely than Boomers or Builders to say they have no friends in their congregations;

they are also more likely to say they have no friends in their neighbor-hoods, and slightly less likely to say they have church friends who live in their neighborhood. We might suppose that these differences among age groups are largely a result of differences in life stage; for instance, younger people may not attend church services or have friends at church or in their

TABLE 3.13

Factors That May Erode Congregation-Based Social Capital
(Percentage in each generation having particular characteristics)

	Busters	Boomers	Builders
Attend religious services			
Weekly	20	30	46
Less than weekly	54	52	41
Never	26	19	13
Friends in congregation (members only)			
None	15	9	9
One or two	11	13	8
Three to twenty	50	65	52
More than twenty	23	22	30
Do any of these (church) friends live in person's immediate neighborhood?			
Yes	52	49	57
How many people in your neighborhood do you know well?			
Almost all	13	11	18
Quarter to a half	29	30	34
Only a few	41	48	41
None	16	10	6
Number	(294)	(620)	(593)

Source: Arts and Religion Survey, 1999.

Note: N = 1,522; Busters born after 1964, Boomers born 1946 to 1964; Builders born before 1946.

neighborhood simply because they are still in school, not married, and have no children. Once they settle down, get married, and have children, they may become more involved in congregations. If that argument were valid, the statistical relationship between age cohort and religious involvement should diminish when these other factors are taken into account. And it does in fact diminish. But not very much.[35] Thus, it seems likely that congregations may not be as strong in the future as they have been in the recent past—at least in the absence of some other factors that may encourage younger people to participate more actively in congregations.

Even if congregational involvement remains strong, we are nevertheless left with two unresolved questions: Are Americans with the greatest needs involved in congregations? And, for these people, what kinds of support do congregations provide? It is possible that congregations function as caring communities for middle-class Americans who live in middle-class neighborhoods but serve less effectively for people in lower-income neighborhoods. It is also possible that congregations provide friends, groups in which people can pray and talk about their emotional needs, and even an occasional pot of soup or ride to the doctor, but not the kinds of financial support or job training needy families truly require. We will return to these possibilities in chapter 6.

The larger implication of the data we have examined in this chapter is that congregations provide a substantial amount of caring and support that has very little to do with the formal service programs they may sponsor or help to sponsor. The caring and support that members experience derives from the fact that congregations function as communities. They draw people in and encourage relatively deep, long-lasting relationships to develop. They are quite different from service programs that may provide assistance through grants to help other service agencies or through specific service transactions, such as a job training program or assistance in securing medical care. As communities, congregations do not require contracts or grants from third parties; they operate from the donations given by their members. Small congregations can often provide as much caring and support for their members, if not more, than large congregations. The principal weaknesses of congregations are that many Americans do not participate actively in them and there are many needs in the wider community that cannot be dealt with through the friendship networks and small groups that congregations encourage.

Religion and Volunteering

Gwen Marshall is a thirty-six-year-old Episcopalian who lives in an upper-middle-class suburb of Knoxville, Tennessee. Several times a year she volunteers for Habitat for Humanity. Habitat recruits volunteers who work with low-income families to construct homes which these families can then purchase at affordable prices. In the Knoxville area, Habitat-built homes would typically cost fifty thousand dollars if sold on the open market, but eligible families purchase them for approximately thirty thousand dollars. Volunteers such as Mrs. Marshall show up for an hour or two on a given Saturday morning if they happen to have time. Students can also fulfill community service requirements this way. Church youth groups can participate on a once- or twice-a-year basis. Busy middle-class professionals who have little control over their work and travel schedules can take part if a business trip or soccer game doesn't interfere. Mrs. Marshall became involved in Habitat several years ago when the traveling required by her job as a bank inspector became too much and she decided to take some time off. She wanted to make a worthwhile contribution without locking herself into too much of a commitment. Neither serving on the altar guild at her church nor undergoing the training to become a deaconess met these criteria. When she consulted her pastor, he advised her to volunteer for Habitat.

John Lee is a Chinese American in his late twenties who works as a teacher and attends church services every week at a large suburban Presbyterian church in eastern Pennsylvania. Through the church he has made close friends with several other people and has gone on church-sponsored trips with them to China and Nicaragua. Several years ago he found himself with time on his hands. His friends at the church encouraged him to talk to the pastor of a large inner-city church in the area that sponsored service projects. Mr. Lee had enjoyed his previous international trips, so was delighted to learn that the church was sending a team of lay volunteers to the Dominican Republic for a week to do repair work at an orphanage. He spent the week there putting screens on windows, cleaning, painting, and getting to know the staff and children. He has now made three of these annual trips.

Volunteering is a way of bridging the gap that may exist between congregations and the needs of the wider society. Congregations make use of volunteers to teach classes, greet newcomers at worship services, put on church dinners, and run committees. They also encourage members to volunteer for service projects that benefit the community. For instance, there may be sign-up sheets in the church vestibule to do volunteer work at a soup kitchen or to help out at an adult literacy program at a nearby prison. Beyond such formal opportunities, congregations also present teachings, as we have seen, that remind participants of their responsibilities to the poor and the needy.

But how many members of congregations actually become involved in volunteering? What kinds of volunteering do they do? Is their volunteering directed toward people with special needs or does it mostly serve their own families, friends, and fellow churchgoers? How many hours per week or per year do they devote to these activities? How does their involvement differ from that of people who are not associated with congregations? Do some religious traditions do a better job of mobilizing volunteers than others? What exactly motivates people to volunteer? And what are the barriers preventing more people from becoming volunteers?

The United States has long been known for its volunteering. No discussion of the subject can avoid Alexis de Tocqueville's observations about volunteering when he visited the United States in the 1830s. Tocqueville was impressed that neighbors helped one another with seemingly abundant generosity and that many of the social activities performed by governments in Europe were done voluntarily in the United States. Whether it was building roads or launching campaigns to curb consumption of alcoholic beverages, Americans seemed to tackle these projects by enlisting volunteers.[1]

Over the past century and three-quarters, many of the activities Tocqueville observed being done by volunteers have become more complex and for this reason have required more investment of government, corporate, and nonprofit organizations. Yet, when surveys are conducted, the United States continues to register relatively high levels of volunteering, compared with many other countries. For instance, in national surveys conducted in sixty-four countries between 1997 and 2000, the United States ranked fourth in the proportion of adults who said they were currently active as volunteers for charitable organizations (surpassed only by Australia, Puerto Rico, and Nigeria).[2]

Social observers have speculated that an important reason for the United States' high level of volunteering may be its high level of religious involvement.[3] Whether this is the case would be hard to say with any degree of accuracy, since religious traditions and practices vary so widely. It is interesting, though, that in the surveys just mentioned the United States also ranks relatively high on the proportion of adults who say that religion is very important in their lives, and there is a positive correlation between this statement and being involved in charitable volunteering. That relationship, although by no means universal, is also present in about two-thirds of the countries studied.[4]

According to the U.S. Census Bureau, 44 percent of Americans age twenty-one or older engage in some kind of volunteer activity each year and the average number of hours volunteered each month is 15.1, or nearly 4 hours per week. Religion appears to be an important part of this volunteer effort. Nineteen percent of the adult public claims to have volunteered for religious activities, a much larger proportion than for any other general category of volunteering. For instance, only about 8 percent of the public volunteers for educational activities and only 1 percent volunteer for political organizations.[5]

These data suggest that volunteering may be an important part of social service effort in the United States and that religion needs to be considered in understanding how volunteering functions. We must look at other surveys and at interviews with individual volunteers, though, in order to understand these relationships more precisely. As in previous chapters, it will be necessary to piece together information from different sources. Studies with the most detailed questions about volunteering often include relatively few questions about religion, while those focusing on religion often provide little evidence about volunteering. Fortunately, the various studies do illuminate different aspects of these relationships and, on balance, yield a picture of both the strengths and weaknesses of American religion's role in generating volunteer efforts on behalf of those who are poor or otherwise disadvantaged.

What Surveys Show

Some of the first surveys in which volunteering was examined were conducted by the Gallup Organization in the 1970s. In Gallup surveys, respondents were asked if they personally happened to be "involved in any charity or social service activities, such as helping the poor, the sick, or the elderly." In 1977, when the question was introduced, 26 percent of the public said they were. By 1991, when the question was discontinued, 46 percent of the public said "yes."[6] It is worth noting that other research casts doubt on whether volunteering actually increased as much during this period as the Gallup figures suggest; observers agree, though, that volunteering was *not declining,* despite erosion in other forms of civic involvement.[7]

I included the Gallup question in a national survey I conducted in 1999. In this survey 35 percent of the respondents said they were involved in such charity or social service activities.[8] The survey also included a question asking people if they currently did any volunteering. By combining the two questions it was thus possible to examine the characteristics of people who were engaged in charity or social service work *as volunteers* (i.e., not just informally, such as caring for a sick or elderly family member). Using that criterion, 17 percent of the public qualified.

In table 4.1 some of the *religious* characteristics that distinguish these volunteers from nonvolunteers are shown. In nearly all of the comparisons, people who are more actively or traditionally religious are more likely to be engaged in charitable or service volunteering than those who are less actively or traditionally religious. Members of religious congregations are twice as likely to be involved in these kinds of volunteer activities as nonmembers. People who attend religious services every week are about twice as likely to be involved as those who attend only a few times a year. Evangelical Protestants are slightly more likely to be involved than mainline Protestants or Catholics. Those who have had a born-again experience are more likely to do volunteer work than those who have not. This pattern is consistent with the difference between evangelical and mainline Protestants. There is no difference, though, between biblical literalists and those who hold a nonliteralist view of the Bible. The largest difference is between those who *read* the Bible regularly and those who do not. There are similar differences between those who pray nearly every day and those who pray less often, between those who meditate nearly every day and

Table 4.1
Charity or Social Service Activity by Religious Characteristics
(Percentage with each characteristic who volunteer and are involved in charity
or social service activity)

	Percentage	Number
Member of a congregation	22	(927)
Not a member	9	(585)
Attend religious services		
Every week	29	(517)
Almost every week	11	(144)
Once or twice a month	14	(199)
A few times a year	11	(399)
Never	7	(263)
Religious tradition		
Evangelical Protestant	26	(205)
Mainline Protestant	21	(199)
Roman Catholic	20	(273)
None	7	(246)
Had a "born-again" experience	22	(655)
Have not had this experience	13	(839)
Biblical literalist	17	(548)
Not biblical literalist	18	(860)
Read Bible nearly every day	31	(355)
Read Bible less often	13	(1,175)
Pray nearly every day	22	(992)
Pray less often	8	(538)
Meditate nearly every day	27	(538)
Meditate less often	12	(992)
Importance of spiritual growth		
Extremely or very important	23	(852)
Less important	9	(678)
Effort devoted to spiritual growth in past year		
A great deal	31	(368)
Less	12	(1,162)

Source: Arts and Religion Survey, 1999.
Note: N = 1,530; all except biblical literalist significant at or beyond the .001 level (Pearson chi-square).

those who meditate less often, between those who value spiritual growth a lot and those who give it less importance, and between those who say they have devoted a great deal of effort in the past year to spiritual growth and those who have not. Further analysis shows that all these relationships (except for the one concerning biblical literalism) remain statistically significant when the effects of age, gender, education, marital status, number of children, and the gregariousness index (discussed in the last chapter) are controlled. When congregational membership and attendance at religious services are controlled, the effects of religious tradition are no longer significant. With these other factors controlled, the effects of Bible reading, prayer, meditation, valuing spiritual growth, and devoting effort to spiritual growth all remain statistically significant.[9]

Some research has given the impression that the reason religiously involved people engage in volunteering has more to do with their social networks than with their religious convictions.[10] The present results suggest otherwise. Doing volunteer work to help the needy is reinforced by what I have elsewhere termed *spiritual practice*.[11] Spiritual practice is different from merely saying that one values being religious. It involves regular intentional activity concerned with strengthening one's relationship with God. Daily prayer, Bible study, meditation, and otherwise expending effort to grow in one's spiritual life are common forms of spiritual practice. People who take them seriously are usually involved in congregations or small fellowship groups. And, as these data suggest, they are also more likely to become involved in volunteering.[12]

The weakness of the Gallup question is that it leaves much unknown about the nature of volunteering itself. Starting in the late 1980s, a more detailed look at volunteering became available through a series of surveys sponsored by Independent Sector in Washington, DC, and carried out initially by the Gallup Organization and eventually by the U.S. Census Bureau. The Independent Sector's Giving and Volunteering Survey in 1996 was one of the most comprehensive in the range of questions it included. In this survey respondents were asked if they had volunteered during the previous twelve months for each of thirteen kinds of social programs, such as health, education, environment, recreation, youth, and foundations. The most relevant category for present purposes was "human services," defined as day care centers, foster care services, family counseling, consumer protection, legal aid, crime and delinquency prevention, homelessness, employment, food, housing, shelter, public safety, and emergency preparedness and relief. The one question about religion in the survey—frequency of church attendance—showed that the more often people attended religious services, the more likely they were to volunteer for human service activities. In fact, those who attended weekly or nearly every week were twice as likely to do this kind of volunteer work as those who did not attend.[13]

Although the Independent Sector surveys were well received, they left gaps in our ability to understand exactly how religious involvement and volunteering might be related. For one thing, the classification of volunteer activities into such large categories as human services or culture meant that it was difficult to know very precisely what people might be doing. For another, it was possible that the surveys encouraged people to exaggerate their volunteering, both because the studies included a number of positively worded questions about volunteering and because it was possible to count the same activity in several categories (e.g., teaching Sunday school as both "religion" and "youth"). Doubt was also raised about the relationship between religious participation and volunteering by an attempt to replicate the Independent Sector study in the 1996 General Social Survey conducted by the National Opinion Research Center at the University of Chicago. In that study, frequency of church attendance was unrelated to volunteering for human services.[14] Whether the discrepancy was because of differences in methodology or some other reason, it suggested that different ways of assessing involvement in volunteer activities might be needed.

In the Civic Involvement Survey I conducted in 1997, I tried to overcome some of these weaknesses by presenting respondents in the survey with a detailed list of activities and asking if they had volunteered for each one during the previous year.[15] Unlike the Independent Sector studies, the list was not intended to evoke all possible ways in which people may have volunteered, but to identify a fairly wide variety of specific service activities. For instance, we asked about distributing food to the needy, about building houses for the poor, and about helping at shelters for abused women and children. We intentionally included these kinds of activities that dealt specifically with helping the needy or disadvantaged, but also included activities that might be of greater benefit for volunteers themselves or their families (such as helping with a neighborhood or homeowners association). From preliminary research, we also knew that the list was likely to include most of the volunteer activities that people mentioned in informal interviews.

Table 4.2 shows the results for the national sample as a whole and for people who attended religious services regularly compared with those who attended irregularly or who did not attend. Church-related activities and activities related to schools top the list, with between one-quarter and one-fifth of all respondents saying they had volunteered for these kinds of programs within the past year. Of the activities specifically concerned with helping the needy or providing social services, distributing food enlists the largest number of volunteers, with nearly one person in five claiming to have done this in the past year. Other service activities command the involvement of fewer people. Some of the more common are neighborhood crime watch programs, community organizing, and helping at shelters for abused women and children. Other programs include AIDS-related activities, building houses for the poor, and assisting with community development corporations. In all cases, people who attend religious services weekly or almost weekly are more likely to have done volunteer work than those who attend between once or twice a month and only a few times a year. Those who attend infrequently are still more likely to have served as volunteers than those who never attend. These differences remain statistically significant when other factors that are related to both religious involvement and volunteering are controlled, such as age, education, marital status, children, gender, and race. Overall, these results give added support to the contention that religious involvement is conducive to service-oriented volunteering (and not just to volunteering that benefits churches or church members themselves). However, the results also suggest that much of what Americans do when they claim to be volunteering may have little direct impact on the poor or other needy people; at least it seems in these data that a large share of the volunteering that occurs in the United States each year is devoted to running churches, schools, youth programs, and neighborhood associations in which volunteers themselves are the primary beneficiaries.

Who Volunteers More?

A question that surfaces repeatedly in discussions of social ministries among religious leaders and observers of American religion is, as we have seen in previous chapters, who does more to serve the needy, Protestants or

TABLE 4.2

Volunteering and Attendance at Religious Services
(Percentage in each category of church attendance who said they had volunteered during the past year for each kind of activity)

	Attend Almost Weekly	Attend Less Often	Never Attend	All Respondents
Church-related activities	54	14	2	26
Activities related to schools	26	18	12	20
Distributing food to the needy	27	18	9	19
Youth activities	24	14	8	16
Informal volunteering	18	14	10	15
Neighborhood crime watch	12	8	6	9
Political campaigns	10	8	4	8
Neighborhood/homeowner assn.	10	7	4	8
Arts or cultural activities	10	7	4	7
Environmental projects	9	8	3	7
Community organizing	8	7	3	6
Shelter for abused women/kids	8	4	2	5
Violence prevention efforts	6	3	2	4
AIDS-related activities	5	3	2	4
Building houses for the poor	5	2	1	3
Community development corp.	4	4	1	3
Number	(595)	(551)	(382)	(1,528)

Source: Civic Involvement Survey, 1997.

Note: All relationships statistically significant at or beyond the .05 level, controlling for age, education, marital status, children, gender, and race (Wald statistic from logistic regression analysis).

Catholics, evangelicals or mainliners? This question also arises when we consider volunteering. It is not quite as self-interested as it may seem. It bears on larger questions about the continuing salience of different theological traditions and with predictions about the future of volunteering, based on which traditions may be encouraging it more and which of these are growing or declining.

The short answer is, it depends. It depends both on how we define religious traditions and on how we think about volunteering. I can illustrate this point most clearly by drawing on the Religion and Politics Survey.[16] That survey has the advantage of asking about religious identity in two ways. People were asked about their religious affiliation in sufficient detail (e.g., including which specific Baptist or Methodist or Lutheran church they preferred) that their identity could be classified as "evangelical Protestant," "mainline Protestant," "black Protestant," or "Catholic."[17] People were also asked to pick a label themselves that best suited their religious orientation. Protestants were given the option of "fundamentalist," "evangelical," "mainline," "liberal," or "none." Catholics could say "traditional," "moderate," "liberal," or "none."[18] The survey has the further advantage of being relatively large (more than 5,600 respondents), so that people could be classified in terms of both affiliation and self-identity. This turns out to be important. For example, among those affiliated with evangelical denominations, only 34 percent call themselves evangelicals or fundamentalists, and among those affiliated with mainline denominations, only 52 percent think of themselves as mainline or liberal.[19] In other words, both ways of thinking about religion are important, especially because, as we know, denominations and even local congregations are quite diverse.

The Religion and Politics Survey contained only two questions about volunteering, so there is a lot we cannot explore with these data. But the two questions are especially important to the question of who volunteers more. We know from other research that participation in evangelical congregations seems to be more conducive to volunteering within the church, while participation in mainline congregations is more conducive to volunteering in the wider community (with Catholics somewhere in the middle).[20] In the Religion and Politics Survey the two questions asked simply whether the respondent had "done volunteer work at a church or other place of worship" in the past year or "for an organization other than a church or place of worship."

Taking only religious affiliation into account, the results are consistent with the previous research.[21] Among evangelical Protestants, a higher proportion (64 percent) volunteered for the church than among mainline Protestants (57 percent). The reverse was true for nonchurch volunteering, where more of the mainline Protestants (54 percent) had done this than of the evangelicals (46 percent). Black Protestants, by these indications, were more like evangelicals than mainliners: 61 percent volunteered at church and 43 percent did nonchurch volunteering. Catholics were lowest on church volunteering (48 percent), but ranked in the middle on nonchurch volunteering (also 48 percent).

Table 4.3 shows the results in more detail, breaking down each of the four traditions according to respondents' self-identities. Among church members affiliated with evangelical Protestant denominations, those who think of themselves as evangelicals are the most likely to volunteer at their church, followed by those who self-identify as fundamentalists. Those who think of themselves as mainliners are only slightly less likely to volunteer at their church, but those who regard themselves as liberals are much less likely to do this kind of volunteering. In contrast, nonchurch volunteering varies little with self-identification, although those who regard themselves as mainliners are slightly more likely to volunteer in this way than the others.[22]

Among the people affiliated with mainline denominations, evangelicals and mainliners are most likely to do church volunteering, suggesting that fundamentalists and liberals may find themselves more peripheral in these contexts. Again, nonchurch volunteering does not vary as much, but it is highest among those who consider themselves mainliners.

Within the historically black denominations, self-identified evangelicals volunteer most often for their church, while self-identified mainliners volunteer most often outside the church. Those who call themselves fundamentalists also volunteer outside the church in fairly high proportions, although there are relatively few members in this category

For Catholics, the traditionalists volunteer most often at the church, compared with moderates or liberals. The three self-identification categories do not differ much in the proportions who volunteer outside the church.

Overall, the results show that there is a strong "net balance" of churched versus nonchurched volunteering among evangelicals, except among those who consider themselves liberals. Among mainline Protestants, the balance

TABLE 4.3
Volunteering by Religious Tradition
(Percentage in each category who volunteered for a church and for a nonchurch
organization during the past year)

Affiliation	Religious Self-Identity			
	Fund.	Evan.	Main.	Lib.
Evangelical Protestant				
Church volunteer	78	82	75	51
Nonchurch volunteer	47	52	58	52
Difference (church-nonchurch)	+31	+30	+27	−1
Number	(194)	(271)	(108)	(222)
Mainline Protestant				
Church volunteer	59	74	67	55
Nonchurch volunteer	52	58	68	58
Difference (church-nonchurch)	+7	+16	−1	−3
Number	(54)	(65)	(106)	(222)
Black Protestant				
Church volunteer	59	80	70	52
Nonchurch volunteer	64	50	70	46
Difference (church-nonchurch)	−5	+30	0	−6
Number	(22)	(20)	(20)	(48)
Roman Catholic				
Church volunteer	—	64	47	43
Nonchurch volunteer	—	52	48	51
Difference (church-nonchurch)	—	+12	−1	−8
Number		(344)	(483)	(407)

Source: Religion and Politics Survey, 2000.
Note: N = 5,603; for Catholics, "traditional" is in the column labeled "evangelical" and "moderate"
is in the column labeled "mainline."

is more even, except among those who consider themselves evangelicals, where the balance is still in the direction of churched volunteering. This is also the case among black Protestants. And, among Catholics, the balance between inside and outside volunteering is again fairly even, except among traditionalists, who are more likely to volunteer for the church.

It will be important to keep these results in mind as we consider more detailed questions about volunteering. On many of those questions, the differences among religious traditions are negligible, and on some it is the individual member's beliefs and practices that seem to matter more than religious affiliation. Chances are that the differences among religious traditions have more to do with whether volunteer work happens in conjunction with the church or elsewhere than with the sheer amount of activity these traditions encourage.

We can now turn our attention back to the question of volunteering that is specifically concerned with helping the needy. If the major religious traditions differ in how much they encourage people to volunteer for churches or for other organizations, they do not seem to differ much in encouraging people to volunteer in some way to help people who are disadvantaged. This is most clearly illustrated in table 4.4, which draws on data from Robert Putnam's Social Capital Benchmark Survey. This survey did not include many questions about religious belief and practice, or even as detailed questions about religious affiliation, as some other surveys, but the questions were sufficient to classify respondents into the same broad categories we have just been considering: evangelical Protestants, mainline Protestants, black Protestants, and Catholics. Because the survey had a large number of respondents, we can also compare Jews and those who fell into a miscellaneous category of other religions. The survey further permits comparing adherents of these various traditions who attended services regularly with those who did not, thus providing a crude indication of whether participation exposes people to the kinds of norms and opportunities that encourage volunteering or not. Finally, the study asked specifically about volunteering during the past year to help the poor or elderly, which has the advantage of somewhat narrowing the meaning of volunteering so that it does not refer to entities such as neighborhood associations or arts organizations.

The figures in table 4.4 reveal two things. First, the people who participate regularly in religious services are significantly more likely to volunteer to help the poor or elderly than people who do not participate regularly in religious services for all six of the religious traditions shown. Second, the differences among religious traditions pale in comparison with those within each tradition between those who attend services regularly and those who do not. The figures do suggest that mainline Protestants at both levels of attendance are slightly more likely to do this kind of volunteer work than are evangelical Protestants, but these differences are relatively small. The differences between these groups and between black Protestants and Catholics are also relatively small. The figures also suggest that among those who do not attend services regularly, Jews are the most likely to do volunteer work. This pattern suggests, as is sometimes argued, that there is a relatively strong ethic of service among Jews in general and that formal religious observance may play a relatively smaller role in reinforcing this ethic than it does among Christian groups.[23]

Data from the Civic Involvement Survey permit examining in closer detail the characteristics of congregations and of church members that influence the likelihood of their volunteering for programs specifically concerned with helping the needy. The figures in table 4.5 are estimates of the likelihood of someone having engaged in any of the following activities

TABLE 4.4
Volunteering for Poor or Elderly by Religious Tradition
(Percentage within each tradition and for each level of attendance who had volunteered during the past year to help the poor or elderly)

Religious Tradition	Attend Weekly	Attend Less	Gamma	Number
Evangelical Protestant	39	23	.359	(5,127)
Mainline Protestant	46	28	.380	(4,851)
Black Protestant	43	26	.368	(2,220)
Roman Catholic	38	23	.349	(7,193)
Jewish	46	37	.183	(423)
Other religion	39	27	.257	(1,811)

Source: Social Capital Benchmark Survey, 2000.

Note: N = 21,625; cases excluded where religious tradition as absent or could not be determined; gammas all significant at .001 level.

within the previous year: distributing food to the needy, helping at a shelter for abused women or children, volunteering for AIDS-related activities, building houses for the poor, helping with a community development corporation, volunteering for a violence prevention effort, or doing community organizing. In all, 27 percent of the public had done at least one of these, and this proportion was 32 percent among church members (I restrict the following to church members because some of the questions were asked only of church members). The coefficients in the table are odds ratios derived from logistic regression analysis. In the column labeled Model 1, we see that the odds of doing this kind of volunteer work are improved if a person attends regularly; specifically, the odds of volunteering to help the needy are almost twice as high for those who attend services weekly or almost weekly as for those who attend less regularly. In the same column, we see how people compare who attend different kinds of churches. These results confirm what we have just seen in the Social Capital Benchmark data. Here, we do not have the opportunity to compare religious traditions in quite the same way, but the data do not suggest that members of liberal Protestant churches or Catholics are any more likely to volunteer than other churchgoers, or that members of conservative congregations are either more or less likely to volunteer than members of other congregations.

Other characteristics of congregations and of members' involvement in congregations do significantly affect the likelihood of their volunteering to help the needy. The figures in the column labeled Model 2 show, for instance, that members of large congregations are somewhat more likely to do volunteer work than members of small congregations. We might suppose that members of churches located in inner-city areas would be more likely to volunteer, too, since there would be more needy people in their community. The opposite is the case, though. Members of inner-city churches are less likely to volunteer than members of churches in suburban areas and small towns. Having more individual and collective resources may be the reason. The data also show (Model 3) that the more programs a congregation sponsors, the more likely members are to do volunteer work. Indeed, once the number of programs is considered, the effect of congregational size on volunteering becomes statistically insignificant.

The data also demonstrate that members who are more formally active in their congregations are more likely to do volunteer work for programs that help the needy (Model 4). It does not seem to make much difference if a person simply attends Sunday school. But if someone serves on a church board or participates in a small group Bible study or prayer fellowship, then that person is significantly more likely to have done volunteer work for a specific program designed to help the needy in the past year. Finally, the data give some support to the view that preaching about social issues and about caring for the poor encourages volunteering (Model 5). At

TABLE 4.5
Volunteering to Assist Disadvantaged Persons by Church Characteristics
(Church members only)

	Model 1	Model 2	Model 3	Model 4	Model 5
Attendance	1.972***	1.862***	1.659***	1.151	1.011
Liberal Protestant	1.268	1.217	1.094	1.051	.922
Catholic	1.082	1.023	1.060	.932	.857
Conservative cong.	.929	.878	.910	.842	.899
Size of congregation		1.283*	1.078	1.254	1.188
Location in inner city		.629**	.468***	.463***	.457***
No. of cong'l. programs			1.213***	1.176***	1.156***
Attend Sunday school				.964	.924
Serve on church board				2.413***	2.071***
Member small group				2.065***	1.940***
Heard sermon on social issues					2.457***
Heard sermon on caring for the poor					1.499*
Constant	.082	.074	.064	.094	.083
−2 Log likelihood	1124.848	1055.296	1013.937	967.629	922.193
Nagelkerke R-square	.043	.057	.120	.187	.249

Source: Civic Involvement Survey, 1997.

Note: N = 850; odds ratios for the likelihood of having volunteered for any activity concerned with helping the disadvantaged.

least there is a strong positive relationship between remembering hearing such sermons and having done volunteer work.

The question of who volunteers more, therefore, may be answered in the following way. Confessional tradition seems not to matter very much. It does matter in how much people volunteer specifically for church work: evangelicals volunteer more than mainline Protestants or Catholics. But it makes little difference to the likelihood that people will volunteer for organizations other than their church or for programs concerned specifically with helping the needy. This result should not be surprising. We know, for instance, that many of the doctrinal "distinctives" separating religious traditions in the past do not matter as much nowadays in shaping the behavior of individual members. This is partly because religious organizations themselves downplay these differences and partly because many people have been affiliated with more than one tradition. The data do suggest that volunteering to help the needy is more common among regular attendees at religious services than among irregular attendees. This may be a function of different kinds of people choosing or not choosing to attend regularly, but it seems more consistent with the idea that people who attend regularly actually hear about the value of serving more often and are more frequently exposed to opportunities for serving. It also appears that congregations may be able to encourage volunteering, if they wish to do so, by getting members involved in small group Bible studies and prayer fellowships and by initiating formal service programs within the congregation.

Is Faith-Based Volunteering Different?

Before we turn to other aspects of volunteering, we can also consider briefly some evidence that will bear on the discussion of faith-based organizations in the next chapter. As we will discuss there, much interest has focused on the differences between special noncongregational faith-based organizations and secular or nonsectarian organizations. This interest reflects questions about performance, administration, and client satisfaction that have arisen in conjunction with government initiatives to provide funding to faith-based service agencies. One of the related questions concerns the possibility that faith-based organizations of all kinds may enjoy advantages over secular organizations because of having greater access to volunteers or being able to draw on a more dedicated pool of volunteers.

How to answer a question like this has stymied investigators because there has been no straightforward way in which to make such comparisons systematically. A question in the Civic Involvement Survey, though, offers a small piece of information that is worth considering.

For the nationally representative sample of volunteers that was obtained through the Civic Involvement Survey, we asked each volunteer if he or she had volunteered during the past year for a program that received funding from various sources. Seventy-eight percent said they had volunteered for a program that received funding from individual donors and 55 percent had volunteered for a program that received funding from religious organizations. Almost as many (52 percent) had volunteered for a program that received funding from other nonprofit organizations and 50 percent had done so for a program funded by corporations. Fewer (39 percent and 36 percent, respectively) had volunteered for programs funded by state or local government or by foundations. And the smallest number (25 percent) had volunteered for programs funded by the federal government. It is important to keep in mind that these figures are not mutually exclusive because many service programs receive funding from multiple sources. It is also important to remember that some volunteers had assisted with more than one program during the year. Nevertheless, these figures suggest that many volunteers do in fact have some contact with programs that receive funding from religious sources.

These programs may be directly sponsored by congregations, or they may be part of separate agencies that are faith-based or that receive funding indirectly from congregations or denominations. The fact that about half of all volunteers have served in programs that receive religious funding and about half have not, though, provides a way of comparing these two groups of volunteers. These comparisons are shown in table 4.6. In the top panel of the table all the other sources of funding to which these volunteers have been exposed are shown. Two things stand out. One is that the programs with which volunteers have worked that receive funding from religious organizations also appear to receive funding from many other sources as well. Or at least the volunteers have been involved with programs with a wide variety of funding. For instance, more than half of these faith-based volunteers say the programs they have been involved with also received funding from corporations, and about four in ten say these programs had received funding from state or local government. The other notable result is that the figures are higher in every instance for the volunteers whose programs have received religious funding than for the volunteers whose programs did not receive religious funding. This difference suggests that volunteers at programs qualifying as "faith-based" in terms of funding are generally not isolated; instead, they are probably more likely than other kinds of volunteers to be exposed to programs that receive funding from other sources. We must be careful not to overinterpret these results, but they do bear on the question of skill and capacity. It is possible, for instance, that the volunteers associated with religiously funded programs have also acquired skill in dealing with government contracts, corporate sponsorship, or foundation support. This is not to say that faith-based programs themselves have such attributes, but that the kinds of volunteers they enlist may have them.

The second panel of the table summarizes some of the religious characteristics that distinguish volunteers at programs with religious funding from volunteers at other programs. Not surprisingly, the former are more likely to attend religious services regularly and to be members of congregations than the latter. However, quite a few of the latter are also church members and attend services regularly. Neither group of volunteers tends to be different from the other in the proportion who are liberal Protestants or Catholics. Personal religious views, however, do distinguish the two groups, with more of the volunteers at programs with religious funding identifying themselves as conservatives or moderates, and more of the volunteers at programs with no religious funding identifying themselves as religious liberals.

In the third panel of the table the two groups of volunteers are compared in terms of the intensity of their volunteering. Volunteers at programs with religious funding are more likely to volunteer at least two hours per week than their counterparts, are more likely to have volunteered for at least three different activities in the past year, and are more likely to have volunteered in a poor inner-city neighborhood. In short, the volunteers connected with religiously funded programs appear to have been more actively involved in service endeavors than the volunteers associated with other programs.

The bottom panel of the table shows the only two demographic factors on which the two kinds of volunteers differed significantly. More of the volunteers at religiously funded programs were women than at the other programs—a result that is consistent with the fact that women are generally

TABLE 4.6
Funding Sources of Human Service Volunteers' Programs
(Percentage of human service volunteers at each kind of program who had each
characteristic)

	Volunteered for Program That Received Money from Religious Organization	Volunteered for Program That Did Not Receive Money from Religious Organization
Said the programs they volunteered for also received funds from		
Individual donors	89	65
Other nonprofits	64	38
Corporations	55	43
State or local government	42	35
Foundations	41	29
Federal government	29	20
Attend religious services almostly weekly	70	32
Church member	84	54
Member of church-affiliated group	44	10
Liberal Protestant	15	16
Catholic	10	10
Religious conservative	26	23
Religious moderate	49	40
Religious liberal	24	37
Volunteer at least 2 hours a week	63	50
Volunteer for at least 3 different activities	81	63
Volunteered in poor inner-city area	41	29
Female	62	48
East	14	23
Midwest	23	23
South	34	29
West	29	25
Number	(231)	(191)

Source: Civic Involvement Survey, 1997.

Note: N = 422; human service volunteers are respondents who during the past year had volunteered distributing food, helped at a shelter, done AIDS-related activities, built houses for the poor, helped with a community development corporation, engaged in a violence prevention effort, or done community organizing; all except liberal Protestant and Catholic statistically significant at or beyond the .05 level (Pearson chi-square).

more involved than men in religious activities of all kinds.[24] Fewer of the religiously funded volunteers were in the Eastern United States, and more were in the South and Western United States. Although these differences are not large, they do correspond partly with impressions about the relatively more churched communities being in the South and the relatively less religious ones being on the East Coast. Since the West Coast is also sometimes regarded as less religious, it is thus of interest that this pattern does not seem evident here.

We will have occasion to consider the organization and activities of faith-based service agencies in greater detail in the next chapter. Suffice it to say here that in terms of religiously funded programs, a majority of volunteers for activities that specifically help the disadvantaged in the United States appear to be associated with such programs. And these volunteers, while more religiously oriented personally than other volunteers, are also relatively diverse and appear to be among the more active of volunteers. For these reasons, there may in fact be some merit to the argument that faith-based organizations, whatever else their limitations may be, hold certain potential advantages in mobilizing volunteers.

Volunteering and Connectedness

Although volunteering is important because of the assistance it provides to people who need it, volunteering is also important for another reason. It connects people. We saw in the last chapter that church members who do volunteer work are much more likely to have made friends with people who are marginalized or disadvantaged than church members who have not done volunteer work. This may not be too surprising, but it does point to the possibility that volunteering builds bridges that span social class differences or racial differences and that may help to connect the kinds of people who attend middle-class suburban churches with people from different backgrounds or neighborhoods. Other possibilities also emerge through volunteering, such as meeting people who run service agencies or who have other positions of responsibility in the community.

Drawing on data from the Civic Involvement Survey, table 4.7 provides some information about the specific kinds of contact in the wider community that volunteers are likely to make through their volunteering. The figures are for people who are church members, so these are people who are already associated with at least one organization in their community. The two columns of numbers compare the contacts of church members who did volunteer work only for church-related activities and of church members who volunteered for at least one program that was specifically concerned with helping the disadvantaged. The latter could have been mainly sponsored by their church or performed at some other organization, whereas the former probably dealt only with their church, such as ushering or teaching Sunday school. Not surprisingly, both kinds of volunteers were likely to say that their volunteer work had put them in contact with a

TABLE 4.7

Community Contacts among Church Members Who Have Done Volunteer Work
(Percentage who said their volunteering had put them in contact with different categories of people)

Types of Contacts	Members Who Volunteered Only for Church-Related Activities	Members Who Volunteered for Programs to Help the Disadvantaged
Clergy	69	62
Social workers	10	33
Health professionals	11	36
Banks	11	18
Nonprofit organizations	20	52
Community development corporations	2	13
Their neighbors	35	61
Service clubs	6	26
Government officials	9	26
Corporation executives	5	19
Teachers	11	54
Lawyers	7	27
Number	(81)	(297)

Source: Civic Involvement Survey, 1997.
Note: N = 915.

member of the clergy. About two-thirds of both groups said this. After that, the similarities end. The people who volunteer only for their church seldom make contact with individuals and organizations in the wider community as a result of their volunteering, other than in some cases with their neighbors. In contrast, the people who volunteer for programs concerned with helping the disadvantaged are much more likely to make contacts in the wider community. Nearly two-thirds make contact with their neighbors. Half make contact with teachers or with nonprofit organizations. One-third make contact with social workers or health professionals. And one-quarter make contact with service clubs, government officials, and lawyers.

Why is this important? Because civil society is held together by networks of this kind. Also because people who need help are more likely to receive the help they need if caregivers are connected to vital sources of service, expertise, and information. In a society fraught with individualism and anonymity, where people can easily stay at home watching television and seldom see anyone besides their immediate family or close friends, volunteering builds bridges. It establishes relationships that people can draw on when they are organizing a community program, when someone needs a referral, or when they themselves need help. Church members, even active ones, can be isolated from the wider community if they take part only in activities at their church. But church members who volunteer for service projects forge links between the congregation and the wider community. It is through such links that others in the congregation find out about community needs and resources.

Motivations for Volunteering

What we know about religion's relationship with volunteering is that religious organizations do not simply serve as a staging ground from which to mobilize volunteers. Religion is also a source of values, including, as we saw in the last chapter, values about caring for the needy. These values are part of all the major religious traditions and are regularly communicated through sermons, classes, small-group discussions, and often more tangibly through the social ministries sponsored by congregations. At the core of these efforts is the idea that values provide potential volunteers with motives to become actively involved in helping the needy.

But motivation is no simple matter. Most people are motivated by multiple and often conflicting values. On the one hand, it is very common, if not universal, for children to learn the value of caring through the sheer experience of being cared for. We know that being cared for benefits us, sustains us, and for that matter is simply a source of good feelings. It may well strike us that our parents are acting sacrificially on our behalf—that they are perhaps benefitting less from the bargain than we are. As we grow older, we learn more explicitly about altruism. In religious contexts, we may learn that it is more blessed to give than to receive. We are exposed to the example of religious figures who behaved sacrificially. In other ways, we are also exposed to ideas that come close to emphasizing altruistic or sacrificial behavior. Idealistic conceptions of romantic love sometimes tell us that we need to put our mate's interests ahead of our own. Marriage vows often include a commitment to love and cherish even if circumstances turn sour. The military and other venues in which patriotism is especially valued encourage us to understand love of country in such altruistic terms that we are willing to die for the good of others. On the other hand, we are also taught from early childhood to look out for ourselves. We are often driven more by self-interest, whether innate or learned, than by altruism. In families, we compete with siblings (and sometimes parents) to get the best of everything for ourselves. In schools, we are taught to take primary responsibility for our own well-being and to compete against other students who are seeking to maximize theirs. The business world reinforces this competitive ethic, surrounding it with economic theories indicating that the pursuit of self-interest may actually be beneficial to the collective good as well. Religion, too, offers messages that may conflict with or at least dampen an altruistic spirit. We learn in some contexts, for instance, that we must take responsibility for our own souls and for our own happiness and personal fulfillment.[25]

The data shown in table 4.8 illustrate the extent to which we value both the goals of caring for others and the goals of looking out for ourselves. These figures are from a national survey conducted in the late 1980s but still relevant in providing unique information about this particular mix of values.[26] I have divided the respondents into those (roughly half) who said they attended religious services fairly regularly (at least several times a month) and those who did not attend religious services as regularly (several times a year or less), as well as showing the results for the whole sample.

The main observation the data reveal is that nearly all Americans hold these values to some degree. On the side of altruism or caring, upwards of nine people in ten say it is at least fairly important to them to make the world a better place, give time to help others, and help people in need. On the more self-interested side, upwards of nine people in ten also say they value taking care of themselves, living a comfortable life, being able to do what they want, and being successful in their work. There are hardly any differences between the more religiously involved and the less religiously involved on these questions. In both columns, the overwhelming majority say that all these values are at least fairly important. Yet people do differ in terms of *how much* they value some of these goals. The simplest way of demonstrating this is by examining the statistical relationships shown in the column labeled gamma. I computed these measures by crosstabulating the full responses for each of the values (ranging from "absolutely essential,"

Table 4.8

Values by Attendance at Religious Services
(Percentage who said each value was at least fairly important to them personally)

	Attend Regularly	Do Not Attend Regularly	All in Survey	Gamma
Taking care of yourself	99	98	98	.027
Living a comfortable life	98	98	98	−.097**
Making the world a better place	97	94	96	.182***
Having a deep religious faith	97	92	95	.653***
Giving time to help others	97	92	95	.274***
Being able to do what you want	93	96	94	−.186***
Helping people in need	90	90	90	.240***
Being successful in your work	90	90	90	−.024
Making a lot of money	71	76	74	−.114***
Number	(1,058)	(1,052)	(2,110)	

Source: American Values Survey, 1989.
Note: N = 2,110; statistical significance, * p < .05; ** p < .01, *** p < .001 (Pearson chi-square).

to "very important," to "fairly important," to "not very important") with the full responses for attendance at religious services (ranging from "about once a week," to "several times a month," to "several times a year," to "only on special occasions," to "never"). Positive gammas mean that regular churchgoers are more likely than less regular churchgoers to say the value is important; negative gammas mean the opposite. Once we look at it this way, religious involvement does seem to go hand in hand with values associated with caregiving: making the world a better place, giving time to help others, and helping people in need. And religious involvement is associated with a slight tendency to *devalue* some of the more self-interested goals: living a comfortable life, being able to do what you want, and making a lot of money.

To the extent that religious involvement reinforces altruistic values and discourages self-interestedness, then, we would suppose that this is one of the reasons why religiously involved people are, as we have seen, more actively engaged in volunteer work to help the needy. Some evidence that bears out this supposition can be seen in table 4.9. However, the evidence is complicated, so we need to consider carefully what the table shows about the ways in which voluntary caregiving, values, and religious involvement intersect. Looking across the first row, we see that the odds of having engaged in charity or social service activities, such as helping the poor, the sick, or the elderly, are more than twice as great among those who attend religious services at least several times a month than among those who attend religious services less often—consistent with what we have seen previously from other surveys. The same is true for having donated time to a volunteer organization in the past year. These two kinds of volunteering could both refer to organized efforts, such as helping at a soup kitchen or homeless shelter (although the one could involve individual caring), and could refer to something sponsored directly by a religious organization. The other two kinds of caregiving—helping someone who had car trouble and giving money to a beggar—are examples of altruistic behavior, but happen outside the context of any formal or informal organization. The odds of having done either of these in the past year are not significantly different for people who attend religious services regularly than for people who attend religious services less often. Unlike the previous two activities, then, these suggest that there may be something about religious involvement that encourages certain kinds of caregiving, but that does not simply lead to the kinds of altruism that are sometimes called "random acts of kindness."

In the second row of the table, the relationships between valuing helping people in need (the clearest example we have of an altruistic value) and each of the four kinds of caregiving behavior are shown. Here again, there is a strong relationship between this factor and having engaged in charity or social service activity. In fact, the odds of having done this in the past year are more than four times as great among those who say helping people in need is absolutely essential than among those who say it is less important. The same is true for the odds of having donated time to a volunteer organization, although the relationship here is weaker. For the two random acts of kindness, though, the relationships are not statistically significant. Whatever drives people to help in these ways, it appears, is indeed sufficiently random as to be unaffected by the value one attaches to helping people. For instance, helping someone having car trouble may have more to do with the chances of having seen someone in this situation, or with traffic

TABLE 4.9

Service Behavior by Values and Religious Involvement
(Adjusted odds ratios of having done each activity within the past year)

Independent variables	Charity or Social Service	Time to Volunteer Agency	Helped with Car Trouble	Gave Money to Beggar
Religious service attendance (only)	2.608***	2.123***	.873	.906
Value helping people in need (only)	4.443***	2.445*	1.016	1.135
Attendance (simultaneous)	2.559***	2.094***	.872	.903
Value helping (simultaneous)	3.757***	2.108*	1.046	1.160
Value doing what you want (only)	.808	1.122	1.160	.852
Value making money (only)	.742**	.982	1.144	1.044
Attendance (with controls)	2.424***	1.962***	.997	.960
Value helping (with controls)	3.581***	1.888+	1.219	1.191

Source: American Values Survey, 1989.

Note: N = 2,110; statistical significance, + < .10, * $p < .05$, ** $p < .01$, *** $p < .001$ (Wald statistic); controls = religious service attendance while growing up, age, gender, education level.

conditions, time of day or night, and so on, than with being an altruistic person. And since most people hold both altruistic and self-interested values to some degree, as we have seen, it may well be these random conditions that prompt a response, more than the mix of values themselves.

The third and fourth rows of the table permit an examination of whether the value people attach to caregiving is the reason for religious involvement seeming to encourage caregiving behavior. The possibility at issue here is the following: religious organizations teach that helping the needy is important, so those who participate in religious organizations more regularly should be more exposed to these teachings, and it is in turn the value of helping the needy that explains why they do in fact help the needy. We already found support for part of this argument in the previous chapter, where we saw that most regular churchgoers do claim to have heard sermons or discussions about helping the needy, and from the evidence presented here about the positive relationship between religious involvement and valuing helping the needy. But it does not seem to be the case that holding this value is *the reason* why religious involvement and caregiving behavior go hand in hand. Were that the case, we would expect the figures in row three to be smaller than the figures in row one. That is, taking account of differences in how much people value caregiving should reduce the strength of the relationship between religious involvement and caregiving behavior. Yet in none of the four comparisons is this the case except to a very slight degree. In fact, there is more of a reduction in the effect of valuing helping the needy (comparing row four with row two). While these relationships remain statistically significant in the same two cases as before, both numbers are somewhat smaller than previously. The differences are not great. But they do suggest that religious involvement may serve a "channeling" effect. That is, people value helping the needy, and then, if they are involved in a religious organization, that involvement helps channel them into actually putting this value into practice.

The next two rows in the table permit us to consider whether or not self-interested values have a negative effect on caregiving behavior in the same ways that more altruistic values seem to have a positive effect. The two values here—being able to do what you want, and making a lot of money—were the two that were most negatively associated with religious involvement. In other words, these may be values that religious involvement discourages (or that discourage people from being religiously involved). Of the eight relationships shown in the table, the only one that is statistically significant is the one between wanting to make a lot of money and having engaged in charity or social service activity. That relationship is negative. Some of the other coefficients are also negative, but are not statistically significant. This is interesting. It suggests that while caregiving values encourage caregiving, self-interested values do not necessarily discourage it.

The last two rows of the table return again to the relationships between religious involvement and caregiving, and between valuing caregiving and doing something about it. It is possible that these relationships have more to do with how people were raised (for example, whether they were raised religiously) or with differences in factors such as age, gender, and education.[27] We know, for example, that better-educated people do volunteer work more often than less well-educated people, and that women may be more likely to care for the sick and elderly whereas men may be more likely to stop to help someone having car trouble. Thus, it could be that these factors either account for or suppress relationships between caregiving and religious involvement or valuing caregiving. The short answer, though, is that they do not. None of the relationships in these two rows is much different from the figures shown in rows three and four.

What we learn from this exercise can be summarized as follows. If people hold some kinds of altruistic or caregiving values, those values do seem to motivate them to engage in volunteer work or other forms of caregiving behavior. But such motives, if they can be called altruism, do not function without limits. They do not seem to affect random acts of kindness. And they do not seem to require that people give up more self-interested values. They do appear more common among people who are religiously involved. And yet religious involvement and altruistic values work hand in hand, rather than one explaining away the effects of the other. If anything, religious involvement probably helps to activate people's caregiving values so that they actually do something to help other people.

The fact that most people hold a combination of altruistic and self-interested values becomes evident again when we consider what people say when asked specifically about motives for engaging in caregiving behavior. The same survey included some questions of this kind. One was a question that asked people to respond to some possible reasons for trying to be a person who is kind and caring (reasons that pertained to them personally), to which one possibility was the statement: "I want to give of myself for the benefit of others." Another question, framed the same way, gave people the option of saying "Being kind and considerate helps me get what I want in life." The first statement, then, serves as a rough measure of an altruistic motive for caregiving, while the second supplies a more self-interested motive. For each statement, people were asked to say if it was a major reason, a minor reason, or not a reason in their own case. The results are shown in table 4.10. In the total sample, about one-third considered the altruistic statement a major reason, and another third considered it a minor reason. But almost as many said the same for the more self-interested statement. One-quarter thought it was a major reason and one-third said it was a minor reason. Again, then, we see that people imagine various possibilities for being caregiving. In the columns that compare caregivers and noncaregivers, it does appear that the former are somewhat more likely to emphasize altruistic motivation than the latter. In contrast, there are no differences

TABLE 4.10
Reasons for Caregiving
(Percentage who give each reason for personally trying to be a kind and caring person)

	Caregivers	Non-caregivers	Total Sample	Gamma
I want to give of myself for the benefit of others				
Major reason	37	28	31	.126***
Minor reason	33	39	37	
Not a reason	30	33	32	
Being kind and considerate helps me get what I want in life				
Major reason	25	25	25	−.001
Minor reason	34	34	34	
Not a reason	41	41	41	

Source: American Values Survey, 1989.
Note: N = 2,110; statistical significance, * p < .05; ** p < .01, *** p < .001 (Pearson chi-square); "don't know" responses omitted; caregivers were respondents who said they had been involved in charity or social service activity within the past year.

between caregivers and noncaregivers in how they regard the more self-interested motivation.

We need to go beyond survey questions, though, if we are to understand the complexities of motivation for volunteering and the role of religion in this motivation. In contemporary thinking, motivation is not so much a predisposing attribute of an individual's personality or value system, as it was once regarded, but a more dynamic constellation of scripts, narratives, and cultural tools that a person uses to make sense of his or her behavior.[28] This is not to suggest that motivation is little more than an after-the-fact rationalization for one's actions. It is rather to say that motivation occurs as a process of self-reflection and discovery—as an internal conversation in which people engage to monitor their behavior, to ensure that they are involved in meaningful activities, and to make decisions about next steps. In this way of thinking about motivation, stories and the elements of which stories are composed play a major role in guiding behavior.

The stories guiding volunteering and other caregiving behavior typically include materials from many sources. Some are accounts of experiences that may have happened during one's youth or within one's family of origin. Others may be taken from observing role models, such as parents or teachers. Still others emerge from caregiving itself and carry forward to future episodes of caregiving. Because of the complexity of our motives, these stories weave together ideas that often emphasize both altruism and self-interest. They do so by asserting selfless motives, but also by taking off the sharp idealistic edge that may be associated with such motives, just as they both acknowledge and deny the role of self-interest.

Religion plays a potential role for many people in shaping their self-narratives about caregiving. Religion is a source of stories about caregiving role models. People learn these stories and incorporate some of the same themes into their personal narratives. Religion also supplies contexts for the telling, retelling, and hearing of stories. In these contexts, the words become more readily available to memory and more easily applied to decisions about caregiving. One remembers hearing a story that makes sense of one's own experience. A person who asks an acquaintance to do volunteer work supplies not only an invitation but also an argument about why that invitation should be accepted. Those arguments can then be used to explain to others and to oneself why it made sense to engage in this activity or to continue engaging in it. Religion is not the only context in which such storytelling occurs. The same processes are often at work in service agencies, and yet religious storytelling also is not restricted to religious settings. Thus, we find instances of people drawing on religious language to explain caregiving in a wide variety of other settings as well.[29]

John Lee, whom I introduced at the beginning of the chapter, provides an interesting case study for understanding how personal narratives forge motivational links between religious involvement and volunteering. Mr. Lee has multiple motives for the work he does each year at the orphanage in the Dominican Republic. One of these motives is to be a better Christian. That, however, is an abstract concept that has motivational power only because Mr. Lee can translate it into more personalized stories. One of his stories provides an account of why he got started doing volunteer work in the Dominican Republic in the first place. This is a narrative about how his friends challenged him to get involved in volunteering. They did not do this simply by inviting him to go on a trip or by telling him there was a need for volunteers. As Mr. Lee tells it, his volunteering was inspired by a larger vision of what life could be. The friends he met were part of a Christian fellowship group that met regularly for prayer and Bible study. They challenged him to think more seriously about his faith in general, and through this process he decided to become involved in volunteering. He recalls, "They were people that I felt were really looking at their faith. They weren't just people who went to church on Sunday and then lived like the rest of the world for the rest of the week." Noting that people learn by imitating others, he continues, "I learned from them that there is a lot more to Christianity than I had originally thought. Getting into volunteer work was just getting into the practical side of what it means to be a Christian and having Christian values. It was curiosity about what I could do to show my faith and learn more about who I am and who God is."

The other part of his story helps Mr. Lee make sense of the personal enjoyment he experiences from working with staff and children at the orphanage. This story directly invokes Jesus as a role model. "That's the way Jesus interacts with us or whomever you want to talk about," Mr. Lee ventures. And then elaborating, he explains: "[Jesus] could have done a lot of things from heaven or wherever you expect him to be and not come down as a human being and interact with other people. So . . . he's a model in terms of helping out, [a model] for me to . . . go to different countries to help out people directly. I think that's the model he set. That's the model I try to live by."

The balance between altruistic and self-interested motives is also evident in Mr. Lee's comments about why he volunteers. When asked as a follow-up to the foregoing to summarize his motivation for getting involved in volunteering, he says, "I think my motivation is partially a little bit selfish in some ways because a lot of the international stuff that I got to do is really getting to see different parts of the world and help people at the same time." It is interesting that he begins this way because he seems to be backtracking from the higher ideals he has just mentioned in talking about his faith. His next remark provides further explanation: "For some people it would be a sacrifice, but I felt like for me it hasn't been a major sacrifice." He acknowledges that "you're not staying in a four-star hotel" and may have no electricity or running water, so some sacrifice is involved. Yet he doesn't stay very long and he enjoys seeing the world. He also considers it personally beneficial to see God working in other countries. "I just see that God is so much bigger than I am."

Being associated with a religious organization doesn't necessarily give volunteers these kinds of stories. Nor do people who volunteer at secular organizations have fewer opportunities to develop such narratives about their motivations. From listening to scores of volunteers describing their motives for becoming involved, the one thing I can say with certainty is that having a story to account for one's volunteering is important *and* these stories generally disclose complex self-reflections about how and why a person became involved in volunteering. In religious contexts, people often suggest motives that sound utilitarian, such as saying that they just enjoy working with children or that serving soup or building houses is a refreshing change of pace from selling software or life insurance. They say they were bored, had time on their hands, or wanted to please a friend who asked them to volunteer. When they mention religious motives, they are often somewhat embarrassed by these connections, downplaying them or (as Mr. Lee did) balancing them with statements that sound more self-interested. In secular contexts, volunteers often mention that they learned altruistic values from their parents or from a teacher or coach. Many mention having been helped at some point in their lives and wanting to return the favor. They, too, emphasize such self-interested motives as being able to relax more when they volunteer than at work or feeling better about themselves than when they only stayed home watching television or were out at bars every evening with their friends.

Where some religious contexts play a special role is by providing volunteers with opportunities to reflect more intentionally or over a more extended period of time about their motives. When they do this, they gradually undergo a process of what the sociologist Rebecca Allahyari has usefully termed *moral selving*.[30] Their self-concept changes. They begin to see themselves as more than volunteers who just happen to have done something helpful on a few occasions. They incorporate messages about the moral worth of volunteering into their self-identity, coming to see themselves as good people and linking this conception of goodness to their volunteering. This is a process that can often happen more effectively in religious contexts, where moral values and the identities of whole persons are involved, than in secular settings, where only the instrumental aspects of getting a job done may be relevant. Our qualitative interviews with volunteers suggest that many engage in very specific activities once or twice a month (such as tutoring at a school or prison or helping with a Special Olympics event) and then never see the recipients of their volunteering or other volunteers on other occasions. They may have received training of some kind prior to their volunteering. But subsequently they are largely on their own to show up at a specified time and perform a specified task. What they receive by being part of a religious group is the opportunity to talk about what they have done and to receive encouragement. They sometimes pray for the people they are helping and hear others pray for them, and, above all, they have opportunities to tell their stories.[31]

Barriers to Volunteering

One of the practical considerations that clergy and service agency administrators face is how to encourage more people to become involved in volunteering. If most people hold altruistic or caregiving values to some degree, it is always possible to think of programs to reinforce the salience of these values. Sermons, small-group discussions, and invitations to participate in specific service activities are among these possibilities. Yet it is also important to consider the barriers that inhibit or discourage people from volunteering. Committee chairs and others in charge of recruiting volunteers often speculate on these barriers, wondering, for example, if there are categories of people they should not approach, such as those who are busy with demanding workplace or family responsibilities or those who are experiencing personal or family crises.

Returning again to data from the Civic Involvement Survey, we see in table 4.11 some comparisons between church members who are currently involved in human service volunteering and those who are not. Being church members, all are associated with at least one organization in their community, but on some of these characteristics volunteers and nonvolunteers are quite different, while on other characteristics the two resemble each other. The factors that distinguish nonvolunteers from volunteers are the following: nonvolunteers are much more likely to belong to no other organizations in the community besides their church, they are less likely to know their neighbors, they are more likely to have moved recently into their current neighborhood, they spend more hours a day watching television, they are more likely to be retired, they are more likely to have meager family incomes, and they are more likely to live in low-income neighborhoods. The factors on which nonvolunteers and volunteers are nearly indistinguishable are the percentage who work more than fifty hours a week, among those who are employed, and the percentage who feel they have hardly any energy left after working. On the three questions about personal crises—health or medical problems, an emotional crisis, or some other family crisis—those who volunteer are actually more likely to have had these experiences in the past year than those who do not volunteer.

These results suggest that some of the stereotypes about why people do not volunteer or about who should not be asked to volunteer are wrong. Having to work long hours or being exhausted by one's work does not seem to interfere with people volunteering, if these results can be generalized. Nor is the view that people should not be asked to volunteer if they are experiencing personal crises. Sensitivity is always necessary in considering the timing of requests to volunteer, but these results suggest that people who have experienced personal difficulties may actually be *more* willing to volunteer than those who have escaped such difficulties. The barriers to volunteering can best be summarized by saying that they involve a lack of social and economic capital. People are drawn into volunteering by participating in community organizations and by associating with neighbors and friends. Not knowing anyone or having recently moved to a new neighborhood is thus a barrier. Staying home and watching television long

TABLE 4.11
Social Factors That Inhibit Volunteering among Church Members

	Members Who Do Not Volunteer	Members Who Volunteer	Adjusted Odds Ratios
Characteristics that are more common among nonvolunteers than among volunteers			
Member of no organizations besides church	53	16	.174***
Know few or no neighbors	51	43	.749*
Lived at present address less than 2 years	25	18	.640*
Watch television 5 hours or more per day	22	12	.472***
Retired	25	15	.499***
Income is less than $20,000 per year	26	16	.494***
Live in low-income neighborhood	16	9	.590*
Characteristics that are not more common among non-volunteers than among volunteers			
Work 50 or more hours a week (if employed)	22	26	1.408
Have hardly any energy left after working	22	22	.934
Had serious health or medical problem during the past year	18	28	1.761***
Had emotional crisis during the past year	13	26	2.328***
Had some other family crisis	16	26	1.734**
Number	(618)	(297)	

Source: Civic Involvement Survey, 1997.

Note: N = 915; volunteers are respondents who during the past year had volunteered distributing food, helped at a shelter, done AIDS-related activities, built houses for the poor, helped with a community development corporation, engaged in a violence prevention effort, or done community organizing; adjusted odds ratios are from logistic regression equations that include frequency of church attendance and gender; coefficients less than 1 indicate that church members with the characteristic listed are less likely to volunteer than members without this characteristic; * < .05, ** < .01, *** < .001 (Wald statistic).

hours a day is also a barrier, although there may be reasons for this, such as being disabled, ill, or caring for young children. The fact that fewer volunteers than nonvolunteers are retired is consistent with other research showing that volunteering declines among people in their sixties and seventies.[32] It is nevertheless a discouraging finding with regard to the future of volunteering. Some observers have suggested that volunteering has increased among older Americans; that research cautions, though, that these increases may not continue.[33] And it may be that better health among older people encourages certain kinds of volunteering, such as caring for one's grandchildren or helping at the church, but retirement is also a time of bereavement for many people, a time of diminished energy and social contacts, and a time when health or safety concerns discourage people from volunteering for programs devoted to serving the poor and needy. The finding that people with meager incomes and those who live in low-income neighborhoods are more common among nonvolunteers than among volunteers is less surprising, but it also runs contrary to some popular arguments. Those arguments suggest that people who are themselves poor will be more likely to help others who are poor.[34] This may be the case, at least if informal caring for neighbors and friends is included. But it is less likely to be the case for volunteering at formal service programs.[35] Those programs may be located in different neighborhoods and, as other research has suggested, many low-income people remain isolated from the networks of recruitment that often seem to operate in conjunction with personal resources such as education and income.[36]

Some Unresolved Questions

Existing research on volunteering suggests that organized religion encourages it not only when it benefits the congregation, but also in ways that provide services to the poor and other needy people in the wider community. Volunteering thus creates links between congregations and people with special needs. It also provides one of the bridges that connect congregations with the other organizations of which civil society is composed, including secular nonprofits, government-funded service agencies, schools, and foundations. Although volunteering is often performed by good-hearted individuals acting alone or working only with others on short-term projects, the connections they provide among community organizations are of considerable importance. These links can function as channels for communication, as sources of information about services and needs, and as networks on which trust can be established. Religious contexts are by no means the only ways in which these networks are created, but religious organizations are one of the most important sources of volunteering in our society and the research suggests that they do enjoy some advantages in terms of enlisting volunteers, motivating them, and keeping them involved.

What we do not have are very precise measures of just how much volunteering is channeled through religious organizations and how much of that effort actually makes its way to people in need. Volunteering has become socially desirable in recent years as a result of highly publicized efforts by political leaders to promote it, not to mention the efforts of clergy and leaders of nonprofit organizations. In surveys and in personal interviews, it is easy for people to exaggerate their involvement in volunteering. Someone who has greeted newcomers at a church or merely attended an exploratory meeting at their workplace to talk about community relations may count themselves as volunteers when they respond to a survey. Questions that ask specifically about volunteering in a low-income neighborhood or helping at a soup kitchen are a step in the right direction. But we also need to consider some of the evidence from recipients and potential recipients (discussed in chapter 6) before drawing any final conclusions about volunteering.

The other unresolved question concerns the management of volunteers. Hardly anything is known about how volunteers at religious organizations are managed. We do not know, for instance, whether certain programs or certain leadership styles are more effective in mobilizing volunteers and deploying them effectively than other programs or leadership styles. What we do know from interviews with volunteers and clergy suggests that congregations typically rely on other organizations to perform much of this managerial function. Congregations largely perform two roles: they encourage people to consider volunteering by reminding them of altruistic and service-oriented values and by organizing meetings where they can hear about opportunities for service; congregations of any size also have mission, outreach, or social ministry committees that serve as liaisons between the congregation and service organizations outside of the congregation. Potential volunteers can thus be identified and encouraged to make their availability known to a service organization that needs them. It is then up to the service organization to provide whatever special training is needed and to schedule specific times for volunteering. Congregations are in this way highly dependent on specialized service organizations, just as those organizations are on congregations for identifying potential volunteers in the first place. At minimum, congregational leaders need to monitor these relationships to make sure that volunteers are properly supported and are indeed being put into effective service opportunities.

Faith-Based Service Organizations

The fact that congregations perform most of their service work either informally or in cooperation with other community organizations means that we cannot fully understand the social role of faith-based services by looking only at congregations. Nor can we understand the relationship between religion and volunteering if we consider only the volunteering that occurs within congregations or in response to appeals from congregations but fail to take account of the many other community organizations through which this volunteering is performed. We need to look beyond congregations to the wider variety of organizations and agencies that provide social services.

Many service agencies are not organized as local congregations but include some aspect of faith in their mission statement and regular activities. Such agencies may have been organized by religious people who felt called to address a particular need in their community (such as providing shelter for the homeless). They may receive funding from religious organizations, have clergy on their boards, draw volunteers from congregations, include prayers among their activities, or encourage clients to reflect more deeply about their own faith and perhaps even to become members of a faith community. These are what policy makers and scholars have in recent years come to refer to as "faith-based service organizations" or simply "faith-based organizations." The literature on these organizations, however, has often failed to distinguish between social services provided by congregations and services offered through more specialized faith-based organizations.[1] Thus, we need to understand what this distinction is and how the two kinds of organizations complement each other.

Much of the interest in faith-based organizations has been generated by public policy debates over the appropriateness of channeling government money to and through these organizations. Questions have been raised about the possibility that such measures violate the separation of church and state and, in response to these questions, various legal arguments and precautions have been generated.[2] A number of larger questions, however, have been raised implicitly or explicitly in these discussions, and we are only now beginning to have evidence with which to address these larger questions.

One question concerns the sheer number of faith-based service organizations that currently exist in the United States. This question is in many ways similar to the one we considered in chapter 2 about the extent of congregational involvement in service provision. It derives from the observation that America is a society in which religion is important and from related claims, uttered variously by religious leaders and government officials, that religion is playing a large role in providing services to the needy. Leaving aside what is being done through congregations, these claims about the importance of religion would appear to be substantiated if faith-based organizations make up a large share of the nonprofit sector more generally, but would be less credible if faith-based organizations constitute a relatively small fraction of the nonprofit sector.

A second question focuses on the possibility that faith-based organizations may be more effective than nonsectarian organizations. This question has typically been raised in connection with arguments about why government should or should not provide funding to faith-based organizations. But it has raised other issues that are interesting in their own right. For instance, are faith-based organizations administered differently than other organizations are? Do they engage in different kinds of activities or include different elements in their programs? Does their effectiveness depend on being able to proselytize? Do they in fact proselytize? And is effectiveness even a relevant question to be asking?

Although these questions assume that a clear line can be drawn between faith-based and nonsectarian service organizations, we also need to entertain questions about that assumption. Some studies have tried to suggest criteria for determining how fully or partially a service organization may conform to the notion of being "faith-based." In this chapter I also want to consider some of the ways in which nonsectarian organizations may include faith or religion among their programs and activities and some of the challenges and strategies that are common to both faith-based and nonsectarian agencies.[3]

How Many Faith-Based Organizations Are There?

In 2003, the Internal Revenue Service reported that there were approximately 1,037,000 registered tax-exempt nonprofit organizations in the United States. Of these, nearly 937,000 were classified as public charities and many of the remaining private foundations were also engaged in charitable activity.[4] Many of these organizations were professional societies, performing arts companies, schools, or advocacy-related agencies that had little direct involvement in providing services to the needy. According to the National Taxonomy of Exempt Entities developed by the National Center for Charitable Statistics, 36,575 nonprofit organizations were directly and primarily involved in human services, such as family services, personal services, emergency assistance, and group home services (not counting organizations concerned only with management, fundraising, professional affiliations, and the like). Collectively, these human services organizations had assets of approximately $142 billion and annual budgets of approximately $93 billion.[5] In addition, many other organizations that were classified differently could also be considered relevant as service providers; for instance, approximately 3,000 organizations specialized in vocational training or rehabilitation and more than 2,500 were youth centers or clubs.

It is impossible to derive estimates of the number of *faith-based* organizations from IRS statistics. The reason is that the National Center for Charitable Statistics does not classify faith-based organizations separately from nonsectarian organizations and the information provided to the IRS is insufficient with respect to mission or administration to permit an independent classification of this kind to be made. Moreover, IRS figures are based only on forms that organizations have filed. Thus, a service agency organized at the national level may be listed as a single organization despite having hundreds of local chapters, whereas another may have filed separate forms for each of its local chapters. In addition, some religious organizations do not file at all because religious organizations can claim exemption from standard IRS reporting requirements.

One estimate of the proportion of nonprofit organizations that may be regarded as "faith-based" comes from a study conducted in New York City by John E. Seley and Julian Wolpert. Through a survey mailed to all nonprofit organizations in New York City, Seley and Wolpert obtained information on 2,797 human service agencies operating in the city. From this information, they determined that 1,045, or 37 percent, could be classified as "religious." Through an examination of financial data, they also determined that approximately 37 percent of the human service sector's total revenues and expenditures were accounted for by religious organizations.[6]

The Seley and Wolpert study is useful because its focus on one city overcomes some of the difficulty of national and local organizations being lumped together in the IRS figures and because respondents in the survey could indicate whether their organization included "religion activities" or not. New York City is not a particularly religious part of the country (unlike the "Bible belt," for instance), so the estimate of 37 percent might actually be conservative if generalized to the whole United States. However, we need to be cautious about this estimate. Some of the organizations Seley and Wolpert classified as religious were congregations and some were apparently included because they were preassigned to the religion category (rather than the human services category) by the National Center for Charitable Statistics's classification scheme. Indeed, when Seley and Wolpert examined results from only the 1,167 organizations from which they received complete information through the survey, they discovered that 631 (54 percent) were secular service organizations with no religious activities, 138 (12 percent) were human service providers under religious auspices, 309 (26 percent) were actually churches or synagogues, and 87 (7 percent) were religious organizations that provided no direct social services to clients. If we are interested strictly in the proportion of human service organizations that are faith-based, then, the best estimate from Seley and Wolpert's research is approximately 18 percent (138 of the 769 human service providers, not counting the congregations and other religious organizations included in the overall study). If this percentage were multiplied by the approximately 36,000 human service organizations in the United States, then the total number of faith-based service organizations would be approximately 6,500. That figure, however, would likely underestimate the actual number of *local* faith-based organizations by as much as 50 percent, since many local organizations are either subsumed under a single national or regional association or have claimed exemption from filing with the IRS. As a proportion, though, 18 percent is probably the best estimate of the share of all private human service provision that comes about through faith-based organizations.[7]

The most interesting finding in Seley and Wolpert's study is that faith-based and nonsectarian service organizations in New York City were virtually indistinguishable in terms of the amounts and the main sources from which they derived revenue. Both derived almost two-thirds (65 and 66 percent, respectively) of their revenue from government grants and contracts. Fees and service charges accounted for 19 and 14 percent of revenue, respectively. Donations and "pass-throughs" made up 9 and 6 percent, respectively. And foundations and corporations provided 3 and 6 percent of revenue, respectively.

The two kinds of organizations nevertheless appeared to specialize in somewhat different kinds of services. The faith-based organizations were more likely to focus on day care, family counseling, mental health, and support groups, while the nonsectarian organizations were more actively involved in job training and advocacy for employment and health. Seley and Wolpert also noted that some of the faith-based organizations appeared to be spread too thin or at least were eager to give the appearance of being involved in a wider variety of services than their modest budgets or staff could adequately provide.

With respect to questions about proselytization or discrimination on religious grounds, Seley and Wolpert found little evidence that the faith-based organizations were engaged in religious advocacy. Their findings led them to the conclusion that most faith-based service agencies deemphasize "religious particularism" in their provision of services. On the whole, they argued that faith-based and nonsectarian organizations provide complementary kinds of services and, to the extent that they compete for the same grants or contracts, this competition is probably healthy for all parties concerned.

How is *Faith* Involved?

If generalizations can be drawn from Seley and Wolpert's study, service organizations may be nominally faith-based and yet be relatively disinclined to emphasize distinctive religious teachings or practices. This possibility has led to several attempts to specify more clearly the ways and degree to which faith-based service organizations actually bring religion into their activities. One approach has been to compare service organizations along a single dimension of religious involvement. A second approach has been to identify several different ways in which service activities may include religion. Both are helpful for understanding more clearly what faith-based organizations are and how they contribute to the provision of social services.

The first approach—comparing service organizations along a single dimension—is most clearly illustrated in a national study of faith-based organizations conducted in 2002 by the political scientists John C. Green and Amy L. Sherman.[8] The study was based in fifteen geographically dispersed states and involved structured interviews (most were done by telephone) with 389 leaders of faith-based organizations that had received government contracts under federal programs. Seventy-eight percent of the interviews were with leaders of faith-based nonprofit agencies and 22 percent were with leaders of congregations, thus making it possible to compare the two. Green and Sherman asked leaders to indicate which of six statements best described the faith dimension of their organization's social service programs:

Not Relevant. Our faith commitments are not revealed in our work with clients in this program.

Passive. Our faith commitments are revealed through the act of caring for our clients rather than by any explicit mention of religious or spiritual matters in the program.

Invitational. Our faith commitments are explicitly mentioned to our clients and they are invited to inquire more fully about religious or spiritual matters outside of the program.

Relational. Our faith commitments are explicitly mentioned to our clients and our staff seeks to establish personal relationships that involve religious or spiritual matters outside of the program.

Integrated. Our faith commitments are an explicit and critical part of our work with clients, but our staff respects the rights of clients to not participate in the religious or spiritual aspects of the program.

Mandatory. Our faith commitments are an explicit, critical, and mandatory part of our work with clients who choose to participate in the program.

At the faith-based nonprofit agencies, 22 percent of the leaders indicated that the faith dimension was "not relevant," 46 percent said it was "passive," 9 percent selected "invitational," 6 percent chose "relational," 16 percent opted for "integrated," and fewer than 1 percent said it was "mandatory." Among the congregational leaders, 9 percent said the faith dimension of their service programs was "not relevant," 45 percent said it was "passive," 6 percent opted for "invitational," 28 percent chose "relational," 11 percent said "integrated," and only 1 percent selected "mandatory."

The main conclusion from these results is that faith-based service agencies (leaving aside those that are part of congregations) vary considerably in how much emphasis they actually place on faith, and the most common option appears to be to downplay the faith dimension. Thus, slightly more than two-thirds of the leaders of faith-based organizations claim not to explicitly mention faith at all, while virtually all of the remainder say that participating in the religious or spiritual aspects of their program is optional. Not surprisingly, congregations bring religion more explicitly into their service programs, but a majority do so without actually mentioning religion or spirituality, and among the remainder who do, the most common option is to establish personal relationships involving religion or spirituality outside of the service program.

Green and Sherman's respondents also answered specific questions about the ways in which religion or spirituality were included in their programs (see table 5.1). The responses largely confirm the conclusion that faith is not prominently emphasized in many faith-based agencies, but the responses do suggest that the leaders of these organizations consider faith important and often try to provide some religious or spiritual input if clients want it. For instance, 38 percent said the spiritual transformation of clients is very important and almost seven in ten claimed they had staff available to discuss religious or spiritual matters (yet only two in ten agreed that their staff regularly ask clients if they would like to join in religious activities outside the program). Once again, congregation-based programs differ significantly from those located in separate nonprofit organizations. This is especially noticeable in the higher proportion of congregation leaders who regard spiritual transformation as very important and who strongly agree that staff are available to discuss or regularly ask clients to be involved in religious activities.

TABLE 5.1

Religious Expression in Faith-Based Nonprofits and Congregation-Based
Service Programs
(Percentage of respondents)

	Faith-Based Nonprofits	Congregation Programs
Spiritual transformation of clients is		
Very important	38	52
Somewhat important	31	25
Not very important	13	8
Not at all important	19	14
Mission statement is explicitly religious		
Strongly agree	21	31
Agree	29	25
Neutral	6	5
Disagree	32	31
Strongly disagree	13	7
Staff are available to discuss religious or spiritual matters with clients		
Strongly agree	19	37
Agree	50	46
Neutral	11	7
Disagree	15	8
Strongly disagree	6	2
Our staff regularly asks clients if they would like to join in religious activities outside of the program		
Strongly agree	3	11
Agree	18	19
Neutral	10	9
Disagree	33	40
Strongly disagree	36	21

Source: Green and Sherman, "Fruitful Collaborations."

The Green and Sherman study also examined the extent to which religious influences are evident in the selection of governing boards, staff, and volunteers. A majority of the leaders of faith-based nonprofit programs (58 percent) agreed that all of the members of their governing board share the faith commitments of the organization, half (50 percent) said all or most of their paid staff shared these faith commitments, and slightly more than half (52 percent) said this about program volunteers. The proportions for leaders of congregation-based programs were consistently higher (respectively, 76 percent, 76 percent, and 73 percent).

As a summary measure, Green and Sherman combined the various responses to specific questions about the role of religious practices, mission, and leadership, and created a single taxonomy with which to classify organizations in terms of how much religion was involved in their programs. Among the faith-based nonprofits, 30 percent were classified as "non-expressive," 26 percent as "quiescent," 23 percent as "vocal," and 21 percent as "fully expressive."[9] Of the congregation-based programs, 15 percent were "non-expressive," 24 percent were "quiescent," 14 percent were "vocal," and 47 percent were "fully expressive." Further analysis showed that the nonexpressive category included a large number of ecumenical agencies and local chapters of Catholic Charities. The quiescent category was the most religiously diverse and included approximately equal numbers of small and large agencies. The vocal category was best illustrated by the Salvation Army, many of the staff of which were evangelical Protestants while many of the volunteers were more religiously diverse. The fully expressive category was the most likely to include organizations sponsored by evangelical and African American groups.

The second approach—identifying several ways in which religion may be included—has been suggested by organizational theorists Steven Rathgeb Smith and Michael R. Sosin in an article based on research conducted in Chicago and Seattle.[10] They argue that *faith-related* is a better designation than *faith-based* and suggest that service organizations can be examined in terms of several kinds of "ties" with religion. Rooting their discussion in theories of organizations that emphasize the institutional arrangements in which organizations are embedded, they identify three ways in which service agencies may be influenced by their relationships with religion: dependence on religious sources of funding, subjection to the authority of religious organizations or individuals, and formal or informal adherence to the cultural norms of religious bodies through mission statements or the convictions of staff and volunteers.

Considering the influence of financing provides one way of determining if an organization is "faith-related," even if that organization does not formally define itself as a religiously oriented agency, but this consideration also muddies the distinction between faith-based and nonsectarian service organizations. In the clearest cases, organizations that claim to promote faith along with service and that also receive all of their funding from churches, for example, would qualify as faith-based organizations. An organization that did not formally regard itself as being faith-based, such as a day care center, might nevertheless operate in a distinct way if all its funding came from a church or denomination. At the other extreme, though, an organization with *church* or *Christian* or *ministry* in its name and mission statement might receive such a large share of its funding from government contracts or fees for service that its distinctly religious mission was overshadowed or hidden.

The kind of authority to which service agencies are subject raises similar considerations. A service program that operates as part of a congregation and is thus governed by the same body of lay leaders and clergy who govern the church is more likely to put its religious convictions into practice than an organization that has been incorporated as a separate tax-exempt entity with its own board of directors and staff. Smith and Sosin suggest that autonomy, rationality, and bureaucracy are all indications that a service agency may not be guided by religious principles, even though it claims to be faith-based.

Cultural ties pose even greater complexity. An agency that includes words such as *Catholic, Lutheran,* or *Baptist* in its title or mission statement reflects the cultural heritage of its founding. Other organizations may describe their commitment to "biblical teachings" or "the love of Jesus" in their mission statements, but these same organizations may go on to declare that they provide services to all people, regardless of faith, and do not attempt to make converts. Cultural influences can also be less formal. An organization that is nominally nonsectarian may convey religious messages to its clients because its director is a priest, for example, or because it is housed in the educational wing of a church.

I want to return later in the chapter to some of the ways in which ostensibly nonsectarian service organizations may be influenced by religion.

For now, though, the main implication of Smith and Sosin's argument is that care needs to be taken in considering how much and in what ways faith is actually a factor in faith-based service organizations. Their research in Chicago and Seattle, involving interviews with directors at twenty-four agencies, shows how agencies' programs differ when they are influenced or controlled by religion to greater or lesser degrees. Although the agencies varied in terms of being influenced more by finances, authority structure, or culture, these three dimensions overlapped considerably, meaning that the greatest differences were between faith-based organizations "tightly coupled" to religious influences and faith-based organizations with only "low or moderate coupling."

The most tightly coupled faith-based organizations typically received few or no government funds, sometimes because of principled concerns about government interference; they appointed board members who were clergy or lay leaders in a particular congregation or faith tradition; they relied heavily on volunteers from churches; they often required staff and volunteers to subscribe to a particular creed and expected them to participate in religious services; they did not, however, restrict services to clients on the basis of religious affiliation, although limited sources of funding did appear to limit the kinds of services that could be offered.

Faith-based agencies with low or moderate coupling to religious organizations depended heavily on government grants or contracts for funding; they ceded control of operations and major decision making to professional staff; they toned down their religious rhetoric in official publications and sometimes denied they were faith-based at all in private interviews; nevertheless, they did benefit from special connections with churches or denominations, such as access to volunteers from local congregations or funding from church offices or individual contributors.

On the whole, Smith and Sosin found faith-based service agencies functioning much like nonsectarian service organizations. The "secular" influences of government regulations, bureaucratic structure, and professional norms appeared to outweigh the influences of being associated with religious traditions and practices. For instance, "secular service technologies," such as following guidelines in monitoring foster care placements and offering in-home services, were evident in many of the organizations. The agencies that succeeded in attracting the largest number of volunteers were not those that drew most heavily from churches for volunteers, despite the fact that churchgoers volunteer at higher rates than nongoers; they were instead agencies with the largest number of professional staff and with the widest range of programs. To the extent that staff or volunteers were "screened" in or out, this screening occurred less through formal proce- dures and more through informal practices, such as opening meetings with prayer. Few of the agencies made public statements framed in specifically religious language; most appealed for public support and legitimacy through more general claims about serving the needy, being trustworthy, and being financially responsible. There was at times a "worker culture" within the organization that included the use of religious language, prayer services, and the like; yet, references to religion generally depicted it as an enhancement of personal fulfillment and of value for contributing to the betterment of society. The organizational culture also emphasized the "dignity and rights" of clients—notions that privileged arguments about equality, nondiscrimination, choice, and self-sufficiency.

The common finding in Green and Sherman's research and in Smith and Sosin's study is that faith-based organizations vary considerably in how much they actually emphasize faith; moreover, both studies suggest that there are pressures within the organizations and from the culture at large that discourage staff at faith-based organizations from being more vocal about their religious convictions.[11] This conclusion in itself neither sup- ports the claim made by some proponents of faith-based organizations that new laws should be passed to make it easier for these organizations to receive government funding even if vocal expressions of religious convic- tions are important nor does it necessarily affirm the view that there is nothing to worry about since few faith-based organizations stress their re- ligious traditions anyway. What we do learn, tentatively at least, is that faith-based service organizations generally emphasize religion much less than congregations do, which underscores the importance of distinguish- ing the two. We also learn, especially from Smith and Sosin's observations, that there are probably norms of service and professional standards in faith-based organizations that erode the distinctions between these orga- nizations and nonsectarian agencies.

How Faith-Based Organizations Function

What studies like Green and Sherman's and Smith and Sosin's fail to provide is a sense of how specific faith-based agencies actually organize their activities. For that purpose, in-depth interviews and ethnographic studies are better. It will be helpful to take a closer look at two kinds of organizations, one that tries explicitly to bring religion or spirituality into its programs, and one that is less expressive about the role of faith.

Salvation Army

The Salvation Army is one of the largest faith-based organizations in the United States. In 2002, it operated 1,369 "corps community centers" (roughly the equivalent of local congregations or service centers). This number was approximately the same as that recorded in 1950, after which the organization experienced several decades of decline but experienced a 27 percent increase since 1980. Among its more specific activities, the Salvation Army operated 1,640 thrift stores, 571 group home or temporary housing facilities, 228 day care centers, 222 senior citizen centers, and 163 rehabilitation centers. Total revenues were approximately $2.3 billion, of which 24 percent came from contributions, 21 percent were classified as "board designated transfers and other income," 18 percent resulted from sales to the public, 13 percent were from government funds, 12 percent were gifts in kind, 7 percent were from program service fees, and 4 percent were from United Way and similar funding organizations.[12]

Officially, the Salvation Army prominently expresses the religious convictions on which it was founded. Its purpose is succinctly articulated in its mission statement, which describes the organization as "an evangelical part of the universal Christian church" and indicates that its ministry is "motivated by the love of God" and its mission "is to preach the gospel of Jesus Christ." The Salvation Army also endorses a number of specific "doctrines," such as belief in the divine inspiration of the Bible, belief in one God, belief in the divinity of Jesus Christ, and belief in the necessity of repentance for salvation and of "faith in our Lord Jesus Christ" as the means of divine grace.[13] Its officers receive training in these doctrines and are expected to ascribe to them personally.

But the Salvation Army also registers the imprint of wider cultural norms governing service organizations. Its stance toward clients comes closer to what Green and Sherman call "invitational" or "relational" approaches than to being "mandatory" about religious involvement, and even its official language stresses the dignity and rights of clients that Smith and Sosin mention. This accommodation to cultural norms is evident in the formally approved position statements that the organization has promulgated on a large number of social issues. For instance, its statement on abortion asserts belief in "the sanctity of all human life" and "deplores society's ready acceptance of abortion, which reflects insufficient concern for vulnerable persons, including the unborn." Yet the statement stops short of outrightly condemning abortion or arguing for it to be outlawed, stating instead that "when an abortion has taken place, the Salvation Army will continue to show love and compassion and to offer its services and fellowship to those involved." Similarly, in its statement on homosexuality, the organization declares itself in support of sexuality "within the context of heterosexual marriage" and in favor of celibacy apart from marriage, stating most explicitly that "scripture forbids sexual intimacy between members of the same sex." The statement also observes, though, that "sexual attraction to the same sex is a matter of profound complexity" and asserts that "the services of the Salvation Army are available to all who qualify, without regard to sexual orientation" and that "worship is open to all sincere seekers of faith in Christ."[14]

Just as important as its capacity for striking a balance between religious teachings and cultural norms, the Salvation Army has also negotiated a complex, hybrid form of organization and activity. From the beginning, Salvationist leaders drew on several models to define themselves and to structure their programs. One of course was the military model, which gives the organization its name and provides a tiered arrangement of discipline and control reaching from the national level down through the various regional offices and influencing daily practice within each local corps. Another has been the church, both in following such familiar practices as training pastors and baptizing members and in organizing caring congregations in local communities. Beyond this, the organization has also borrowed performative technologies from the wider culture and innovated technologies of its own. As the historian Diane Winston has shown in her account of the Army's first half-century, these borrowings and innovations ranged from street theater to uniforms and brass bands and from creative definitions of gender roles to clever exploitations of publicity.[15]

At the local level, Salvation Army staff reveal the same combination of emphasis on religious teachings and commitment to wider practices of professionalism and nondiscrimination and the same hybrid of organizational models. Leaders speak in distinctly religious language about their mission and about their personal goals and motives. "We're a Bible-preaching, holiness movement," explained one leader. "What we're all about [is] bringing people to know Jesus Christ as their personal savior." Another leader, who echoed that the main goal at his center is to "preach the gospel of Jesus Christ," said he became involved because "the Lord God Almighty called [me] to do this work." The commander at another center told how he was raised Catholic but joined the Salvation Army as a young adult because the organization "blew me away" and had a totally different view of what religion should be. "People share what God's doing in their life." Soon after, both he and his wife decided to work full-time for the Salvation Army. He recalled, "The spirit of God just fell upon my wife and me. . . . I knew God was speaking to me very clearly." The same leaders, nevertheless, deny that they impose their views on clients and emphasize the rational, service-oriented approach that governs their work. As one remarked, "We shouldn't force our own beliefs onto people." Or as another explained about showing God's love to clients, "It doesn't have to come out overtly, it can be very subtle." The language leaders use to describe their activities also reflects the hybrid structure the Salvation Army has developed over the years. They emphasize Christian development, pastoring, and fellowship, but they also emphasize wider community involvement, fund-raising, mobilizing volunteers, and specific programs, such as day care, foster care, thrift shops, and programs for the homeless. One leader evoked the mixed missions and models of the organization even in choosing a few words to describe it: "It's a charity. A charity and a church. It's a service that takes care of human needs, physical needs."

But local Salvation Army centers vary considerably in how these combinations of faith and service are put into practice. Some closely resemble local churches, drawing people into what they hope will be long-term and life-transforming social relationships, while others operate service programs that meet specific needs either off-site or on a short-term basis and they deal with clients more through arms-length transactions than under the auspices of a caring community. At the Salvation Army center in a community I will call Eastside, the emphasis is on the former, that is, drawing people from the community into activities that resemble those of a religious *congregation*. One of its main programs is called "Golden Agers" and brings a group of older adults age fifty-five through ninety-five to the center once a week for a hot meal, fellowship, and perhaps a guest speaker or discussion. Another program is called "Home League" and consists of three different groups of women (two English-speaking and one Spanish-speaking) who meet weekly to build relationships, support one another, and help as volunteers and fund-raisers. The weekly tutoring program for children that meets on Tuesdays is also organized as much to build relationships as it is to help students with homework. After approximately an hour of tutoring, the forty or so children in the program eat dinner together and then break into age-graded clubs that engage in "character-building activities" similar to those provided by scouting troops. Virtually every other program at the center—parenting classes, a dance and drama group, a choir, a Friday night youth group, and prayer meetings—are oriented toward building long-term relationships. People in the low-income neighborhoods surrounding the center are served mainly by drawing them into a congregationlike experience through which specific needs are addressed but which also seeks to integrate participants into a set of long-term relationships. The norms governing interaction here are similar to those Rebecca Allahyari observed in her study of a Salvation Army center in Sacramento. Allahyari described a set of activities that focused on rehabilitation and recovery from alcoholism among homeless men. The center provided shelter, enlisted the men in an Alcoholics Anonymous–type program of abstinence and sobriety, and drew them into volunteer activities, such as doing kitchen work. The result was what Allahyari called "moral selving"—a redefinition of clients' selves around norms of personal discipline and hard work, an image of being a good provider, and separation from former acquaintances who remained homeless.[16]

Other Salvation Army centers are organized less around the congregational model and more in terms of a *service provider* model. The center in a community I call Westside illustrates this second approach. This center is in a low-income, mixed Hispanic and English-speaking neighborhood much like that of the Eastside center. Its annual budget of $1.2 million is about one-third larger than of the other center and has increased by nearly 50 percent in the past five years. Whereas the leader at Eastside thinks of himself as a minister and refers to his job title as "pastor," the Westside center brought in a pastor six years ago who had formerly worked as a certified public accountant and more recently has replaced him with two leaders, a pastor who describes his position as "city coordinator" and a business administrator who holds a graduate degree in taxation. Westside's leaders reflect the more service-oriented manner in which the center's programs are organized. The contrasts with the other center are striking. Whereas Eastside has a Golden Agers group, Westside runs a "senior nutrition program" through a government contract and has a staff person to coordinate the program. Eastside helps homeless people by inviting them to the center for meals; Westside operates a shelter at a location separate from the center. At Eastside, providing hot meals at the center's kitchen, much as a church might in the church basement, assists people who cannot pay their bills; at Westside, the center cooperates with the local utilities company through a contract with the state to identify people who have fallen behind on payments and assists them in securing temporary financial assistance. Whereas Eastside's groups focus on long-term involvement, Westside specializes more in programs that meet short-term needs, such as through its emergency assistance program, or that deal with clients around a clearly defined event, such as through its adoption program.

What we see in these two examples, then, are illustrations of how faith-based organizations with strong connections to religious teachings and practices may nevertheless be structured in quite different ways because of the mixed organizational models on which faith-based agencies can draw. The differences have less to do with financing and authority or the degree to which religious convictions are vocalized than they do with the relationships that are cultivated between caregivers and recipients. The congregational model emphasizes group interaction over an extended period that not only meets needs but also forges informal bonds of intimacy and loyalty through which personal identities are reshaped. The service-oriented model is guided more by the desire to organize programs that meet diverse needs, including ones that can often be dealt with more effectively off-site or through short-term interaction than by cultivating extended relationships.

The congregational model does not strictly reproduce the activities of local churches (at least in the Eastside case, the two "congregations" that meet at the center are clearly identified as programs separate from the center's service activities). This model nevertheless makes use of ideas and resources that are familiar to many staff, volunteers, and clients because they so closely resemble those of local churches. Providing hot meals cooked in the church kitchen and served in its fellowship hall is just one example. The service model also differs from the approach one might find at the welfare department or at a nonsectarian agency insofar as religious language is evident, staff have pastoral training, and the organization also sponsors a worshipping congregation or prayer meetings and makes these opportunities known to its clients. This model, though, is potentially effective because it differentiates the organization from churches in the same community, treats clients in ways that may be familiar through dealings with other service agencies, provides opportunities for professionally trained staff, and encourages cooperation with other organizations and more diverse sources of funding. In these ways, then, even faith-based organizations that are tightly linked with religious traditions engage in activities that differ from those offered through congregations.

Church Service Agencies and Councils of Churches

As examples of faith-based organizations that are less tightly linked to religious traditions, we need to consider agencies such as Catholic Charities and Lutheran Social Services that have been established specifically to supplement and administer service activities of the kind that cannot adequately be supplied through local congregations and church councils that provide the same kind of services but in most cases within a single community through an interdenominational or ecumenical alliance. In Green and Sherman's study, these organizations generally fell into the nonexpressive or quiescent categories of faith-based agencies. A closer look at several of these organizations will show why they appear to be less religiously expressive and how they in fact negotiate the relationship between their faith tradition and their role as service providers.

Catholic Charities is a prominent example of a church service agency. With approximately 1,400 local agencies under its jurisdiction and an annual budget of approximately $7.5 billion, it is one of the largest networks of private service providers in the United States. It serves as a specialized organization through which Catholic parishes can more effectively meet the needs of people in their communities. It can thus be regarded as an arm of the Catholic church and an extension of its programs into particular areas of need. At the national level, it provides management assistance, technical help, training, resource development, and a disaster response office. At the local level, Catholic Social Agency offices operate a wide range of programs including parenting classes, counseling, adoption services, foster care placement, schools for children with developmental disabilities, and assistance for immigrants and refugees.[17]

Lutheran Social Services functions similarly, although on a smaller scale than Catholic Charities. Through local, statewide, and regional organizations, Lutheran Services is a network of approximately 280 service agencies with about 138,000 employees. Its efforts focus especially on children and families, older people, and people with disabilities. In local communities it typically offers counseling services, foster care and adoption programs, food and shelter, and disaster relief. It also provides consultation and training for pastors and operates hospitals, assisted living centers, and prison ministries. It is thus a resource that congregations can rely on for service programs that are not as efficiently run through congregations themselves.

Councils of churches and other ecumenical or interfaith organizations form another category of faith-based service agencies.[18] There are approximately five hundred of these, mostly organized at the local or statewide level, that are incorporated as tax-exempt nonprofit agencies to provide social services. They provide refugee services, operate emergency shelters and food programs, help families with mental illnesses, build affordable housing, operate nursing and extended care facilities, and coordinate service efforts among local churches and other religious bodies. These organizations vary widely in budgetary size and scope of programs and in terms of how directly involved they are in service delivery. For instance, an organization I will call the Smithville Council of Churches has an annual budget of more than $700,000, employs twenty-two full-time staff, and draws on the assistance of seven hundred volunteers to operate a homeless shelter, a mental health program, activities for at-risk youth, and several other programs. In contrast, the Jonesville Council of Churches has a budget one-tenth as large and operates no service agencies of its own, but has served as a coordinating network among local churches and over the years has helped spawn several freestanding service agencies. Both councils grew from efforts early in the twentieth century to promote cooperative relationships among local clergy. Ecumenical and interfaith service organizations have often emerged more recently and for more specific purposes. For instance, an organization I will call Focus came into being in the late 1960s as a joint effort among Protestants, Catholics, and Jews in one community to launch a food bank and then gradually added other programs, such as tutoring and adult literacy.

In all of these examples, the faith component is clearly present. Besides having words such as *Catholic, Lutheran,* and *churches* in their names, these organizations typically include religious language in their mission statements, and the staff draw on religious language to explain the organization's goals. For instance, at one local chapter of Catholic Social Agency, the sister in charge explained, "We are a Christocentric organization that definitely journeys with the concept that what we do we do in the name of Christ." Similarly, the director of the Jonesville Council of Churches noted that "our mission statement is faith-based, to witness to Jesus Christ through loving care in the community, service projects, cooperation with the churches, cooperation with the community, and to help people to hold joint worship services on occasion." He added, "Our whole thrust is to bring about an understanding among people and to witness to Jesus Christ." Yet these organizations fall closer to the end of the spectrum that Green and Sherman call nonexpressive or quiescent than they do to the end in which faith is vocal or mandatory.[19] Their mission statements sometimes take the faith connection implied in their name for granted, rather than elaborating, and staff often speak in general humanitarian terms instead of emphasizing only religious language. Another Catholic Social Agency director, for example, insisted that "our mission is to provide compassionate human services with respect for the sanctity of all life" and preferred not to reformulate that goal in words more specific to Christianity. Similarly, a homeless shelter that was initiated by the Jonesville Council of Churches describes itself as "religion-related," but defines its mission as "providing shelter and social services to disadvantaged persons in the form of an emergency shelter and transitional housing for homeless individuals."

Unlike faith-based agencies that follow the congregational model of drawing people into a tightly knit, long-lasting community (like the East-side Salvation Army), these church agencies and ecumenical organizations typically follow the service provider model. Having been started in most cases by clergy or lay people who viewed them as supplements to the programs of local churches, these organizations usually avoid activities that might compete with congregations. Programs are typically short-term and specific, rather than aiming to cultivate communal relations among clients. People come to food banks or tutoring programs for assistance, not fellowship, and insofar as needs for community are concerned, these recipients are typically advised (if they are advised at all) to seek that through a church. The exceptions are nursing care and assisted living facilities, in which people may live for extended periods and for this reason be provided with prayer groups, worship services, and the like.

Arguments about Effectiveness

Having considered the variety and functioning of faith-based organizations, we are now in a better position to examine the arguments that have been advanced about the effectiveness of these organizations. We should distinguish between arguments defending the existence and significance of faith-based organizations simply as one among other kinds of private nonprofit service organizations and arguments that suggest faith-based organizations may be *better* than nonsectarian agencies. There are many reasons to think that faith-based organizations should continue to exist as service providers alongside nonsectarian organizations. Some faith-based organizations may have a distinctive clientele. For instance, even though most faith-based agencies offer services for clients of any religious orientation, it stands to reason that Catholics may be drawn to Catholic organizations, Jews to Jewish organizations, and so on. In addition, these agencies may have access to special sources of funding or volunteers by virtue of their ties to a particular denomination or having been initiated by a coalition of churches. Certainly the overall scale of human service provision would shrink significantly if faith-based agencies ceased to exist.

The arguments suggesting that faith-based organizations are *more* effective than other organizations are of a different sort, though, and they require closer scrutiny. These arguments take several forms, but typically they emphasize that people need to undergo personal transformation in order to overcome their problems and can be aided in this process by religious teachings, or that religiously motivated caregivers do a better job of caring for the whole person, are more altruistic, or are more dedicated and trustworthy. For instance, Robert Woodson, president of the National Center for Neighborhood Enterprise, has been quoted by John DiIulio as suggesting that "faith-based social-service providers, armed with a religious sensibility, often go above and beyond the call of duty and act in ways that inspire an unusual degree of trust among program beneficiaries."[20] Similarly, in an interview at a Catholic service agency the director emphasized an "internal energy" rooted in the faith commitments of the agency's staff and volunteers that was invisible but went "way beyond rational reality." And some proponents of faith-based services go considerably further; for example, Charles Colson, the founder of Prison Fellowship Ministries, asserts that "only Jesus Christ can truly transform the hearts and change the future for those caught in the web of crime."[21]

The research that has been conducted among faith-based organizations, although quite sparse, suggests that it is probably their ability to forge encompassing whole-person, personally transforming relationships with clients that accounts for any special success they may have. For instance, a study conducted by the National Opinion Research Center at the University of Chicago for the National Institute on Drug Abuse found that 67 percent of the graduates of a drug rehabilitation program sponsored by Teen Challenge were drug-free seven years after participating in the program, a rate much higher than the 10 to 15 percent cure rate for other federally funded drug rehabilitation programs.[22] Teen Challenge, founded in 1958, is a faith-based network of 178 Christian substance-abuse prevention and treatment programs.[23] The organization's leaders believe that the program achieves a high success rate because of the personal transformation that accompanies a client's "decision to surrender his or her will to Jesus Christ and to establish a personal relationship with him."[24] Transformation is effected through an intensive year-long, in-residence program that includes participation in daily prayer services, church services, religious instruction, volunteer activities, and vocational technical training. Through these activities, participants find themselves so intensively involved in a morning-to-night regimen of structured group activity that they focus more on the activities and less on staying sober. These activities are accompanied by strict codes of moral conduct (requiring honesty and encouraging loyalty), counseling about anger management and dealing with emotions, a system of rewards and punishments, and close mentoring by program staff who serve as role models.

Other studies of faith-based organizations often stress similar efforts to promote personal transformation and to cultivate social ties that reinforce or monitor desired behavior. For example, Byron Johnson conducted a comparison of the recidivism rates of inmates released from two prisons in Brazil. At Humaita prison, inmates participated in a faith-based program organized by Prison Fellowship Ministries and involving regular Bible studies, interaction with chaplains, and emphasis on religious conversion. At the Braganca facility, a secular nonprofit organization provided a program of job training and placement. Both programs had lower recidivism rates than at Brazil's other prisons. But Humaita achieved better results than Braganca. Among low-risk offenders, the recidivism rate for Humaita was 21 percent, compared with 36 percent for Braganca; and among high-risk offenders, the rates, respectively, were 12 percent and 38 percent.[25]

What studies like these suggest is that faith-based organizations work best at producing change in individuals and communities when these organizations imitate congregations. That is, the vital ingredient includes religious teachings about hope and redemption, but also grounds these teachings in social relationships that resemble those that occur in congregations. These social relationships are sufficiently personal and happen over a long enough period that people develop new attitudes, new understandings of themselves, and new friendships.[26] Adequate research has not yet been done to sort out the relative effects of the teachings and the social relationships, but chances are that each reinforces the other. Thus, teachings in the absence of relationships would not have the same effect, nor would extensive social interaction be as effective without religious teachings.

But if this argument about the advantages of faith-based organizations is correct, it is very important to recognize that *relatively few* faith-based organizations actually fit this model.[27] Significant as they may be to the people who are helped by them, the number of Teen Challenge centers, Prison Fellowship ministries, Ten Point Coalition programs,[28] and the like, make up a small fraction of the faith-based service agencies that exist nationally. Even the Salvation Army (as we have seen) may emphasize a service provider model more than a congregational model at many of its locations. Thus, there may be little reason to expect that faith-based organizations in general are more effective than nonsectarian organizations. Moreover, the kinds of faith-based organizations that do cultivate intense communal, life-transforming social relationships appear thus far to have concentrated on a particular kind of client, whereas the wider variety of needs being met by service organizations may not be so easily met in this way. The situation of teenagers who can be supported for a year in a Teen Challenge rehabilitation program or of inmates in the context of a prison is clearly different from that of working mothers who need day care assistance or of the person coming off welfare who needs job training or of the physically impaired person who needs transportation to the doctor. In those cases, few of the specific arguments that have been advanced about the special advantages of faith-based organizations may apply.

The Role of Faith in Nonsectarian Organizations

The research and examples we have considered thus far suggest that faith-based organizations often function in ways that depend little on their connections with religious traditions. The implication of this observation is that the faith component of the service sector may not be as pronounced or distinct as might be suggested by the mere presence of faith-based organizations. The other side of the coin, though, is that so-called secular or nonsectarian service agencies may include faith and may communicate messages about faith despite not being formally organized around religious traditions. I want to consider briefly five ways in which faith may be a factor in nonsectarian service organizations.

Founding

The fact that religion has been such an important part of American society throughout our nation's history means that religious organizations and religiously motivated people often played a role in founding service organizations. Even when these organizations have ceased qualifying in any distinctive way as faith-based organizations, they owe their existence to the influence of faith, and this legacy may still guide their mission and values. The YMCA is probably the best example of an organization that was founded on religious principles but has become disconnected from specific religious teachings in most communities. Although its mission statement refers to "Christian principles," its local chapters function separate from religious ties and provide services, such as swimming lessons and after-school day care, on a fee-for-service basis, with charitable contributions and volunteer labor significantly subsidizing the fees charged to low-income families. The YMCA is sometimes viewed by social scientists as an example of a general trend in service provision toward secularization—a view that has been supported by some research showing a secular drift in local service organizations.[29] However, churches and religiously motivated people also play a role in founding new service organizations that are intentionally secular from the start. For instance, a program to provide guidance in conflict resolution for at-risk teenagers grew out of a Bible study group at a Presbyterian church where the pastor had been an active advocate of peace and social justice in the local community. The guidance program was never formally affiliated with the church, though, and has been funded largely through grants from a family foundation.

Governance

We can extend Smith and Sosin's observations about the degree to which faith-based organizations may be controlled by clergy and other religious representatives by recognizing that clergy also frequently serve on the boards of nonsectarian service organizations. Although the boards of nonprofit organizations remain an understudied topic, examples of secular service agencies with clergy among their board members are not hard to find. At one chapter of Meals on Wheels, for instance, two members of its twenty-five-member board are clergy. Similarly an organization in a largely Hispanic community that provides employment training and educational services through government contracts and fees-for-service includes two clergy on its twenty-one-member board. Religiously involved board members who are not clergy are harder to identify from published materials, but judging from what we saw about volunteers in chapter 4, it is likely that religiously oriented lay people are often represented on the boards of nonsectarian organizations. The extent of such involvement is almost certainly less than in faith-based organizations where, according to Smith and Sosin, half to all board members may be required to be clergy or religiously active lay leaders; this representation nevertheless facilitates ties between churches and nonsectarian organizations.

Resources

We saw in previous chapters that congregations often donate small contributions from their budgets to service organizations (chapter 2) and that congregations are an important source of volunteers for these agencies (chapter 4). This giving and volunteering may be disproportionately directed to faith-based organizations, but there are plenty of examples of nonsectarian organizations benefitting from it as well. Meals on Wheels is again a case in point. The organization typically covers less than half its expenses from government contracts and fees paid by clients (who pay on a sliding scale); the remainder comes from charitable donations and is supplemented by free labor supplied by volunteers. Churches are an important source of giving and volunteering to Meals on Wheels. Other nonsectarian organizations also make use of churches and faith-based organizations to help with the administration and distribution of services. An interesting example is America's Second Harvest, the nation's largest distributor of emergency food relief. With an annual budget in excess of $400 million (much of which consists of donations of food), the organization's major challenge is to get food into the hands of people who need it most. Typically, volunteers from neighborhood food pantries come to Second Harvest warehouses where they collect and repackage food, and then make it available to local clients. For instance, at one Second Harvest warehouse, the director explained that her distribution network included 165 nonprofit agencies with nearly three hundred local sites across a six-county area. Many of these distribution points, she said, were churches or food pantries operated by coalitions of churches. These organizations have to meet certain standards established by Second Harvest and cannot discriminate among recipients on religious grounds, but they do not have to remove religious artifacts or refrain of talking about religion with recipients in order to qualify.

Personal Convictions

We also need to recognize the many ways in which individual staff members and volunteers bring religious convictions into their activities at nonsectarian service organizations. Although there are often norms of professionalism and tolerance that inhibit the expression of these convictions (which I discuss further in chapter 8), agency personnel are often motivated by faith commitments and these commitments may be communicated directly or indirectly to the agency's clients. A good example is Albert Janzen, who heads a large multipurpose service agency called the Action Committee. Janzen is a lifelong Presbyterian who remains active in his church but considers his real work for God to be taking place through his role at the Action Committee. He joined the organization in 1980 and became its director in 1990, and has played a significant part in building its assets to $3.2 million and its annual program budget to $3.7 million. Among other things, the Action Committee operates a large food distribution program, a homeless shelter, a mortgage program, a business development organization, and a low-income home energy assistance program. Janzen is adamant that no service organization should proselytize, and he is glad to be working in an organization that has no formal ties to churches; still, his own religious convictions clearly influence his work. Besides teaching Sunday school and occasionally serving on committees at his church, he frequently speaks at churches in his community. He regards them as an important source of volunteers and contributions and he wants them to be more involved in the community than they often are. After welfare reform legislation was passed in 1995, he helped launch an interfaith coalition on poverty. Through this organization, more churches and synagogue members have become involved, not only in helping poor people, but also in public advocacy for economic justice. Janzen is thus an example of someone who is inspired by religious teachings and makes use of congregations for support, but who also chafes at the limitations of trying to work only through the church and is thus pleased to work more directly in community development. As he explained during one interview, "I've got my place in the pew, the whole deal. But I don't mind saying that I think the church is far too institutionally oriented and because of that just not speaking the truth enough."

Ambience

Finally, the influence of religion may be communicated to clients of non-sectarian organizations in subtle ways that may best be described as ambience. Bibles on desks or bookshelves, crosses, paintings of Jesus, leaflets and announcements of church services, and other markers of religion are not uncommon at nonsectarian service organizations. These may be personal items in the offices of staff, much like family photos, or they may be displayed on bulletin boards as public announcements or among the brochures and other literature on tables in entry halls. Sometimes the connection with religion is hard to hide, even if it is not actually an official one. For instance, at an AIDS counseling center the appearance of ties to a church is unavoidable because the center is located in a building adjacent to the church and owned by the church. The same is true at a nonsectarian organization that specializes in job training. Although it has no religious connections, it is located in a building that formerly served as a church, complete with gothic arches and stained-glass windows. Prospective clients might well assume the organization is faith-based, just from the building's appearance.

One important implication of these ways in which religion may be a part of nonsectarian organizations is that the sharp line that some observers have tried to draw between faith-based and nonsectarian service organizations is probably exaggerated. From a legal standpoint, it may be important to write bills or pass executive orders that specify the ways in which service organizations may be religious and still qualify for government contracts. But arguments that claim special privileges or advantages for faith-based nonprofits need to be regarded with caution.

Challenges and Strategies

Because faith-based and nonsectarian service organizations are in many cases so similar, the challenges they face and the strategies they adopt to meet these challenges also frequently exhibit close similarities. With the exception of those faith-based service agencies that model themselves on congregations, the practical considerations that guide activities in the nonprofit sector more generally are the ones that also prevail among faith-based organizations. The contrast with congregations is again instructive. In those settings, the fact that members and attendees—who come for worship, religious instruction, and fellowship—also do most of the work is paramount. Classes, prayer groups, church dinners, and service activities all depend on volunteer efforts from the congregation. The situation in nonprofit service agencies is quite different. These organizations typically provide services to clients who are not members, who only occasionally serve as volunteers for the organization, and whose fees (if there are any) have to be supplemented by payments from so-called third parties, such as government, foundations, or individual contributors. The major administrative challenges facing nonprofit service agencies derive from these arrangements.[30] They can be grouped under three headings.

Resource Generation

Because of the important role played by third-party payers, nonprofit service agencies are heavily influenced by the need for funding, staff, and volunteers that come from sources other than the recipients of services. It is for this reason that most nonprofit service agencies of more than modest size, faith-based and nonsectarian alike, employ at least one fully paid professional staff person with some expertise in grant writing and fund-raising as well as administration or direct service provision. The directors of these agencies typically rely on volunteers for assistance, but it is less common at these agencies than at churches to hear that programs have not been initiated because of a lack of volunteers. It is also relatively uncommon for directors to say they initiated a program simply because there was a need for it in the community. Instead, the availability of funding sources is a more prominent consideration. Organizations with a larger professional staff and with a track record of having received funding before are in a better position, therefore, to obtain grants and contracts in the future.

Public Relations

Establishing and maintaining goodwill in the larger community is the second major administrative challenge that nonprofit service agencies face. Public relations are especially important because of nonprofit agencies' dependence on third-party payments. Directors typically give lectures at churches and at other community organizations and often serve on boards or committees at other organizations. Some larger organizations have established a "speakers bureau" for this purpose, while smaller agencies sometimes enlist board members. Publicity through newspaper stories, local television coverage, and Web sites is also important. The challenge is not only to spread word about what the organization is doing, but also to maintain the public's trust that the organization is financially and professionally responsible. In some cases attracting clients also depends on the organization's visibility in the wider community. Faith-based organizations benefit from the general goodwill toward religious organizations and leaders that is typically evident in public opinion polls. These organizations also benefit from having natural constituencies, as it were, among church members. However, faith-based service agencies sometimes compete with churches for contributions from the same donors. Nonsectarian organizations, such as the Children's Defense Fund, Amnesty International, and the American Red Cross, have also made extensive use of contacts with church members.

Programmatic Decisions

Then there are the day-to-day decisions about which services to provide, how best to provide them, and what programs to initiate or expand in order to supply these services most effectively. Just as in for-profit organizations, the challenge is to identify markets that can be served and programs that can serve these markets effectively. This challenge entails being aware of community needs and of funding opportunities. Insofar as third parties are involved, demonstrating that the organization's programs are effective is also important. It may be less important than in for-profit organizations, however, to show that these programs are *efficient*. This is partly because profitability for shareholders is not a factor in decision making and because service outcomes are often more difficult to reduce to dollars-and-cents calculations. In this respect, nonprofit service agencies are like churches, where calculating the cost-effectiveness of a worship or prayer meeting seems almost to profane the sacred character of those activities. At service agencies, though, more of the activities are likely to be reducible to measurement (such as meals served, foster children placed, or teens rehabilitated from drugs) and for this reason questions of efficiency and effectiveness are more likely to surface, especially in securing resources from third parties.[31]

The strategies that nonprofit service agencies use to meet these various challenges reflect the geographic level at which the agencies has been organized, the scale of operations to which it has grown accustomed, how recently it was formed and the competition it faces from other agencies, and its sense of mission or distinctive values. Despite the differences that emerge from these considerations and constraints, the strategies at nonprofit service agencies are largely shaped by norms of rationality, effectiveness, organizational survival, and fairness (what Smith and Sosin call "dignity and rights"). These norms influence the strategies pursued at faith-based organizations and at nonsectarian organizations.

With the exception of the few faith-based organizations that claim exemption on grounds of being religious, most nonprofit service agencies are incorporated as 501(c)3 tax-exempt organizations. The decision to incorporate in this way is a strategy for protecting whatever assets the organization may have or acquire, limiting the legal liability of its officers, and securing access to financial resources. Even in the case of service programs initiated by and wholly controlled by congregations, it appears that separate incorporation is increasingly common. From the standpoint of directors and staff, this step also provides for greater autonomy in decision making. It goes without saying that such organizations also have boards of directors and that these board members often contribute funds and help with public relations.

Another strategy that is commonly employed in nonprofit service agencies is to develop formal programs around functionally defined activities. For instance, one agency initiated a program called Daybreak for people with mental health problems, one called Linkage that alerts homeless people to dangerous weather conditions, another called Guardianship for people who would otherwise be wards of the state, another simply called Soup Kitchen, and so on. Differentiating programs this way is helpful for bookkeeping purposes, since separate accounts are often required because of separate funding sources; it also assists in signaling to potential donors and clients that a targeted activity has been added.[32] The importance of adding new programs is evident in the fact that the number of different programs operated by a service agency appears to be one of the closest correlates of agencies' overall size in terms of annual expenditures.[33] But new programs sometimes also become separate 501(c)3 entities. An unintended consequence of this kind of functional specialization is that meeting the needs of clients increasingly becomes a matter of referrals. Unlike a congregation in which the whole person is integrated, service agencies meet specific needs and refer clients to other agencies to meet other needs. Some of this functional specialization is driven by funding sources targeted toward specific needs, but, as one agency director explained, it also works well for clients whose schedules are increasingly hectic or who are transient to the community, and who for these reasons do not have the time it would take to get help from a church that might expect them to participate more extensively in its activities. For those with multiple needs, functional specialization also means, as we shall discuss more fully in chapter 6, that clients develop portfolios of service providers from which to seek assistance, and the composition of their portfolio may be as important as the effectiveness of any single organization.

A related strategy on the part of directors and staff members is to develop informal and formal institutional linkages with other organizations. These linkages are partly necessitated by the functional specialization present among different programs and organizations. It is also a way of securing resources and of protecting access to these resources. Service agencies contract with utility companies to help low-income families, with the human services or welfare department to handle clients with special needs, with schools to operate before- and after-school programs or to provide tutoring, with an organization like Second Harvest to distribute food, and so on. Increasingly, service agencies are developing computerized databases that link major service providers in the community with one another so that records on individual clients can be maintained. These databases facilitate referrals but also prevent clients from exploiting resources by obtaining the same assistance from several agencies. In addition, local organizations are often linked to regional and national federations, and personnel are typically involved in professional associations of various kinds. In the case of faith-based organizations, these links mean that they are seldom likely to be influenced only by the norms of their particular religious tradition. Through conferences, newsletters, competitive bidding for contracts, and partnerships, faith-based and nonsectarian organizations are likely to be integrated into a wider network of service providers.

Government is inevitably involved in these networks. Whether nonprofit agencies seek grants or contracts directly from government or whether they refrain from doing so, their programs and access to funding are influenced by public policy. Examples include welfare reforms that increase the demand for job training or day care for working mothers, agricultural or Food and Drug Administration policies that make it easier or harder for food pantries to obtain subsidized food, state-mandated policies that require utility companies to supply heat and electricity to low-income residents, or decisions to mainstream persons with physical or mental disabilities. Administrators are thus faced with needing to be aware of government policies, and faith-based organizations are affected by government in larger ways than just by Charitable Choice legislation or executive orders concerning nondiscrimination in hiring. Indeed, it is not uncommon for directors at large organizations to say they have started new programs primarily because some change in government policy opened a new opportunity. For instance, the agency I mentioned that started the Guardianship program did so because of a change in state law permitting organizations as well as individuals to be appointed as legal guardians. The relationships between faith-based agencies and government are also more complicated than simply working through grants and contracts. In one community, for example, the local council of churches is part of a consortium that operates a gym and provides low-income apartments in a large inner-city building. The consortium includes the YMCA, the city's health bureau, the city's housing authority, a government-funded child care program, and a nonprofit management group. The church council raised about a third of the money to renovate the building and its director is on the consortium's board.

The other strategy that is commonly adopted in nonprofit service organizations is to emphasize professional norms. These include hiring and promoting staff on the basis of training, experience, and accomplishments rather than on the basis of other personal characteristics such as race, gender, or religion. Just as the occupation of pastor has been professionalized to the point that administrative abilities and advanced education sometimes outweigh personal spirituality, so has providing services through nonprofit organizations. Clients may appreciate staff who are congenial and who go out of their way to be helpful, but these are as much professional expectations as they are rooted in religious teachings. Faith-based organizations may have an advantage over nonsectarian organizations if they can also appeal to clients' religious values. But it is likely that staff at faith-based organizations will also be expected to demonstrate competence, to have requisite training, and to be effective. Among other things, these professional norms undergird the emphasis that staff at faith-based organizations place on nondiscrimination, fairness in dealing with clients of all religious persuasions, and refraining from being promoting one's own convictions. As the director of one faith-based agency explained, "It's not the fervency of your doctrine that counts, it's the quality of your compromise."

Conclusions

Faith-based service organizations have become the focus of heated discussions because of government policies concerning whether or not and in what ways these organizations should be eligible for government funding. In this chapter I have tried to step away from those discussions in order to give a larger and less partisan perspective on the social role that these organizations currently play. I have suggested that noncongregation faith-based organizations devoted specifically to human services make up a significant proportion of all such service providers (perhaps one-fifth), but that this proportion is smaller than some analysts have suggested by deriving guesses simply on the basis of religion's prominence in the United States more generally. I have also examined the distinctions that studies of faith-based organizations are beginning to identify among these organizations, and through these distinctions I have suggested how faith-based organizations may be similar to nonsectarian organizations and how to specify more critically the kinds of faith-based organizations about which claims of special effectiveness have been made.

The comparison between faith-based organizations and congregations becomes especially important for making broader observations about the role of religion in providing social services. The fact that some faith-based service organizations are incorporated nationally (and thus subsume many local centers) while others are incorporated locally makes it difficult to compare their numbers with that of congregations, but even the most generous estimates would suggest that there are far fewer of these organizations than there are congregations. In terms of spending, though, faith-based service organizations probably make up a substantially larger share than congregations. Estimates are at best difficult, but we can arrive at a conservative calculation of total spending by faith-based organizations from the following figures: total expenditures by nonprofit human service organizations in 1999 as reported by the National Center for Charitable Statistics (NCCS) were $93.1 billion (this is a conservative estimate because it does not include spending on service activities by organizations classified differently by the NCCS); 18 percent of the human service organizations in Seley and Wolpert's study were faith-based; Seley and Wolpert also found that faith-based and nonsectarian organizations had similar budgets; and thus, the total expenditures of faith-based organizations nationally may be estimated at approximately 18 percent of $93.1 billion, or $16.8 billion. We may also want to adjust this figure to take out administrative expenditures. These usually do not run more than 20 percent, but if we assume they are 50 percent, that leaves $8.4 billion that goes directly to the recipients of social services.

How does that compare with congregations' spending on social services? We saw in chapter 2 that Chaves estimates that only half of all congregations spend anything on the direct support of formal social service programs; and he estimates that among this half, the *median* amount spent may be as little as $1,200, or approximately 2 percent of total expenditures. We also noted, though, that this estimate does not take account of volunteer time, and that the median masks the fact that some churches provide an extraordinarily large share of total congregational spending on social services. If we use the mean rather than the median, the proportion of total church budgets devoted to the support of social service programs is about 5 percent. Applying this percentage to the total of $74.3 billion that is considered the best estimate of total congregational spending in the United States, we arrive at a figure of $3.7 billion.

Thus, a conservative estimate of the financial contribution of faith-based organizations suggests that this contribution is more than twice as great as that of congregations and, if administrative costs are not subtracted, more than four times as large. If we want to think of the comparison a different way, it is also helpful to note that the total expenditures of *all* nonprofit human services organizations ($93.1 billion) are larger than the total that churches spend on all of their activities ($74.3 billion). What needs to be remembered in making such comparisons is that the amount spent by churches comes almost entirely from charitable contributions, whereas much of the amount spent by faith-based organizations comes from fees for service and government contracts. The point, then, is not that nonprofit organizations are more charitable than churches but that nonprofit organizations in general and faith-based nonprofit service organizations in particular make up a larger financial share of total human service provision than congregations do.

I have also suggested that the faith component of nominally faith-based organizations is most likely to be a significant factor when these organizations emulate congregations by drawing clients into long-term social relationships that make them feel as though they are part of a community and that effect some sort of personal transformation through new friendships and explicit exposure to religious teachings. But the best research to date indicates that the congregational model probably characterizes only about one-quarter of all faith-based service organizations. The remainder vary in the extent to which they express religious themes, but they generally appear to follow a service provision model that emphasizes meeting specific needs and running programs organized around these needs, rather than providing a communal set of social relationships in which clients are encouraged to become involved. The service provision model probably "gets the job done," so to speak, much as it does at nonsectarian organizations in that it involves professional staff and a rationally organized program devoted to serving clients with specific needs. In comparison, the more inclusive model of aiming to transform whole persons is likely to be far more costly and thus require either substantially more financial resources per client or the kind of informal, voluntary assistance found in congregations.[34] At Teen Challenge, for instance, each center handles only twenty-five clients per year, on average, and there is a full-time staff person for every 2.5 clients. This level of investment makes it possible for Teen Challenge to achieve a high rate of recovery among clients, but the same level would not be possible (or necessary) at the many faith-based or nonsectarian organizations that provide shorter-term services to larger numbers of clients.

The larger point to be emphasized is that faith-based service organizations play an extremely important role in facilitating the service activities that religiously oriented people wish to provide through their churches and denominations. As worshipping communities, congregations are limited in what they can do to alleviate problems in the wider society. Even if they had unlimited budgets and were willing to spend a much larger proportion of these budgets on service activities than they presently do, congregations would seldom be able to accomplish these aims through the congregation itself. They would form new nonprofit organizations or support existing ones. These organizations have the legal and budgetary autonomy to secure funding in more diverse ways than congregations can, and they provide places where staff can utilize special skills to assist clients with a variety of needs. In an increasingly professionalized society, staff with such skills are needed to be effective in the provision of social services.

The relationships between faith-based and nonsectarian service organizations are more ambiguous. As Seley and Wolpert suggest, faith-based organizations probably have a niche in the larger market of service providers that at least somewhat reduces the amount of competition that might otherwise be present between them and nonsectarian organizations. My interviews with agency directors suggest that service organizations more generally adapt to market conditions by trying to develop a niche that gives them access either to a distinct pool of clients or to a distinct source of funding. These strategies do not eliminate competition or prevent a certain amount of redundancy from being present among service providers. It does, though, mean that faith-based organizations fulfill a number of significant needs. The larger, better-established organizations (such as the Salvation Army or Catholic Charities) have facilities, financial assets, and skills that can be deployed when new programs need to be initiated. Through their connections with churches or through the entrepreneurial activities of individual churchgoers, smaller faith-based organizations also emerge.

In chapter 6 we will consider the question of effectiveness from the standpoint of clients. Here, though, I want to underscore the fact that relatively little research has been done to compare faith-based organizations with nonsectarian organizations, and the studies that have been done and that are often mentioned in conjunction with arguments about the special advantages of faith-based organizations appear to represent only a small fraction of faith-based organizations in terms of how those organizations are structured. This is because faith is never simply about mission statements, crucifixes, pictures of Jesus, an occasional prayer, acting kind, or even evangelization—many of which can also be present in nonsectarian organizations. Faith is principally about community, a community of belonging and identity that involves deep friendships and caring and that puts religious teachings into practice. A few faith-based service organizations aim to provide that kind of community, but most do not. Most faith-based service organizations are better understood as specialized agencies that supplement, rather than duplicate, the activities of congregations.

The Recipients of Social Services

Despite all the interest that has been shown in welfare needs and social services over the years, it is surprising how little we know about the recipients of these services. We do have some information about the demographics of low-income families and an occasional study of low-income neighborhoods. But we know little about how people go about seeking social services, why they choose some service organizations rather than others, what they understand the motives of those from whom they seek assistance to be, and whether they regard these caregivers as trustworthy and effective. These are the topics I consider in this chapter and in the following two chapters.

Listening to the voices of those who are the beneficiaries of service organizations is especially important if we want to understand the place of these organizations in our society. From the reports of clergy, church members, and volunteers, we may be persuaded that faith-based organizations are providing an enormous array of services to their communities. But is this the way people who need these services feel? Do they consider the help they receive adequate? Are they happier about the services they receive if these services come from people of faith than if they come simply from professionals for whom faith makes no obvious difference?

Through the research I conducted in the Lehigh Valley in northeastern Pennsylvania, I was able to explore the views of low-income families about their needs and about the services of organizations they turn to in trying to meet these needs. The information comes mainly from a survey of the Lehigh Valley that collected responses from approximately two thousand people living in low-income neighborhoods and from 140 in-depth interviews conducted as a follow-up to this survey. Before turning to that information, though, I want to consider briefly what we know nationally about the characteristics of Americans who are the most likely to seek assistance from service organizations.

Census Bureau Information

The U.S. Census Bureau calculates the percentage of Americans living in poverty each year as a way of estimating the likelihood of people needing public assistance or services of various kinds. Definitions of the poverty level are adjusted annually to take account of changes in cost of living and are based not only on income but on family size and age. Thus, in 2000 the poverty line for an unrelated individual under age sixty-five was $8,959; for an unrelated individual age sixty-five or over, $8,259; a householder in a two-person family under age sixty-five, $11,590; a householder in a two-person family age sixty-five or over, $10,419; a family of three, $13,738; a family of four, $17,603, and a family of five, $20,819. The Census Bureau also reports the proportions of Americans whose incomes fall within various intervals below or above the poverty line, such as 50 percent, 150 percent, or 200 percent.

Table 6.1 shows the percentage of people for each year between 1975 and 2000 whose incomes were defined as being less than half of the official poverty level, below the poverty level, below 150 percent of the poverty level, and below 200 percent of the poverty level. Over this quarter-century period, persons below the poverty level averaged 13.3 percent of the population, with annual fluctuations between 11.3 percent and 15.2 percent. On average, 5 percent had incomes below 50 percent of the poverty level, 23 percent had incomes below 150 percent of the poverty level, and 33.1 percent had incomes below 200 percent of the poverty level.

Data from the Census Bureau are also helpful for identifying categories within the U.S. population in which poverty is disproportionately concentrated. Table 6.2 shows the percentage of persons living below the poverty line within selected categories of the population. As a way of indicating the range of these proportions, I have included figures for 2000, the year in which the poverty rate nationally was lower than at any time since 1975, and for 1993, which had the highest poverty rate (except for 1983) during the same period. The data show that poverty is significantly more likely

Table 6.1
Percentage of People by Ratio of Income to Poverty Level, 1975 to 2000

	Ratio of Income to Poverty Level			
	0.50	1.00	1.50	2.00
2000	4.4	11.3	20.2	29.2
1999	4.6	11.8	21.0	30.1
1998	5.1	12.7	21.5	30.8
1997	5.4	13.3	22.5	32.1
1996	5.4	13.7	23.4	33.5
1995	5.3	13.8	23.5	33.6
1994	5.9	14.5	24.3	34.3
1993	6.2	15.1	25.0	35.2
1992	6.1	14.8	24.5	34.4
1991	5.6	14.2	23.8	33.5
1990	5.2	13.5	22.7	32.3
1989	4.9	12.8	22.0	31.4
1988	5.2	13.0	22.2	31.7
1987	5.2	13.4	22.3	31.7
1986	5.3	14.0	23.9	33.9
1985	5.2	13.6	23.9	33.9
1984	5.5	14.4	24.3	34.6
1983	5.9	15.2	25.6	36.1
1982	5.6	15.0	25.5	36.6
1981	4.9	14.0	24.7	35.7
1980	4.4	13.0	23.1	33.9
1979	3.8	11.7	21.1	31.3
1978	3.6	11.4	20.5	31.0
1977	3.5	11.6	21.8	32.7
1976	3.3	11.8	22.2	33.5
1975	3.7	12.3	23.3	34.6
Average	5.0	13.3	23.0	33.1

Source: U.S. Census Bureau (www.census.gov/income/histpov/hstpov05.txt).

among people living in unrelated subfamilies than among people living in families; that it is higher among women than among men; and higher among blacks and Hispanics, the foreign-born who are not naturalized citizens, and persons living in central-city areas. There are also minor variations in poverty rates among age groups and by geographic region.

Although figures like these are helpful for identifying population groups in which social needs are especially likely, care must be taken in interpret-

TABLE 6.2
Percentage of People by Ratio of Income to Poverty Level within Selected Categories

| | *Ratio of Income to Poverty Level* | | | |
	0.50	*1.00*	*1.50*	*2.00*
Total 2000	4.4	11.3	20.2	29.2
Male	3.9	8.3	18.1	26.7
White	3.1	9.9	16.0	24.2
Non-Hispanic	2.6	6.5	12.7	20.0
Hispanic	6.3	19.5	35.4	49.3
Black	8.6	19.6	30.6	42.2
Female	4.9	12.5	22.2	31.5
White	3.9	10.5	19.6	28.5
Non-Hispanic	3.3	8.5	16.4	24.4
Hispanic	8.2	22.9	39.3	53.3
Black	10.0	24.1	37.4	50.0
Under 18 years	6.4	16.1	26.8	37.4
65 years and over	2.2	10.2	24.3	37.3
Native	4.2	10.7	19.2	28.0
Foreign-born	6.1	15.7	28.1	39.1
Naturalized citizen	3.2	9.7	19.2	28.2
Not a citizen	7.8	19.4	33.7	45.9

Source: U.S. Census Bureau.

ing them. For example, they do not indicate that *most* poor Americans are black, noncitizens, or people living in unrelated subfamilies. Those are all minority groups among the poor, just as they are in the general population. Thus, only 25 percent of persons below the poverty line are black, 12 percent are noncitizens, and fewer than 2 percent live in unrelated subfamilies.

Drawing further on data from the 2000 census, table 6.3 shows the percentages of persons living in households that received various kinds of public assistance.[1] I compare those whose incomes were less than 50 percent of the official poverty level with those whose incomes were 50 percent to less than 100 percent of the poverty level, and with those whose incomes ranged from 100 to 150 percent or between 150 and 200 percent of the poverty level. The differences between those in the two lowest income

TABLE 6.3
Percentage of Persons Receiving Public Assistance by Income Relative to Poverty Level

	Income as Percentage of Poverty Level			
	Less than 50%	*50% to Less than 100%*	*100% to Less than 150%*	*150% to Less than 200%*
In households that received means-tested assistance	63.3	68.1	53.0	39.7
In households that received means-tested assistance, excluding school lunch	56.7	58.2	41.2	27.6
In households that received means-tested cash assistance	25.6	24.9	12.4	7.9
In households that received food stamps	35.9	32.5	14.0	6.1
In households in which one or more persons were covered by Medicaid	49.5	50.1	34.8	23.1

Source: U.S. Census Bureau.

categories are relatively small. After that, the percentages decline for those with incomes between 100 and 150 percent of the poverty level, and are still lower for those with incomes between 150 and 200 percent of the poverty level. We need to pay special note of two aspects of these figures that might otherwise be overlooked. The first is that even among those in the highest of these four income groups, a substantial proportion (approximately 40 percent) receive some kind of means-tested assistance. This proportion highlights the fact that many people living slightly above the official poverty line still rely on public assistance and probably are in need of private assistance as well. The other observation is that among those in all four income categories, even those in the lowest income category, a large minority (approximately 37 percent) do not receive public assistance. They are either self-sufficient or rely only on private assistance when they need help.[2]

Evidence from Other Sources

Additional evidence about the needs of American families was collected by the Urban Institute in a large study that included more than forty-six thousand families living in thirteen states. The Urban Institute data are not strictly representative of the United States, but the families within each state were selected through a random sampling procedure and the states themselves are diverse geographically and socially. Of the families studied, approximately 22 percent had received food stamps at one time or another, 21 percent had qualified at some point for the Earned Income Tax Credit (EITC), nearly 8 percent had qualified at some point for Aid to Families with Dependent Children (AFDC) or Temporary Assistance for Needy Families (TANF), and at the time of the survey (in 1999) 5 percent were on food stamps and 3 percent qualified for the Earned Income Tax Credit.

By comparing families who had ever or who were currently receiving assistance of these various kinds with all families, it is possible to see some of the needs that low-income families mentioned in the survey (see table 6.4). Among the families who had received various kinds of public assistance, approximately one-third said they had been unable to pay their rent at some point during the preceding year, compared with 14 percent of all families in the study. About four in ten, on average, among the low-income families said they had been worried that food would run out, compared with

two in ten among all families. The proportion who said the food they purchased hadn't been adequate was also about twice as high among the families receiving public assistance as in the total sample. Other concerns that
were expressed by somewhere between 11 percent and 29 percent of the
low-income families included worrying about the availability of medical
care, being dissatisfied with the quality of medical care received, and post-
poning dental or medical care or prescription drugs.

The Urban Institute data underscore three important conclusions about
the social needs of American families. First, the proportions currently qualifying for public assistance through food stamp programs or EITC are

TABLE 6.4
Selected Needs of Low-Income Families
(Percentage reporting each type of need)

| | *Families Having Received Assistance* | | | | | |
	AFDC TANF (ever)	*Foof Stamps (ever)*	*Food Stamps (1999)*	*EITC (ever)*	*EITC (1999)*	*All Families*
Unable to pay rent last year	32	31	39	26	30	14
Worried food would run out	44	44	59	34	43	20
Food bought didn't last	36	38	54	28	35	16
Not confident could get medical care if needed	12	14	12	11	12	9
Dissatisfied with quality of medical care received	15	15	12	14	14	10
Dental care postponed	29	27	25	26	25	17
Medical care postponed	17	16	14	15	16	10
Prescription drugs postponed	14	15	15	12	14	7
Mean years as adult on AFDC	4.1					
Mean years as adult on food stamps		4.1				
Number	(3,579)	(10,104)	(2,539)	(9,991)	(1,628)	(46,705)

Source: Urban Institute Survey of Families, 1999.

much smaller than the proportions identified by the U.S. Census as having incomes below the poverty line or within 200 percent of poverty levels. In short, there are clearly many low-income families who are not on public assistance and who are evidently fulfilling their needs by themselves or through nongovernmental means. Second, the average number of years that families in the Urban Institute study who had ever been on AFDC were on AFDC was approximately four, and this was the same number of years that families who had ever been on food stamps had received food stamp assistance. In other words, receiving these kinds of public assistance was relatively short-term, rather than being sustained over long periods of time, meaning that people either improved their situation enough to no longer qualify or turned to other sources for assistance. And third, a significant minority of those who had received or who were currently receiving public assistance were nevertheless experiencing needs such as shortfalls in paying rent or purchasing food, receiving inadequate medical care, or having to postpone such care. Nationally, as many as one in seven of all the families in the study were having trouble paying rent, as many as one in five were experiencing concerns about food, and at least one in ten were having problems with health care.

The Urban Institute study included no questions that shed light on where American families are seeking assistance when they experience these kinds of needs, nor did the study include questions about religion or religious organizations. One question, however, is suggestive. The study was partly timed and designed to learn about families who were going off welfare assistance as a result of the 1996 welfare reform measures. A very small percentage of families in the study went off welfare during the year preceding the survey, but since the study was so large this number totaled nearly 1,200 persons. And of this number, approximately one-quarter had received assistance from some source while making the transition. Table 6.5 shows the percentage of all families who went off welfare and the percentage of such families receiving assistance who received assistance from various sources. Ten percent of all the families who had gone off welfare reported having received assistance from government programs (44 percent of those who had received assistance from any source). Approximately 9 percent had received help from churches, about 12 percent had received help from their families, and about 5 percent had been helped by community centers.

TABLE 6.5
Sources of Assistance for Families Going Off Welfare

	As Percentage of All Families Who Went Off Welfare during the Previous Year	As Percentage of Only Those Families Who Received Any Assistance
Government programs	10.0	44.4
Churches	8.7	38.5
Family	11.7	51.8
Community centers	4.8	21.5
Number	(1,198)	(270)

Source: Urban Institute Survey of Families, 1999.

From these figures, we gain a sense of the *relative* role that churches may have played as families went off welfare. Nearly four in ten of those who received some kind of assistance had been helped by churches. This proportion was not as large as that receiving informal assistance from families. But it was about equal to the percentage that had received government assistance. And it was about twice as large as the proportion that had received help from community centers. Of course we do not know the dollar amounts or what kinds of assistance these families may have received from various sources. But the evidence does suggest that religious organizations were one of the sources to which many people turned as they left welfare programs.

Does it make sense that so many of those leaving welfare would have turned to religious organizations for help? One indication that it does comes from the Urban Poverty and Family Life Survey of Chicago, which was conducted by the sociologist William Julius Wilson in 1987.[3] Although Wilson himself never emphasized the role of religion among the respondents in his study of low-income neighborhoods in Chicago, his survey reveals a surprisingly high level of religious involvement in these neighborhoods. Among the more than 1,500 women in Wilson's study, the proportions who attended religious services at least a few times a year ranged from 75 percent among white non-Hispanics, to 82 percent among Puerto Ricans, to 83 percent among African Americans, and 94 percent among Mexican Americans. The proportions of men who attended a few times a year or more were nearly as high, ranging from a low of 63 percent among non-Hispanic whites, to 76 percent among Puerto Ricans, to 78 percent among African Americans, and 93 percent among Mexican Americans. In other words, most of the families in Wilson's neighborhoods had at least some connection with churches. Whether this might still have been true a decade later and whether it was the case nationally are, of course, questions that can only be addressed with other data.[4]

Religious Characteristics of the Lower-Income Population

By law, the U.S. Census Bureau is not permitted to collect information about religion, and studies such as the Urban Institute survey that focus on government programs often pay little attention to religion. Thus it is necessary to turn to other sources to gain an understanding of the religious characteristics of America's low-income population. The reason for being interested in these characteristics is that they help us know whether or not churches and other faith-based service organizations are likely to be of interest to low-income families. It has traditionally been assumed that religion had special appeal for people in less privileged strata of society.[5] Having fewer material advantages, the argument goes, encourages people to look for solace to the teachings and practices of religious organizations.[6] If this argument is correct, then low-income families might be especially interested in religious organizations as a source of social services. These families would at least have connections to churches and thus be in a good position to seek services from churches, perhaps preferring them to secular organizations. A counterargument can also be advanced, namely, that people in poor communities no longer have as much interest in churches as they probably did in the past. This argument is rooted in speculation that religious organizations mostly develop programs oriented to the middle class, are often ineffective in reaching out to low-income neighbors, and have fled from the inner-city neighborhoods where many low-income families live.[7]

The figures shown in table 6.6 are drawn from the General Social Survey, a large nationally representative survey of the English-speaking population of the United States that is conducted every two years. I have combined the surveys conducted in 1996, 1998, and 2000. Doing so yields more than eight thousand respondents, of whom 2,650 earned annual incomes of less than $25,000. This proportion is approximately the same as the one derived by the census for persons living below 200 percent of the official poverty level. Although it is not adjusted for family composition as the census figures are, it provides a way of assessing the religious characteristics of that part of the population with low incomes. The religious classification included in the table is based on respondents' answers to questions about their religious preference and includes sufficient detail to distinguish between evangelical Protestants (e.g., Southern Baptists, Free Methodists, Missouri Synod Lutherans, and the like) and mainline Protestants (American Baptists, United Methodists, Evangelical Lutheran Church in America members, etc.), as well as historically black Protestant denominations (such as National Baptists and African Methodist Episcopal members), Roman Catholics, Jews, others, and the unaffiliated.[8] Evangelical Protestants and Roman Catholics are the largest categories among those who earn low incomes, comprising 26 percent and 22 percent of the population, respectively. Mainline Protestants and black Protestant denominations each make up 14 percent of the low-income population. And Jews, affili-

TABLE 6.6
Religious Affiliations of Americans with Incomes Less than $25,000
and of Total U.S. Sample
(Percentages)

	Income Less than $25,000	Total U.S. Sample
Evangelical Protestant	26	24
Mainline Protestant	14	18
Black Protestant	14	9
Roman Catholic	22	24
Jewish	1	2
Other religion	6	6
Unaffiliated	13	13
Unclassified	4	4

Source: General Social Survey, 1996-2000.

Note: Total N = 8,553; N with incomes less than $25,000 = 2,650; religious affiliation classified according to Steensland et al., "The Measure of American Religion."

ates of other religions, and those who could not be classified make up another 11 percent. Thus, only about one person in seven (13 percent) among low-income adults claims to have no religious affiliation. As can be seen in the table, these percentages are very similar to those for all adult Americans regardless of income. The most significant differences are that fewer of those with low incomes are mainline Protestants and more are affiliated with black Protestant denominations. The important point is that, at least by this indication, religion plays some role in the identities of nearly all low-income Americans. Religious affiliation is not more extensive than in the general population, but it is no less extensive, either.

We can use this classification of religious identities in the General Social Survey data to paint a more detailed picture of the nation's low-income population than is possible from other sources. If a religious leader associated with one of the four major religious traditions just considered (evangelical Protestant, mainline Protestant, black Protestant, or Roman Catholic) wanted to minister to the needs of low-income families within his or her own tradition, what kinds of people would he or she expect to be dealing with? Would they mostly live in cities or elsewhere, would they be young or old, would they have children or not? Table 6.7 presents this information. It includes some conclusions that may not have been expected. Except for those affiliated with black Protestant denominations, most low-income people in these religious traditions do not live in inner-city areas. They are, for the most part, urban, but they are scattered mostly in small- or medium-sized cities rather than being concentrated in the heart of the largest cities. In marital status, they are diverse. Except for evangelical Protestants, they are no more likely to be married than is true among all low-income people. More than one-quarter are divorced or separated, as many as one in six is widowed, and a large minority (especially among Catholics) have never been married. Only about half are in the labor force, and one-third of this number work only part-time. But relatively few have been laid off or are unemployed. Nearly one-quarter are retired (more among mainline Protestants) and another quarter are doing something else (such as keeping house or going to school). The proportions who have children living at home range from 45 percent among black Protestants to only 22 percent among mainline Protestants, a pattern in keeping with the fact that mainline Protestants are also more likely to be older and black Protestants younger.[9] Our hypothetical religious leader

TABLE 6.7
Characteristics of Low-Income Population by Religious Tradition
(Percentages)

	Evangelical Protestant	Mainline Protestant	Black Protestant	Roman Catholic	All Low-Income
Residence					
Central city	18	20	49	33	30
Suburb	12	13	16	23	16
Other urban	53	50	22	40	43
Rural	17	16	13	5	11
Marital status					
Married	33	21	21	22	23
Widowed	18	25	25	15	16
Divorced or separated	29	29	29	26	27
Never married	20	25	25	38	33
Employment					
Working full time	36	31	38	37	37
Working part time	12	12	11	14	14
Unemployed or laid off	4	4	5	6	5
Retired	23	34	17	21	20
Other	25	19	29	22	24
Children					
Has children at home	30	22	45	32	32
Age					
18 to 29	22	19	22	30	27
30 to 49	33	24	41	33	34
50 to 64	15	16	18	14	14
65 and older	30	42	18	25	25
Gender					
Male	35	33	27	40	36
Female	65	67	73	60	64
Health					
Poor or fair health	37	36	42	33	34
Number	(699)	(378)	(599)	(599)	(2,588)

Source: General Social Survey, 1996-2000.

Note: Respondents with incomes less than $25,000; religious affiliation classified according to Steensland et al., "The Measure of American Religion."

would be interested to know that women outnumber men by almost two to one in this low-income segment of the population. And it would be important to know that as many as one-third in each religious tradition claim to be in poor or only fair health.

Besides religious affiliation, the General Social Survey also provides evidence about the frequency with which people actually participate in religious services. In table 6.8 I show both the percentages who attend services at least several times a year and the percentages who attend services nearly every week. I do so for people affiliated with each of the four religious traditions as well as for all low-income persons and divide both according to level of income. We see that there is a slight tendency for persons with incomes below $15,000 to be less actively involved in religious services than persons with incomes between $15,000 and $25,000. However, these

TABLE 6.8
Religious Participation of Low-Income Population by Religious Tradition

	Evangelical Protestant	Mainline Protestant	Black Protestant	Roman Catholic	All Low-Income
Among those with incomes between $15,000 and $24,999					
Percentage who attend services at least several times a year	70	57	77	58	58
Percentage who attend services nearly every week	44	29	38	32	33
Number	(351)	(168)	(291)	(291)	(1,182)
Among those with incomes less than $15,000					
Percentage who attend services at least several times a year	63	55	72	57	54
Percentage who attend services nearly every week	38	20	28	30	26
Number	(232)	(121)	(179)	(179)	(1,468)

Source: General Social Survey, 1996–2000.
Note: Respondents with incomes less than $25,000; religious affiliation classified according to Steensland et al., "The Measure of American Religion."

differences are quite small. The more important differences are among religious traditions. Evangelical and black Protestants have the highest rates of religious observance, while mainline Protestants and Roman Catholic rates are significantly lower. Nevertheless, between one-half and three-quarters in all the categories attend once in a while, and about one-third in most of the categories attend regularly. Thus, if we were to think of religious involvement as a kind of tie to religious organizations that might make these organizations aware of needs in their community or make individuals inclined to seek assistance from religious organizations, we would have to conclude that a large share of American's low-income families do have such connections.

Another large national survey also provides some useful information about America's low-income families. This is the Social Capital Benchmark Survey conducted by Robert Putnam. Because of the large size of this study (more than thirty thousand respondents) and because it included questions about religion, we are again able to make comparisons among evangelical Protestants, mainline Protestants, black Protestants, and Roman Catholics, as well as all respondents with annual incomes less than $25,000. These data show that a majority of those affiliated with each tradition are actually members of their local congregation (see table 6.9). The highest percentage is among black Protestants and the lowest is among Catholics. On average, about four persons in ten claim to have given at least one hundred dollars to their church during the preceding year. Nearly half claim to have a friend who has been on welfare. More than one-third express alienation in the sense of feeling that community leaders do not care about them. Distrust of neighbors is especially evident among black Protestants and Catholics, and it is notable that far fewer in any of the categories distrust people at their church than distrust their neighbors. Finally, about one in five reports doing volunteer work to help the needy. The profile that emerges from these data is thus one of active connections with churches among at least a sizable minority of the low-income population. These connections seem to indicate both that low-income churchgoers know people who are needy and that some of them do volunteer work to help the needy. If religious involvement is viewed as a kind of network of personal ties and associations, then it seems to extend among a significant number of people with lower incomes.

TABLE 6.9

Social Characteristics of Low-Income Population by Religious Tradition
(Percentage)

	Evangelical Protestant	Mainline Protestant	Black Protestant	Roman Catholic	All Low-Income
Church members	56	63	68	49	56
Give $100 or more to church	52	55	53	37	41
Have a friend who has been on welfare	46	40	54	36	46
Feel community leaders don't care about people like them	37	36	42	47	43
Distrust neighbors	20	15	39	39	30
Distrust people at church	5	4	15	20	11
Volunteer to help the needy	20	27	20	18	21
Number	(776)	(563)	(442)	(1,009)	(3,069)

Source: Social Capital Benchmark Survey 2000.

Note: Respondents with incomes less than $25,000; religious affiliation classified according to Steensland et al., "The Measure of American Religion."

Needs and Services in a Small City

The difficulties in trying to actually learn about the need for social services and the organizations that provide these services are immense. Although asking about needs may be possible on a national scale, it is inconceivable to collect information on that scale about the kinds of organizations lower-income families contact for assistance. Even within a large metropolitan area, the possibilities for systematic research of this kind are limited by the fact that people may contact any of thousands of organizations scattered across the city.

For these reasons, I focus in the remainder of this chapter on information collected in one small urban community. The community is the Allentown-Bethlehem Metropolitan Statistical Area, otherwise known as the Lehigh Valley, in northeastern Pennsylvania. This is a community of approximately 616,000 people. Allentown and Bethlehem are essentially a single cluster of urban neighborhoods, divided by the Lehigh River, which separates Lehigh and Northampton counties; Easton is a smaller urban area some ten miles to the east. In size, the Lehigh Valley thus resembles approximately fifty other smaller cities scattered around the country, such as Charlotte, El Paso, Mobile, Omaha, and Syracuse. I selected the Lehigh Valley as the location for an intensive community study of low-income families for several reasons. First, I had been studying service agencies and churches there for nearly a decade and thus had quite a bit of information already about the community and the services that, from the standpoint of agency directors and clergy, were being provided. Second, I wanted a geographically autonomous community of a size that would make it possible to ask specific questions of recipients about the particular organizations from which they had sought assistance; this meant focusing on a small city rather than a large city or neighborhood within a large metropolitan area. And third, I wanted to understand more about small cities since nearly all previous studies of low-income families have been conducted in large cities (such as Chicago and Philadelphia).[10] My hunch was that service organizations in the Lehigh Valley were doing a fairly good job of meeting the needs of people in the community, but newcomers were also being attracted to the area and welfare reform was adding to the number of clients being served.

In 2002 I conducted a survey among 2,077 respondents in the Lehigh Valley. The respondents were randomly selected residents of the fifteen census tracts in the area with the lowest average family incomes. Table 6.10 compares the respondents in the survey with census data for the Allentown-Bethlehem Metropolitan Statistical Area (MSA) as a whole. The figures show that the respondents are indeed much worse off financially than are families in the area in general. Median family income of respondents was $26,364, compared with $49,848 for the MSA; 36.4 percent of respondents had incomes below the poverty level, compared with 9.5 percent in the MSA; the unemployment rate was twice as high among respondents as in the MSA; and among all families with children, nearly half of those in the sample were headed by a single parent, compared with only one-quarter in the whole MSA. Demographically, the Lehigh Valley includes a relatively smaller African American population than in many urban areas (only 8 percent of the sample were African American), but for a city in the

northeastern United States it includes a fairly large proportion of Hispanics (27 percent of the respondents were Hispanic), and for this reason interviews were conducted in Spanish as well as in English. The Hispanic
community includes an established population, largely from Puerto Rico,
who settled during the 1960s and a more recent and diverse population
who have moved to the Lehigh Valley from New York or Philadelphia in
search of cheaper housing and safer neighborhoods. Economically, the
Lehigh Valley has suffered from the downscaling and then closing of Bethlehem Steel, which for many years had been the largest employer in the
area and one of the largest steel plants in the world. Currently, the largest
employers are several light manufacturing companies, two hospitals, and
several discount retail stores.

Having data from randomly selected respondents in low-income neighborhoods thus provides us with an opportunity to learn what kinds of
problems they experienced, what kinds of needs they sought to fulfill, and
which service organizations they contacted. Unlike studies of the clients of
only one or two organizations, these data also permit us to examine whether
or not clients thought the agencies they contacted were *effective,* taking into
account the fact that different kinds of clients contacted different kinds
of agencies. The same procedure permits us to examine whether clients
thought some agencies were more *trustworthy* than others. In addition to
the survey, I obtained detailed qualitative information from 140 respondents who provided extensive narratives about themselves and their experiences with service organizations through in-depth interviews.

TABLE 6.10
Comparison of Survey Respondents and Lehigh Valley Metropolitan Statistical Area

	Low-Income Survey Respondents	Lehigh Valley MSA
Median family income	$26,364	$49,848
Percentage of families with incomes below the poverty level	36.4	9.5
Unemployment rate (percent)	9.2	4.6
Percentage of families with children headed by single parent	46.8	25.4

Source: Lehigh Valley Survey, 2002; U.S. Census Bureau, 2000.

Table 6.11 shows the kinds of problems respondents in the survey said they or someone in their immediate family had experienced within the past two years. For purposes of comparison, I have included the responses for persons whose family incomes during the year prior to the survey were less than $20,000, those for persons whose family incomes were at least $20,000 but less than $30,000, and those for persons whose family incomes were $30,000 or more. Approximately one-third of the respondents fell into each of these three family income categories. In interpreting these results, we need to remember that the two years prior to the survey included almost all of 2000, when the economic boom of the 1990s was still largely in effect, and all of 2001, which included the economic downturn which began in January of that year and which deepened after the attacks on the World Trade Center and Pentagon on September 11, 2001.

The problems that respondents in these fifteen low-income neighborhoods were most likely to report having experienced were "being seriously ill or hospitalized"; "falling behind in your gas, electric, or phone bills"; "being seriously depressed"; "being laid off from work or losing your job"; and "having too little money to buy enough food." Between one-quarter and one-fifth of the respondents mentioned each of these problems. In addition, approximately one in ten mentioned "falling behind in your rent or mortgage payments" and "being a victim of a crime." Fewer (only 4 percent) reported "having a problem with alcohol or drug abuse" or "being in trouble with the police." And 13 percent said they had experienced some other serious problem, difficulty, or decision.[11]

It is interesting that, despite living in the poorest neighborhoods in the Lehigh Valley, relatively few of the people surveyed had experienced most of these problems. Most, or at least a large minority, seemed to be living in ways that might not require them to seek assistance for any serious family problems. In fact, as shown in the bottom panel of the table, 40 percent said they had experienced none of the problems listed (including the open-ended "other" kind of problem).

The other way of looking at the data, though, is that a large number of people in these neighborhoods *did* experience at least some serious problem in the previous two years. Sixty percent had experienced at least one such problem, 36 percent had experienced two or more problems, and 13 percent had experienced three or more problems. In addition, the comparisons among the three income categories demonstrate clearly that most

Table 6.11

Family Needs Experienced in Low-Income Neighborhoods
(Percentage of families in which member experienced problem in previous two years)

	Income < $20,000	Income $20,000 to $29,999	Income ≥ $30,000	All Respondents
Being seriously ill or hospitalized	29	24	16	23
Falling behind in your gas, electric, or phone bills	32	22	15	22
Being seriously depressed	30	20	15	21
Being laid off from work or losing job	24	17	19	20
Having too little money to buy enough food	33	17	7	19
Falling behind in your rent or mortgage payments	16	12	8	12
Being a victim of a crime	8	7	10	9
Having a problem with alcohol or drug abuse	4	3	6	4
Being in trouble with the police	4	4	4	4
Some other serious problem, difficulty, or decision	16	12	12	13
Index				
No problems	29	41	47	40
One problem	24	25	24	24
Two problems	26	21	21	23
Three or more problems	20	12	8	13
Number	(645)	(688)	(743)	(2,077)

Source: Lehigh Valley Survey, 2002.

of the problems listed were experienced more commonly among people with the fewest economic resources. For instance, about one-third of those whose annual incomes were less than $20,000 indicated having fallen behind on utilities bills, having too little money for food, or being seriously depressed, whereas these proportions were lower among those with incomes between $20,000 and $30,000, and were markedly lower among those with incomes of $30,000 or more.

Family income is not the only factor affecting the likelihood of experiencing these problems. In multivariate analysis of these questions, I discovered that the number of serious problems respondents reported was greater (taking family income into account) for respondents who were mothers heading households with children, for respondents who were elderly, for those who were African American or Hispanic, for those who did not speak English, and for those living in census tracts with lower average incomes and higher rates of unemployment. In short, these are largely the same factors that have been identified in other studies with higher rates of dependence on welfare programs or public assistance. They also point to the importance of contextual (neighborhood) factors as well as individual characteristics.[12]

In table 6.12 we see the kinds of assistance that respondents in the survey said they had sought during the two years preceding the survey. "Medical assistance, such as medical treatment, finding a doctor, or transportation to the doctor" was the most common kind of assistance, sought by 23 percent of the respondents. Next in order were "financial assistance, such as a loan, welfare, or assistance paying your bills" (16 percent); "food or shelter, such as groceries, meals, food stamps, or temporary housing" (14 percent); and "spiritual assistance, such as prayer, clergy visits, or religious instruction" (13 percent). Ten percent said they had sought "employment assistance, such as finding a job or job training." Least often mentioned were "emotional assistance, such as counseling, support, or help overcoming an addiction" (8 percent); "child-related assistance, such as day care, baby sitting, or tutoring" (6 percent); and "legal assistance, such as with police matters, divorce, or child custody" (5 percent).

Although we should be careful about generalizing too broadly from these data, it is perhaps worth noting how infrequently emotional assistance was mentioned in comparison with some of the other kinds of assistance (especially medical assistance, financial assistance, and food or shelter). This is notable in view of the relatively higher percentage seen in the previous table who said they suffered from serious depression and in view of the impression one gains from studies of the society at large that suggest that interest in emotional problems and psychological therapy is widespread. In a lower-income population like this one, material needs clearly take precedence over emotional ones. It is also interesting that so few respondents sought assistance for child care and other child-related needs. Of course such needs pertain only to families with children of a particular age and, for those families, having these needs met is crucial to parents being able to seek gainful employment. In view of our interest in faith-based social

TABLE 6.12
Kinds of Assistance Sought in Low-Income Neighborhoods
(Percentages of respondents seeking assistance)

	Income < $20,000	Income $20,000 to $29,999	Income ≥ $30,000	All Respondents
Medical assistance	32	20	17	23
Financial assistance	27	12	9	16
Food or shelter	30	11	4	14
Spiritual assistance	16	12	12	13
Employment or job assistance	15	10	8	10
Emotional assistance	12	7	7	8
Child related assistance	7	5	5	6
Legal assistance	7	4	4	5
Index				
None of these kinds of assistance	48	63	68	60
Only one kind of assistance	12	16	15	14
Two kinds of assistance	14	8	7	10
Three or more kinds of assistance	26	13	10	16
Number	(645)	(688)	(743)	(2,077)

Source: Lehigh Valley Survey, 2002.

services, it is also of interest to note that the proportion seeking spiritual assistance ranks as high as it does among the kinds of assistance sought.

In all, 40 percent of those surveyed had sought at least one of these kinds of assistance, 26 percent had sought assistance of more than one kind, and 16 percent had sought assistance of at least three kinds. In view of the problems described in table 6.11, it is worth noting that a large share of those who experience problems appear to be self-sufficient in dealing with these problems, at least as measured by having sought assistance. It is also important to emphasize that a majority of those who seek assistance are people with multiple needs or interested in gaining help of more than one kind. Finally, as in table 6.12, people with lower family incomes are significantly more likely than those with higher family incomes to have sought all of the kinds of assistance listed (specifically, among those with incomes below $20,000, 52 percent have sought at least one kind of assistance, compared with only 32 percent among those with incomes of $30,000 or more).

Multivariate analysis shows that the other factors affecting the likelihood of having sought assistance include being a mother heading a household with children, being elderly, and being black or Hispanic. Unlike the factors affecting the number of serious problems a person experiences, contextual factors (such as average income or unemployment in one's census tract) do not have a significant effect on seeking assistance. With all of these factors (including income) taken into account, level of education is *positively* associated with seeking assistance.[13] This relationship suggests that seeking assistance stems not only from need but also from the kind of training or cultural exposure that may make one more aware of the availability of sources of assistance in the community.[14]

Before turning to a consideration of the kind of organizations from which people in the survey sought assistance, it will be helpful to look briefly at the religious characteristics of respondents in the Lehigh Valley study. Table 6.13 presents this information. For comparative purposes, I have divided respondents into evangelical Protestants, mainline Protestants, black Protestants, and Roman Catholics using the same criteria I did before in considering national data. I also show information for people in the survey who said they have no religious affiliation. Among the lower-income people surveyed in the Lehigh Valley, all but 16 percent claim some religious affiliation: 16 percent identify with an evangelical Protestant denomination, 16 percent with a mainline Protestant denomination, 4 percent with a historically African American denomination, 36 percent are Roman Catholics, and 14 percent indicate some other affiliation (mostly Christian but unspecified). Compared with the two national studies considered previously, therefore, these respondents are less likely to be evangelical Protestant (probably because of living in older, inner-city neighborhoods where relatively few evangelical Protestant churches have been founded), less likely to belong to historically African American churches (because the community has a slightly smaller African American population than in the nation at large and because African Americans also identify with other religious traditions in the community), and more likely to be Roman Catholic (partly because of the large number of Hispanics living in the neighborhoods surveyed).

I have shown the kinds of problems experienced by people within each religious tradition to demonstrate that each tradition includes a substantial number of lower-income families with needs. Nearly one-quarter of those in each of the four traditions, for instance, mention that they or someone in their family has been seriously ill or hospitalized in the past two years. At least one-fifth in each tradition have been seriously depressed. About the same proportion, or more, have had trouble paying their utility bills, have been laid off from work, or have had too little money for food. In all, approximately six people in ten within each tradition have experienced at least one of the problems listed. The percentages are sometimes higher among those who identify with African American churches than among those associated with the other traditions (especially on matters of money, work, and food); otherwise, the similarities across the different traditions outweigh the differences. Nor does being identified with a religious tradition seem to protect people from experiencing these problems, at least judging from the comparisons provided by those who are religiously unaffiliated.

The bottom half of table 6.13 provides some other comparisons. It shows that approximately two-thirds of those associated with each tradition in these neighborhoods have annual incomes less than $30,000 and that about one-third have incomes less than $20,000. It shows that mainline Protestants have more older people than the other traditions and fewer young people, while the other three traditions are fairly similar to one another. The unaffiliated are most likely to include young people and least

TABLE 6.13

Needs and Other Characteristics by Religious Tradition (Percentage of respondents)

	Evangelical Protestant	Mainline Protestant	Black Protestant	Roman Catholic	No Affiliation
In the past two years, someone in family had a serious problem with					
Being seriously ill or hospitalized	23	29	20	22	17
Falling behind in your gas, electric, or phone bills	28	16	34	20	24
Being seriously depressed	20	19	20	20	24
Being laid off from work or losing job	19	19	27	16	24
Having too little money to buy enough food	22	16	30	20	15
Falling behind in your rent or mortgage payments	10	9	18	11	14
Being a victim of a crime	9	7	7	7	11
Having a problem with alcohol or drug abuse	5	5	6	3	5
Being in trouble with the police	4	3	7	3	5
Some other serious problem, difficulty, or decision	17	13	16	11	14
At least one of the above problems	64	60	67	57	57
Other characteristics					
Income less than $30,000	64	60	63	68	64
Income less than $20,000	32	29	37	33	27
Age 18 to 29	22	11	22	22	41
Age 30 to 49	45	35	37	37	41
Age 50 and over	33	54	41	41	19
Female	62	65	53	66	48
Children living at home	44	31	42	42	39
African American	3	4	96	3	8
Hispanic	41	2	10	36	25
Attend religious services at least almost every week	59	33	51	49	9
Attend religious services at least a few times a year	89	87	90	88	51
Number	(339)	(342)	(73)	(748)	(327)

Source: Lehigh Valley Survey, 2002.

likely to include older people. Women are somewhat more common than men among those who have a religious affiliation, while men are relatively more common among the unaffiliated. In all the traditions, a substantial minority (one-third or more) have children living at home. Not surprisingly, the different religious traditions remain relatively distinct racially, but ethnically it is notable that evangelical Protestants are composed of a somewhat higher percentage of Hispanics than are Roman Catholics. Lastly, the table shows that a large minority (if not a majority) of those who claim affiliation with each religious tradition attend religious services regularly and nearly all affiliates attend at least a few times a year. Even among those with no religious affiliation, half attend religious services at least a few times a year.

The conclusion to be drawn from this table is twofold. On the one hand, none of the religious traditions represented in these low-income neighborhoods is immune to the kinds of needs that families experience in these neighborhoods. If the leaders of these various traditions are interested in trying to help needy families, they have no shortage of such families within their own traditions. On the other hand, if we think about the population living in these low-income neighborhoods, religion would appear to be a very relevant consideration. Nearly everyone has a religious affiliation and nearly everyone has some connection with religious organizations by virtue of attending religious services.

People in low-income neighborhoods in the Lehigh Valley sought assistance from a variety of service organizations. Twenty percent of the total sample (or 36 percent of those who contacted any organization for assistance) sought assistance from the public welfare department. A slightly larger proportion (22 percent of the total sample and 40 percent of those seeking any assistance) contacted one or more of eleven secular service agencies for help. These organizations included local chapters of well-known national organizations such as United Way, Habitat for Humanity, and Meals on Wheels, as well as purely local organizations specializing in job training, food distribution, shelter, or a more eclectic range of services. There were also eleven faith-based organizations in the community that provided social services. Unlike the secular nonprofits, these organizations were explicitly sponsored by religious groups and included religious activities in their mission. They included clergy or church councils, neighborhood shelters or missions, and local units of national organizations such as the Salvation Army and Catholic Charities. Sixteen percent of the total sample (28 percent of those who sought any assistance) had contacted one of these organizations. Finally, 12 percent of the respondents (22 percent of those seeking any assistance) said they had contacted a religious congregation for help.

Table 6.14 compares the people who sought assistance from each kind of organization in terms of the kind of assistance they were seeking. It should be kept in mind that many people sought several kinds of assistance and contacted more than one organization. Thus, the figures shown in the table do not mean that people *specifically* sought a particular kind of assistance from a particular kind of organization. What the figures provide is a sense of whether people generally flocked to certain kinds of organizations because they had distinctive needs or whether the various organizations attracted similar clienteles.

The latter appears to be the case. On the whole, the proportions among those in each of the four columns who had sought each kind of assistance listed are more similar than different. And the exceptions are fairly predictable. The highest percentage seeking spiritual assistance, for instance, occurs among those who sought help from local congregations, and the next highest percentage is among those who contacted a faith-based organization. The other generalization that can be ventured from these results is that faith-based service organizations resemble secular nonprofits (and even the public welfare department) in clientele needs more closely than they resemble congregations. This is especially evident with respect to financial assistance and food or shelter: 48 percent of those who contacted faith-based organizations were seeking financial assistance, compared with only 28 percent of those who contacted churches; and 47 percent of the former were seeking food or shelter, compared with 22 percent of the latter.

The bottom panel of table 6.14 sheds light on another question that has been discussed in the policy literature on faith-based social services.[15] Some have argued that faith-based organizations should be encouraged because some clients might strongly prefer to deal only with such organizations. Others have argued that faith-based organizations should *not* be encouraged because they might monopolize some corner of the service market and thus force clients to come there because they had no choice to go elsewhere. Neither argument seems to be supported by these data. To the contrary, the data suggest that people who sought assistance from one

TABLE 6.14
Kinds of Assistance Sought by Type of Service Organization Contacted
(Percentages)

	Public Welfare Department	Secular Nonprofit Organization	Faith-Based Organization	Local Congregation
Kind of assistance sought				
Medical assistance	59	44	50	42
Financial assistance	54	42	48	28
Food or shelter	59	41	47	22
Spiritual assistance	25	31	38	53
Employment assistance	26	32	27	19
Emotional assistance	20	21	26	25
Child-related assistance	16	15	17	10
Legal assistance	12	13	13	12
At least two of the above	74	63	69	56
Three or more of the above	50	43	51	41
Also sought assistance from				
Public welfare department	—	47	56	27
Secular nonprofit organization	52	—	65	40
Faith-based organization	44	46	—	34
Local congregation	17	22	26	—
Any other kind of organization	86	85	85	78
Number	(415)	(460)	(325)	(253)

Source: Lehigh Valley Survey, 2002.

kind of organization generally sought assistance from other kinds as well. For instance, among those who sought assistance from the public welfare department, 86 percent had also sought assistance from at least one of the other kinds of organizations. Similarly, 85 percent of those who had contacted a secular nonprofit or a faith-based organization had also contacted one of the other kinds, as did 78 percent of those who sought help from a church. The data also cast doubt on the idea that there might be some collusion or special relationship between churches and faith-based organizations, as far as clients are concerned: only 26 percent of those who sought help from a faith-based organization also sought help from a congregation, and only 34 percent of those who sought help from a congregation also sought help from a faith-based organization. To the extent that there is an overlapping clientele, it is between faith-based organizations and secular nonprofits (65 percent of the former's clientele had contacted the latter, and 46 percent of the latter's clientele had contacted the former). The data do, however, suggest (as other research has indicated) that nonprofit service organizations probably supplement the activities of local public welfare agencies.[16] Thus, 52 percent of those who had contacted the public welfare department for assistance had also contacted one of the secular nonprofit organizations, and 44 percent had contacted one of the faith-based organizations.

Another set of comparisons among the clients of the various kinds of organizations is shown in table 6.15. In this table I show the social characteristics, problems experienced, and religious characteristics of people who had contacted each of the four kinds of organizations for assistance. The figures in the top third of the table show even more clearly than in the previous table that the clients of public welfare, secular nonprofit, and faith-based organizations resemble one another. On income, age, gender, having children at home, race, ethnicity, and language, they are virtually indistinguishable. Those who contact local congregations for help, though, are distinctive. Compared to the clients of the other three kinds of organizations, they are less likely to be poor, less likely to be female, less likely to have children at home, less likely to be African American or Hispanic, and less likely to be Spanish speakers. Multivariate analysis of the social characteristics associated with selecting different kinds of service organizations also support these conclusions: being older is significantly associated with seeking help from a congregation, but not with seeking help from the other

Table 6.15
Social Characteristics by Type of Service Organization Contacted (Percentage)

	Public Welfare Department	Secular Nonprofit Organization	Faith-Based Organization	Local Congregation
Social characteristics of respondents who sought assistance from each kind of organization				
Income less than $30,000	86	73	79	64
Income less than $20,000	59	43	50	27
Age 18 to 29	28	27	26	25
Age 30 to 49	44	45	44	49
Age 50 and over	28	28	30	26
Female	74	68	70	63
Any children at home	62	57	58	51
African American	12	13	16	11
Hispanic	48	46	41	30
Spanish primary language	19	15	17	7
Problems experienced				
Falling behind in gas, utilities	50	45	46	32
Too little money to buy food	46	35	41	28
Seriously depressed	38	34	38	29
Laid off or losing job	36	33	34	27
Seriously ill or hospitalized	34	30	34	32
Falling behind in rent/mortgage	25	24	25	18
Victim of a crime	11	14	14	13
In trouble with the police	6	7	8	8
Alcohol or drug abuse	6	6	8	8
Other serious problem	24	20	24	25
Three or more problems	36	31	35	25
Religious characteristics				
Attend religious services at least almost every week	35	42	46	65
Attend religious services a few times a year or more	78	85	89	94
Evangelical Protestant	21	18	17	29
Mainline Protestant	12	14	14	14
Black Protestant	5	5	6	5
Roman Catholic	35	37	37	33
Unaffiliated	17	16	15	9
Number	(415)	(460)	(325)	(253)

Source: Lehigh Valley Survey, 2002.

three kinds of organizations; having more education is more strongly associated with seeking help from a congregation than with any of the other three; and, in contrast, having lower income and being Hispanic or African American are generally associated with seeking help from the other three but not with seeking help from churches.[17]

The problems people have experienced, as shown in the middle part of the table, follow a similar pattern in relation to the kind of organizations from which they have sought assistance. Clients seeking help directly from congregations are less likely than clients of the other three kinds of organizations to mention financial problems such as having too little money for utilities, rent, or food. Where clients of congregations most resemble clients of the other organizations is on illness and hospitalization, being a victim of crime, being in trouble with the police, and having alcohol or drug abuse problems in their family.

It is important not to overinterpret these results, but they point to the importance of distinguishing between congregations and faith-based organizations. If the pattern evident here is true in other communities, congregations may not be well equipped to deal with the needs of clients with severe financial problems. For those problems, clients probably gravitate more naturally to public agencies and secular or faith-based private agencies. Churches, however, may be a more attractive option for people experiencing emotional, spiritual, or health-related problems.

In the lower portion of table 6.15 we see how clients of the four kinds of organizations compare in terms of religious characteristics. If faith-based organizations have a special role to play in relation to highly religious clients, or if these organizations are so explicitly focused on religious content that they attract such clients, then we would expect their clients to resemble those of churches. This is not the case. Although it is true that the clients of faith-based organizations are somewhat more likely to attend church services and to attend regularly than clients of the public welfare department, there are virtually no differences between these clients and those of secular nonprofit agencies. In contrast, clients who seek help from churches are significantly more likely to attend church services regularly than clients who seek help from faith-based organizations. The figures shown for religious affiliation also run counter to the argument that faith-based organizations may be serving only a particular kind of client, most likely an evangelical client. It is the case that a relatively high proportion of the clients of churches (29 percent) are evangelical, but the proportion of faith-based organization clients who are evangelical (17 percent) is actually lower than the percentage of public welfare clients who are evangelical (21 percent). Nor does it appear that the religiously unaffiliated are being underserved by faith-based organizations. At least the proportion who seek help from these organizations is about the same as the proportion who seek help from other organizations, whereas fewer (as might be expected) seek help from churches.

Table 6.16 shows how people who had contacted the various kinds of service organizations rated them in terms of perceived effectiveness. This information was obtained in the survey by asking any respondent who indicated having contacted a particular organization for assistance to rate that organization "in terms of its effectiveness in meeting your need." Respondents were asked to provide a grade ranging from A to F. The virtue of this approach, besides the fact that it registers clients' perceptions, is that anyone who *contacted* a particular organization was given an opportunity to provide a grade, rather than only those who had actually received assistance. Thus, if a potential recipient was turned away, that person could still register his or her opinion of the organization. Because there was only one public welfare department, and because respondents were asked to indicate which specific religious congregation they had contacted, a single grade was given for each of these two kinds of organizations. Because respondents provided separate grades for each of the secular nonprofits or faith-based organizations they had contacted, those grades were averaged. Looking first at the grades given by people who had contacted the public welfare department, we see that there is considerable variation: about one-quarter gave the highest grade (A), another quarter gave a grade of B, almost one-quarter gave a grade of C, and the remainder split equally between grades of D and F. On a 4-point scale, the average grade for the public welfare department was 2.47. In comparison, the grades given to secular nonprofits and faith-based organizations were significantly higher: 38 percent and 44 percent, respectively, gave grades of A, and the average grades, respectively, were 3.10 and 3.13. Finally, the grades received by religious congregations were higher still: 70 percent gave a grade of A, only 7 percent gave a grade of C or lower, and the average grade was 3.59.

These results suggest that different kinds of service organizations actually do differ in terms of how people who contact them perceive their effectiveness. Public welfare is perceived least positively, churches are perceived most positively, and the various private nonprofit organizations score in the middle. As for faith-based organizations, there is little evidence that they are perceived as being *more effective* than secular nonprofits (although the proportion who receive A's is slightly higher, the overall GPA is nearly the same). At the same time, there is no evidence in these results that clients perceive faith-based organizations to be *any less effective* than secular nonprofits.

There are several possible reasons why the welfare department may be perceived as less effective, the various nonprofit organizations as more effective, and churches as the most effective. One is that the various organizations actually performed more or less well at meeting the needs of people who contacted them. Another is that people had choices among the various nonprofit organizations or churches they contacted, whereas they did not have a choice about the welfare department, and thus were able to shop

TABLE 6.16

Effectiveness Ratings by Type of Service Organization Contacted
(Percentage of respondents giving each grade for effectiveness in meeting his or her need)

	Public Welfare Department	Secular Nonprofit Organization	Faith-Based Organization	Local Congregation
Grade of A (4.0)	27	38	44	70
Grade of B (3.0)	25	40	34	22
Grade of C (2.0)	21	12	14	4
Grade of D (1.0)	11	5	6	1
Grade of F (0.0)	11	1	1	2
Mean GPA	2.47	3.10	3.13	3.59
Standard deviation	1.33	0.98	1.06	0.78
Number	(398)	(446)	(311)	(178)

Source: Lehigh Valley Survey, 2002.

around among the other organizations until their needs were met. Yet another possibility is that the welfare department served more clients and was thus understaffed or confronted clients with more bureaucracy and impersonality than they experienced at the other organizations. Or the differences may be due to people with more serious needs going to the welfare department, while people with less serious needs sought help from churches.

We cannot sort out many of these possibilities with the data at hand. We can, however, compare the various kinds of organizations on some of these factors to see if they are plausible explanations for the differences in perceived effectiveness. For one thing, because we knew the address of every respondent in the survey as well as the address of each service organization, we were able to compute the average distance a person might have to travel to contact various kinds of agencies. The average distance between respondents' homes and the welfare department for those who contacted it was 4.3 miles. Of course they might have contacted it only by telephone or mail or indirectly through some other office or program, but if they actually went in person, it was a considerable distance away—requiring several bus changes, as some respondents told us. In contrast, the distance between respondents' homes and the closest secular nonprofit they contacted was only 1.7 miles, and for the closest faith-based organization 1.2 miles. (We were unable to secure good information for enough of the churches, but their number suggested that the average distance between home and church for most respondents was probably less than one mile.) We have already seen, too, that respondents who contacted the various kinds of organizations differ in terms of the kinds of problems they had experienced and the kinds of assistance they were seeking.

To tease out the effects of some of these factors, we must confront the fact that most of the clients did not seek help from only one organization or even one kind of organization. As we saw previously, nearly all the respondents who sought help from one kind of agency also sought help from at least one other kind of agency. It will be helpful to think of this phenomenon as a *service portfolio*. When economists write about families' financial resources, they often refer to the idea of "income packaging." An income package may consist of the earnings from one's job, interest on savings, alimony payments, gifts from family members, and public assistance such as Social Security. Similarly, in seeking the assistance they may need from community organizations, families are likely to put together a service portfolio. They may go to the welfare department to see about financial assistance of some kind, contact a nonprofit organization to secure job training, drop the kids off at a church-run nursery school, and go to a food bank if food runs low. In thinking about perceptions of effectiveness, therefore, the real question is not so much whether a particular organization is regarded as being effective but whether the service portfolio overall is considered effective.

Thinking in terms of service portfolios also solves the methodological problem of figuring out how to compare respondents' perceptions when respondents have contacted different kinds of organizations. Instead of trying to make calculations based on various combinations of agencies contacted, we simply compute the average effectiveness score for each respondent's service portfolio. Then we examine whether these scores are elevated or reduced when a person has contacted a particular kind of organization for assistance. We can also control for respondents' social characteristics and the kinds of problems or needs they had, thereby determining if the type of organization contacted is related to average effectiveness scores independent of these other factors. Because we are taking into consideration all the kinds of organizations a person has contacted, we also correct for any bias that may be introduced by respondents having different points of reference in mind based on having contacted different organizations (e.g., a person who has contacted a secular nonprofit organization and the welfare department versus one who has contacted a secular nonprofit organization and a church).

The results are shown in table 6.17. The first row of numbers are the standardized multiple regression coefficients for the effects of having contacted each kind of service organization on the average perceived effectiveness rating for each respondent's service portfolio (only those respondents who contacted at least one organization are included). The negative coefficient (−0.329) for the public welfare department means that average service portfolio effectiveness ratings were lower for people who had contacted the public welfare department than for people who had not contacted it. The coefficients in this row for secular nonprofits and faith-based organizations are not statistically significant, meaning that average service portfolio effectiveness ratings were neither higher or lower among respondents who had contacted these two kinds of organizations compared with those who had not contacted them. The positive coefficient in this row for congregations means that average service portfolio effectiveness ratings were higher among people who had contacted a congregation than among those who had not. These results are thus similar to those obtained previously from looking separately at the effectiveness ratings given to particular kinds of organizations; that is, churches are more favorably regarded than the two kinds of nonprofits, the public welfare department is less favorably regarded, and faith-based organizations are not regarded differently from secular nonprofits.

The remaining numbers in table 6.17 are derived from multiple regression equations in which additional factors are included to determine, as it were, if the differences among the kinds of organizations can be explained away by these other factors. In the second row of the table, the social characteristics that are controlled include gender, race, ethnicity, age, income, education, children, the number of problems a person mentioned having experienced in the past two years, whether that person had received informal support from family and friends, how often the person attended religious services, and the total number of agencies contacted for assistance. Of these factors, age and having received informal support were associated

TABLE 6.17

Effects of Contacting Different Types of Service Organizations on
Perceived Effectiveness Rating of Respondents' Service Portfolios
(Standardized multiple regression coefficients)

	Public Welfare Department	Secular Nonprofit Organization	Faith-Based Organization	Local Congregation
Controlling only for type of organization contacted	−0.329***	−0.015	0.001	0.234***
Also controlling for social characteristics of respondents	−0.169*	0.083	0.098	0.270***
Controlling for above and type of assistance sought	−0.232**	0.110	0.094	0.297***
Controlling for all of the above and kind of problems experienced	−0.172*	0.077	0.105	0.278***

Source: Lehigh Valley Survey, 2002.
Note: *$p < .05$ **$p < .01$ ***$p < .001$.

with higher effectiveness ratings and the number of problems experienced was associated with lower effectiveness ratings. From comparing the figures in the second row with those in the first row, it can be seen that the coefficient for the effect of having contacted the public welfare department is smaller when these social characteristics of respondents are taken into consideration. This suggests that some (perhaps as much as half) of the negative effect on effectiveness ratings that comes from contacting the welfare department can be explained by the fact that people who contact the welfare department differ from those who do not (especially in the number of problems they have experienced). None of the other three figures in the second row differ very much from the corresponding numbers in the first row. The positive effect of having contacted a church, these comparisons suggest, is not simply a function of the fact that people with different backgrounds or different problems have contacted a church for assistance. The numbers in the third and fourth rows simply provide further substantiation for these conclusions. When special problems, specific needs for assistance, and social characteristics are all taken into account, the coefficient for having contacted the public welfare department is still negative and significant (although not as strong as when none of these factors are controlled), the coefficient for congregations is positive, and the coefficients for secular nonprofits and faith-based organizations are not significant.

On balance, these results suggest that there are probably a variety of reasons why people who seek assistance from public welfare departments are less inclined to think they have been effectively helped than people who seek assistance elsewhere. The problem is partly that different kinds of people seek assistance from welfare departments than from private service agencies. Without attempting to infer too much from these data, closer inspection of some of the results, for instance, shows that people seeking financial assistance and employment or job training are the least likely to have felt that the assistance they received was effective. These are among the needs that most often lead people to seek assistance from the welfare department and they are also among the needs that are most difficult to fulfill. In contrast, people who say they were looking for spiritual assistance tend to give higher effectiveness ratings than people looking for other kinds of help, and of course these people are the most likely to seek help from churches. It may be, too, that seeking help from churches means that people receive support from friends, neighbors, and others they happen to know as a result of going to church, and that this kind of informal support makes them feel better. The data at least indicate that effectiveness ratings are higher among those who received informal support than among those who did not.

Conclusions

The evidence presented in this chapter demonstrates the difficulty in determining precisely what the kinds of needs are that may lead American families to seek assistance from others, how many people experience these needs, and how exactly these needs are related to income levels and other demographic characteristics. National data do indicate that about one person in eight (slightly more during economic downturns) has an income that places him or her below the official poverty level and that about one person in three has an income below 200 percent of the official poverty level. The data also show that the likelihood of families receiving public assistance is closely related to whether their income is below, at, or slightly above the poverty level.

I have emphasized, though, that national data also reveal the lack of any one-to-one correspondence between income levels and public assistance or between public assistance and perceived needs. As many as one-third of those with incomes below the official poverty line receive no means-tested public assistance. And of those who do receive public assistance, as many as one-third still experience needs for money, food, help in securing medical care, and the like. Although the exact percentages are hard to determine, one thing is clear: both among those who receive public assistance and among low-income families who do not, there are significant needs that people fulfill either on their own or with assistance from family members, churches, faith-based organizations, and other community agencies.

The religious characteristics of America's low-income population has received little attention, but the evidence we can piece together from large national surveys suggests that most low-income Americans do have some connection to religious organizations. About five people in six claim to have a religious identity, and at least three-quarters of those who claim a religious identity attend services once in a while. Even among those who do not claim a religious affiliation, about half have some contact with religious organizations each year. From this evidence alone, it would not be surprising if low-income families turned to churches or faith-based service organizations for help. And, from the standpoint of religious organizations, it is clear that there are large numbers of people within each of the major religious traditions who have needs and who could thus, potentially at least, be helped by religious organizations.

Among the people living in low-income neighborhoods in my study of the Lehigh Valley, more than half had sought assistance of one kind or another from a service organization in the community during the two years prior to the survey. The most common problems reported by people in these neighborhoods concerned illness and hospitalization, difficulties in paying for utilities and food, experiencing serious depression, and losing their jobs. The kinds of assistance sought followed the same pattern: medical and financial assistance, food or shelter, spiritual assistance, and employment or job assistance topped the list. Even among people with the lowest incomes, a large minority were self-sufficient. Yet it was equally clear that needs in the community were pervasive enough that service agencies were in high demand.

The public welfare department played an important role in the community, as evidenced by the fact that approximately 20 percent of the people surveyed had sought assistance from it in the past two years and by the fact that most of these people had several serious needs, including financial or medical problems and needs for food, shelter, or employment. But few people sought help only from the welfare department. For every six people who went to the welfare department for help, five also went to some other community organization for assistance. Secular nonprofit organizations, faith-based organizations, and congregations all played significant roles, at least judging from the kinds of organizations people in the survey indicated having turned to for assistance. Moreover, the kinds of problems people had experienced and the kinds of assistance they sought tended to be similar, whether they had turned to the public welfare department or to secular or faith-based service organizations. Only congregations differed significantly from the other kinds of organizations, chiefly because people with spiritual needs turned to them more often whereas people seeking financial assistance, food, or shelter, were less likely to seek help from congregations than from the other kinds of organizations.

The Lehigh Valley information suggests that people seeking assistance from community organizations may be less likely to regard public welfare departments as being effective and somewhat more likely to view congregations positively in these ways. Nonprofit organizations fell in between on these measures, but we found no evidence on the whole of recipients viewing faith-based organizations more favorably than secular nonprofits. In considering how effective people regarded the overall portfolio of organizations from which they had sought assistance, we saw that some demographic factors and the number and kinds of problems people had experienced were the significant influences, rather than whether an organization was faith-based or secular.

If faith-based nonprofits were not perceived as *more* effective than secular nonprofits, the data nevertheless gave considerable indication that faith-based organizations do have an important place alongside secular organizations. The substantial number of people who were seeking spiritual assistance turned more often to faith-based organizations than to secular organizations, just as they did to churches. Despite the fact that there were similar numbers of secular and faith-based organizations in the community, and despite the fact that the two kinds of agencies were used by about the same number of people, there was also some evidence in the survey that people may have *preferred* to deal with faith-based organizations if they could. Thus, when asked if they would prefer dealing with an organization sponsored by a coalition of churches or an organization not sponsored by such a coalition, nearly five to one opted for the church-sponsored organization.

Religious considerations do influence which service organizations people contact for help, but these are only some of the considerations that matter. For instance, regular churchgoers and evangelical Protestants are more likely to seek help from congregations than people with different religious profiles, but the people who seek help from faith-based organizations differ little on these characteristics from those who seek help from secular nonprofit organizations. Judging from the survey, a majority of people would like to deal with someone who believes in God when they seek assistance from a service organization, but only a minority care if the person they deal with shares their religion or is of a different religion.

Information from recipients and potential recipients about their perceptions does not answer questions such as whether job training programs actually give people the skills they need to earn a better income or whether drug rehabilitation programs actually help people to recover from addictions. This information about recipients' perceptions is nevertheless a valuable piece of the puzzle in thinking about the contribution of faith-based services to the future of civil society. Religion is probably more important to the lives of more lower-income people than the typical study of poverty or welfare programs would lead us to believe.[18] Lower-income families with needs turn not only to the welfare department but also to private nonprofit organizations for assistance. Congregations may not have the resources to deal with serious economic needs, but lower-income families do turn to congregations for spiritual and emotional assistance and, when they do, generally come away feeling that they have been well served. Those with more serious needs are more likely to turn to specialized service agencies. The recipients of faith-based agencies do not seem to differ much in kinds of needs or in feelings about effectiveness from the recipients of nonsectarian nonprofit organizations. This lack of difference between the two kinds of agencies, then, is similar to what we suggested may be the case in the last chapter, given the reasons why both kinds of agencies may include some expressions of faith but on the whole be guided by professional norms.

Promoting Social Trust

Most of the discussion of faith-based social services has focused on questions about the actual supply of services. But the way in which services are provided can also make a broader impact on the well-being of communities. Service provision can build trust in communities. It can restore people's faith in their fellow human beings and in themselves. Or it can undermine that faith, resulting in broken relationships, failure to seek the assistance one's family needs, or even a desire for revenge.[1] The usual way in which trust enters discussions of service provision concerns the possible untrustworthiness of recipients: are they telling the truth about their needs, are they cheating to get services they do not deserve?[2] Those are important questions whenever public monies are being spent. Here, though, I wish to turn the question around: do recipients regard caregivers as trustworthy, and if they do, what are their reasons for believing that caregivers can be trusted?

Understandably, scholars and policy makers have been concerned about the effectiveness of service organizations because these organizations are usually supported by tax dollars and philanthropic donations. Yet, from the perspective of clients, effectiveness is only one of the characteristics of service organizations and of individual caregivers that matter. Dealing with someone who is trustworthy, whom one knows well, or who shares one's background and values may also be important, especially because a person seeking assistance is in a subordinate or less powerful position than the person from whom assistance is sought. As a person having lost my job and needing help feeding my family, I may understand if the service agency I contact tells me I do not qualify under their guidelines or that they do not offer the kind of assistance I am seeking. But I do not want to come away feeling that I have been cheated or that the person I contacted was not sincere about wanting to help me.

Trust is at once totally straightforward, almost banal, and quite complex. If I say I trust my spouse, it is fairly simple to define what I mean. I consider her reliable, someone I can count on, and indeed I consider her to be trustworthy in keeping her word, meaning what she says, carrying out the responsibilities she agrees to, and so on. We have the same intuitive sense of what trust means when we say we trust our neighbors, trust the people we know in our congregations, trust our doctor, or trust our elected officials. At the same time, it is not always clear whether trust is a kind of emotional state, whether it is rooted in information or is a wager of faith, or whether it is influenced by our experiences with specific groups of people or is a more general outlook on life rooted in broader values and childhood training.[3]

The one thing about which social scientists agree is that trust is an important consideration in thinking about civil society.[4] It is a social norm that enhances the likelihood of cooperative relations taking place and that increases the chances of people helping one another, contacting those with whom it may be desirable to exchange goods or information, and being willing to maintain those relations even when they may not prove immediately beneficial or gratifying.[5] When trust is present, people feel that it is worthwhile to forgo immediate gratification. They give others the benefit of the doubt, all the while assuming that leaders and other citizens in their community will generally refrain from doing evil and try to do good. When trust breaks down on a large scale, as it sometimes does when public leaders are caught lying or when business executives steal from their shareholders, institutions suffer the consequences even if these leaders and executives do not. Institutions that have been sullied need to be cleansed so that the public's faith is restored and business as usual can return.[6] Trust is in this sense the cultural glue that keeps civil society together. It is also a barometer that we can use to judge how well civil society has been working and whether it is likely to work well in the future. This is why studies of national trends in levels of trust toward government and elected officials typically show that trust declines when economic conditions are bad, when crime is perceived to be rising, and when highly publicized scandals occur.[7] It is also why community leaders worry about signs of erosion in trust and argue that it is important to find ways to maintain and restore trust. If people are willing to trust others, at least when that trust is warranted, then we may suppose that they will give others the benefit of the doubt when things go wrong and will continue to interact with them. But if trust deteriorates, as some evidence suggests is happening, then we may worry that civil society will not be as strong in the future.[8] In the absence of trust, people have to look out more for themselves and take a skeptical attitude about their society to the extent that the social contract devolves into a Hobbesian war of all against all.[9]

Trust among Lower-Income People

In national studies, trust has generally been found to be lower among people in disprivileged segments of the population than among people with greater advantages, and this finding underscores worries that civil society may be eroding from the bottom, even though it may still be working fairly well for those at the top or in the middle.[10] Some evidence to this effect can be seen in table 7.1, which includes responses about trust from two of the national surveys considered in chapter 6. In the General Social Survey, only about one-quarter of people whose annual incomes were less than $20,000 thought most people could be trusted, compared with about one-third among those with incomes between $20,000 and $30,000, and more than four in ten among those with incomes of $30,000 or more (data from the 1996, 1998, and 2000 surveys, excluding persons who did not report their income). When the same question was asked in Putnam's Social Capital Benchmark Survey, the percentages in each category were higher (probably because of a different sampling scheme), but the pattern was the same: persons with lower incomes were less likely to express trust than those with higher incomes.

From this evidence, we might conclude that people with lower incomes—the people most likely to seek assistance from service organizations—would be predisposed to be distrustful of those with whom they had dealings at these organizations. Thus, it might be especially important for the staff at these organizations to demonstrate their trustworthiness. Yet the additional questions in table 7.1 from Putnam's survey suggest that people in the various income categories discriminate among different kinds of people when such questions about trust are included, and that the responses to some of these questions are relatively stable across the various

TABLE 7.1
Expressions of Trust by Level of Income (Percentage of respondents)

	Income < $20,000	Income $20,000 to $29,999	Income ≥$30,000	All Respondents
General Social Survey				
Most people can be trusted	24	34	43	36
(Number)	(1,473)	(833)	(3,079)	(6,140)
Social Capital Benchmark Survey				
Most people can be trusted	36	42	56	51
Trust people in neighborhood a lot	35	38	54	49
Trust coworkers a lot	40	46	57	54
Trust people at your church or place of worship a lot	65	69	76	73
Trust people who work in stores where you shop a lot	32	29	29	30
Trust local news media a lot	18	17	12	14
Trust police in your local community a lot	48	48	55	53
Agree people running my community do not really care what happens to me	43	40	28	32
(Number)	(3,321)	(3,145)	(15,330)	(21,664)
Lehigh Valley Survey				
Agree most people can be trusted	53	57	70	57
Disagree you can't be too careful in your dealings with people	10	8	6	8
Trust people in your immediate neighborhood whom you know well a lot	24	28	33	28
Trust people in your neighborhood whom you do not know well a lot	2	3	3	3
Trust people who serve as volunteers in your community a lot	17	16	18	17
Trust the leaders at your church or place of worship a lot	54	52	57	54
Agree I have a great deal of confidence in myself	68	72	74	72
Disagree I often do not trust myself	58	60	76	65
Agree government officials here in the Lehigh Valley don't really care much what happens to people like me	52	51	44	49
(Number)	(645)	(688)	(744)	(2,077)

income categories. The question that shows the greatest differences among income groups is about trusting one's neighbors. On questions about church people, shops, media, and police there are only small differences or no differences in the responses of people with lower or higher incomes. In fact, it is probably the dangers low-income families perceive in their neighborhoods that account for the differences in responses to the general question about trustworthiness.[11] And, as the more specific questions asked in the Lehigh Valley survey show, neighbors one knows well are much more likely to be trusted than neighbors one does not know well.

Two other observations from these data are especially relevant. One is that people with the lowest incomes are especially distrustful of community leaders—at least they feel that community leaders do not care much about what happens to them. This is a sense of powerlessness that could also be operative when people seek assistance from service agencies run by community leaders, but such agencies could play a large role in mitigating this feeling of not being cared for if they did demonstrate a caring response. The other observation is that people with low incomes in both the Putnam study and the Lehigh Valley study were much more likely to trust people or leaders at their churches or places of worship than almost any other target group. This level of trust might be explained in a number of ways—shared values, specifically religious values, affinity, personal familiarity, or religious people simply being more trusting in general—but they suggest that churches or service agencies sponsored by churches may have an advantage as far as garnering the trust of clients is concerned.

A word about self-trust is also in order. When respondents in surveys are asked questions about generalized trust ("most people can be trusted"), their answers may be projections of whether or not they believe themselves to be trustworthy. We might think of this self-trust variously as self-confidence, willingness to follow through on one's hunches or impulses, or even an indication of self-sufficiency. The two questions about self-trust from the Lehigh Valley survey suggest that as many as one-third of the people living in these low-income neighborhoods entertained some doubts about their own trustworthiness. And, although the data are mixed, one of the two questions shows a slight tendency for the lowest-income group to express these doubts more than those in the higher-income groups, and the other question shows a marked tendency in this direction.

Concerns about self-trust, then, pose yet another reason for thinking that the perceived trustworthiness of service agency personnel may be especially important. Consider the following example. A woman from one of the lowest-income neighborhoods in the Lehigh Valley who speaks no English had recently been to the hospital when she was interviewed. When the interviewer asked her if she felt she could probably trust the people at the hospital when she went there, she replied, "I don't really trust many people; no way, I don't even trust myself." But she was treated well at the hospital, and came away feeling better about people in general and about herself. In contrast, an untrustworthy staff person can conceivably erode not only the generalized trust of clients but also clients' confidence in their own judgment. We cannot, of course, know exactly what the causal influence may be, but it is also likely that people whose trust in themselves and others has been reinforced in the past will be more confident about seeking the help they need or will be more likely to believe that the service workers with whom they have dealings are trustworthy. Whatever the process, perceptions of trustworthiness would seem to be in the best interest of clients and service agencies alike.

Desirable Traits of Caregivers

The figures shown in table 7.2 reveal some important information about the characteristics of caregivers that are actually valued by people whose incomes and neighborhoods make them likely to be in need of social services. At the top of the list is a caregiver who is "the kind of person you can trust." Five-sixths of those surveyed in the Lehigh Valley said this was quite important to them in dealing with someone trying to help them. And the percentages were about the same among people in each of the three categories of income. Thus, it may be that people in low-income neighborhoods are distrustful of their neighbors, people in general, or even of themselves, but this does not mean that they devalue trust; indeed, they probably value it all the more.[12]

What does trust mean, though? The other items shown in table 7.2 give us some clues about the characteristics that might make a caregiver seem trustworthy (trust, after all, is a vaguely defined word that can take on a number of different meanings). When we think about trust, it is certainly common to think about *affability*—someone we get along with and feel comfortable being around. In the survey, a caregiver who is "friendly and easy to talk to" was especially valued by four out of five respondents, putting it second only to trustworthiness itself. *Sincerity* is another mark of a trustworthy person. A sincere caregiver is not only affable but a person who means what he or she says. Sincerity in the case of a caregiver may also mean being sincerely devoted to giving care or being sincerely interested in

TABLE 7.2

Characteristics Desired in Caregivers

(Percentage who say it is quite important to deal with someone trying to help you who has each characteristic)

	Income < $20,000	Income $20,000 to $29,999	Income ≥$30,000	All Respondents
Is the kind of person you can trust	82	81	86	83
Is friendly and easy to talk to	76	77	83	79
Seems sincere	72	74	75	74
Has a lot of knowledge and training	65	66	66	66
Has a lot of experience	65	62	61	63
Has a deep faith in God	61	53	38	50
Is someone you have known for a long time	59	49	37	48
Has faced similar problems in his or her own life	46	40	36	40
Is located close to where you live	46	37	28	37
Has religious beliefs similar to your own	42	37	26	35
Is well known in the community	36	29	14	26
Is of the same race or ethnic background as you	26	24	12	20
Is willing to break the rules to help you	23	17	13	17
Number	(645)	(688)	(743)	(2,077)

Source: Lehigh Valley Survey, 2002.

clients' problems. In the survey, three persons in four said this was quite important to them. Another basis for judging the trustworthiness of a caregiver is *competence*. I may appreciate the fact that my surgeon is friendly or sincere, but I especially want my surgeon to be competent. The survey suggests that competence is also among the most valued characteristics of caregivers: about two-thirds of the respondents said it was quite important to them for a caregiver to have a lot of knowledge and training or to have a lot of experience—two of the best ways to judge whether the person you are dealing with is competent.[13]

Then there are a number of other considerations that may enter into one's assessments of trustworthiness. *Faith*—faith in God, or a shared faith—is one. This may not be an important criteria for people in general, especially those who do not themselves believe in God. But there has been such an emphasis on religion in American culture that many people may associate faith in God with being altruistic or at least with having the kind of moral scruples that make one dependable. We shall consider this possibility again when we return to questions about churches and faith-based organizations, but for now, it is notable that about half of the survey respondents indicated that having a deep faith in God was quite important in a caregiver. *Familiarity* is another such consideration. It may not be important to everyone; indeed, as the old adage suggests, familiarity may breed contempt, so familiarity alone may not be a good indication of trustworthiness. Yet, if other things are equal, it is fairly common to hear people say they trust someone or prefer to deal with someone simply because they know that person or have had dealings with that person in the past. In short, familiarity generates the kind of trust rooted in having a good track record. In the survey, about half of the respondents picked having known a person for a long time as an important trait in caregivers. *Affinity* is another possible basis on which to make judgments about trustworthiness. Especially in a society of strangers, as ours is, we may seek markers that tell us people can be trusted because they are like us, have shared experiences, or share our values. In the survey, four people in ten said they valued having a caregiver who had faced problems similar to their own—a response that possibly suggested the importance of *empathy* as a basis for trust as well. Almost as many said this about having a caregiver who was located close to them—suggesting not only affinity, perhaps, but also *proximity* or *accessibility*. And at least one-third of those surveyed said it was important for a caregiver to share their religious beliefs, and one in five said the same thing about sharing a common racial or ethnic background. A caregiver who was well known in the community was considered an important trait by only one-quarter of those in the survey. This response could suggest that *prestige* or *reputation* is a basis for trust to some people. Interestingly, the trait least likely to be valued in the survey was willingness to break rules. This response is revealing because, although it might be grounds for trusting someone to know that this person was not rule-bound or would do special favors, it seems that rule breaking is probably also a reason to think that someone is *not* trustworthy.

The comparisons among income groups in table 7.2 are worth pondering as well. The characteristics of caregivers that were most frequently considered important in the survey varied only slightly among the three income groups (bear in mind that all the respondents lived in low-income neighborhoods). Regardless of income, the large majority valued trustworthiness, affability, sincerity, and competence. But the rest of the characteristics were all valued most by those in the *lowest* income category. Faith, familiarity, and affinity of various kinds were all valued more commonly among those with lower incomes than among those with higher incomes. Why? A likely explanation is that people with fewer resources feel a stronger need for cues about whom they can trust and whom they cannot. They have more at stake. Or have more to lose. For instance, if I have money, education, wide social networks, and other resources, I can take the risk of dealing with someone who merely seems to be affable, sincere, or competent. My resources help ensure that I will have found someone who is trustworthy and, if not, they provide me with a safety net of sorts. But if I have very few resources, I may want some additional assurances: someone whom I have known for a long time, whom I know I have easy access to, and who shares my values or background. And it may even be the case that my needing these extra assurances goes hand in hand with my being less trusting of people in general or less trusting of myself: give me some good reasons based on location and affinity to trust someone, and then I will, but ask me about people in general or about myself, and I will insist on the need to be careful in one's dealings. In short, one's resources may affect not only the likelihood of being trusting but also the *grounds* on which one is trusting. It may be too, of course, that people with different levels of resources are also exposed to different subcultures that influence their reasons to trust others. For instance, people with more resources may have more training and thus value competence more, while those with fewer resources may be more culturally isolated and thus value affinity and familiarity.

We can pin down these possibilities somewhat more precisely by examining the figures shown in table 7.3. These are from logistic regression analyses. From the longer list of caregiver characteristics we have been considering, I selected the five that showed the greatest differences among income categories (not including the two about religion, since those are probably influenced more by religious orientations than anything else). In the first row of the table, I show the coefficient (odds ratio) for the odds of saying each characteristic is quite important for those who say most people can be trusted compared with the odds among those who disagree with the idea that most people can be trusted, controlling for level of income (in thousands of dollars). In the second row, I do the same thing but substitute self-trust (disagreeing strongly with the statement "I often do not trust myself"). We see that in only one of the five comparisons is generalized trust associated with valuing these characteristics—and this relationship is not in the expected direction (i.e., preferring a caregiver who is close by is associated positively with generalized trust, not negatively). However, self-trust is significantly associated with valuing these traits in three of the five cases, and in all five comparisons the relationships are negative. In other words, if I trust myself, I am less likely to value these special or particularistic bases of trusting a caregiver. In contrast, if I lack confidence in myself (perhaps in my ability to make judgments on more universalistic grounds), then I value traits in caregivers such as familiarity, proximity, and affinity.

The remaining rows of table 7.3 show odds ratios for logistic regression models that include selected demographic variables. These results help in determining what kinds of resources (or the lack thereof) may be associated with valuing these special or particularistic traits in caregivers. Income remains significantly associated with valuing these traits in three of the five comparisons, meaning that even among people living in these relatively poor neighborhoods, each dollar of income reduces the likelihood of wanting a caregiver whom one has known for a long time, who lives nearby, or who is well known in the community. Put differently, even when all the other demographic characteristics are taken into account, people with lower incomes seem to rely more or place more importance on familiarity and proximity. Level of education, however, is even more consistently associated with valuing these traits. In all five comparisons, those with higher levels of education are less likely to value these traits than those with lower levels of education. The reason may be that education gives people the skills to seek caregivers based on more general criteria, such as expertise, or that it gives people more confidence in making judgments in the absence of personal familiarity or affinity. Age is also consistently associated with the likelihood of valuing these traits. One might imagine that older people would be more rooted in the community and thus would be more likely than younger people to value caregivers on the basis of knowing them for a long time or living close by. As it happens, this is the case. Older people actually do attach more importance to these traits than younger people do

TABLE 7.3

Logistic Regression Analysis of Selected Caregiver Traits
(Odds ratios for saying each trait is quite important)

	Known for a Long Time	Shared Similar Problems	Located Close By	Well-Known in Community	Same Ethnicity or Race
Controlling only for income					
Generalized trust	1.015	1.017	1.120***	1.001	1.054
Self trust	.737***	.952	.973	.639***	.511***
All variables simultaneously					
Income	.991***	.996	.991***	.991**	.994
Education	.887***	.949**	.949***	.851***	.837***
Age	1.012***	1.007*	1.014***	1.016***	1.016***
Female	1.283**	1.024	1.207*	1.036	1.013
Black	1.179	1.462*	1.280	2.053***	2.147***
Hispanic	1.849***	1.258*	1.838***	3.344***	3.054***
Self trust	.890	1.045	1.148	.813*	.652***

Source: Lehigh Valley Survey, 2002.
Note: *p < .05 **p < .01 ***p < .011.

(taking into account differences in income, education, etc.). The reason may be that younger people may feel confident or capable of making judgments on grounds other than personal ties. Gender is associated with valuing only two of the five traits. Women are more likely than men to value caregivers they have known for a long time and who are located close to where they live. The results for race also vary. Being African American is associated with valuing caregivers who have shared similar problems, are well known in the community, and are of the same racial or ethnic background. Being Hispanic is associated with valuing all of these traits. Hispanics are almost twice as likely as white Anglos to attach importance to knowing a caregiver for a long time and dealing with a caregiver located close to where they live, and they are more than three times as likely to value caregivers who are well known in their community and who are of the same racial or ethnic background. Finally, I have included self-trust in these models to see if the demographic factors explain away the relationships between a lack of self-trust and valuing these traits. One of the relationships (for knowing a caregiver a long time) does become insignificant, but the other two remain significant, indicating that low self-confidence is a factor in preferring a caregiver who is well known in the community or of the same racial or ethnic background, even when major demographic factors are taken into account.

Trustworthiness of Service Providers

Having examined some of the factors that affect how people think about trust, we can now return to the main question of how clients of service organizations perceive the trustworthiness of staff with whom they have dealings at these organizations. Table 7.4 shows the results obtained in the Lehigh Valley survey when people who had contacted specific service organizations were asked "how much did you feel you could trust the people you dealt with at [name of organization]—a lot, some, only a little, or not at all?" The results for the public welfare department refer to that specific agency; those for secular nonprofits and faith-based organizations are averages for all of the relevant agencies each respondent may have contacted; and those for local congregations refer to any particular congregation a respondent mentioned having contacted. The trustworthiness of staff at the public welfare department received the most variable ratings of the four kinds of service organizations. Although "trust a lot" was the modal response, it was given by only 38 percent of those who had contacted the welfare department within the past two years. Almost as many (33 percent) said they felt they could trust the people there only a little or not at all. At the other extreme, local congregations received the highest trustworthiness ratings: an overwhelming 84 percent said they felt they could trust the people they dealt with a lot, while only 6 percent felt they could trust people there only a little or not at all. Secular nonprofits and faith-based organizations fell in between. For both, slightly more than half of the people who had contacted these organizations gave them the highest possible trust ratings. Faith-based organizations were slightly more likely than secular nonprofits to receive the highest trust ratings, but they were also more likely to receive low ratings; thus, the mean ratings of the two kinds of organizations were virtually the same.

In table 7.5 I present results for respondents' service portfolios similar to the ones we considered earlier in chapter 6 for perceived effectiveness. In this table, multiple regression coefficients are shown for the effect of having contacted different kinds of organizations for assistance on the average

TABLE 7.4

Trustworthiness Ratings by Type of Service Organization Contacted
(Respondent's rating of the trustworthiness of people he or she dealt with at organization)

	Public Welfare Department	Secular Nonprofit Organization	Faith-Based Organization	Local Congregation
Trust a lot (4.0)	38%	55%	58%	84%
Trust some (3.0)	28%	31%	21%	11%
Trust only a little (2.0)	21%	8%	13%	4%
Trust not at all (1.0)	12%	4%	8%	2%
Mean trustworthiness rating	2.92	3.35	3.29	3.76
Standard deviation	1.04	0.78	0.93	0.60
Number	(389)	(437)	(309)	(177)

Source: Lehigh Valley Survey, 2002.

trustworthiness ratings respondents gave for all the organizations from which they had sought assistance.[14] In the first row, we see a pattern similar to the one we saw previously for effectiveness: trustworthiness ratings are negatively associated with having contacted the welfare department, unrelated to having contacted a secular nonprofit or faith-based organization, and positively associated with having contacted a church. It may be, of course, that people are simply predisposed to trust the people they deal with at service organizations because they trust people in general. To check out this possibility, the figures shown in the second row are from multiple regression equations that take into account whether a person agreed that people in general can be trusted, said he or she trusted people in the neighborhood (whom he or she did not know well), and generally trusted himself or herself. Each of these factors was significantly associated with the trustworthiness ratings people gave to those they had dealt with at service organizations. When these factors are taken into consideration, trustworthiness scores are still lower among those who have contacted the welfare department, but the positive coefficient for having contacted a church for

TABLE 7.5

Effects of Contacting Different Types of Service Organizations on Average Trustworthiness Rating of Respondents' Service Portfolios
(Standardized multiple regression coefficients)

	Public Welfare Department	Secular Nonprofit Organization	Faith-Based Organization	Local Congregation
Controlling only for type of organization contacted	−0.141***	−0.002	−0.043	0.067*
Controlling for other trust variables as well as organization	−0.141**	0.027	−0.068	0.094
Also controlling for social characteristics of respondents	−0.063	0.092	−0.016	0.119
Controlling for above and type of assistance sought	−0.131	0.098	−0.030	0.134
Controlling for all of the above and kind of problems experienced	−0.069	0.089	−0.015	0.118

Source: Lehigh Valley Survey, 2002.
Note: *p < .05 **p < .01 ***p < .001.

assistance is no longer statistically significant. The three remaining rows in the table introduce controls for the social characteristics of respondents, types of assistance sought, and kinds of problems experienced. When these factors are taken into consideration, none of the coefficients remains statistically significant.

These results suggest that whatever differences there are between the ways in which recipients perceive the trustworthiness of personnel at various kinds of service organizations are probably more a function of the recipient than of the differences in type of service organization. Perceptions of the trustworthiness of service organizations are (not surprisingly) higher among people who are inclined to trust others in general and who trust themselves and people in their community. These views about the trustworthiness of organizations tend to be lower among African Americans than among white Anglos or Hispanics. They are also lower among people who seek financial or employment assistance and who have lost their jobs or been laid off. They are, however, higher among people who have received informal sources of support, and there is some indication that they may be higher among people seeking food or shelter than among people seeking other kinds of assistance.

One final set of results from the Lehigh Valley survey will round out the picture of how much or how little people with low incomes are likely to trust various kinds of service organizations. The previous questions dealt with the perceptions, after the fact, of people who had actually contacted specific service agencies in the community. We also asked all respondents, whether they had sought assistance or not, how much they felt they could trust various organizations in their community. This is relevant information because it suggests that some organizations may have better reputations than others and, if nothing else, suggests that potential clients may be more predisposed to trust some more than others. It also provides some additional evidence on possible differences between religiously sponsored and secular organizations. In table 7.6 I show the percentages of people within each of the three income groups and in the total sample who said they felt they would trust each kind of organization or group listed either a lot or some; in other words, everyone who seemed favorably disposed toward trusting the organization or the people running that organization. About half the respondents say they would trust the people who run the public welfare department in their community this much, and the percentages are

fairly similar for each of the three income categories. Comparing these figures with the proportions of clients of the welfare department who gave
similar responses, it appears that the welfare department's reputation for
trustworthiness is lower in the general community than it is among people
who have actually been in contact with it. In short, contact may improve
rather than dampen people's perceptions of its trustworthiness. As table 7.6
also shows, though, the welfare department's reputation in the sample at
large appears to be lower than that of the Salvation Army—which was one
of the larger and more visible faith-based agencies in the community. In
turn, more people said they would trust the Salvation Army than said they
would trust United Way—one of the more visible secular nonprofit organizations. The table also shows that more people seemed willing to trust
"community organizations that help the needy" in general than was true of
either the welfare department or United Way. The remaining items in the
table asked for people to make choices between particular kinds of organizations. As between an organization that got money from private donors
and one that got money from the government, about one-third favored the
former, one-third favored the latter, one-fifth said it made no difference,
and the remainder were unable to respond. People with higher incomes
were more likely than those with low incomes to favor an organization
sponsored by private donors. The other comparison is between an organization sponsored by a coalition of churches and one not sponsored by a
coalition of churches. Here, there was a strong preference for the faith-
based organization: 63 percent favored it, 13 percent favored the non-
faith-based option, and 23 percent said it made no difference.

A Closer Look at Trust

The foregoing suggests that recipients of social services in the Lehigh
Valley generally felt that the service providers with whom they had dealt
were trustworthy. This is good news for service agencies, and there is no
reason to think the Lehigh Valley is distinctive in this regard. Conversations with agency directors show clearly that they recognize the value of
trust and make deliberate efforts to cultivate it. As one director observed:
"Especially in a volunteer or nonprofit organization you have to convince
people that you're worthwhile. It's not like in a business [where] people are

TABLE 7.6
Perceived Trustworthiness of Various Groups

	Income < $20,000	Income $20,000 to $29,999	Income ≥$30,000	All Respondents
Percentage who say they trust each of the following a lot or some				
People who run the public welfare department in your community	48	40	46	45
People who run the Salvation Army in your community	63	62	69	65
People who run the United Way in your community	48	52	63	55
People who run community organizations that help the needy	68	68	79	72
Percent who would trust more				
An organization that got money from private donors	26	36	42	34
An organization that got money from the government	38	30	27	32
No difference/it depends/don't know	35	33	31	34
Percent who would trust more				
A community organization sponsored by a coalition of churches	62	66	62	63
A community organization not sponsored by a coalition of churches	15	12	12	13
No difference/it depends/don't know	22	21	27	23
Number	(645)	(688)	(743)	(2,077)

Source: Lehigh Valley Survey, 2002.

going to look at the bottom line. With us, what they have to look at is, 'Do I really believe in this?' and that's why I think [trust] is extra important." Or, as another director put it: "People trust you if you deliver on the services. It's better to say 'I can't do that,' if you can't deliver. It is never good to promise things to people that you can't deliver on. If you deliver, people respond to that positively. They trust. They refer others. Most of our stuff is word of mouth, so the trust factor is very, very important."

Directors try to cultivate trust in a variety of ways. One says he spends a lot of time getting to know people in the community and listening to their concerns. He participates in public meetings and writes articles for the newspaper because he believes having a good public image is an important aspect of trust. Another (who works more directly with clients) says she emphasizes respect and dignity in her relationships with clients. "From the moment they come in our front door they are greeted in a positive manner. It's 'how can we help you?' People often come to us very angry and upset and frustrated. They may not be able to convey what they need. They may not understand it themselves and so we try and identify what their immediate concern is and then through conversations develop that relationship."

The most commonly mentioned strategies for cultivating trust are carrying through on one's commitments, expressing genuine care and compassion, listening, communicating well, avoiding scandals that would damage the organization's reputation, and simply being a reliable provider of services. Other activities that directors sometimes mention include keeping information confidential, planning well, having staff who can speak clients' native languages, cultivating good relationships with community leaders and other agency directors, holding regular staff meetings at which problems are discussed openly, and conducting self-studies or commissioning independent audits of the organization.

From these comments it is evident that agency directors want to be perceived as trustworthy and want their organizations to be regarded that way. Some of them also recognize the larger role they can play in promoting self-trust among their clients and in cultivating trust within wider circles throughout the community. But it is less clear whether anyone, community leaders and scholars alike, has thought very deeply or systematically about what trust actually is. Most recent studies of trust, although useful, have focused less on understanding the nature of trust in real-life relation-ships and more on the significance of trust in larger societal contexts.

Too often, trust is treated as if it were a single, easily quantifiable vari-able. This assumption is readily evident in data from surveys, such as those we have just considered, where groups of people are compared in terms of how much or how little trust they have in certain target groups. Although the target groups—neighbors, volunteers, politicians, people in general—may vary, it is assumed that trust is simply a matter of degree, not some-thing that differs in content. In the remainder of this chapter, I want to challenge that assumption by examining in greater detail how the recipi-ents of social services understand trust.

My central argument is that trust is as much a reflection of *culture* as it is of behavior. What I mean by this is that we are more or less inclined to trust someone, not only because of how that person has treated us, but also because of how we frame our thinking about that person. For instance, a particular political leader may have never done anything to harm me or to violate my confidence in his or her ability to govern, yet I may be inclined to distrust that leader simply by virtue of the fact that he or she is a politi-cian. In contrast, one of my close friends may disappoint me again and again by being late for appointments, but I continue to trust that friend—even saying that I trust him or her to be late—because I have other reasons for considering this person trustworthy, such as our lengthy acquaintance, our having been through hard times together, or our sharing a number of common interests.

As these examples suggest, trust involves having reasons, or what we might term "warrants," for trusting. Warrants are descriptions of the un-stated assumptions that provide backing for decisions or arguments.[15] They often remain implicit because they reflect deep-seated values, but they emerge in response to "why" questions, such as why did you feel you could trust someone? Warrants are often evident in public argumentation, especially when issues or positions are explicitly contested. For instance, political leaders seek to show the public that they are trustworthy by gar-nering endorsements from influential newspapers, by shaking hands and kissing babies, and sometimes by making appearances at their houses of worship. These strategies give us warrants for believing that whatever trust we may place in these leaders is reasonable. If our trust seems warranted, then we are likely to continue in the conviction that someone is trustworthy. But if we cannot find such warrants, our trust can easily be dismissed as gullibility (as in the case of someone who "trusts" that they will win the lottery).

The evidence we considered earlier in the chapter about the traits of caregivers that recipients value provides a starting point for thinking about warrants. *Effectiveness* is the most common reason people give for saying they trust caregivers or service organizations. When pressed to say why they trusted a caregiver or a service organization, recipients often point simply to the fact that they were helped, as if to say that no other warrant is necessary. A woman who received help from a faith-based organization, for instance, said she had no expectations at the start, but gradually came to trust the people there "because of the way they were handling my case." She added that she knew she "was going to get some good results back." It is not surprising that someone is willing to trust an organization that produces desired results. In contrast, the organizations people say they do not trust are typically ones that failed to produce results. As one welfare recipient remarked about a job placement agency, "They're no good. They ain't helping nobody get jack." But people sometimes find ways to express trust that do not depend so directly on results. Effectiveness can also be a judgment made on the basis of means, for example. They "go through the procedures and the standards" was how one welfare recipient put it. It was reassuring to this recipient that the office did pay careful attention to these procedures and standards.

Besides effectiveness, another common warrant for trusting a caregiver is the belief that the caregiver is a person of *integrity* or an *altruistic* person who is sincerely trying to help. A remark about not trusting a caregiver at a child services agency illustrated the former: "They tell me one thing and then write down something else on the forms." Altruism is a complicated notion that we will consider in greater detail in chapter 8, but a good example of how it can be a warrant for trust comes from a woman who said she trusted the Salvation Army because "they weren't knocking at your door and trying to sell you something." She explained that "they weren't taking anything" and were just "there to provide a service." As if to suggest that she worried that she might be gullible for believing this, though, the woman added that "when you have no other choice and your back is against the wall, you have to trust, no matter how you feel about it." Integrity and altruism, we should note, suggest that trust has a moral dimension. We trust someone because we believe that person to be of good moral character.

Competence or training, as we saw, were among the more commonly mentioned traits of caregivers that people said they desired in the survey. When asked specifically about their reasons for trusting or not trusting caregivers, though, recipients were less likely to associate competence or training with trust. They usually seemed to believe that the caregivers they dealt with were competent, and thus did not base their trust as much on this factor as on other traits. The few exceptions were people who had been in the hospital or had other dealings with the medical system. They knew that special competence was necessary and for this reason expressed misgivings if this level of expertise was not evident. "They're not doctors, they're interns" was how one recent surgical patient explained why she felt obliged to "double check everything." She considered it only reasonable to be suspicious: "How would you feel going to an intern? This is a person learning to be a doctor. I'm on oxygen and all this stuff. Would you feel safe?" In contrast, a man who had been in the hospital said he went to the hospital he did because "they just seemed more skilled," whereas he distrusted the staff at another hospital because he knew people who had been misdiagnosed there.

Apart from the specific competence of the caregiver, the status or reputation of the service organization sometimes makes a difference, as the second example suggests. A woman who received meals from Meals on Wheels said she trusted the people who brought meals "because they're from the County." She lived in a neighborhood where it was unsafe opening the door for just anyone. Another woman who went to a government agency for help after everything else failed, for instance, said she wasn't sure how much the agency would actually help her, but she did trust the people she talked to at the office. Asked why, she replied, "Big Brother, you're supposed to be able to count on them." She acknowledged the irony in her statement by chuckling as she said it. She knows that many people do not trust the government, so she then points out that besides thinking she could trust the organization because it was the government, she had also heard good things about the agency from people in her neighborhood.

The importance of *affability* comes through in comments about trusting caregivers because they are friendly or simply likeable for some reason.

"They just seemed friendly" or "I felt comfortable" are common remarks about trusted caregivers. It is difficult from brief comments in interviews to know exactly why clients regard some caregivers as more likeable than others, but being on the same wavelength or sharing the same mannerisms is often implied, and these characteristics are associated with social class and with the status differences between clients and professionals or middle-class volunteers as well. For instance, a lower-income woman who had taken classes taught by volunteers at a nonprofit organization in her community complained that she did not trust the volunteers because she "didn't know them." Then she elaborated by saying she "did not like the people" and further explained that the volunteers were people with money. "They're snobby," she asserted. A man who had been on welfare also provided a revealing comment about the status differences he perceived between himself and the case worker. "I just felt like I was being violated because of the questions they asked," he commented. He understood at one level that these questions were required, but he resented being asked them because they were not what he was used to among people he considered equals.

Besides the sheer fact of being friendly or unfriendly, caregivers are trusted or not trusted because of other personal attributes that, if they were physicians, would be described as bedside manner. "They seemed to be really down to earth" was the way one woman described the people who helped her at a neighborhood service agency. In contrast, she complained about the impersonality of another agency. "They got machines. Machines don't help too much. You call and you want to talk to an individual, and you never get to talk to an individual. They say hold the line and we'll let you talk to somebody and the next thing you know they disconnect you."

The last comment points to the importance of *accessibility* as a warrant for trust. It is easier to trust someone if that person is available when you need assistance. Accessibility also has metaphoric uses in discussions of service agencies. Talking about another agency, the woman who was getting meals from Meals on Wheels backtracked a couple of times when asked if there were any organizations she did not trust. She didn't want to seem critical, but then she mentioned one, explaining that "they're never there for me." She did not mean literally that she was unable to speak to someone at the agency, but she implied that people there were unavailable.

Affinity is, as we noted in discussing the survey results, more often valued as a basis for trust among people with few resources and especially among African Americans and Hispanics. Experiences of discrimination and skepticism about the intentions of caregivers from different backgrounds seem to be part of the reason why affinity is especially valued. A mother who had not only received help from a food bank but volunteered there, for example, said she came away with "a sour taste in my mouth" because nobody there was Puerto Rican and whenever she took her children with her and something happened, it was her children who got blamed.

The other argument I want to propose is that warrants are *domain-specific*. How we think about trust within families, for instance, is different from how we think about trust in business or politics. This is because we do not make up our warrants from whole cloth. Rather, we contextualize our thinking about trust in the same way that we talk differently about ourselves to our family and to people at work. Our warrants are composed of scripts that weave meanings from conversations we have in specific settings or about those settings. We learn that different kinds of behavior are expected in different places, so we base our warrants for trust on those expectations. To say that a thief can be trusted is, for example, not simply a cynical statement but one that acknowledges certain predictable kinds of behavior among thieves. We would give quite different reasons for trusting a thief than we would for trusting our best friend. The difference is not simply one of degree, that is, the likelihood of saying that family members or business associates are trustworthy. It is rather a difference of kind: we base our trust in family members on different reasons than we do our trust in business associates. In the one instance, we have expectations about intimacy, love, caring, and support. If we can think of ways in which family members behave or can be expected to behave in keeping with those expectations, then our trust in these family members is warranted. In the business context, intimacy and support will be less important than expectations about competence, training, or dependability.

Although warrants for trust are domain-specific, these domains are nevertheless permeable. The expectations we develop in one domain may be applicable in other domains, or we may at least think they are. For instance, we may trust our business associates because they seem like family, and our employers actually may try to cultivate this expectation by having parties, sending birthday and holiday greetings, and talking about their employees as "one big family." Thus, we must pay attention not only to the distinctive language people use to explain trust in particular settings, but also their use of language that seems out of place, or that is even deliberately out of place, as in the case of some comparisons or metaphors.

These considerations are relevant for thinking about the reasons people may give for trusting some service providers more than others and for making sense of the broader contributions that congregations and other faith-based organizations can make to levels of trust and trustworthiness in communities. My argument is that families serve as the primary domain in which people learn to trust and thus provide a common set of warrants in which to think about trust.[16] Congregations draw on this primary language, likening themselves to families and, through their association with families, encouraging people to use family-oriented warrants in their thinking about trust within congregations. Congregations extend family-oriented warrants through notions of common belief, familiarity, and long-term commitment. Faith-based service organizations can draw on some of these warrants, but they are hybrid entities that also require other warrants, such as reliability and professionalism. Non-faith-based service organizations are also hybrid organizations: relying on language about professionalism but also communicating messages about familiarity, caring, congeniality, and the like. In short, it is an empirical question to determine whether faith-based organizations have some special advantages in cultivating trust or whether the warrants they communicate are similar to those of other organizations.

Trust within Families and among Friends

Children learn to trust through interacting with their parents, siblings, and childhood friends. Much of why we trust or do not trust others probably depends on these relationships. A child who has been abused or who has felt betrayed by the death of a parent will often find it difficult to trust others.[17] Barring such experiences, family relationships are likely to reinforce trust, at least in comparison with the interaction one may experience later in the wider world. It stands to reason that most people trust members of their own family, even if they don't trust their neighbors, politicians, or people in general. There are good reasons to trust family members, at least we would suppose so from what surveys tell us about people's likelihood of trusting family, friends, and neighbors, compared with politicians or business leaders.[18] But what are these reasons? Surveys tell us only that most people trust their families, not why they do so or what the common language is in which people describe their trust. Are people able to discriminate among different family members or friends, saying why they trust some more than others? How do people explain why some of their most intimate associates are more trustworthy than others? And what do these comments tell us about trust more generally?

When people provide warrants or explanations for the various relationships or activities in which they are involved, their language often takes the form of narratives. They may say only that they trust someone because that person "is there" or "is dependable," but they typically have a story (or several stories) to which they can resort if asked to elaborate. And the more there is to explain, the longer or more complex these narratives become. For instance, warrants for choosing a career, risking one's life to help another person, or converting to a different religious faith usually require telling a story that accounts for something unexpected, out of the ordinary, or life-changing.[19] It is notable, therefore, that warrants for trusting family members and friends are usually brief, even terse. What is being communicated by this brevity is that trusting family members and friends is *not* something that requires much explanation. Trustworthiness is to be expected of family members and friends. Still, even the briefest of explanations include warrants, and these explanations often become longer when people articulate their reasons for picking one family member or friend rather than another.

The most common warrants for trust among family members and close friends focus on characteristics of persons, rather than on specific deeds or aspects of the relationship. These characteristics include being "kind," "sweet," "honest," and "sincere." Other such qualities include being non-judgmental, hard working, responsible, law-abiding, objective, open, and straightforward. Sometimes people refer to qualities that specifically connote trustworthiness, such as "helpful" or "dependable." The fact that such a wide range of words is evident, though, suggests that trust is being warranted, not so much by someone being specifically trustworthy, but by that person being of good moral character in general. One woman illustrated this point rather clearly in explaining why she picked her mom as the person she trusted most: "She's a good person." In short, our most trusted associates among friends and family are not necessarily the people who will help us out of a jam (although we hope they will), but those who are *good* people—the kind we want to have as friends and who we believe will help us if they possibly can.

Good people are trustworthy because their goodness is genuine, real, or authentic. This is probably why words such as *honest, sincere,* and *open* surface as often as they do. An authentic person can be trusted because there is little danger of deceit, false pretenses, or misunderstanding. An authentic person is, as one woman explained, "someone you can believe in." Such people are mirrors of our best selves. We feel implicitly that we can trust them because they know us and we know them in a way that precludes artifice. One man provided an interesting illustration of this emphasis on authenticity in explaining why he and his brother trusted each other so deeply. "More than anybody else he knows the kind of person I am. He's more than willing to just deal with the fact of things, things that I hide from other people. It's so hard to describe. Like, there's two different individuals in me: one that I would show to people at work or to people I just met, and then the actual me. I'm free to be that actual me with [my brother]."

When relationships with family members or close friends are mentioned, it is usually the strength, quality, or durability of the relationship that is mentioned as a warrant for trust, rather than a specific instance of assistance or support. A woman who says she trusts her family says simply: "because they are here all the time." An older woman who trusts her children describes them as "the closest things to me," adding "I've had them all my life." Another older woman picks a longtime friend, explaining, "She's that type of person; she's never, never let me down."

Warrants for trusting family members also reveal that *membership* is an important factor in many people's minds. When explaining why they trust certain family members, people make statements such as "they are just family," "mom is mom," "they're part of my family," "she's my sister," and "he's my brother." Comments about friends are less likely to emphasize membership or roles. But people often use family terms as ways of explaining why they trust friends. For example, one man says his friend is like a brother. A woman picks a friend who, she says, is "like a mother, like a sister." Membership, it appears, trumps actual behavior. We do not base our trust in family members in calculations about their willingness or capacity to serve our interests. Rather, we place them inside a collectivity in which we also are members, and the fact of our common membership, our common identity, is enough to convince us that these persons can be trusted. One of the people in our Lehigh Valley study actually captured this idea quite nicely: "It's a circle. When you're inside the circle, you're under my trust. When you're out, you're out."

We might summarize, therefore, by saying that the trust that exists within families and among close friends is warranted in terms of unconditionality. The person who is trusted is there unconditionally, so temporality is not a concern, and that person is present as a whole being, or as someone who has deep and enduring traits, such as kindness. This kind of trust, we might say, is robust in the sense that it is difficult to break. There may be specific instances in which trust is violated, such as a time when someone is not physically present or when that person fails to behave in a loving way. But trust involves taking the long view, or taking a holistic view, and thus disregarding these exceptions.

Our primary language of trust—the language we learn about trust as children—is thus a language that accounts for our willingness to trust others in terms of who they are as persons. We have that information because of the durability of our relationships with them. We have interacted with them in different settings and thus have seen different sides of their personalities and different aspects of their characters. This information, based on observations not only in different settings but over a period of time, enables us to make generalizations about their behavior, and it is further validated by the fact that we have mutual acquaintances who can vouch for our conclusions. In these ways, trust is deeply embedded within the social relationships in which we regularly engage with our families and friends.

Trust in Congregations

Congregations are like families in that relationships are often long-term and involve the sharing of intimate details of one's personal life.[20] This may have been more true in the past than it is today, when congregations are larger and when many people have switched congregations or moved to new communities. From the evidence we considered in chapter 3, though, we know that congregations typically are still places where people establish close friendships, participate in small groups, share their stories in these groups, and come to depend on one another. Like families, the relationships that take place in congregations typically presume certain shared experiences and values, such as working together on committees or participating in the Eucharist and listening to sermons that reinforce common beliefs. The religious teachings communicated in most congregations, as we saw in chapter 3, encourage members to care for and support one another, just as family members are expected to provide care and support. For all these reasons, we often think of congregations and families as having much in common. Clergy frequently refer to their congregations as families and encourage members to treat one another as family members; as one pastor put it: "I like to operate believing that we are all part of a large family of God and that we need to operate not as a dysfunctional family but as a functional family." We would not be surprised, therefore, to find people talking about trust within congregations in terms of the same warrants they use when talking about trust in families. In addition, trust within congregations can be warranted with reference to specifically religious language, such as trust based on common convictions or Christian love.

The frequency with which people use the same language in talking about congregations as they do in talking about family and friends suggests that the same warrants for trust are involved. People say they trust the caregivers at congregations from whom they have received help because these caregivers actually are their friends or at least behave in exactly the same way friends do. Congregational caregivers are good people who not only try to be helpful, but also are nice, familiar, safe, and easy to talk to. They are sincere, caring, and easy to get along with. "I feel like they're my friends," says one woman who has received help from her congregation. "I'm able to talk to [them]." Another woman says she trusts people at her church for help "because I have known them for years." A man says he trusts church people who have helped him "because they would never do anything to hurt me intentionally." Recipients of help from congregations also reveal the importance of friendship in explaining why they were guarded in how much they felt they could trust church people. A woman who had sought help because she had too little money for food explained that she trusted people at her church for assistance "because they've been my friends." But she added: "I'm not in a deep friendship with them [so] I'd never tell them personal things. I'm not that close with them." Similarly, an older woman who had been in the hospital said she didn't completely trust people at her church, even though they had helped her, "because I didn't really know them. I knew of them, but I didn't know them." Another woman admitted that she did not trust people at her church, explaining that "they think they're friendly" when in her experience they were not.

When talking about religious congregations from which they have received help, people often mention something about shared values. A woman who had been relying on people at her mosque for help with child care and periodic financial assistance said she trusts these people "because we have the same religious values." An older man who is a longtime member of his church and who had been ill recently said he trusts the "majority" of people at his church because "you know what they're like" and "they have the same purpose as you have." People also signal shared values by emphasizing that they belonged to the congregation from which they received help or were regular participants. It was evident that their trust was contingent on their continuing membership or participation. They knew that if they ceased participating, they would be less likely to receive help. A woman who had received help from a Catholic church when she was ill articulated this point in describing how people from the church "were always there" and "would call me to see how I was doing." But she no longer attends that church and now says "they call me once in a long while, but before they used to call me more."

Thinking about this emphasis on shared values in relation to what we just considered about trust in families is helpful for gaining a clearer sense of why people talk about shared values. With family members, affinity is implied by common membership, by the sheer fact of being in the same family. This warrant for trust makes it unnecessary to talk about shared values in that context. A congregation is a larger social unit; affinity among its participants cannot be assumed, and this is even more clearly the case for those outside the congregation or less actively involved in it who may receive assistance. Shared values become a way of affirming affinity, or common membership, and thus trust. People understand these values to be religious or rooted in religious teachings and practices. But it is not so much the substance or content of these values that seems to matter as it is the perception that they are *shared*. For instance, it is rare for someone to say that "we believe in Christ" or "they follow the Bible," whereas it is more common to hear more generic references that imply sharing or membership ("they're from the church") without spelling out what exactly is shared.

Another warrant for trust that occurs with surprising frequency in the language recipients use to talk about their trust in congregations concerns privacy. Their reason for trusting pastors or others from whom they receive help in congregations includes the perception that their needs, or the help they have received, will be kept confidential. This warrant sometimes occurs in remarks about trust within families, but is less evident in those remarks, apparently because people assume that what is said or done within families stays within families. In contrast, congregations are what sociologists call secondary groups, meaning that they are large enough that one does not know all the members intimately, yet important enough that it matters what people think. Thus it is potentially embarrassing to receive help from a congregation because word can spread around about one's problems. Knowing that one's problems will be kept confidential is thus an important aspect of trust. One woman provided a nice illustration of this point as she talked about being "down" and "needy" and seeking help from people at her church. "I went to those people and [they] just kept it right in the house of the Lord. It didn't go no further. I felt as though I could go to one of the pastors or one of the sisters and pour my heart out to them." Another woman talked about her priest in much the same way. "As far as I know," she observed, "he's not known to gossip."

The fact that recipients of assistance from congregations so rarely talk in explicitly religious language about their reasons for trust has important implications for thinking about the differences between faith-based and non-faith-based social services. As we saw in the survey results, receiving assistance from congregations seems to be associated with more positive feelings about the trustworthiness of caregivers than receiving assistance from other kinds of organizations. The qualitative data from interviews, though, suggests that this trust is rarely understood or explained in terms of the actual faith-content or religious beliefs of congregations. It is more often understood by recipients as a matter of congregations being like family and friends—congregations are places where friendships develop and where friends help one another, and trust of caregivers in congregations is thus warranted in terms of knowing people well or over a long period of time, feeling a common bond with them, and feeling safe in their presence. To be sure, these qualities of the social relationships within congregations are rooted in religious beliefs and practices. Were it not for these beliefs and practices, congregations would lose their distinctive identity and purpose. Yet it is the social relationships, and the language for understanding these relationships, that seems to matter more than religion itself. Thus, as we consider how people explain their trust in other faith-based or secular service organizations, we will want to see if faith is emphasized in those contexts or whether trust is embedded in different understandings.

Trust in Service Agencies

The language people use to talk about the trustworthiness of caregivers at service agencies is quite different from how they talk about trust in families and congregations. Although they still mention personal traits such as sincerity and friendliness, these warrants for trust are much less important than aspects of the service transaction itself. A Spanish-speaking man who took English classes at a service organization in his community said he really had no expectations in advance about whether he could or could not trust the organization, but afterward he came away trusting it principally because the class was helpful and the teacher was good. A woman who needed a wheelchair heard from an acquaintance about a civic organization that would provide one free of charge. She trusted her friend enough to contact the organization; she now trusts the organization itself because it came through for her. A man who sought help from a faith-based service agency said he really did not feel he could trust the people there before he contacted the agency. "I was just gambling. If they help me, fine. If they don't, I'll look for somebody else." Because the agency helped him, he feels he might trust it enough to contact it again if he ever needs help.

As these examples suggest, and as I discussed previously, the warrants people give for trusting service agencies mostly emphasize the agencies' effectiveness in meeting their needs. The relationship people have with these agencies is like a business transaction; if an initial transaction is successful, then trust is established and further dealings can be imagined. As in the business world, trust is further reinforced by knowing in advance or learning through interaction that the caregiver is competent. Caregivers' credentials help, as in the case of doctors, therapists, and social workers. In addition, referrals play an important role. The word of a trusted acquaintance matters, especially if that acquaintance has credentials or has had good experiences. Not many people mention efficiency, but this too, as in business, is a warrant some people give for explaining why a particular service agency was trustworthy. As one man noted in discussing the skills program he had attended: "They're like a banking organization; they seemed to be very organized." Other warrants, such as affability and competence, come into the picture as well, but it is clear that the initial contact with a service organization is generally like an arms-length transaction that results in trust if the transaction is effective and generates mistrust if it is not.

The kinds of trust people experience in their families (and often in their congregations) provide a reference point for how they talk about the trustworthiness of service organizations. The typical formulation is for someone to say that she received the assistance she needed and, yes, the people she dealt with at the service organization were helpful and trustworthy, but not in the same way that friends or family members are. For instance, a man who went to a program offered by a service organization in his neighborhood for people joining the workforce after being on welfare remarked that he trusted the staff at this organization as much as he could: "I trusted them, but not like I trust my friends. I trusted them like business people who are getting paid to help other people."

It helps people to trust service organizations if they have some reason to regard people at these organizations like friends or family. Volunteering for the same organization from which one receives assistance is a way of making this connection. Volunteering establishes personal contact with staff members and other volunteers, and this contact becomes a basis for trust. For instance, a woman who received assistance from a community development organization explained that she trusted the people there, even before she received help, because she "knew the girl that ran the program" as a result of having volunteered at the program.

The public welfare office provides people with a different frame of reference for talking about trust. As we saw in chapter 6, most people who seek assistance from the welfare department also seek assistance from private service agencies. For these people, then, it is possible to compare the two. The language they use to describe their encounters at the welfare office is one of rights or, perhaps more accurately, *entitlement;* as one woman remarked in talking about going to get help for her son: "I did trust them; it was just something [my son] was entitled to." Usually people do not speak explicitly of rights and entitlement, but they describe going to the welfare office with a sense that they can trust people there because they are asking for what is rightfully theirs. The welfare office is only one kind of agency that generates this language of entitlement-based trust. Other government agencies do, too. For instance, a woman who needed insurance to pay for medical treatment for her baby sought help from her congressman; when asked if she went trusting that he would help, she replied, "Yes, well, it's the government; you're supposed to be able to count on them." A man who got a loan from the city's real estate department had been told by someone he knew that he was entitled to the loan; as he filled out the paperwork, he trusted that the staff person was doing the right things, and when the loan came through, he felt that his trust was warranted. The sense of entitlement that undergirds (and sometimes undermines) people's trust in government agencies is generally absent from the language people use to describe their interaction with private organizations. At these organizations, caregivers seem more trustworthy because they behave differently from case workers at the welfare department. Instead of enforcing the rules, even if those rules are fair, they take a more personal approach. They seem trustworthy because the client has *chosen* the organization, usually on the basis of having heard good things about it from friends and neighbors, rather than being required to seek assistance from this particular organization.

The warrants people offer for trusting in faith-based service agencies do differ in some ways from those given for nonsectarian agencies. People sometimes mention that they selected a faith-based organization in the first place, or that they had more confidence in it, because it was religiously oriented. For instance, a woman who had misgivings about some of the service organizations she had dealt with observed: "I can't say that about the Salvation Army, because Salvation Army is Christian people and they help out and they make you feel welcome." But the religious dimension of faith-based organizations is by no means a safeguard against mistrust. Clients of these organizations talk about trust in much the same way that clients of secular organizations do. The religious element may provide a bond or sense of commonality that overcomes disappointments or misgivings. The presence of faith, though, can also be a source of greater disappointment and even mistrust if other problems arise. A woman who had sought marital counseling from a counseling organization provided an illustration of this dynamic. In her case, the organization was not faith-based, but the therapist and the woman shared the same faith and this was one of the reasons why the woman trusted the therapist. Eventually, however, the therapist and the woman fell into disagreement because the therapist wanted the woman to leave her husband and the woman wanted to preserve her marriage. The woman felt more betrayed than she would have otherwise because the religious bond had led her to expect the therapist to give different advice.

When Trust Is Broken

A common understanding of trust is that it is fragile enough that it can easily be broken by misdeeds in private life or can even be damaged on a large scale by public scandals or a sagging economy. We may have an instinctive desire to trust other people, but we learn quickly that human nature is frail. We schedule an appointment with a friend and our friend fails to show up. We vote for a political candidate who a short while later becomes embroiled in an ethical scandal. We seek help from a service agency and the help is inadequate or endlessly delayed. It is for these reasons that social observers have expressed so much worry over the declining levels of trust in our society. Trust is apparently so fragile that it is hard to maintain, especially in the face of rising divorce rates, crime, political corruption, and the like.

But we probably gain a better understanding of trust, especially in relation to social services, if we take a different view. Given the many ways in which trust can be broken, it seems to me that trust is actually remarkably robust. Despite disappointments and broken relationships, most of us continue to trust our friends and families.[21] We may believe that public leaders do not have our best interests at heart, and yet we often express high levels of confidence in their ability to govern, especially in times of national crisis. We may be struggling financially and receiving relatively little from the service agencies in our community and yet, as the survey results suggest, remain convinced that the directors and caregivers at these agencies are worthy of our trust.

Part of the reason that trust is this robust can be found in the warrants for trust that we have been considering. These warrants are seldom based only on precise calculations about the likelihood of receiving assistance from someone or from some organization. In the interview material we have considered, we heard people talking about trust rooted in perceptions of effectiveness. But we also noted how people were willing to withhold judgments, or to trust because they had no other choice, or to anticipate the best because of the agency's reputation. Warrants for trusting caregivers also reflect assumptions about human goodness, or at least the goodness of people with whom we are acquainted, and about sincerity, honesty, and authenticity. These warrants sometimes borrow from the primary language we learn to use about our families and friends and we extend this language into more impersonal spheres. Thus, even when people have been disappointed with the results of seeking help at a particular service agency, they generally say they would seek help from other agencies, and they sometimes find ways to excuse the particular caregiver who disappointed them.

Still, trust is often broken, and everyone can think of examples of people or organizations that are not trustworthy. This is where additional arguments and understandings come into play. We may call these arguments and understandings "secondary warrants." They explain why some breach or violation of our expectations has taken place, providing an excuse, as it were, that permits us to continue trusting even in the face of evidence for why we should not. Secondary warrants are a common, although little-studied, aspect of our culture. They function much as rituals do: for instance, we have small rituals in everyday life that provide ways for apologizing, saying excuse me, and covering over embarrassing mishaps such as calling someone by the wrong name.[22] Secondary warrants are the verbal equivalents of these rituals. They provide explanations (for ourselves or for anyone who may ask), not why it was appropriate to trust in the first place, but why it is appropriate to continue trusting even when there is evidence that one should not. We find ways to tell ourselves that the violation we experienced was the exception rather than the rule. It was, for instance, some bureaucratic snafu that caused the problem, or the caregiver was having a bad day, or the incident was overshadowed by another event that was more favorable. Secondary warrants are less common when transactions occur at arms length, though, and this insight probably helps us understand why levels of trust in congregations seem to be higher than toward more specialized service agencies.

The trust that people express toward congregations is remarkably robust, and it is not because congregations are such good providers of care (although they may be), but rather because we have a well-stocked supply of secondary warrants with which to explain away the apparent miscues and breaches of trust that occur in our interactions with congregations. In the first place, people who have been disappointed in the help provided them by congregations point out that this is only one of the reasons why congregations exist. A woman who attends a Roman Catholic church, for instance, observed, "I'm not going to let it stop me from going to church, because I go to church for the Lord. I don't go to church [to receive help], although I feel that's part of what the church should do." Being places of worship and fellowship, as well as sources of assistance, is thus reason enough for churches to still be trusted, even if they falter in providing help. The same woman illustrates a second way of excusing her congregation. Despite not getting the help she needed, she says, "Well, I don't feel, I mean, I didn't go to them and ask them." Her comment could be interpreted as blaming herself for not asking. It also reflects something deeper about congregation-based services. Most of the people we talked to who had received help from congregations said they had not asked explicitly for this assistance. Someone helped them just because they were already friends or a friend in the congregation learned about their need and told the pastor. Sometimes the need became known because someone prayed about it. Their experience of receiving help was thus quite different from having to go to a service agency and explicitly ask for help. We shall consider this point again in chapter 8, but for present purposes the importance of not asking is that congregations can also be more easily excused for not providing. Another way of escaping the possible ill effects of damaged trust is to separate the congregation from a particular person in the congregation, such as the pastor. An elderly woman who had received a visit from her pastor when she was in the hospital, for instance, said she would trust him less if he hadn't come, but would not feel any differently about the church. Although this way of exculpating an organization from blame is not unique to congregations, it does reflect the fact that people think of their congregations as communities. No single individual, even the pastor, represents the whole community; thus, they can blame a person for violating their trust without blaming the entire congregation.

Of course secondary warrants are not completely effective in maintaining people's faith in congregations when congregations let them down. People admit that they do (or would) feel "rejected," "let down," "hurt," "upset," and even "resentful." Yet, if such feelings weaken their trust in a particular congregation, the presence of other congregations in the community helps. Disgruntled people can simply vote with their feet, as it were, and relocate to a new congregation that their neighbors say is more trustworthy. Or they can continue going to their church but seek help from a different service agency, as one man said he would do if he found that the drug-abuse program sponsored by his church was not keeping him clean. In this way, the presence of alternative service organizations may keep people involved in their congregations even when their congregations fail to provide help. This does not mean that religious involvement is in general immune to the ill effects of slights, misunderstandings, and missed opportunities. We know from other research that people certainly do cease participating in religion after some unfortunate episode in which their faith in God, friends, or the pastor is destroyed.[23] If we ask why trust in congregations is as resilient as it is, though, we have to acknowledge the role played by secondary warrants.

When service agencies fail to live up to people's expectations, there seem to be fewer ways of excusing their failure, which may account for levels of trust in these organizations being lower than for congregations. Prior to their contact with these agencies, people are either inclined to trust them on the basis of good reports from people they know or to withhold judgment. The eventual assessment of trustworthiness, therefore, depends much more on how the organization actually performed. If the service provided was unsatisfactory, then secondary warrants for maintaining trust in the organization are needed. These typically take the form of offering some reason for the organization's inability to meet one's needs. For instance, people who have been denied food assistance, loans, or financial help sometimes excuse the organization they contacted by explaining that the organization had rules or limited funds. Their faith in the organization is maintained if they feel the caregivers were "doing all they could." But if the organization's response seems arbitrary, or if staff do not offer reasons for being unable to help, then people are likely to come away feeling that they probably cannot trust the organization to help them in the future. One man illustrated this breakdown of trust in describing why he distrusted the Salvation Army. "They promise to help you and then they turn around and knife you in the back." His mistrust was only partly rooted in feeling aggrieved about not receiving help. It was rooted more in feeling that he had not been given an adequate reason: "No explanation, just no." Had he been in a long-term relationship with the Salvation Army, as he might have been with his church, he could very likely have received a satisfactory explanation from someone else, or he might have felt more comfortable pressing for an answer. But because he was in an arms-length relationship, he simply went away feeling dissatisfied.

Service agencies are like congregations in one respect: people can excuse the organization for failing to help them by blaming the performance of a particular staff person or volunteer at the organization. But, unlike in congregations, one staff person or volunteer is likely to be the only person with whom recipients have dealings. Thus, when people say they like their caseworker at a service agency, they usually report that they trust the organization. But if they do not like their caseworker, they have little basis on which to say they still trust the organization.

The Social Contribution of Trust

From the qualitative interviews, we have thus seen in more detail how recipients of caregiving view the traits of caregivers. The recipients of caregiving not only want caregivers to be trustworthy but are usually predisposed to think they will in fact be trustworthy (or are at least willing to suspend judgment until the results are in). This predisposition is partly rooted in generalized trust of humankind and is further conditioned by the fact that service organizations are safe places (relative to the neighborhood in general) with positive reputations in the community. Thus, it is striking to hear the *many* different ways in which the clients of these organizations support their belief that caregivers are trustworthy. If one caregiver is especially friendly, then friendliness becomes a basis of trust. If another is particularly competent, then competence provides a rationale for trust. Proximity, affinity, and availability also provide such rationales. This is not to say that recipients are always pleased with the caregivers with whom they have dealings, but stories about unsatisfactory dealings are often told reluctantly or are volunteered as points of contrast to show why another caregiver was indeed trustworthy. It is disturbing, therefore, for a client to have experienced dealings with a caregiver who violated the expectation of trustworthiness. When that happens, many clients are quick to provide explanations, such as attributing the problem to some flaw in the organization rather than in the caregiver or even blaming themselves for being gullible. Such explanations restore and maintain faith in the overall trustworthiness of caregivers.

The role of faith in all this may be to provide recipients of caregiving with a special language in which to understand why they have been helped. But it is hard to say if faith-based interpretations of caregiving carry any special advantages or implications compared to secular interpretations. Either may give recipients of assistance reasons to trust caregivers. If the caregiver is perceived as a person of faith, then it may be easier to assume that he or she is altruistic, a person of good moral character, or someone who shares your values if you happen to be a person of faith also. What does seem abundantly clear is that recipients do try to make sense of caregivers' behavior and to determine whether or not it is warranted to trust these caregivers. Service organizations need to be attentive to this interpretive process. Although cynical interpretations of assistance may be difficult to prevent in some instances, such interpretations can sour clients' views and perhaps even damage their sense of who can be trusted. Being able to provide positive interpretations of caregivers' behavior matters to clients. Believing that a caregiver is altruistic, sincere, knowledgeable, or religiously motivated provides a basis for trust, not only of the caregiver, but also of oneself—trust that one's faith in human nature is justified and that if one needs assistance, it is only natural to seek it.

Experiencing Unlimited Love?

The one thing that religious organizations claim to be doing that truly makes a difference in the world is communicating love—unconditional love, the kind that comes from God and has been exemplified by great people of faith throughout the centuries. By serving the needy, religious organizations put into practice their traditions' teachings about love. Faith-based social services are surely one of the ways in which religious organizations demonstrate the value of love. Even if faith-based services had no special purchase on being effective or in solving the problems of low-income families, we would need to consider the possibility that they convey important messages to the world about the value of love.

Like trust, love is an important part of what holds civil society together.[1] We may not think of it immediately in this context. Love is more typically associated with romance and sexual intimacy. Yet the broader meaning of love includes the bonds of respect and acceptance that we sometimes refer to as filial relations and the selfless caring that we refer to as altruism.[2] Civil society depends on these kinds of love. Even though many of our actions are driven by self-interest, it is necessary at times to show that we care for people for reasons other than the short-term benefit we may derive from them. We want the best for them, we want to alleviate suffering, and we want our world to be a better place. Unlike the marketplace (which is oriented toward self-interest) or government (which operates through its capacity to coerce), the vast domain of civil society is where expressions of love in its many forms must prevail if civil society is to flourish.

Love is chiefly evident in how we behave. If we only talk about love and do nothing to carry through on our fine language, then love is hardly present at all. It is for this reason that most of what interests us about service organizations is whether they actually provide services and do so effectively. The deeds are primary. And yet they are not all. If someone assists me in getting to the doctor, that may be an act of kindness that I interpret as love. But if the person who assists me is a taxi driver I pay, then my interpretation will be quite different. The activities of service organizations seldom involve cash payments like this; they fall into a gray area in which messages about love may or may not be present. As a caregiver, I may simply be doing my job and, indeed, do it in such a way that clients receive help but have no sense that I actually care for them. It is in this sense that messages matter. Love involves both deeds and the interpretation of deeds; it involves sending and receiving explicit and implicit messages, especially about motives and feelings. Motives convey whether love was intended by the caregiver and whether it was perceived by the recipient. Feelings help to communicate whether important aspects of love are present in a relationship, such as empathy and emotional investment. It is thus not only the deeds but the connotations of these deeds that must be considered in thinking about service organizations as mechanisms for conveying love.

Scholars have become interested in the social benefits of unlimited or unconditional love.[3] Some argue that many of the world's problems would disappear if we just had more love and if we understood better how to practice unlimited love. In this view, expressing love in social relationships is a way of encouraging cooperation and thus mitigating the ill effects of unrestrained competition, not to mention being closely allied with trust, solidarity, maintaining long-term commitments, serving others, and working to help the disadvantaged. Faith-based organizations are of particular interest in view of such claims. Grounded in religious teachings and motivated by these teachings, the staff and volunteers at these organizations should be in a position to communicate unlimited love. That is one of the added benefits such organizations may have. Besides simply providing services, they explicitly emphasize love, providing opportunities for caregivers to explain why they are motivated to be compassionate, and encouraging recipients to see that they are loved and worthy of love. But do these organizations function this way?

One does not have to look far to find anecdotal evidence of someone being pulled from a fire or saved from drowning by a complete stranger and being so inspired by this act of sacrificial love that he or she goes on to be a better person and to help others. Inspirational books, sermons, and even newspapers frequently recount such anecdotes. And these stories often include references to religious values as motives for helping. But we should be skeptical about such accounts. We do not know if they are typical or if it is because they are so rare that they are told. Often we do not know exactly how the person saved in these stories understood what had happened or whether that person's understanding was at all similar to how the rescuer understood his or her motives for helping.[4]

The same uncertainties arise when we think about the potential role of faith-based service organizations in communicating unlimited love. It may be that these organizations do communicate such messages. After all, they do provide services and, from what we have seen in previous chapters, do so in a way that garners positive evaluations from most clients. If we think about love similarly to how we looked at trust, then we would want to emphasize that love is not simply about behavior but about cultural understandings of behavior. Thus, the message communicated by an act of service may be richer, and more likely to be perceived as unlimited love, if it is accompanied by religious language than if it is not, especially because love, compassion, charity, and related topics have been stressed so heavily in religious teachings. Yet it may be that caregivers at faith-based organizations *think* they are communicating these messages, and are even genuinely motivated by a desire to show godly love, but somehow fail to get these messages across to recipients. Or perhaps they do, but perhaps the idea of love—or related notions of caring and compassion—are so common in the culture that caregivers at non-faith-based organizations are able to communicate the same messages.

Let us be more systematic about what exactly is at issue. There are three basic questions needing to be addressed with empirical evidence if we are to understand the role of faith-based organizations in communicating messages about unlimited love. The first is whether caregivers at service organizations perceive themselves to be motivated by unconditional love and, if so, whether they try to communicate unconditional love to those who receive their care, either by talking about their faith or through other means. The second is whether clients of these organizations perceive the caregivers they deal with to be motivated by something resembling unlimited love, such as genuine concern and compassion, altruism, or sacrifice. As part of this question, we can also ask whether clients perceive the motives of caregivers at faith-based organizations in terms of distinctly religious teachings and, if so, whether clients of faith-based organizations experience something about unlimited love that clients of non-faith-based organizations do not. And the third question is whether the various kinds of service received and the organizations involved differ in the degree to which implicit limits or conditions are actually associated with love. This last question requires further explication.

The idea of unconditional or unlimited love may be an ideal associated theoretically with being godly or with being the perfect parent or caregiver, but in practice it is doubtful that love is ever truly unconditional.[5] Parents who love their children unconditionally are more demonstrative about that love at certain times than at others, and these variations send subtle messages to children about parent's expectations concerning desirable and undesirable behavior. Similarly, a caregiver at any service organization may attest to being motivated by unconditional love for the needy, and yet in practice caregivers find it necessary to place limits on their caregiving because truly unconditional love would strain the financial resources of the organization, compromise their ideas of professionalism, or rob them of the time and energy they need to care for themselves, their children, and other loved ones. It does not require taking a cynical attitude toward caregiving to recognize that "unlimited" love is in fact always limited. Indeed, there are good reasons, as we shall see, for caregivers to deny that what they are doing involves unlimited love and to use other language to describe their behavior.

If love is in some ways limited, then the important questions should focus on how exactly it is understood to be limited by those who receive it. One possibility is for recipients to *believe* that the love they have received is unconditional, even though it is not. For instance, they may insist that caregivers expect nothing of them in return and that caregivers were motivated purely by the highest altruistic ideals. If this is the perception, it may have interesting and even positive consequences for recipients' behavior. Another possibility is that recipients recognize that certain expectations are associated with the care they receive and that these expectations are important in guiding subsequent behavior, as, for example, in the case of an organization that encourages its recipients to abstain from alcohol, or one that expects recipients to join a church and profess faith in Jesus.

We need to be especially sensitive to the ways in which understandings of love and caring are shaped by the culture in which we live. Our culture provides us with many ways of thinking about *caregiving:* through our families, schools, the mass media, and even the bully pulpit occupied by political leaders, we hear constant refrains about why we should give care, how we can be more caring, and the good this caring will do not only for others but also for ourselves. Whether these messages are framed in religious or in secular terms, they are abundant. The cultural role of the caregiver, we might say, is well defined. We know what a caregiver is and how a caregiver is supposed to behave; most important, we know that giving care is good. In contrast, our culture gives us far less to go on for thinking about *receiving* care. The popular aphorism reminds us that it is more blessed to give than to receive. And receiving, in consequence, is a kind of cultural black box. It could be a role in which only gratitude is important. Or it could require repayment. It could be a source of embarrassment or shame. Or it could be fraught with such uncertainty that we pass over it because we have no ways of thinking about it. To speak of unlimited love, then, may be to describe an attitude, lifestyle, or state of being that can be understood in terms of caregivers, and yet not be a concept with clear meanings as far as recipients are concerned.[6]

There is an important sociological dimension to be considered, too. Unconditional love or whatever most closely approximates it is usually associated with families or other intimate relationships in which a long-term attachment is involved.[7] It is in these relationships that the relative unconditionality of love can be demonstrated (as expressed in marriage vows pledging commitment in bad times as well as in good times or in parents' promises to children to "be there" for them). From what we have considered about trust, congregations may resemble families in their capacity to generate and sustain relationships that are sufficiently deep and long-lasting to connote unconditional love. The question is whether other kinds of service organizations, faith-based or not, can do the same. These organizations are enough like the ones we deal with in the marketplace that it may be hard to believe that unconditional love is involved.

The large question that we confront in thinking about unlimited love, then, is whether it can be communicated somehow within the context of relatively impersonal, arms-length, market-oriented social relationships. If it cannot, arguments about unlimited love as a solution to human problems become more difficult to entertain seriously. We might still argue for heavier doses of love in families, but the dominant social relationships we experience in the marketplace and other public settings would need to be considered in terms of rational calculations, self interest, and legal restraints, rather than unlimited love. But service organizations may be an interesting and important exception. Perhaps they are places in which unlimited love is communicated despite the fact that many of the characteristics of the marketplace are present. If so, we can benefit from understanding how love is communicated and in what ways it is important.

How Caregivers Talk about Love

Caregivers certainly regard themselves as being engaged in service activities that demonstrate love. Through the services they provide, and in the manner in which these functions are performed, the staff and volunteers at service organizations try to show care and compassion. For instance, the head of one agency says she tries to be pleasant no matter how nasty someone may be to her and just assure them that "I'm still here" if they need her help. Another agency director says she is very direct with clients. She likes to say, "Okay, you're here because you want this kind of stuff, and I'm here because it makes me happy to see people get this stuff." A man who provides direct services to a large number of clients understands his role in terms of "establishing the rules and guidelines" for clients, being available to help them, "offering things," and indeed treating them "like they're part of a family." An elderly man who does volunteer work almost every day at his church and visiting the sick at a nearby hospital says he just tries to appreciate and value the people he helps as if they were "a brother or sister," "with no suspicion whatever," just "quietly" and "affectionately." These remarks are typical. Caregivers generally do not regard their work as "just a job" or as simply a way to make a living or create time for things they would rather do. They also deny that they are making special sacrifices, but they take for granted that their activities are a way of expressing genuine concern about the needs and well-being of others.

It is clear from talking with caregivers that understandings of caring and the motives for caring do not have to be made up from scratch; they are part of a rich cultural tradition, a tradition so rich, in fact, that the motives for caring are often, as it were, overdetermined.[8] That is, caregivers have many options for explaining why they are engaged in service work, and these options individually and collectively provide reason enough to be a caring person; it seems almost natural to be one. In table 8.1 I have listed some of the more commonly mentioned reasons offered by caregivers for being caring and compassionate, and included a verbatim quote from our interviews in the Lehigh Valley to illustrate each one. It is clear from this list that caregivers have a large repertoire from which to draw in making sense of love and compassion. Faith or religion is one. But only one. Popularized versions of psychology and sociology provide ample alternatives. People talk about upbringing, role models, social class, behaviorist and instrumental reasons, and a variety of other factors. A few talk specifically in terms of the mission of their service organization. But most resort to wider arguments that are not linked to a specific organization.

The fact that reasons to be caring are simply "out there" in the culture, as it were, and readily available to caregivers is also evident in the frequency with which popular sayings and aphorisms appear in caregivers' remarks. One man says "caring is like stopping to smell the roses." A woman asserts, "You get further with honey than you do with vinegar." After talking for awhile about her personal experiences, she also offers a paraphrase of the Golden Rule: "Treat others the way you would want to be treated yourself." Another recites, "What would Jesus do?" Other remarks are less formulaic, but are phrases that roll so easily from people's tongues that it is certain they have used these phrases before and heard others using them. A woman says being a caregiver gives her a "sense of well-being" as she drifts off to sleep at night. A man says it's his "relationship with Jesus Christ" that motivates him to be caring. People also draw on stories, books, or movies they know will succinctly communicate something about why they are caring (such as *Pay It Forward* and *Saving Private Ryan*).

Yet it is important to recognize that caregivers hardly ever use the specific language of "love" to describe what they are doing. The ones we talked to were more comfortable talking about caring, caregiving, helping, assisting, serving, and in some cases showing compassion. Some of the volunteers we interviewed actually became agitated by being asked questions about love that just seemed out of sync with the service activities they had been doing. Love connoted too much intimacy. It was a word reserved for one's family and close friends. As one woman remarked, "My mind is racing about [love] because you mostly think about it in more family or intimate types of relationships." To speak of love in the context of one's

TABLE 8.1
Caregivers' Reasons for Being Compassionate

Reason	Example
Personality/personal nature	"It's just a part of my nature and how I do my work."
Socialization	"I was raised that way; that's what I experienced in my family, and it just seemed like a natural thing."
Role model	"My grandmother . . . was the most caring person in the world and helped me through any troubling times I had; I think I just carried that on."
Reinforcement	"We all want to be accepted in life and I think the feedback you get from others by being a caring person is positive and reinforces itself."
Social class	"When you come from humble beginnings and you've had to struggle and you've had to face life experiences that weren't always the most positive, it compels you to want to give back and make it a little bit easier for others."
Happiness	"I want other people to see that this is a good life and you will be happier."
Health	"More and more research is showing that having caring relationships . . . is tied to health."
Professionalism	"You won't hear foul language here [or] people having a bad day. . . . They're professional."
Human nature	"I'm not on an island somewhere; I have to interact [and] it's not going to kill me to be nice to somebody or be compassionate."
Faith/religion	"Christ called us to be loving, compassionate, and kind; that's what we try to do."
Organizational mission	"[Our] overall mission is to be able to show compassion and caring to the people who are coming through our doors."

Source: Lehigh Valley Caregiver Interviews.

clients was almost a breach of professionalism. It violated the psychological and emotional distance caregivers felt they needed to maintain between themselves and their clients.

This sense of professional distance is a norm that most caregivers learn at some point in the course of their training and is one that many volunteers seem to accept as well. It not only discourages caregivers from talking about love, it also puts them on their guard about disclosing too many of their personal motives. Thus, it is acceptable to be friendly and to express interest in clients' problems, but not acceptable to talk candidly with clients about why one became involved in caregiving and how that relates to one's deeper values. There are some variations in how caregivers understand these norms. For instance, the sense that one should refrain from disclosing personal motives and values came through most clearly in our interviews with staff associated with the public welfare department. As representatives of a government agency, they felt it inappropriate to get too "close and personal" with clients. For instance, one man said that communicating his motives was determined by the "job function basically." He meant that just working at the job showed clients as much as he needed to about his motives. One of his colleagues felt this wasn't quite enough, but in her view treating clients "honestly" and being genuine and courteous, rather than being "abrupt" or appearing too busy, were the acceptable ways to demonstrate one's motives. But caregivers at nonprofit service agencies (secular and faith-based alike) were also reluctant to talk about their motives and values with clients. Most of them shared the view of the man at the public welfare department that deeds were enough. The director of a homeless shelter observed simply, "I don't [communicate my motives]," adding that he just tries to help people. A woman who held the same view said she just tries to express that she cares through her "body language" and "facial expressions."

The conviction that it is unacceptable or at least unnecessary to talk about one's motives and values was especially evident among the caregivers we talked to at faith-based organizations. They were often sensitive to the expectation (or criticism) that they would talk about their faith to clients and thus went out of their way to deny that they did so. For instance, the head of one faith-based agency said he is sure some people think they have to join a church or believe in a certain way to get help from his organization and he has been criticized by religious people for not giving religious teachings more publicity; but he asserted, "We don't come out and say 'In Jesus' name' or anything like that. We're in the business of helping people, and if they don't know why we did it, then so be it." Another director of a faith-based organization chuckled and said he had talked about his religious values for purposes of the interview, but he does not try to communicate those values to the people he assists. "We just help; it's there, the caring is there." In fact, he explained, people who come to him for help sometimes try to beg special favors by saying, "Aren't you a religious person?" And he responds by saying he's here to help them but is unable to provide the kind of assistance they want.

Caregivers grant that whatever they are doing is offered without conditions and is, in this sense, unlimited or unconditional. It is not the kind of favor that has to be earned. Clients can be ill-tempered, ungrateful, or suspicious and still qualify for help. It doesn't matter, as one man explained, whether you like a client or not, and you certainly can't ask those you don't like to "jump through more hoops or do more." Those who receive help are not expected to pay back, at least not by doing volunteer work for the organization or by joining it. If recipients feel a desire to care for others, that is commendable, but it is not a condition of receiving care in the first place.

We should nevertheless see that caregivers explicitly or implicitly place limits on their caregiving. The "love" they express through their work or volunteering is, in this sense, not at all unconditional. It comes with strings attached; that is, with expectations that the people they care for will do something or respond in certain ways—possibly on penalty of receiving no further help if they do not. In some cases, such as the public welfare department, these expectations are "written down in black and white," as one staff person explained. In other cases, the expectations go unstated but are nevertheless present. "Help themselves" is how one caregiver put it. "Become self-sufficient," said another. Caregivers also expect clients to observe common standards of moral decency. Although it may be excusable for clients to be abrasive or ill-mannered, they are expected to be honest, truthful, and trustworthy. If they are not (if they "play us for fools," as one director said), they are less likely to receive assistance again in the future.

The expectation that most clearly shows the imprint of cultural norms is that people who receive assistance from service organizations must take responsibility to get back on their own feet. "This is your life," one program director said, repeating her standard advice to clients. "I'm here and I can help guide you a little bit, but you ultimately will make your own decisions." Unlike the love that exists between marriage partners, there is no sense of shared destiny. Individual clients are on their own. There are no lasting relationships with a service organization, no mutual decisions, no collectivity or common unit to which both the clients and providers belong. Another agency director put it this way: "I'm not your mother. I'm not your husband. I'm not your child. I'm none of those things. I'm here. I'm running a program. I would love to have you avail yourself [of it], because I think it will do you [good]. If you don't want it, that's okay with me." In short, the relationship between caregivers and clients is not only emotionally different from the love people have in mind when they think about families; it is sociologically different as well.

Caregivers also restrict the idea of unconditional love in more subtle ways. When we pressed them in our interviews to say whether they really tried to express unconditional love, many of these unstated restrictions came out. One is the idea that you may try to love someone unconditionally, but it isn't necessary to feel good about it. As one man explained, he sort of grits his teeth and tries to squelch the repulsion he may feel for a client. In this sense, what matters is how one behaves; the positive inward feelings that typically accompany love may not go all the way down. Another way of limiting love is almost the opposite. It emphasizes feelings, but stops short of saying that attraction has to be present; respect is good enough. Unconditional love is thus a feeling of respect for someone as a human being, even though one may disagree with or dislike some of the things that person does.[9] And respect may actually be rather different from love, as one woman decided after wrestling with the ideas for awhile: "It's a very touchy-feely term for me," she concluded. Another woman, who also found herself struggling with the idea of love, decided that what she was really practicing was not love, but acceptance. Unconditionality, therefore, involved a feeling of what Alan Wolfe has termed "nonjudgmentalism," a kind of rapport, but not one based on much knowledge or familiarity.[10]

In our culture we tend to psychologize love, turning it into what various scholars have termed an "expressive," "therapeutic," or "subjective" feeling, and this tendency also affects how caregivers understand unconditionality.[11] For instance, a man who tries explicitly to follow biblical principles in his role as an agency director explains that there is a tension in the Bible between what God says, which is often judgmental, and the example of Christ, which is "unconditional." This man prefers the example of Christ and for this reason tries to be unconditional in relating to clients. What he means is that he tries to cultivate an attitude of acceptance and to communicate that attitude by treating everyone fairly. He illustrates his point by saying he has some "issues" with people being gay, based on his reading of the Bible, but in trying to be unconditional he does not look down on gay people or treat them differently when they come for assistance.

This example, which was similar to ones that came up in other interviews, is helpful for understanding what exactly caregivers mean when they talk about unconditionality in the context of providing social services. Their love is certainly not unconditional in the sense of giving up one's life to help others. It is not unlimited in the sense of giving people all they ask for or always devoting extra hours to helping them. At the same time, it is not merely an attitude without consequences, as critics of the emphasis in our culture on expressivity or subjectivity sometimes suggest. It is nevertheless largely an attitude or a point of view that emphasizes acceptance and fairness.

More than they probably realize, caregivers define unconditional love in a way that fits neatly with the norms in our society that emphasize tolerance of diversity. Caregivers may be inspired by religious teachings and they may use the language of faith in describing their motives. But the way in which unconditional love is actually defined is more in keeping with ideas about diversity, acceptance, and fairness that are pervasive in the culture at large, rather than in terms that are distinctly religious. Unconditionality is nevertheless a concept that provides a standard of comparison for what caregivers actually do. If they deny that they really care for clients unconditionally, there are at least aspects of unconditionality to which they aspire. Respecting, accepting, and not judging people who are down on their luck, even if they are rude and ungrateful, is part of what it means to relate in a truly caring manner. Being open to the possibility that their values may be different from one's own is another important mark of unconditional acceptance. One draws the line, but does so liberally, perhaps at the point where one's personal safety is compromised, rather than expecting compliance with one's values.

From the perspective of caregivers, then, serving people who are in need is an act of kindness or compassion, which makes it something like love, even though love itself is not a common way of describing service activities. Caregivers typically downplay notions that what they are doing is special or particularly worthy of commendation, but they do consider it important to be loving and to communicate signals of kindness or compassion in conjunction with their service functions. There is little evidence, though, that working or volunteering for faith-based organizations encourages caregivers to communicate about love differently than in other kinds of service organizations. Professional and more general cultural norms discourage disclosing motives and values, the realities of service work require placing limits on one's caring behavior, and the ways in which unconditional love are shaped by the culture encourage it to be understood less in religious terms and more in terms of fairness and respect.[12]

The exception to these patterns is congregation-based caregiving. Clergy and lay volunteers in congregations are much more likely than other service workers to say explicitly that they try to communicate unconditional love and that Christ is their model for doing so. For instance, one pastor explained that the caregiving at his church was quite explicitly intended to demonstrate unconditional love: "It's the love that we read about in the New Testament that God has toward all mankind. . . . And when Jesus dies on the cross he dies for the sins of all mankind from the whitest lie to the darkest, horrific action anyone has taken. Without conditions. Without conditions. Now that's what makes God God. He's that infinitely powerful and that wonderful. We aspire to mirror that as best we can." Pastors also define unconditional love less in terms of filling specific needs and more as cultivating relationships that include the whole person—emotionally, spiritually, and socially. Thus, being friendly and welcoming strangers may be as important as helping people get back on their feet financially. Observing that his congregation "does a pretty good job" of showing unconditional love, another pastor explained: "If you're the visitor, the first thing is that you have at least five or six people coming over to you who start introducing you to folks and saying, 'Nice to have you here,' and not asking real private questions. That's not our business. So I'd say definitely unconditional love." Others, though, stressed that compassion required more than being friendly. As one caregiver noted, compassion "means suffering with—staying with people in their suffering." This, he said, is possible only because of "the love that God has for me" and is best communicated through the image of Christ on the cross. The contrast between caregivers in congregations and those in faith-based service organizations in these respects is marked. Despite the fact that faith-based service providers are often personally religious and are motivated by their faith, the norms against talking to clients about faith carry into the ways they communicate messages about love. Congregational caregivers, in contrast, worry less about the possibility of offending recipients who may not be religious and are not constrained in what they say by being ecumenical. Caregivers in congregations also believe that the messages they try to communicate are reinforced by the familylike atmosphere of the congregation. This at least is how they perceive the situation.

Do Recipients Experience Love?

If experiencing love is defined as perceiving that one has been helped, then there is no question that nearly all recipients of social services experience love in some degree. Just as caregivers do in giving assistance, recipients understand that something of value has taken place in receiving it. The short-term loan, food basket, transportation to the doctor, job training, or day care program for their children is a tangible expression of being cared for. Apart from the goods or services they receive, recipients also participate in a social relationship that is often affirming, congenial, and conducive to realizing that they are not alone when help is needed. Comments such as "It's people helping people," "It warmed my heart," "The woman [who helped me] was lovely," "[She] was very nice and understanding with me," and "The people [there] are very friendly" point to the positive social relationships that recipients experience.

The love that recipients experience is not unlimited in the sense of being perceived as abundant or even adequate. In formal interviews, recipients are reluctant to criticize the organizations or individuals who have helped them. But recipients are keenly aware of the limited resources, the regulations, and the time constraints that restrict the assistance they can expect to receive. Examples are not hard to find. A woman who received food from a local food bank said, "you can't possibly pull together a balanced diet" from what the food bank makes available. A woman who had received help once a month from a nonprofit organization through a children's assistance program said it was difficult to keep her appointments because the organization was open only during the same hours she was working. A man who missed a deadline for help from another organization complained that the staff person there told him "You were supposed to call yesterday. You missed the day, we can't help you. Good-bye."

Despite these limitations, the love recipients experience is at least unconditional in the sense that they seldom feel that they have had to promise to do anything to receive assistance. Most recipients deny that anything was expected of them in return for the help they received, generally taking it for granted that this is normal, although in a few cases expressing surprise or particular gratitude that nothing was asked of them. Fairly typical of these views was the comment of a man who had received help finding a job and explained that the service organization did not expect anything "because they are always helping people in need without expecting anything in return." Those who do acknowledge that they incurred a debt or implicitly made a promise to do something in return usually diminish the significance of this obligation. "Just do a good job," a woman who had received job training observed. Another woman, a recipient of free meals delivered to her home, acknowledged that she did feel as though she owed the organization something ("because they did a great thing for me"), but what she owed was gratitude, rather than needing to pay back by doing anything. The exceptions to feeling that no obligations had been incurred are usually associated with loans, in which the obligation to pay off the loan is explicit, or in conjunction with meeting government welfare qualifications, such as promising to meet with one's caseworker or undergo job training. Otherwise, it appears that recipients do sense that they have been helped freely, and this sense seems to be as common among recipients of secular organizations as among recipients of faith-based organizations.

But if love is regarded as something involving sacrifice on the part of the caregiver, then recipients uniformly deny that this kind of love has been part of the assistance they have received. There seem to be two underlying reasons for thinking that sacrifice is not involved. One is that the agencies from which assistance is received are known to be in existence to provide such assistance. Thus, the staff at these agencies are simply doing their job. The other is that recipients regard staff and volunteers as helping them because they enjoy doing it. As one woman explained, "They just seemed like they were happy to [help]." The love that is experienced presumably benefits the caregiver as well as the recipient—another reason why few recipients feel an obligation to pay back. This is not to say, however, that recipients are unmindful or unappreciative of the fact that caregivers are expending effort and sometimes going the second mile in order to be of service. For instance, one woman had received assistance from one of the local coalitions of churches in getting medical treatment. Her comments are revealing because she does believe that the man who helped her was making a sacrifice. "I think he was volunteering his time, his effort. And I do think he was giving up his time that he could have been doing something else." She also insisted that volunteering was something one did because you "wanted to do it." Thus, it was important to her to have been helped by a volunteer rather than by someone who simply worked for a service organization.

Like caregivers, recipients seldom use the word *love* to describe what they have experienced. And, unlike some caregivers, they seldom focus on the warm feelings that the caregiver may have tried to communicate. Not surprisingly, they view the assistance they have received mostly in concrete terms, such as food, clothing, job training, help with paying bills, programs for children, and the like. It is the deeds that matter, more than the words surrounding those deeds. And yet they interpret the deeds in different ways because of the contexts in which they have been given assistance.

The recipients who received help from the welfare office did not understand the help they had received as an example of love or compassion. They understood that they had been given help, and they appreciated this assistance. But they understood the transaction less in terms of a gift that had been given because someone cared about them and more in terms of receiving something to which they had a right. A mother who had received $350 per month from the welfare office through a cash assistance program illustrated this perspective explicitly and implicitly in her remarks. She said the reason the welfare office gave her the money was that she qualified for it. "I figured if I qualify, I'm going to try to get what I can get. I know people who take advantage of it and they get it for years and years, so I just felt like I should qualify so I was going to try and get it." When asked to elaborate, she repeated that "I fit the qualifications" and went on to discuss some of the specific aspects of her finances that made her eligible. She also implicitly suggested her sense of entitlement by referring to the cash assistance as "my daughter's money." The assistance did not fit her idea of a gift that was freely given because she had to ask for it, had to qualify, had to keep the welfare office informed about her sources of income, and was expected to enroll in a job training class. She says she hasn't learned anything about love, acceptance, or compassion from the experience. She thinks the people at the welfare office are just doing their jobs and, for them, "it's not really like they're helping people, like one-on-one; they're nine-to-five and they do it because they have to, not because they really want to help." The concerns that are uppermost in her thinking focus on fairness, especially whether the welfare office's rules are fair and whether there are people who are exploiting the system.

The recipients who had been assisted by nonprofit organizations spoke in quite different terms about their experiences than those who had been helped by the welfare office. They were more likely to have experienced personal caring or compassion and were more likely to express gratitude in return. A man who had received food and gifts at Thanksgiving and Christmas through a coalition of churches recalled "that just kind of had me in tears; no offense, I'm not ashamed to say, yeah, I do cry." He said his "whole heart was warmed." A woman whom the same coalition had helped by providing a security deposit so she could rent an apartment said she felt not only "relieved" but "grateful." A woman who had received money from a church to tide her over until her next check said she felt "humbled" and could only explain why she had been helped by thinking that the caregivers were "just good people."

Recipients generally offered no comments about whether the agency from which they had received help was faith-based or non-faith-based or whether its sources of funding influenced its programs. There was some indication in the interviews (just as in the survey), though, that recipients felt differently about nonprofit programs funded by the government than about nonprofit programs with no obvious connections to government. For instance, a woman who mentioned receiving financial help from the local hospital in the form of medical bills being forgiven said she felt "wonderful" about the hospital voluntarily doing this without her having to ask, but she also suspected the hospital had "to do so much charity [for low-income people] to get state help." Her understanding of the hospital's motives, therefore, was mixed; the hospital was doing good work, but it was functioning under government mandate as much as from an intrinsic commitment to serve.

The only times recipients seemed to single out religious organizations in their descriptions of caregivers' motives were when they had received assistance directly from congregations. In these cases, distinctly religious motives seem to have been communicated visibly enough that recipients could not escape saying something about them, unlike the cases involving faith-based nonprofits. For instance, one man who had received counseling on several occasions from a pastor said the church was probably willing to help because it was interested in promoting peace in the world. Another man who had sought help from a church while recovering from an addiction remarked, "Well, they are religious people, and they comfort everybody, not only me." There is a hint of altruism or unconditional love as a motive in remarks such as these, but it was more common for people who had been helped by pastors or church volunteers to say they had been helped just because they needed help.

The reason that recipients often seem disinclined to ponder the motives of caregivers more deeply than they do is that the existence of these agencies is itself sufficient reason not to question motives. That is, the establishment of an organization for the purpose of serving needs in the community is an act of legitimation. The organization is simply there to serve. And it gives caregivers a reason for being involved. Thus, recipients go for help expecting to receive it and not having to question why someone is helping them. This is similar to being helped by a family member. It simply stands to reason that a family member or loved one will try to help. What is problematic is if a stranger who is merely a passerby tries to help. An act of that kind deviates from the norms of ordinary social life. In contrast, serving is normal behavior for a service organization and thus does not require effort to make sense of. One woman, a recipient of counseling from a faith-based organization, expressed this understanding quite clearly: "They help people if you need the help." For her, that was the bottom line.

If recipients generally do not focus deeply on the motives of caregivers, they do sometimes talk about their own moral qualities as a reason for being helped. For instance, a woman who had become well acquainted with a staff member at a secular nonprofit organization from which she had received help observed that this staff member could "look at people and tell good people" as soon as they walked in the door. In this woman's view, the reason she had been helped was that the staff member "knew I was a good person when she laid her eyes on me." A recipient of help from another nonprofit organization responded similarly. When asked what motivated people at this organization to help her, she replied, "I was telling the truth when I went there." Another woman thought it was her "sincerity" that motivated the caregivers at a faith-based organization to help her.

These comments are interesting because they reveal a broader point about the relationship between social assistance and understandings of unconditional love. The conditions we place on love are often moral. We want our children to grow up to be persons of good moral character, so we give or withhold expressions of love in relation to particular aspects of moral character, such as being truthful, fair, and kind. Receiving assistance from service organizations, at least those that give assistance voluntarily rather than on the basis of entitlement, does sometimes raise questions in recipients' minds about why they have been helped. If the assistance is experienced as a gift, then some justification for this gift becomes necessary. One is faced with the question, "What did I do to deserve this act of kindness?" The answer can conceivably be, "Nothing, the kindness came about entirely because the caregiver was a good person." But the answer is likely to imply something about the recipient as well. Thus, recipients assert that they are good people, that they are honest, that they are hard-working, or that they deserve to be helped because of other morally desirable traits.

Of course we do not know enough about recipients' lives from brief interviews to say whether these self-perceptions are justified. But we are left with an intriguing possibility about unlimited love. If assistance is given freely so that it is in this sense experienced as unconditional love, then it may encourage recipients to feel that they are morally justified in receiving it. The outcome may be the same we imagine when considering unconditional love in the context of childrearing. A child who experiences unconditional love rises to meet those expectations. And when this happens, the response is in some ways ironic. We might suppose that unconditional acceptance leads to an attitude of anything goes—to misbehavior in the case of spoiled children or to misuse of social services in the case of adults seeking assistance. Yet a more favorable outcome derives from the fact that a free gift is so difficult to understand that we feel compelled in some way to earn it. This is akin to the argument that free gifts generate good behavior because of gratitude and the need to show gratitude. Bringing in the idea of moral worth, though, alters the argument. Good behavior in this view is not so much a way of showing gratitude as of demonstrating to oneself that the kindness received was deserved. These self-perceptions can be false or, at minimum, little more than self-justifications. Yet it is often the case that self-justifications become self-fulfilling prophecies; that is, we behave in ways that conform to how we think we should behave. By evoking reasons why we deserve to be helped, therefore, caregiving can reinforce the value we attach to moral behavior.

The Role of Faith

Religious teachings and religious convictions play an important role in shaping our understandings of caring and compassion, and one way of interpreting what we have considered thus far is that these understandings are sufficiently pervasive in the United States that they do not depend specifically on faith-based service organizations to be communicated. Thus, recipients need not become clients of faith-based organizations to see the hand of God in the help they receive. If they are deeply religious themselves, they are more likely to think of assistance as a manifestation of divine love, regardless of its source. At the same time, the norms that inhibit caregivers at faith-based organizations from talking openly about their beliefs and values keep clients of these organizations from concluding that faith was particularly important at these organizations. Judging from their stories about the help they have received from various nonprofit service organizations, it does not appear that the auspices under which assistance is given have very much to do with the likelihood of recipients experiencing unconditional love or compassion. In short, the recipients of faith-based organizations from which we collected information *did not* have noticeably different understandings of love and compassion than the recipients of non-faith-based organizations.

Faith-based organizations nevertheless reinforce the *cultural* connection between faith and caring, even though this link is not restricted to the recipients of those organizations. In the most obvious sense, people who walk past a service organization that contains *Catholic, Lutheran, churches,* or similar words in its name can make a connection between faith and service, whether they get help from this organization or not. The consequences are social. In the community at large, religion is linked to helping the needy, even if individual recipients do not hear very much about religion at those organizations. If these same services were replaced by the activities of nonreligious organizations, the services would remain, but the cultural role played by religion would diminish. Thus, we need to ask whether this cultural role is important and, if so, why it may be important.

The main role that religious teachings play in relation to compassion and various understandings of unconditional love is to *legitimate* caring as a human activity. Put simply, they persuade people that it is right and good to be caring. They do not do this, as we have seen, by providing specific language for people to use in describing their reasons for caring. Religious teachings are part of the first language that most people learn in their families and while receiving religious instruction. It is at this deeper level that these teachings usually function.[13] Only when asked specifically about religious understandings of caring do people bring them to the surface, but when they do, it is clear that these ideas reinforce the conviction that it is simply valuable, even natural, to be a caring person.[14] Religious teachings contribute to this way of thinking through explicit references to God's love, which, by implication, suggest that people should behave the same way. Religious teachings also undergird the value of caring by creating "an aura of factuality," in Clifford Geertz's memorable phrase, about the relationship between sanctity and compassion.[15] This aura of factuality is realized through specific teachings such as the Golden Rule, but also through subliminal associations such as images of Christ's death on the cross or clergy mentioning the need for volunteers at a local homeless shelter. Other ways of legitimating care and compassion are certainly present in contemporary culture as well (as evident in the list of caregivers' motives we considered earlier), and yet the religious teachings that invoke an authoritative divine being and vivid examples of divine sacrifice are capable of cloaking caring with unrivaled legitimacy.

Although the idea of love being freely given is an important aspect of religious teachings, the role of faith in communicating understandings of love goes beyond this. Receiving something that is completely free is, as I have suggested, a difficult concept. Perhaps this is because we are so influenced by our culture that we believe it is necessary to work for what we earn or to somehow deserve what we are given.[16] Religious leaders sometimes draw contrasts between godly love and human behavior in these terms. But it is revealing that recipients of assistance from religious organizations also draw on religious language to explain why they deserve the help they have received. We saw, for instance, how the man who had received food during the holidays from a coalition of churches was grateful to the point of tears for what he had been given. Yet when asked his understanding of why he had been helped, he voiced the following interpretation: "The Lord had said in the Bible a long time ago, 'You obey my commandments and do as I ask, and you shall be rewarded.' Well, I've been, for the last four years, getting into church very heavily, and he's shown me [this] in a lot of ways." In other words, the food was still a gift, but one that the man could take some responsibility for having earned because he had, as he discussed elsewhere in the interview, become actively involved in his church and seriously engaged in studying the Bible, talking to the pastor, and trying to lead a better life.

I suggested earlier that religious teachings appear to be associated more clearly in our culture with giving care than with receiving it. In our interviews, we found that caregivers and recipients alike could readily accede to the idea that God was loving and that they, too, should try to help other people. But we found more confusion (and silence) when it came to religious teachings about how to receive help. There were no simple formulas, like the Golden Rule, that encouraged people to think about receiving help in a particular way. Religious teachings did not, for instance, tell people that they should be grateful, that they should limit their requests, or that they should try to pay back what they had been given. The role of religion is thus indirect. By influencing understandings of caregiving, it helps recipients to make sense of how they should behave, but not directly. Because caregiving should be universal, natural, human, and beneficial, some of the onus is taken from receiving it. One does not have to respond in a particular way because care is just "there," the same way as air and water are there. It is the sheer abundance of such care (the fact that it is available to everyone) that reduces my need to feel any particular obligation in response to it. Abundant love is thus different from love freely given. The former is given to everyone; the latter is given freely, but not to everyone. And it is that sense of being singled out for special treatment that evokes a clearer obligation to be morally deserving.

Restating this point in more sociological terms, religious teachings encourage people to think of caring as a universal or generalized good, rather than as a good that engenders any special obligations on the part of those who have received it. Caregiving is beneficial not only because it takes care of a needy person's needs, but because God wants us to be caring and because caregiving benefits the helper and the whole society. The recipient can benefit, therefore, feeling grateful, to be sure, but not feeling that strings are attached as would be the case in, say, an ordinary business transaction.

The deflection from having to repay, as it were, that arises from the possibility of thinking about caring as a generalized good also resolves or reduces the problem of moral dependency in the receiving of care. One of the challenges that arises from the inequality present in all societies is the need for ways of providing assistance to those in need without undermining their sense of moral worth. As we have seen, a gift that is freely given may encourage a high sense of moral worth. Yet the danger of robbing people of their basic dignity is always present when assistance is given. As caregiver, I affirm my own worth by helping others less fortunate than myself. But as recipient, I may sense my inadequacy in that same transaction. I am unable to pay back. I am weak. Perhaps I have fallen short in my responsibilities to myself and my family. The concept of rights and entitlements has been one way of compensating for the moral fallout that may arise from receiving assistance. If the help I receive is my right—that is, if it is something to which I am entitled simply by virtue of my being a citizen or having a need—then I need not experience a sense of moral weakness in exercising this right. Any person can qualify for assistance without judgments about moral worth being involved.[17]

This way of avoiding moral fallout has worked better in theory than in practice. Brian Steensland's extensive research on public policy debates about social welfare programs between the 1960s and 1990s shows that moral issues were nearly always a significant part of these debates.[18] Policy makers struggled to identify the kinds of recipients who were truly deserving. They did so by arguing that some recipients were morally worthy, generally by virtue of having done what they could to get jobs and keep them, and that other recipients were at least free of moral fault (for example, because they were children or were physically handicapped), while others did not meet appropriate moral standards, as indicated by not working or having too many children. Thus, arguments about rights and entitlements turned out to focus on the rights and entitlements of those who were morally deserving.

Not surprisingly, such arguments leave recipients of assistance in a quandary about how to think of their own moral standing. On the one hand, the sense of entitlement is attractive because it focuses entirely on need and, at least on the surface, implies nothing about moral deficiency. On the other hand, it is at best awkward to defend oneself in moral terms against the suspicion that some failing is the reason for one's need or in response to the idea that receiving assistance entails some responsibility to pay back.

Religious arguments about the relationship between needs and moral worth provide an alternative to this quandary. I do not mean religious arguments in the narrow sense of ones focusing specifically on church doctrines or arising only in the context of religious services. I mean instead the arguments about universal or intrinsic values that we commonly find in religious traditions but that in the modern world are also abundantly evident in more secular versions of humanitarian claims. In the simplest formulations, these arguments suggest that it is simply of value for human beings to care for one another. The grounds for this argument recognize that those in need are entitled to be helped, but emphasis shifts from recipients' rights to the *responsibility* of caregivers. That is, anyone who is capable of assisting others has a responsibility to do so.

Consequences of Receiving Care

Finally, I want to consider more specifically the consequences of receiving care and the possibility that these consequences may be different for those who receive care from faith-based organizations than for other recipients. We have seen that recipients generally deny feeling obligated to pay back for the help they have received. Yet there may be other consequences. We know from research on volunteers, for example, that the language of obligation is not a popular way to think about motives for volunteering, and yet volunteers often report an increased *desire* to help others because of someone helping them.[19] Among recipients, we might expect to find greater involvement in volunteer work and other forms of caregiving. In the literature on caregiving, some speculation has also been given to the possibility that receiving help from faith-based organizations encourages clients to become more spiritual and to grow in self-confidence.[20]

We gain some insights about the consequences of receiving care by looking again at the results from the Lehigh Valley Survey. Table 8.2 shows these results. We have four indications of possible consequences of receiving care in the survey: whether or not someone is currently engaged in charity or social service activities, such as helping the poor, the sick, or the elderly; whether or not a person does any volunteer work at an organization in the community; whether or not the person says spiritual growth is extremely important; and whether or not the person regards himself or herself as trustworthy. There are arguments for thinking that receiving any kind of assistance might encourage or reinforce each of these consequences and that help received from a faith-based organization or congregation might be especially conducive to these outcomes. Receiving assistance could encourage informal service activity or formal volunteering because the recipient has experienced love and thus feels an obligation or desire to pass this kindness along to others. Faith-based organizations or congregations may encourage this feeling more clearly than other kinds of service organizations because of religious teachings about loving others (or because of opportunities provided to serve others). An interest in spiritual growth could be encouraged by having received assistance from any organization if the love experienced prompted thoughts about godly love or possibilities of spiritual rebirth. Religious organizations would of course be expected to encourage such interest most clearly. And self-trust, as we considered in chapter 7, may be reinforced because receiving assistance restores one's faith in humanity and validates one's self-worth. Faith-based organizations and congregations may be especially oriented toward these kinds of self-affirming messages.

In considering the data, we should bear in mind that data like these cannot tell us whether one thing causes another. The data can only inform us about the relationships between activities or attitudes. Thus, we need to consider the possibilities here, for instance, that people who receive help from churches may already have been involved in service or volunteer activities, that recipients of faith-based organizations may have selected these organizations for help because of a prior interest in spiritual growth, and so on. We can, however, reduce the possibility of these alternative interpretations by taking into account other factors, such as age, gender, and frequency of church attendance, that we know are associated both with the likelihood of receiving assistance from particular kinds of organizations *and* with the outcomes under consideration.

Table 8.2 reports the odds ratios from logistic regression equations for each of our four dependent variables, first, for only the effect produced by having or not having received assistance from each kind of organization,

TABLE 8.2

Dependent Variables Associated with Having Received Assistance
from Specific Kinds of Service Organizations
(Odds ratios from logistic regression models for each dependent variable
and for having received assistance from each kind of organization)

	Zero-Order Odds Ratios	With Control Variables
Engaged in service activity		
Public welfare department	.720**	.841
Secular nonprofit organization	1.089	1.001
Faith-based organization	1.158	1.043
Local congregation	2.305***	1.594**
Doing volunteer work		
Public welfare department	.600***	.785
Secular nonprofit organization	1.022	1.107
Faith-based organization	1.159	1.255
Local congregation	1.927***	1.093
Spiritual growth is important		
Public welfare department	1.225	1.278
Secular nonprofit organization	1.664***	1.716*
Faith-based organization	1.690***	1.274
Local congregation	2.965***	1.906***
Self-trust is high		
Public welfare department	.891	.936
Secular nonprofit organization	1.092	.978
Faith-based organization	1.114	1.068
Local congregation	1.441**	1.077

Source: Lehigh Valley Survey, 2002.

Note: *p < .05 **p < .01 ***p < .001; control variables = female, black, Hispanic, age, income, education, number of children, number of needs, church attendance, number of organizations from which assistance was sought, and each kind of organization from which assistance was sought; service activity means currently being involved in charity or social service activity to help the sick or needy; volunteer work means being involved in doing work for any voluntary organization; spiritual growth means saying that spiritual growth is extremely important, and self-trust is strongly disagreeing that "I often do not trust myself."

and second, for these same effects after a large number of other factors have been statistically controlled. The results include some surprises. We see, for instance, that having received assistance from a faith-based organization is *not* significantly associated with any of the four outcomes (other than a zero-order relationship with interest in spiritual growth). In contrast, having received assistance from a congregation is positively associated with all four of the outcomes when only the zero-order relationships are considered, and remain positively associated with two of the four outcomes when the control variables are taken into account. Having received assistance from the public welfare department or from secular nonprofit organizations are generally unrelated to these outcomes (except for the anomalous result that recipients of secular nonprofit organizations are more interested in spiritual growth than nonrecipients, even when controls are taken into consideration). In sum, there is some evidence here, just as in the qualitative interviews, that congregations generate different outcomes than other kinds of organizations, including faith-based organizations.

Although we need to be cautious, we can venture a possible substantive generalization from these results. Receiving assistance from faith-based organizations probably encourages some people to be more altruistic or interested in spiritual growth or self-confident, but it does not encourage others in these ways and, indeed, is no more conducive to such outcomes than receiving assistance from secular nonprofits or the welfare department. In contrast, receiving assistance from congregations *does* seem to go hand in hand with engaging in informal service activities to help others and, not surprisingly, with being more interested in spiritual growth. It also appears that recipients of assistance from congregations are more likely to do volunteer work in their community, and this may well be volunteer work for the congregation itself (suggested by the fact that the relationship becomes statistically insignificant when frequency of church attendance is taken into account). Insofar as faith makes a difference, therefore, it does so in the context of congregations, not simply when it is part of the mission of a task-oriented service organization. The reason, as I have suggested, is probably that congregations are structured differently. They function as communities, rather than as organizations in which relationships focusing specifically on assistance predominate. As communities, congregations provide people with opportunities for formal and informal service to others, reinforce the value of such behavior, and include occasions for worship and for thinking about spiritual growth.

Our qualitative interviews are helpful for pinning down these observations. As people describe the consequences of having received assistance from various kinds of organizations, we see why some people are more likely to experience these consequences than others, no matter which organization has helped them. The qualitative interviews also suggest some of the reasons for congregations having a greater impact on attitudes and behavior than faith-based and other kinds of service organizations.

The recipients we talked to were mixed in terms of saying that receiving care had resulted in their becoming more interested in helping others. The ones who said this had not been the case fell into two categories. One category was composed of people who said they were already loving, caring people and thus had not been motivated to do more as a result of receiving assistance. The other category was made up of people who simply said they had not tried to help others and, in most cases, offered little explanation other than the fact that they felt the assistance they had received had been something they deserved in the first place. The people who said they *had* been motivated to help others were typically ones who felt a special bond with or sense of gratitude toward the caregiver who had helped them. Long-term relationships that become close and personal seem to be an important factor in some of these cases. For instance, a woman who has received assistance from the same caregiver long enough to talk about this caregiver as if she were a "sister" or a "friend" says she wants to do something for the caregiver to show her appreciation. "She's constantly doing for me. I feel I want to be able to do something for her. . . . I want to be able to take her out to a nice dinner or a nice movie or a nice hockey game to show her more appreciation." Doing this has not been possible, given the professional-client relationship between the two, so the woman has tried harder to help others. For instance, after receiving her unemployment check recently, the woman saw a homeless man and decided to give him some money to get a meal since she felt so much appreciation for having received assistance herself. Another woman knew two of the staff at the food bank that helped her with her groceries because she went to the same church they did; through this connection, she tried to do volunteer work occasionally in return for the help she received. "The more I'm helped, the more I want to help others," she explained. But then she also backtracked, saying, "But I've always wanted to help others."

As far as spiritual growth is concerned, none of the recipients we interviewed said they had become more interested in spirituality or more committed to their faith as a result of receiving help from a faith-based organization. In keeping with what we have already considered, the role of faith in these relationships was generally too oblique or restrained to have encouraged spiritual renewals or awakenings of this kind. Congregations were a different matter. It was more common for recipients of assistance from congregations to have been influenced spiritually. Of course some went to congregations explicitly seeking spiritual help, and others claimed they were already about as devout as they could be. But there was evidence of people seeking help for other needs, such as depression, illness, or lack of money, and finding themselves drawn into the spiritual life of the church. The difference between congregations and faith-based service organizations in this regard was a combination of factors: congregations were much more explicit in communicating religious messages, they provided mechanisms specifically for doing this (such as classes or individual meetings with clergy), and they functioned as communities in which deeper and more long-lasting friendships developed.

The effects on self-image were harder to gauge from personal interviews, but some recipients did say they felt more confident and had greater self-esteem. These effects had less to do with the type of organization from which they had received help than with how they interpreted their situation and the extent of their interaction with caregivers. Transactions involving specific, short-term assistance, such as advice about getting a job or help negotiating a loan, generally resulted in little change in self-image. Longer-term relationships with caregivers or participation in self-help groups or congregations were more effective.

Limited Love and the Realities of Social Life

One of the conclusions that emerges from these results is that the worry expressed in policy circles about faith-based (or other) service organizations attaching "strings" to the assistance they offer, such as requiring recipients to come to church or become Christians, is not substantiated by any of the information from our interviews with recipients. Indeed, faith-based organizations seem not to be any more effective than other service organizations in communicating ideas about faith in general or about unconditional love in particular. At the same time, this result could be interpreted as evidence that restrictions on faith-based organizations should be eased. In this view, it has been the fear of losing public money that has inhibited caregivers at these organizations from speaking more openly about their motives. As I have suggested, though, there are many other factors involved in these inhibitions, including professional norms, concerns about religious diversity and tolerance, and the lack of longer-term or communal relationships that exist in congregations.

The larger conclusion from these considerations is that unlimited love is highly complex, both in the manner in which it is understood and in the degree to which it is communicated through service organizations. We need to reckon with the concern expressed by many of the caregivers we talked to that the term *love* is not quite right in these contexts at all. We also need to acknowledge that *unconditionality* is not really an accurate term, either. There are many restrictions on the ways in which care is given and received. Caregivers and recipients understand this and in both cases see the difference between such restrictions and being obligated to pay back or meet certain expectations. More interesting are the ways in which the perceptions surrounding assistance are associated with understandings of moral worth and responsibility. We have seen evidence of strong norms encouraging fairness, respect, and honesty in giving and receiving care, as well as clear expectations about personal responsibility and self-sufficiency. It is also evident that moral worth is culturally associated with giving care, and that in ironic ways with receiving it as well, at least in the sense that the care one has received has been deserved because of good behavior. Religious teachings intertwine with these broader cultural understandings of caring. They legitimate the value and naturalness of caring, easing the burden of shame that may derive from feeling dependent on caregivers. They also undergird religious communities in which longer-term and more personal relationships can grow than those which usually take place through service organizations.

Public Policy and Civil Society

When social scientists write about the relationship between public policy and civil society, they usually emphasize how civil society can shape public policy. A vibrant civil society in which citizens trust one another and are interested in the good of their communities is one in which people can be mobilized to shape public policy. They learn civic skills in their churches and social clubs, get out to vote, and write letters to their elected officials about issues they care about. It is less common for social scientists to ask questions about how public policy shapes civil society. Yet we know it does. In the extreme case, repressive policies by totalitarian leaders seriously suppress the activities of voluntary associations and thus the vitality of civil society. In less extreme situations such as in democracies, public policy may make it harder or easier for civic groups to speak freely (minority religious groups champion First Amendment freedoms for this reason). Public policies can threaten civic groups enough that they become more politically active (for instance, opponents of abortion became more active after the Supreme Court's 1973 ruling in *Roe v. Wade*). The hope of receiving government funding or of legislation making it easier to do business is also a "carrot" that public officials can use to mobilize certain constituencies within civil society.

In this concluding chapter, I want to consider how the debate about faith-based social services has influenced—and may continue to influence—civil society in the United States. It would appear that Charitable Choice and the subsequent faith-based initiatives generated support from some constituencies and opposition from others. If public debate mobilizes support or opposition, we might say that civil society is better for it. Whether they like or dislike the policies, citizens are paying attention. They may be angry enough to voice their opposition or eager enough to express their support in the public arena. But we need to look closer to see who exactly has been mobilized (or might be mobilized) and at the kinds of coalitions or voting blocs that may be emerging. Civil society is always about coalitions. Individual citizens matter, and their opinions may matter even without being mobilized because pollsters can measure these opinions. Yet it is the capacity to weld individual citizens into voting blocs, identity groups, and coalitions that influences elections and the outcome of legislative proposals.

One way to think about the effect of public policy on civil society, therefore, is to consider the influence of political rhetoric and of policy proposals on the responses of the electorate. In the case of faith-based programs, we would want to know who has been most in favor of them, whether these supporters constitute an identity group of some kind, and whether these identity groups might form coalitions or voting blocs that would be more favorable to one candidate or party than another. Viewed this way, proposals about faith-based services are a political tool. Public officials can use these proposals to attract voters. Whatever else may be accomplished, the very act of proposing ideas about faith-based services can have an impact on civil society, whether those proposals ever become realities or not.

We must also consider the realities of faith-based programs. Apart from the rhetoric, the programs themselves have the potential to influence civil society. Most straightforwardly, they can help poor people get back on their feet. They can make people more self-sufficient. They may produce life-transforming experiences, as supporters hope and as opponents fear. Faith-based programs can promote faith and thus influence civil society by generating more believers who flock to churches. These programs can also shape the public by extending norms of professionalism and principles of fairness into areas that have previously been guided by other norms and principles.

My argument will be that the rhetoric about faith-based programs has had one kind of impact on civil society while the reality of these programs has had quite a different effect. These differing consequences concern the *diversity* of civil society; that is, the degree to which different interests reflecting the heterogeneity of the United States are expressed or the degree to which standardization and even uniformity is the result. It is perhaps odd to emphasize diversity when the purpose of faith-based and other social programs is ostensibly to alleviate misery. Yet, it is often the unintended consequences of public policy that turn out to be most important. In the case of faith-based services, proponents have argued that these programs should be supported (whether they are more effective or not) because *not* to support them would amount to discrimination, whereas supporting them respects and upholds the inherent religious and cultural diversity of the United States. The question is, thus, are there reasons to think this is happening and, if so, what kind of diversity is being upheld? What about faith-based organizations does encourage diversity and what about them may not be as conducive to diversity?

The *rhetoric*—or if one chooses to think about it as more than rhetoric, the concrete proposals that have been put forward by public leaders—has been especially attractive to certain constituents. For these constituents, faith-based programs seem, among other things, to be a way in which their distinctive values are being recognized by leaders in Washington. Faith-based programs are thus reinforcing the identities of particular constituencies and they are in this way, I will suggest, reinforcing the diversity of civil society by drawing these groups in and encouraging them to express their values. The *reality* of faith-based programs probably has the opposite effect. From what we know about the operations of these programs, it makes sense to suggest that they do more to promote homogeneity than they do to encourage diversity. And if this is the case, it is an ironic consequence, for it is diversity ("choice") that the proponents of faith-based initiatives have often seen as the special advantage of these programs. To see how these differing, even competing influences on civil society have taken form, we must first consider public support for government-funded religion-based service programs, and then return to what we have learned in previous chapters about the content of these programs.

Support for Government-Religion Partnerships

The most controversial aspect of faith-based social services has been whether government should help pay for these services. When churches initiate social ministries through their own finances, people can decide for themselves whether they want to help pay for these programs. When government spends tax dollars on them, all citizens become involved in their financing, and for this reason, these programs become items of contestation. The constituencies who want them most are eager to get everyone to pay for them, while those who dislike them prefer not to be required to pay. As we have seen in previous chapters, the answer to the question of whether government should fund faith-based programs probably depends to a great extent on which kinds of agencies are at issue and on what exactly those agencies are doing. The ones that are nominally faith-related but that do not expect clients to become converts have little reason not to seek and obtain government funding. The ones that help clients by providing life-transforming experiences through intensive involvement in religious training are more problematic with respect to government funding. They at least must walk a fine line between claiming that government should fund them because they are effective and arguing that the funds they receive are not being used for religious purposes. But the question of funding is as much about public rhetoric as it is about such practical considerations. How members of the public *view* the role of religion in connection with social welfare has a lot to do with their stand on larger issues—from how important religion is in their personal lives to whether they think the society as a whole is in need of more religion. Like other issues, support for government-religion partnerships in social service provision is an indication of the deeper values around which the public is willing to mobilize, vote, or in other ways be guided in their roles as citizens.

One of the best sources for examining public opinion about government funding of faith-based service organizations is a national survey conducted in 2002 by Princeton Survey Research Associates for the Pew Research Center for the People and the Press.[1] When asked their opinion about "allowing churches and other houses of worship to apply, along with other organizations, for government funding to provide social services such as job training or drug treatment counseling to people who need them," 26 percent of those surveyed said they were strongly in favor, 44 percent said they were in favor, 18 percent said they were opposed, 9 percent said they were strongly opposed, and 3 percent said they were unsure.[2] In short, more than twice as many people were in favor of government funding as were opposed.

The survey did not ask separately, as I have suggested we need to, about possible differences between congregations and more specialized faith-based service agencies. Focusing as it did on "churches and other houses of worship," the question is actually useful for our purposes, though, because it was direct government support to congregations with which much of the discussion of faith-based initiatives was concerned at the time the survey was conducted. Including the phrase *along with other organizations* was helpful because supporters of faith-based initiatives were increasingly trying to emphasize that they merely wanted a level playing field for church-based programs. At the same time, mentioning job training as well as drug treatment counseling in the question helpfully provided balance because job training was less often mentioned in public discussions than drug programs as an area in which faith might be especially beneficial.

That so many people were at least mildly in favor of government funding of this kind is probably not surprising. In my Religion and Politics survey, 74 percent of the public said they were in favor of religious congregations in their community "receiving government funds to help provide services to the poor." Despite its pervasive unease about government, the American public is often in favor of government taking an active role (even in concert with religion) to accomplish desired ends (from educating children to encouraging people to get married). And we know that in public opinion surveys it is easy for people to agree with statements that seem reasonable, especially if these statements (as this one does) seem to imply evenhandedness, inclusiveness, or tolerance. What is more interesting than the large number who mildly favor government funding of faith-based programs is the quarter or so of the public who are *strongly* in favor of such funding. These are the people who may feel strongly enough about it to write letters to public officials, vote on the basis of candidates' views about this issue, or press community leaders to form closer ties between government agencies and churches.

Who are these people? It is the answer to this question that will begin to address the larger question of how faith-based proposals may be affecting the climate of public opinion and the potential for various constituencies to be mobilized. Let me suggest four possibilities, each consistent with a popular interpretation of what is *really going on* with the debate about government funding of faith-based services. The first is that government-funded programs of this kind are—as their advocates in Washington argue—a way to help poor people and are thus attractive to poor people themselves, especially those who may be religiously inclined. The second is that supporters of these programs are hard-core conservatives. They are conservative in self-defined political ideology. They are Republicans, probably on the far right of their party. They voted for George W. Bush. They like his views about faith-based services. And they may even be carryovers from the Reagan era who are skeptical about big government and thus see in the faith-based initiatives a way to scale back government's role. The third possibility is that these supporters are more specifically opposed to what has been called "welfare as we know it." They oppose government assistance for the poor, or at least they oppose expanding it, and so they favor government funding of faith-based agencies as a way of privatizing public welfare. They probably favored the 1996 welfare reforms for the same reason, and they probably think welfare programs have done more harm than good. Moreover, they may think the reason such programs have had ill effects is that poor people are lazy or in need of moral reform, rather than viewing them as victims of social conditions and thus deserving of public assistance. The fourth possibility is that support for government funding of faith-based programs has more to do with religion than anything else. In this view, people who are religiously involved themselves want religious organizations to do more, and they apparently feel this could happen with government funding. They may not just be religious, but conservatively religious, too. That is, they are evangelical or born-again Christians who perhaps think that faith-based agencies *not* getting government help is a form of religious discrimination. Perhaps they have had transformative religious experiences and thus think the way to correct social ills is to fund religious organizations to help others have those experiences.

The figures shown in table 9.1 help us to choose among these possible interpretations. The breakdown by race and ethnicity shows that government-supported faith-based programs are especially attractive to African Americans. In these data, African American respondents were three times as likely to have been receiving welfare benefits or currently be receiving these benefits as white respondents. Thus, it is not surprising that they would be supportive of government funding for church programs, at least if they thought this would be a way of providing more assistance to people like themselves or to others in their community.[3] It is interesting, however, that Hispanic respondents were scarcely any more likely to favor government-funded religious programs than white non-Hispanic respondents, despite being about twice as likely to have received welfare benefits themselves. The view that government funding of faith-based programs is most strongly supported by hard-core conservatives is partly supported;

for instance, 33 percent respond "strongly in favor" to the survey question among those who say their political views are very conservative—the highest proportion among any of the categories of political views. Yet the next highest proportion is among those who say they are very *liberal.* Moreover, Republicans and Bush voters are only slightly more likely to express support than Democrats, Independents, and Gore voters. The third possibility—that support for this kind of government funding is really a referendum against public welfare in general—also is consistent with only some of the data. People who think welfare makes people dependent on government, for instance, are slightly more likely to favor government funding of faith-based programs than people who have a more positive view of welfare. But the highest percentage in favor of such funding is among those who strongly favor more generous government assistance to the poor. The fourth interpretation seems to be most consistent with the results. People who say religion is very important in their lives and people who say they are born-again or evangelical Christians are the most likely to favor this kind of government funding.[4]

Suppose a poll like this had been taken prior to the 2000 election by a firm hired to advise political candidates. The question would have been: Will coming out in favor of government funding for church-based programs be a political asset or a liability? Clearly, it would be difficult to provide a conclusive argument on the basis of what we have just seen. Conservatives might be attracted, but so might liberals. Republicans might be, but so might Democrats. African Americans might be supportive, but Latinos might not be. And so on. We would thus need to know more before positing an answer.

The place to start would be the two groups who show the highest proportions of support for government-funded church programs and who are also identifiable constituencies with some possibility of voting as a bloc or being mobilized collectively. One is African Americans. The other is white evangelical Christians. In table 9.1, these are the groups in which support for government-funded church programs is strongest. There is also a minority among white nonevangelicals who support such funding. We need to look at these three groups to gain a clearer picture of where support for government funding of faith-based services lies. Doing so offers a way of understanding why each group includes people who strongly favor such funding.

Table 9.1

Support for Government Funding of Faith-Based Service Programs
(Percentage who strongly favor allowing churches and other houses of worship to apply,
along with other organizations, for government funding to provide social services such as
job training or drug treatment counseling to people who need them)

	Strongly Favor
All respondents	26
White non-Hispanic	23
Black non-Hispanic	50
Hispanic	26
Republicans	28
Democrats	26
Independents	26
Voted for Bush	26
Voted for Gore	23
Very conservative	33
Conservative	29
Moderate	24
Liberal	22
Very liberal	30
More generous government assistance to the poor	
Strongly favor	49
Favor	19
Oppose	16
Strongly oppose	23
1996 welfare reform works better	28
1996 welfare reform works worse	26
Welfare makes people dependent on government	28
Welfare helps people unable to support themselves	23
Poverty reflects society's failures	26
Poverty is because of individual failures	27
Religion is very important in own life	32
Religion is fairly important	18
Religion is not very important	9
Born again or evangelical Christian	34
Not born again or evangelical Christian	23

Source: Religion and Public Life Survey, 2002.
Note: Weighted data, N = 3,626.

Among African Americans, those who have been on welfare themselves are significantly more likely to favor government-funded church programs than those who have not been on welfare (table 9.2). This is probably not surprising, but it does suggest that one reason for African Americans' interest in policies favoring faith-based initiatives is the perception that their own families or neighbors may benefit. More speculatively, this result may also suggest that African Americans who have received welfare tend *not* to perceive government funding for church programs as a way in which welfare services as a whole may be *reduced*. The other factors that seem to be associated with favoring faith-based initiatives among African Americans are being politically conservative or moderate (Republican or Democrat) rather than being a liberal Democrat, having voted for Gore (which seems at odds with being politically conservative), being favorable to Christian conservatives, agreeing that people should do more to help the needy, disagreeing that government should help more needy people, and thinking that the welfare system makes people dependent.

Our political pollster-consultant would probably conclude that African Americans are a potential constituency that could be mobilized by offering faith-based initiatives as a political incentive.[5] Which particular appeals would work best might be unclear, though. For instance, it might be best to appeal to African Americans who have been on welfare, but it might also be best to appeal to African Americans who are unhappy with the welfare system. It also might be easiest to attract political conservatives or moderates, but Democratic candidates might be more attractive than Republican candidates. Still, the possibility that Republican candidates could draw away some of the African American support for Democratic candidates might be a reasonable conclusion. The most tantalizing result is the high level of support for faith-based programs among African Americans who strongly favor the Christian conservative movement (whatever that may mean). This is tantalizing because the Christian conservative movement, *as movement,* could be the vehicle for attracting African Americans to certain candidates or issues.

The Christian conservative movement also emerges as an important factor in the results for white evangelicals. We shall want to consider what the Christian conservative movement is, but for now it is worth noting that how favorable evangelicals say they feel toward the movement is the strongest predictor of how they feel about government funding for church

TABLE 9.2

African Americans' and White Evangelicals' Support for Government Funding
(Percentage who strongly favor allowing churches and other houses of worship to
apply . . . for government funding to provide social services such as job training or drug
treatment counseling to people who need them)

	African Am.	White Evan.	White Other	All Resp.
All	48	30	21	26
Welfare recipient — yes	58	36	28	38
Welfare recipient — no	43	29	20	24
Conservative Republican	57	31	26	28
Moderate Republican	50	38	22	27
Conservative/Moderate Democrat	56	19	22	27
Liberal Democrat	34	3	19	20
Voted for Bush	35	32	22	26
Voted for Gore	47	23	16	23
Very favorable to Christian conservatives	60	49	32	47
Mostly favorable to Christian conservatives	52	30	29	33
Unfavorable to Christian conservatives	34	15	15	15
Agree people should do more to help the needy	53	32	22	28
Disagree people should do more to help the needy	36	18	16	18
Agree govt should help more needy people	38	27	23	26
Disagree govt should help more needy people	46	27	18	22
Welfare makes people dependent	56	31	25	28
Welfare helps people who can't support themselves	50	26	14	23

Source: Religion and Public Life Survey, 2002.

Note: Weighted data, African American (N = 408), white evangelical (N = 970), white nonevangelical (N = 1,509), total (N = 3,628).

programs. Otherwise, the factors that influence their views about such funding appear mostly to be political party (Republican) and thinking that people should do more to help the needy. Although it is the case that white evangelicals who have been on welfare are more likely to favor government funding for churches than those who have not been, this number is relatively small among white evangelicals. How they feel about government helping people or about welfare seems hardly to matter.

Among white respondents in the survey who were not evangelical Christians, being favorable to the Christian conservative movement is again one of the strongest predictors of support for government-funded church programs. Party identification makes relatively little difference among this group, but those who think welfare makes people dependent are significantly more likely to favor government-funded church programs than those who think welfare helps people who cannot support themselves.

If a single conclusion can be drawn from these results, it is that support for the Christian conservative movement and support for government funding of church-based service programs are closely related. Of the relationships shown in table 9.2, this one is the strongest and indeed is the only one that is consistently strong in all four columns when all the various factors are taken into account.[6] The implication is that a political candidate who wanted to mobilize support for policies favorable to faith-based initiatives would do well to enlist the help of the Christian conservative movement. The additional implication is that the Christian conservative movement may be an especially powerful political tool because of its potential for generating common ground (and perhaps even cooperation) between African Americans and white evangelicals.

The possibility of common political interests or a coalition between African Americans and white evangelicals is one that should not be taken lightly. In their book *Divided by Faith,* Michael Emerson and Christian Smith argue that white evangelicals claim to be interested in racial reconciliation but generally do little to promote it because they fail to see the social structures that perpetuate racial inequality.[7] The implication of this argument is that African Americans and white evangelicals are by no means natural allies in American politics. For their part, white evangelicals may not be overt racists, but they have done little to help the cause of racial justice, according to Emerson and Smith, because they think racial divisions can be healed by bringing individuals to a closer walk with God. Paradoxically, African Americans and white evangelicals do share many of the same religious beliefs, yet the two groups are sufficiently different and are separated to the point that common interests are difficult to identify. Few attend the same churches or belong to the same denominations. Few live in the same neighborhoods. Whereas African Americans have overwhelmingly voted Democratic, white evangelicals have included large (and apparently increasing) numbers of Republicans. And there are continuing disparities in levels of income. These differences are evident in the Pew survey. Three times as many African Americans as white evangelicals said they were currently on welfare and more than twice as many of the former had been on welfare in the past. African Americans were twice as likely as white evangelicals to have earned less than $10,000 during the previous year and only half as likely to have earned more than $100,000. Only 7 percent of African Americans described themselves as Republicans, whereas 43 percent of white evangelicals did; in contrast, 64 percent of African Americans said they were Democrats, compared with only 25 percent of white evangelicals. In the 2000 presidential election, African Americans had voted for Gore by a margin of ten to one, while white evangelicals had voted almost three-to-one for Bush. The one thing on which the two groups were most similar was support for the Christian conservative movement: 27 percent of African Americans said they were very favorable toward it (with another 42 percent favoring it) as did 23 percent of white evangelicals (and 57 percent more saying they favored it).

Were one a *Republican* candidate for president, figures like these might suggest little hope of garnering support among African Americans. To the extent that there was hope, though, it would be through those who sympathized with the Christian conservative movement.[8] Indeed, in the Pew survey, African Americans who said they were very favorable toward the Christian conservative movement were four times as likely to have voted for Bush in 2000 as those who were only mildly favorable or opposed to the movement.[9]

The Christian Conservative Movement

What is the Christian conservative movement? The phrase *Christian conservative movement* comes from the Pew survey. It is not the title of any particular organization, instead connoting the cluster of groups and religious leaders who emerged between the early 1980s and late 1990s as a force in American politics. The Reverend Jerry Falwell's Moral Majority spearheaded the movement in the early 1980s and television preacher Pat Robertson's bid for the presidency in 1988 became emblematic of the movement's efforts to gain political power. Opposition to abortion and concerns about homosexuality were among its most frequently emphasized positions.[10] As I mentioned in chapter 1, self-identified religious conservatives were also distinguishable in surveys as early as 1984 by opposition to government spending for social welfare programs.[11] The 1996 Charitable Choice provision was formulated by Senator John Ashcroft (R-Missouri), an active member of an Assemblies of God church who was haled by conservative evangelical leaders as an ally on Capitol Hill. Early support for Charitable Choice came from the National Association of Evangelicals, an organization that had avoided taking stands on public policies until the 1980s, but became increasingly favorable toward working with government to achieve its agenda on issues such as abortion and school prayer.[12] In Texas as early as 1997, then-governor George W. Bush began holding regular meetings with conservative clergy, including T. D. Jakes and Tony Evans, the state's best-known African American preachers, and in 1999 he became a defender of Teen Challenge against the state drug-control agency's threat to shut down the popular religious program for failing to meet health and safety standards.[13] Subsequently, the Bush administration's efforts in Washington to expand faith-based initiatives were supported by a variety of conservative religious and political leaders. Some of these leaders, including Falwell and Robertson, voiced concerns about funds going to non-Christian organizations, but for the most part conservative leaders continued to be active backers of White House policies.

Leaders of prominent African American congregations and denominations also became strong advocates of the Bush administration's faith-based initiatives. These leaders generally did not identify themselves with the Christian conservative movement and, indeed, were sometimes critical of the movement because they viewed its white evangelical leaders as moving too slowly to support an expansion of faith-based initiatives.[14] Yet, in so doing, they made common cause with leaders such as Senator Ashcroft and Prison Fellowship leader Charles Colson, who had championed faith-based initiatives. These African American leaders included the Reverend William J. Shaw, president of the National Baptist Convention; the

Reverend Walter Fauntroy, head of the Black Church Communications Network; the Reverend Cecil Bishop, senior bishop of the African Methodist Episcopal Church; and the Reverend Gilbert Patterson, presiding bishop of the Church of God in Christ.[15]

The figures in table 9.3 show where the strongest grassroots support for the Christian conservative movement was located in 2002. These figures are from logistic regression analysis of strong support ("very favorable") versus weaker support or opposition to the Christian conservative movement. They show that the odds of being very favorable toward the movement were three times greater among white evangelicals than among other respondents. They also show that these odds were almost that much greater among African Americans than among respondents who were not African American. In addition, the odds of favoring the movement were more than twice as great among conservative Republicans as among other respondents. And these odds were about one and a half times as great among people who were critical of the welfare system (say it promotes dependency) as among those who were not critical of it. Each of these factors continues to have a statistically significant relationship with favoring

TABLE 9.3
Support for the Conservative Christian Movement

	Model 1	Model 2	Model 3	Model 4	Model 5
White evangelical	3.013***	—	—	—	3.550***
Black		2.769***	—	—	5.642***
Conservative Republican			2.260***	—	2.071***
Critical of welfare				1.475***	1.415**
No college education					1.313*
Attend church weekly					1.684***
Intercept	.073***	.092***	.090***	.082***	.022***
−2 Log likelihood	2234.762	2278.248	2285.654	2316.121	2068.353
Nagelkerke R-square	.052	.027	.023	.006	.145

Source: Religion and Public Life Survey, 2002.
Note: Weighted data, N = 3,628; *p < .05; **p < .01; ***p < .001.

the Christian conservative movement when all the others are taken into account and when level of education and church attendance are taken into account.

We might summarize these results by saying that there are at least four constituencies that find the Christian conservative movement attractive: white evangelicals, African Americans, conservative Republicans, and people who are upset about the welfare system. There are probably other constituencies as well that the Pew data do not show (for instance, people who are concerned about abortion or homosexuality). For present purposes, though, these results suggest that the Christian conservative movement may be a banner under which criticisms of the welfare system can be combined with support from Christians and conservatives who might well be expected to favor such a movement, but also from African Americans. Indeed, when all the factors are examined (model 5 in table 9.3), the odds of favoring the Christian conservative movement among African Americans are more than five times greater than among respondents who are not African American.

The information shown in table 9.4 provides a way of understanding the beliefs and values that are especially prominent among supporters of the Christian conservative movement. These are a particular combination of views about government, religion, and individual responsibility. With respect to government, Christian conservatives are more willing than other Americans to breach the line separating government from private life and from religion. They are more likely in the survey than other respondents to approve of government being used as a tool to promote marriage and more likely to approve of churches endorsing political candidates. Supporters of the Christian conservative movement are also more likely than opponents to regard their own religion as the one true faith, to believe that the strength of American society is based on religious faith, and to doubt that people can be good Americans without religious faith. Consistent with these favorable views toward religion, they believe religious organizations can do a better job of providing services to needy people than other organizations can.[16] Supporters are also more likely than opponents to emphasize individual responsibility—saying that poverty is the result of individual failures rather than social or economic structures and that children living in poverty are the result of the individual failures of their parents. This em-

TABLE 9.4
General Views of Supporters of the Christian Conservative Movement
(Percentages)

	Very Favorable	Favorable	Unfavorable	All Resp.
Government should start up programs that encourage people to get and stay married	36	21	10	18
During political elections, churches and other houses of worship should come out in favor of one candidate over another	42	22	19	24
Churches and other houses of worship should not keep out of politics*	72	65	35	53
Right for clergy to discuss political candidates or issues from the pulpit*	46	32	27	31
My religion is the one true faith leading to eternal life	39	24	9	20
The strength of American society is based on religious faith	84	68	40	59
A person cannot be a good American if he or she does not have religious faith	27	12	10	14
Religious organizations can do the best job of providing services to people in need*	61	43	28	39
Most poor people are poor because of their own individual failures	69	66	54	62
Children are being raised in poverty these days because of the failure of their parents as individuals	59	52	45	50
People should do much more than they do now to help others who are in need, even if it costs them their own time and money	49	30	30	33

Source: Religion and Public Life Survey, 2002.
Note: Weighted data, (N = 3,628); *Results from a Pew Religion and Public Life Survey conducted in 2001, in which approximately half of respondents were asked specific questions (weighted data, N = 1,703).

phasis on individual responsibility, however, does not deter supporters of the Christian conservative movement from thinking that more should be done to help the poor. They think it is important to help others in need, at least by giving of their own time and money.[17]

There is, then, a set of beliefs and values that would make it reasonable for Christian conservatives to be in favor of government policies oriented toward the support of faith-based social services. Government initiatives that may encourage individual morality by channeling money to churches are not likely to be viewed as a violation of the separation of church and state. Religion is thought to be true and necessary for the social good. And if poverty is the result of individual failures, then faith-based organizations are presumably a good solution because they can change the minds and hearts of individuals.

If Christian conservatives think churches can do a good job of providing social services for the reasons just suggested, they nevertheless draw distinctions among the kinds of services they consider churches especially well qualified at providing. Not surprisingly, they overwhelmingly believe churches are better than secular organizations or government agencies at mentoring young people and counseling teens about pregnancy (table 9.5). By a large margin, they also think churches are better than these other organizations at counseling and educating prisoners. Slightly more than half think churches have an advantage in treating drug and alcohol addictions and in feeding the homeless, and nearly this many feel the same about child care services. Literacy training, job training, and health care, though, are different matters. Relatively small proportions of Christian conservatives think churches can provide these better than other organizations.

These findings are consistent with Christian conservatives' views of social problems. Many of these problems are, they believe, the result of individual failings. The way to overcome these failings is by developing a new set of values and a new belief system. Christian conservatives believe the church is the way to help people do this. Counseling and mentoring programs are the best examples. When people need other skills, though, such as medical care and job training, early research has prompted some observers to acknowledge that churches may have no special advantages.[18]

In emphasizing the role of Christian conservatives, I do not mean to imply that they are the only force behind policies favorable to government funding for faith-based service programs. The data are striking, neverthe-

Table 9.5

Views of Supporters of the Christian Conservative Movement on Social Service Provision (Percentages responding to the question: Who does the best job providing each kind of service?)

	Very Favorable to Christian Conservatives	All Respondents
Treatment for drug and alcohol addiction		
Religious organizations	57	28
Nonreligious community-based group	15	37
Federal or state government agency	24	30
Literacy training		
Religious organizations	21	12
Nonreligious community-based group	20	31
Federal or state government agency	56	50
Mentoring programs for young people		
Religious organizations	77	41
Nonreligious community-based group	10	38
Federal or state government agency	10	15
Feeding the homeless		
Religious organizations	52	40
Nonreligious community-based group	15	26
Federal or state government agency	32	28
Counseling teens about pregnancy		
Religious organizations	66	40
Nonreligious community-based group	14	42
Federal or state government agency	13	12
Child care		
Religious organizations	45	30
Nonreligious community-based group	19	34
Federal or state government agency	36	29
Health care		
Religious organizations	29	10
Nonreligious community-based group	20	29
Federal or state government agency	46	54
Job training		
Religious organizations	8	6
Nonreligious community-based group	23	28
Federal or state government agency	67	61
Counseling and educating prisoners		
Religious organizations	70	41
Nonreligious community-based group	9	20
Federal or state government agency	20	34

Source: Pew Religion and Public Life Survey, conducted in 2001, in which approximately half of respondents were asked specific questions (weighted data, N = 1,703).

less, in the consistency they suggest between holding favorable views of the Christian conservative movement and believing that government funding should be available for church-run social programs. With leadership, access to the White House, and a network of local clergy and lay members who sympathize with it, the Christian conservative movement is also in a strong position to mobilize support for government funding of faith-based initiatives.

From a broader perspective, faith-based services represent a way to connect two segments of the population—African Americans and white evangelicals—who have often been (or felt) disenfranchised by the political process and by values that have strong resonance with some strands of the American heritage.[19] African Americans and white evangelicals can feel that faith-based services are being championed by the White House and other government officials. Their own pastors or other religious leaders whom they identify as Christian conservatives support these programs. And the programs make sense because religion is good, it corrects the deficiencies of individuals in poverty, and it is something that government should help to promote.

Although critics of the Christian conservative movement often view it as a kind of incipient totalitarianism that threatens cultural diversity, the movement could just as easily be portrayed as an influence that is promoting greater diversity in civil society as a whole. African Americans and white evangelical Christians still have distinctive interests, forms of religious expression, and values. There is little reason to think that either would blend into the other or that efforts to impose particular religious practices on the rest of the population would succeed. Through the Christian conservative movement and through public debate about faith-based initiatives, they are simply drawn into the public arena and given reason to think that their voices have been heard.[20]

The benefit of including minority voices in civil society is hard to disagree with from the perspective of democratic principles. The discussion of faith-based programs has perhaps succeeded even better than some of their proponents had anticipated in this regard. If diversity and the representation of diverse interests is good for democracy, then the discussion of faith-based service programs has apparently served America well. We must, however, consider whether the actual functioning of these programs is likely to have the same consequences.

Is Civil Society One-Dimensional?

The larger question we are left with is whether faith-based service organizations, once in operation, have the same effects on civil society as policy discussions about them do. Do the ways these organizations are staffed and funded contribute to the diversity that has long been a strength of American society or are they monochromatic and becoming more so as a result of recent government policies? Let us think about how each of these possibilities may be true. Religion in the United States reflects the great historic divisions among racial and ethnic groups, immigrants of different national origins, social classes, and regions—the divisions H. Richard Niebuhr wrote about so clearly in the early twentieth century—and religion is thus one of the mainstays of social diversity.[21] The fact that congregations and faith communities do not try to serve everyone, but continue to be distinguishable in terms of membership, loyalty, and internal friendships means that their historic cultural distinctiveness is preserved. They provide places, as we have seen, where people make friends and join small groups. Their strength lies in their ability to draw friends and neighbors together and to involve them in worship services and Sunday school classes and to enlist their energy in staffing committees and caring for the needy in their midst. The communities of which congregations are composed are often racially and ethnically bounded. They attract people of the same racial background, of similar income and education levels, and from similar national origins. Congregations function less well in encouraging ties across social class lines or among different racial and ethnic groups. As such, local houses of worship are places where distinctive Pentecostal or Orthodox styles of worship may be found, where resounding lectures given by African American preachers are heard, or where Muslims gather on Fridays for the *khutbah* (sermon) and *salat* (prayers). The argument for giving government funding to these houses of worship to develop special programs for people associated with these worshipping communities is that such funding upholds the local diversity represented therein. An even stronger argument can be made: that to give funding to secular programs while denying such funding to religious ones is to privilege the former at the expense of the latter.[22] The society thus becomes more organized around secular values, the action shifts to secular service organizations, and religiously motivated people who want to serve have to go to those organizations rather than being able to serve at their houses of worship. If instead government funding goes to congregations as well as to secular agencies, government benefits by making use of the resources and skills these congregations can provide. Especially if none of the religious trappings need be removed and the programs can be staffed by people chosen because they live by the faith community's values, then an infusion of public funds would seem only to help these groups do more of what they would like to do anyway. Furthermore, the funding of religious organizations in communities that have been discriminated against, such as African American churches, may be a way of channeling much-needed resources to these communities and of placing these resources under local control. That, too, would seem to reinforce diversity. The possibility that faith-based organizations may contribute less to diversity than these scenarios suggest, though, needs to be entertained as well.

The monomorphic quality of faith-based organizations is one that we have seen in a number of the studies we have considered. It is especially evident in Smith and Sosin's research on faith-based service organizations in Chicago and Seattle, where not only government funding but also norms of professionalism, bureaucratic structures, reporting requirements, and an emphasis on the rights and dignity of clients inhibited distinctive expressions of faith. The same uniformity may be evident in Green and Sherman's findings that upwards of three-quarters of ostensibly faith-based service organizations actually give little indication that faith is present at all, except perhaps in the personal motives of staff. In my study of the Lehigh Valley, recipients' perceptions of service agencies, both in the survey and in personal interviews, suggested little difference between faith-based agencies and nonsectarian agencies. Only among those who received help directly from congregations or from specialized agencies that functioned like congregations was there evidence of identity-transforming or identity-reaffirming relationships. Yet congregations in the Lehigh Valley were not as well equipped to deal with the serious needs of people in lower-income neighborhoods as the separate faith-based and nonsectarian service agencies were. These agencies brought a different kind of diversity to the community. Some specialized in job training, others in food distribution, and so on. They were diverse in the same way that banks are different from supermarkets. Had there been more government funding available to the faith-based organizations, it is not clear that the variety we typically associate with religious communities would have been greater.

Does it matter? The reason to be concerned about the diversity or lack of diversity associated with faith-based social services is that the character of civil society itself hinges on the larger question of what values are being encouraged and what values are not. Few would disagree that there needs to be a certain level of uniformity in society. Standardized time zones, a single national currency, fixed airline schedules, and a shared language are examples. The fact that we share these aspects of our culture means that the business of social life can be conducted more easily. We benefit from other public uniformities as well. For instance, agreed-upon procedures for passing laws that pertain to everyone or rules for conducting public meetings with a minimum of confusion assist in dealing with the complex decision making our society requires. But there is another kind of uniformity that is more dubious in its effects. This is the standardization associated with least-common-denominator values that Tocqueville worried about, the conformity to mass opinion he believed characteristic of democratic societies in which everyone was the equal of everyone else. In our time, this uniformity is evident in the prepackaging of news by the two or three large communication syndicates that results in television and newspaper news coverage being nearly always the same in style and content while very rarely including stories critical of these syndicates or their corporate affiliates. The homogenization of civil society is equally apparent in the growth of fast-food chains, the fashion industry, prefabricated home construction materials, and many other realms of the consumer market. We may feel that in these areas we can at least opt out of the market. In public discussions about public values, though, the terms in which important aspects of civil society are framed may be harder to keep varied. Thus, it may be, as critics fear, that the meanings of *freedom* become increasingly vague and even vacuous or that public policy is decided more on the basis of what is cost-effective than in terms of what is beneficial to all.

There is little evidence that government funding is an effective tool for promoting greater diversity or inhibiting the march of uniformity. Government funding takes money from the public and thus must be used in ways that are accountable to the public. It necessarily requires the application of standards that can be agreed upon by all the public, such as fairness, efficiency, and effectiveness. No matter what the intentions are in support-ing diverse groups, the norms by which that support is given or adminis-tered will impose a degree of uniformity that may not have been present before. In the case of religious organizations, this will be true as well. The standards of professionalism and considerations about rights will be rein-forced by concerns about public accountability. We as the public are will-ing to strike this bargain with government in a growing number of areas. We want children to be educated well, so we go along with programs that require national testing standards, even though these compromise the free-dom of local school districts to determine their own curriculums. We may be in favor of government funding for faith-based service programs for the same reasons. These specialized agencies, and even congregations, may have the capacity to operate foster placement services or teen pregnancy counseling centers that the public wants. We would permit government officials to negotiate contracts with these agencies as long as the programs are effective and money is not diverted to religious uses. But we should be under no illusions about what is involved. Contracts are legally enforceable relationships. They are very different from the informal, personal relation-ships that have been the hallmark of religious congregations.

Where public policy can play a more positive role in encouraging diver-sity is in protecting local groups from government intervention and in up-holding standards of civil liberties and nondiscrimination that might otherwise be in jeopardy in the case of weaker and less dominant groups. That has been the role government has played most effectively in protect-ing the religious freedoms of all Americans. Rather than trying to support religious groups or their programs, government has protected the rights of these groups to pursue their goals voluntarily. It has done so through legis-lation and judicial opinions preventing particular religious groups from imposing their programs on others and by withholding actions by govern-ment that might unduly limit the ability of religious groups to worship freely. In the case of racial discrimination, the government's role has been more controversial because of efforts to remediate the effects of past dis-crimination, but the underlying principle has remained that of encourag-ing the opportunities of diverse groups by applying standards of fairness and fair treatment.

In all this there is of course room for disagreement about the impor-tance of diversity itself. A Christian fundamentalist, for example, might argue that the United States would be better off if everyone were Christian than if large numbers were Jews or Muslims, let alone atheists or secular humanists. Yet this same fundamentalist would want there to be sufficient diversity that Baptists could do things differently from Pentecostals and that the rights of all fundamentalists would be protected against the possible hegemony of secularists. The more pertinent question, therefore, is not diversity as such but whether the kinds of professional and procedural norms necessitated by government support are inimical to genuinely diverse religious and cultural expressions.

The answer to this question is that it depends greatly on the goals of particular religious organizations and the means by which they achieve those goals. For a large majority of faith-based service organizations, as we have seen, the service-provider model is already sufficiently in place that government is often already a source of their funding, and even when it is not, these organizations try to provide services to the broader community in a way that upholds fairness and is consistent with standards of efficiency and effectiveness. Many of the services that people need can be supplied in this manner and there is no particular reason why they need to be provided by organizations that are either different from or similar to their constituencies in religion, race, or other social characteristics. However, the same is not true for congregations and for the small segment of specialized faith-based organizations that function like congregations. In these instances, faith is essential, not simply as an item of personal conviction, but as the basis for communal interaction and life-transforming experiences. Faith communities of that kind should jealously guard their freedom to be different and for this reason should be wary of government support. If they accept it at all, they would be wise to demarcate carefully its uses and to establish a firewall between these uses and the communities' religious activities.[23]

In the final analysis, though, the role of faith communities in American civil society is not as much about government support or public policy as it is about social relationships. Religious organizations are important as anchors for many of the relationships that tie civil society together. They are more enduring than many of the ephemeral task-oriented projects that develop in local communities or that increasingly appear on the Internet. They may not involve people as deeply as the workplace does, but they hold more possibility for being there when illness or bereavement strikes or after one retires. The volunteering that religious organizations promote appears to be relatively extensive and often connects volunteers with other organizations in the community. Among lower-income families, religious organizations are at least present in their neighborhoods and many of these families do participate regularly in them. But religious organizations should not be credited with doing more than they actually do. Many congregations are too small to operate specialized service programs. Much of the volunteer work initiated by congregations is not directed to the needy. And there is little evidence that faith-based service organizations necessarily function better than nonsectarian organizations. The challenge is for religious organizations to do their part alongside other private organizations and for government to continue doing its part. The special challenge for religious organizations is that the coming generation of community leaders may be less committed to these organizations than previous generations have been. That challenge will require religious organizations to be even truer to their mission than they have been in the past.

METHODOLOGICAL NOTE

The research for this book began in 1995 and took specific shape in 2000 but was heavily influenced by a line of scholarly inquiry I began in the late 1980s. In the earlier work that was published in 1991 (*Acts of Compassion: Caring for Others and Helping Ourselves*) and in 1995 (*Learning to Care: Elementary Kindness in an Age of Indifference*) I combined national survey data and information from in-depth qualitative interviews to examine the motives, values, and self-understandings of volunteer caregivers. In 1995 I initiated a research project that resulted in my 1998 book *Loose Connections: Joining Together in America's Fragmented Communities*. That book also combined national survey data and in-depth qualitative interviews. The interviews were conducted among directors and staff of service agencies as well as among volunteers and among people who did no volunteer work in their communities. Some of these interviews were conducted among the kinds of religiously sponsored or religiously initiated organizations that subsequently came to be called "faith-based service agencies." This of course was prior to the welfare reform legislation of 1996 that included the Charitable Choice provision through which such organizations could more easily receive government funding. With the ensuing debate about faith-based service organizations, I decided to stay in contact with some of the service agencies I had studied in the Lehigh Valley in northeastern Pennsylvania. I was also subsequently able to conduct several national surveys.

I have described the surveys in the chapters and in notes to the chapters at the points where I draw information from them. The main surveys from which I draw information are the Civic Involvement Survey, conducted in 1997; the Arts and Religion Survey, conducted in 1999; the Religion and Politics Survey, conducted in 2000; and the Small Groups Survey, conducted in 1999. These were all based on samples drawn to be representative of the adult (age eighteen and older) noninstitutionalized population of the continental United States. Two of the surveys (Civic Involvement and Religion and Politics) can be downloaded or analyzed online at the American Religion Data Archive (www.thearda.com), as can an earlier version of the Small Groups Survey, and any of the data sets or codebooks can be obtained directly from me as well. Publishing considerations prevent me from reproducing the full survey instruments here, but those can be obtained in the ways just mentioned. In the chapters, tables, and notes to chapters, I have provided as much detail as possible about the questions, levels of statistical significance, and results of multivariate analysis, perhaps to the point, I fear, of trying the patience of some readers.

The same goes for the Lehigh Valley Survey, from which I draw in chapters 6 and 7 particularly. As I say in those chapters, this was a survey conducted among a sample drawn to be representative of the adults (age eighteen and older) living in private residences in the fifteen lowest-income census tracts in Lehigh and Northampton counties (at the time of the 1990 census). It is relatively rare to have information from a representative sample of the community for such a geographically concentrated population as this. The study made it possible to ask questions about specific service agencies in the community and to do so without resorting to referrals from those organizations. The information thus makes possible comparisons of recipients and nonrecipients and permits us to examine the characteristics of people who were relatively casual or intermittent recipients rather than the kind whose names might appear on organizational lists. We were also able to circumvent concerns that organizations may have had about granting access to client lists. Because the survey included questions about specific organizations in the community, though, we decided to protect the confidentiality of those organizations by not referring to them by name.

I have also disguised the identities of individuals with whom qualitative interviews were conducted. Several kinds of individuals were interviewed. Agency directors (or, in a few cases, agency staff) were interviewed between 1995 and 2002. Some of the interviews on which I have drawn here were part of the broader study conducted in 1995, which I mentioned previously, but most were done in the Lehigh Valley and thus provided a way of knowing which organizations to include in our survey of the community and which were faith-based and which were secular. Some of the agency directors were interviewed two or three times. That information provided a basis for some of the tentative arguments I make in chapter 5 about how new programs are initiated, but the multiple interviews were not intended to provide longitudinal information as they were necessitated by securing information about a number of different topics, such as the organization's founding and auspices, sources of funding, relationships with churches, dealings with recipients, and ways of cultivating trust. The clergy who were interviewed were mostly interviewed twice. They were selected randomly to be representative of the approximately six hundred congregations in the Lehigh Valley. The 140 recipients with whom qualitative interviews were conducted were selected from the respondents to the survey and were chosen to provide information about contacts with the full range of service organizations asked about in the survey. Half were asked questions about trust and half were asked questions about altruism. Finally, 120 volunteers provided qualitative interviews. Half were from the survey and thus were lower-income residents who said they had done some volunteer work, and half were selected through referrals from agency directors or clergy.

The qualitative interviews were all transcribed. Collectively, they provided more than six thousand pages of information. I made extensive notes from these interviews, reading the transcripts both person by person and question by question. The material included in the chapters is based on that analysis. I have tried not only to distill the most important themes and to provide summaries, but also to include a few specific examples that illustrate these main conclusions and provide texture. Qualitative information of this kind is most useful in conjunction with large-scale surveys that can be used to substantiate generalizations and for examining the specific language and narratives that people use to make sense of their decisions and experiences.

Chapter 1. "Why Faith-Based"? Why Now?

1. Inglehart and Baker, "Modernization, Cultural Change and the Persistence of Traditional Values," Pew Research Center, "Among Wealthy Nations U.S. Stands Alone." See also evidence presented in chapter 4.

2. Examples of many of these indicators of religious commitment, along with national data, are given in Gallup and Lindsay, *Surveying the Religious Landscape*.

3. Data about welfare recipients is available from the U.S. Department of Health and Human Services at www.acf.dhhs.gov/acf_policy_planning.html#stats.

4. Two recent collections that provide helpful overviews of cultural sociology for those not acquainted with this field are Spillman, *Cultural Sociology*, and Cerulo, *Culture in Mind*. Besides my essays in these volumes, my approach to sociology of culture is also presented in my edited volume *Vocabularies of Public Life* and in Wuthnow, Hunter, Bergesen, and Kurzweil, *Cultural Analysis*.

5. Trattner, *From Poor Law to Welfare State*, chapter 1; Day, *A New History of Social Welfare*, chapters 1–2, 3; Axinn and Stern, *Social Welfare*, chapter 1. On patron-client relations, see Schmidt, Guasti, Lande, and Scott, *Friends, Followers, and Factions;* and on moral economy, James C. Scott, *The Moral Economy of the Peasant*.

6. Parsons, *Talcott Parsons on Institutions and Social Evolution*. For a critical examination of the modernization thesis, see the essays in Bruce, *Religion and Modernization*.

7. Skocpol, *Protecting Soldiers and Mothers*.

8. Orloff, *The Politics of Pensions*.

9. The most widely cited source of these arguments was Olasky, *The Tragedy of American Compassion*.

10. See also Clydesdale, "Toward Understanding the Role of Bible Beliefs and Higher Education in American Attitudes toward Eradicating Poverty."

11. Axinn and Stern, *Social Welfare*, chapter 9.

12. Steensland, "The Hydra and the Swords."

13. O'Neill and Hill, "Gaining Ground?"

14. See Seib, "Bush and Gore Find the Faith in Social Policy."

15. Bush, "Rallying the Armies of Compassion."

16. Particularly helpful on these issues are Gilman, "'Charitable Choice' and the Accountability Challenge"; and Lupu and Tuttle, "Government Partnerships with Faith-Based Service Providers."

17. A helpful overview and annotated bibliography is available in Jason D. Scott, "The Scope and Scale of Faith-Based Social Services."

18. Casanova, *Public Religions in the Modern World.*

19. Embeddedness is a central concept in economic sociology; see for example Swedberg, *Principles of Economic Sociology.*

20. See Ammerman, *Congregation and Community.*

21. DiMaggio and Powell, "The Iron Cage Revisited"; Thomas, *Revivalism and Social Change.*

22. The importance of understanding faith-based services as one component of complex, local service networks has been emphasized by Robert Wineburg in *A Limited Partnership.*

23. Skocpol and Finegold, "State Capacity and Economic Intervention in the Early New Deal"; Skowronek, *Building a New American State.*

24. This may have been particularly true as government contracts with private service providers became increasingly widespread. See Lynn, "Social Services and the State."

25. Some have suggested that a substantial number of existing faith-based services (particularly those sponsored by mainline churches) developed in response to cuts in human services during the 1980s. See Wineburg, *A Limited Partnership,* especially chapter 1, and Cnaan, Wineburg, and Boddie, *The Newer Deal,* chapter 1.

26. Hart, *What Does the Lord Require?*

27. Cohen and Arato, *Civil Society and Political Theory;* Wuthnow, *Between States and Markets.*

28. See Park and Reimer, "Revisiting the Social Sources of American Christianity."

29. Tocqueville, *Democracy in America.*

30. See, however, recent contributions such as Small, "Culture, Cohorts, and Social Organization Theory."

CHAPTER 2. CONGREGATION-BASED SOCIAL SERVICES

1. Mitchell, "Clinton Urges a Jobs Role on Churches."

2. Among adults who volunteer, 20.3 percent do so at both religious and secu-

lar organizations and contribute nearly one-third of all volunteer hours. See "Faith and Philanthropy: The Connection between Charitable Behavior and Giving to Religion," report available at www.independentsector.org.

3. Hodgkinson, Weitzman, and Kirsch, *From Belief to Commitment;* see especially p. 2 on methodology. The study included non-Christian as well as Christian congregations; no details are provided about Jewish, Muslim, and other non-Christian congregations but in all likelihood the number of such congregations included in the study was quite small.

4. Ibid., pp. 18, 23, 25.

5. Ibid., p. 18.

6. Ibid., pp. 27, 28, 44.

7. This table is derived based on tables 3.1 and 3.2 in Ibid., pp. 18, 20; size of congregation partly reflects differences between Catholic and Protestant definitions of membership; see also Ibid., p. 8, for further detail on size.

8. Ibid., p. iii.

9. Cnaan, Boddie, Handy, Yancey, and Schneider, *The Invisible Caring Hand.*

10. Ibid., pp. 299–300.

11. Ibid., pp. 60–61, 86–87; Cnaan does not report the percentages of congregations sponsoring each specific activity.

12. Ibid., pp. 64–65.

13. Ibid., pp. 71–72.

14. Ibid., p. 81.

15. Hodgkinson et al., *From Belief to Commitment,* pp. 22–23.

16. The National Congregations Survey is described in Chaves, Konieczny, Beyerlein, and Barman, "The National Congregations Study"; full conclusions from the study are presented in Chaves, *Congregations in America;* the data are available online at the American Religion Data Archive (www.thearda.com).

17. The data presented in the table are from my analysis of the National Congregations Survey.

18. The figures are not exactly comparable because *From Belief to Commitment* (p. 8) reported size based on a question that asked, "Currently, what is the estimated number of members in your congregation, that is, people who are on your membership rolls or who have made a formal commitment to belong?" whereas the National Congregations Survey figure is based on asking "How many adults—people 18 years or older—would you say regularly participate in the religious life of your congregation?"

19. Chaves, *Congregations in America,* chapter 3.

20. The *Faith Communities Today* research report is available online from the Hartford Institute for Religion Research at http://fact.hartsem.edu.

21. The numbers here differ somewhat from those reported in Chaves et al.,

"The National Congregations Study." My numbers are taken from the official counts in the 1998 General Social Survey, whereas the Chaves numbers were the best counts available at the time of the survey and do not take into account subsequent changes resulting from cleaning the data or recoding miscoded responses.

22. We should also keep in mind the possibility that when presented a list, clergy overestimate or "double count" some of their service programs.

23. These figures are from my analysis of the National Congregations Study data, excluding cases in which number of regularly participating adults was not reported.

24. Chaves et al., "National Congregations Study," p. 468.

25. U.S. Census Bureau, *Statistical Abstract of the United States: 2001* (Washington, DC: Government Printing Office, 2001), table no. 561, p. 360 (www.census.gov/prod/2002pubs/01statab); total funds from individuals based on Internal Revenue Service reports of individual charitable deductions in 2001 were $152.1 billion, of which $74.3 billion was allocated to religion. Because this counts only the charitable deductions claimed by taxpayers who do not take the standard deduction, it may significantly understate both the amount and the proportion going to churches.

26. Vallet and Zech, *The Mainline Church's Funding Crisis*, p. 3.

27. Linder, *Yearbook of American and Canadian Churches*, table 4.

28. The estimates reported here are from my analysis of data from the National Congregations Study. I used the weight provided to compensate for oversampling of larger congregations. Readers should be aware that the financial figures are affected by the relatively large number of small congregations in the study and by the large proportion of pastors who said their congregation sponsored no service programs.

29. See, for example, the discussions of "distant missions" in Bartkowski and Regis, *Charitable Choices*.

30. Cnaan et al., *Invisible Caring Hand*, pp. 88–100.

31. Chaves, *Congregations in America*, chapter 3.

32. Cnaan et al., *Invisible Caring Hand*, p. 113.

33. Chaves used a combination of denominational affiliation and leaders' perception of whether the congregation was conservative or liberal, but does not say exactly how these measures were combined; Cnaan's multiple regression models include a number of variables besides conservatism, but none of these variables (other than budget size) show significant relationships.

34. These data are from my Religion and Politics Survey, conducted in 2002. Denominational affiliation was coded on the basis of a set of questions that asked for specific detail about the denominations with which respondents were affiliated; the analysis is restricted to members; the controls for region and respon-

dents' residence serve only as general proxies for the location of the church itself (which was not asked), while the controls for respondents' attendance at religious services and level of education compensate for the possibility that regular attendees or those with higher levels of education may be more aware of the existence of congregational service programs. Odds ratios greater than 1 indicate positive relationships, and those less than 1 indicate negative relationships.

35. Food distribution appears to be so nearly universal in these data that it is as likely to be part of suburban congregations' activities as of inner-city congregations, and congregations' low-income housing programs, judging from anecdotal evidence, may be largely composed of sending volunteers to help with Habitat for Humanity projects; the controls for congregations' location here were two dummy variables, one for location in an inner-city neighborhood (as reported by members), and one for location in a suburb (the comparison category was thus location in a small town or rural area).

36. Hodgkinson et al., *From Belief to Commitment*, pp. 22–24, find that liberal theological orientation is somewhat positively associated with the likelihood of congregations sponsoring service programs, but more so on some programs than others; those results do not take account of congregation size, location, or other factors.

37. David Roozen, Hartford Seminary, personal communication, January 6, 2003.

38. Ammerman, *Pillars of Faith.*

39. This may prove particularly true for congregations with fewer educational and economic resources who seek federal funds for social ministries; see Bartkowski and Regis, *Charitable Choices*, especially chapter 8.

40. See Ammerman, *Congregation and Community*, especially pp. 43–62; and Warner, "The Place of the Congregation in the Contemporary American Religious Configuration."

CHAPTER 3. CONGREGATIONS AS CARING COMMUNITIES

1. See the discussion of congregational mutual aid in Bartkowski and Regis, *Charitable Choices,* chapter 3.

2. Chaves, *Congregations in America*, chapter 5.

3. Guth, Green, Smidt, Kellstedt, and Poloma, *The Bully Pulpit*, 82–95.

4. I discussed some of this information in my book *The Crisis in the Churches.*

5. Civic Involvement Survey, 1997; based on logistic regression of a dummy variable indicating having heard a sermon about caring, frequency of attendance is the strongest single predictor, the effect of congregation size is significant and positive, the effect of congregation's theological orientation is not significant at the

.05 level (is marginally significant in a direction indicating greater likelihood of hearing a sermon about caring in moderate or liberal congregations), and location of congregation is not significant, nor are age, race, and gender of respondents.

6. In the Religion and Politics Survey, only members were asked these questions; the additional results mentioned in the chapter are from logistic regression analysis for the three dependent variables shown in the table and including dummy variables for Hispanic, black, urban neighborhood, evangelical Protestant, black Protestant, and Catholic, and controls for frequency of attendance and size of congregation. For the two questions about the poor, the odds of Catholics having heard discussions are about 30 percent greater than the odds for mainline Protestants, and for all three questions, the odds for blacks are between 1.6 and 2.4 times greater than the odds for whites.

7. Chaves, Giesel, and Tsitsos, "Religious Variations in Public Presence"; see especially 114–17.

8. See Davidson and Koch, "Beyond Mutual and Public Benefits."

9. Chaves et al., "Religious Variations in Public Presence," 117.

10. For example, Djupe and Grant, "Religious Institutions and Political Participation in America"; see also Jones-Correa and Leal, "Political Participation."

11. Verba, Schlozman, and Brady, *Voice and Equality,* p.18.

12. Wuthnow, *Sharing the Journey.*

13. Wuthnow, "Learning Forgiveness," machine-readable data available from the author; the survey was conducted between November 1998 and February 1999 among 4,292 respondents who were identified and contacted through random-digit dialing.

14. For these comparisons, I use results from the Forgiveness Survey and the Civic Involvement Survey.

15. The criticisms are discussed in Wuthnow, "United States."

16. See, for example, Worthington, Sandage, and Berry, "Group Interventions to Promote Forgiveness"; also Krause and Ellison, "Forgiveness by God."

17. Much of the recent research literature is summarized in Worthington, *Dimensions of Forgiveness.*

18. Putnam, "Introduction," pp. 1–19 in *Democracies in Flux.* See also Putnam, *Bowling Alone.*

19. Based on the Civic Involvement Survey, these results are from logistic regression analysis of the effects on having ten or more friends in one's congregation of congregation size, theological orientation of congregation, frequency of attendance, location of congregation in an inner-city neighborhood, location of congregation in a suburb, age, race, and gender.

20. Religion and Politics Survey, conducted in 2000; my analysis of responses from 3,045 members; in this study the question about number of close friends in

the congregation was open-ended, which I why I report the median numbers; specifically, the figures are 20 for evangelical Protestants and black Protestants, 15 for mainline Protestants, and 12 for Catholics.

21. In the Religion and Politics Survey the median proportion of congregants who were close friends in small congregations (fewer than 200 members) was 25.3 percent; in medium-sized congregations (between 200 and 1,000 members), 10.0 percent; and in large congregations (more than 1,000 members), only 1.9 percent.

22. Arts and Religion Survey, 1999, N=1,530, my analysis; for instance, the respective percentages for members who have one or two close friends in their congregation and for those who have more than twenty friends are: very satisfied with the fellowship at their church, 38 percent and 72 percent; very satisfied with the sermons, 42 percent and 72 percent; very satisfied with the music, 44 percent and 71 percent; say attending services at their place of worship is very important to their spiritual growth, 49 percent and 79 percent; felt close to God while being with close friends, 35 percent and 51 percent; and go with friends from church to plays, galleries, or concerts, 32 percent and 54 percent.

23. Civic Involvement Survey; from logistic regression of saying that one could count on church members on the following variables: congregation size, theological orientation of congregation, location of congregation in inner city, location of congregation in suburb, frequency of attendance, age, race, gender, and number of close friends in congregation.

24. Ordinary least squares regression analysis for the three categories of church attendance as the dependent variable yields standardized regression coefficients of .131 for the Gregariousness Index, .213 for age, .067 for education level, and .145 for gender (female), all significant at the .01 or .001 level.

25. From ordinary least squares regression, the standardized coefficients are: for the Gregariousness Index, .119, and .115 for age, -.049 for education, and .084 for gender, all significant at the .001 or .01 level, except for education, which is not significant; these relationships also hold when frequency of church attendance is added to the model; number of close friends in the congregation in this survey was precoded into six categories ranging from none to more than twenty; to compute means, I converted the categories using midpoints of categories involving ranges (such as fifteen for "eleven to twenty").

26. See Krause, Ellison, and Wulff, "Church-Based Emotional Support, Negative Interaction, and Psychological Well-Being," and Krause, Ellison, Shaw, Marcum, and Boardman, "Church-Based Social Support and Religious Coping," respectively.

27. This was one of the findings of my research on small groups (Wuthnow, *Sharing the Journey*); in research on the relationships between faith and work, I also found that women dealt with work-related stress more often than men did by

talking with their friends (Wuthnow, *God and Mammon in America*); additionally, see Krause, Ellison, and Marcum, "Effects of Church-Based Emotional Support on Health."

28. See, for example, Pope, *Millhands and Preachers;* and Wallace, *Rockdale.*

29. For a more complete presentation of the results that are summarized in the table, see Wuthnow, "Religious Involvement and Status-Bridging Social Capital."

30. Putnam, "Social Capital Benchmark Survey, 2000, machine-readable data file.

31. An alternative interpretation may be that people who already have friends who have been on welfare or who are members of racial and ethnic minority groups are more likely to be in situations where they feel an impulse to do volunteer work (taking account of other aspects of their own social status).

32. For recent contributions to this large literature, see Hackney and Sanders, "Religiosity and Mental Health," and Smith "Theorizing Religious Effects among American Adolescents."

33. Some research has begun to explore the complex relationship between social ties (e.g., church attendance) and various religious coping measures, for example, Krause et. al., "Church-Based Social Support and Religious Coping," and Maynard, Gorsuch, and Bjorck, "Religious Coping Style, Concept of God, and Personal Religious Variables in Threat, Loss, and Challenge Situations."

34. One of the more useful empirical studies of cohort differences in American religion is Carroll and Roof, *Bridging Divided Worlds;* larger generational differences in civic responsibility are discussed in Putnam, *Bowling Alone*, especially chapter 14; other discussions of the possible consequences of generational erosion in religious commitment include Barna, *Baby Busters,* and Mahedy and Bernardi, *A Generation Alone.*

35. For the four dependent variables in the table, the regression coefficients for cohort only and for cohort controlling for being in school, being married, and having any children, respectively, are .179, .146; .078, .054 (not significant); 061 (not significant), .092 (not significant); and .106, .101.

Chapter 4. Religion and Volunteering

1. Tocqueville, *Democracy in America,* 513–17.

2. *World Values Surveys, 1997–2000* (machine-readable data file); my analysis. The data were collected from more than 118,000 randomly selected respondents in the sixty-four countries; the surveys included nearly all western European countries, many in Latin America and Africa, and many in the former Soviet Union and East Asia. Further information about the surveys, copies of the questions, and downloads of the data are available online at www.worldvaluessurvey.org.

3. Greeley, "The Other Civic America."

4. *World Values Surveys*; Pearson correlations between actively volunteering for charity and saying that religion was very important were statistically significant in forty-four of the sixty-four countries.

5. U.S. Census Bureau, *Statistical Abstract of the United States: 2002* (Washington, DC: U.S. Government Printing Office, 2002), p. 362, table 558.

6. *Public Opinion Online*, April 18, 1977, and February 7, 1991; available online from Lexis-Nexis.

7. See especially Gross, "Volunteering and the Long Civic Generation."

8. *Arts and Religion Survey, 1999* (machine-readable data file); the lower figure than in the 1991 survey may indicate a decline in volunteering, but it may also reflect differences in sampling and methodology. Further information about this survey is available in my book *All in Sync.*

9. From logistic regression analyses.

10. For example, Becker and Dhingra, "Religious Involvement and Volunteering."

11. Wuthnow, *After Heaven.*

12. Positive relationships between volunteering and measures of devotional activity similar to those discussed here have also been reported by Lam, "As the Flocks Gather."

13. *Giving and Volunteering 1996* (machine-readable data file), N=2,718; my analysis. See also Hodgkinson and Weitzman, *Giving and Volunteering in the United States.*

14. *General Social Survey, 1972–2000, Cumulative File* (machine-readable data file); my analysis. Additional information about these surveys can be found online at www.icpsr.umich.edu/GSS.

15. See Wuthnow, *Loose Connections.*

16. Described in Wuthnow and Evans, *The Quiet Hand of God.*

17. This classification scheme was developed by Steensland, Park, Regnerus, Robinson, Wilcox, and Woodberry, "The Measure of American Religion."

18. These questions followed those developed by Smith et al., *American Evangelicalism.*

19. For this analysis I relied on the first label chosen, rather than including responses to a second question that pressed them for an answer even if they preferred none; those who said "other," "none," or "don't know" are excluded.

20. Wuthnow, "Mobilizing Civic Engagement"; also Hoge, Zech, McNamara, and Donahue, "The Value of Volunteers as Resources for Congregations."

21. Wuthnow, "Mobilizing Civic Engagement"; see also Uslaner, "Religion and Civic Engagement in Canada and the United States."

22. See Park and Smith, "'To Whom Much Has Been Given. . . .'" Park and

Smith's analysis focuses on religious self-identification among churchgoing Protestants; they find that religious self-identification affects the likelihood of volunteering through a church program but not the likelihood of volunteering through a nonchurch program.

23. Previous research suggests this is particularly true with regard to philanthropy; see Rimor and Tobin, "Jewish Giving Patterns to Jewish and Non-Jewish Philanthropy."

24. A concise review and recent contribution to the literature on gender differences in religious involvement can be found in Stark, "Physiology and Faith."

25. I have written more extensively about questions of motivation in *Acts of Compassion* and *Learning to Care*.

26. The survey is described in *Acts of Compassion*.

27. The relationship between such factors and volunteering is summarized in Wilson, "Volunteering."

28. Swidler, "Culture in Action"; Swidler, *Talk of Love*.

29. Careful analysis of religious narratives in a diverse caregiving context is presented in Bender, *Heaven's Kitchen*.

30. Allahyari, *Visions of Charity*.

31. The redefinitions of self that come about through prayer have been described by Griffith, *God's Daughters*.

32. Gross, "Volunteering and the Long Civic Generation"; however, see also Wilson, "Volunteering," for studies finding an increase in hours worked among established volunteers upon their retirement.

33. Gross, "Volunteering and the Long Civic Generation."

34. Other studies have shown that low-income people rely heavily on networks of friends and families for assistance with both routine and emergency needs; see, for example, Stack, *All Our Kin*, and Newman, *No Shame in My Game*.

35. See Wilson and Musick, "Who Cares?" This research found that although formal volunteering was positively influenced by socioeconomic status, informal helping was primarily determined by age, gender, and health status.

36. Musick, Wilson, and Bynum, "Race and Formal Volunteering." For a related discussion of socioeconomic status differences in church volunteering, see Schwadel, "Testing the Promise of the Churches."

CHAPTER 5. FAITH-BASED SERVICE ORGANIZATIONS

1. For an overview of the literature and an annotated bibliography, see Scott, "The Scope and Scale of Faith-Based Social Services," available online at www.religionandsocialpolicy.org.

2. See chapter 9.

3. Besides material from other studies, I draw in this chapter on sixty-eight interviews with service agency directors that my research team conducted between 1996 and 2003. The interviews lasted from one and a half hours to three hours and included open-ended questions about agency programs, funding, clients, relationships with other agencies and churches, and changes in the community. Some of the directors were interviewed several times during these years in order to obtain a sense of change in their organizations.

4. IRS figures are available at www.guidestar.com.

5. The financial figures are for 1999, as reported by the National Center for Charitable Statistics (www.nccs.urban.org).

6. Seley and Wolpert, "Secular and Faith-Based Human Services."

7. I address the question of finances later in the chapter; the relatively small proportion of service providers that appear to be faith-based in Seley and Wolpert's research is consistent with the conclusion drawn by Campbell, "Beyond Charitable Choice"; Campbell writes, "Overall, faith-related organizations are still minor players, dwarfed by secular nonprofit service delivery, private contractors, and by the government itself" (p. 223). A study conducted by the General Accounting Office in 2002 found that only 8 percent of Temporary Assistance for Needy Families funds were being administered by faith-based organizations; the study, however, did not explain how faith-based organizations were identified (United States General Accounting Office, "Charitable Choice: Federal Guidance on Statutory Provisions Could Improve Consistency of Implementation," September 2002, Report GAO-02-887).

8. Green and Sherman, "Fruitful Collaborations"; the scale of religious intensity used by Green and Sherman is similar to that suggested in Unruh and Sider, "Religious Elements of Faith-Based Social Service Programs."

9. This conclusion (that only one-quarter of faith-based organizations are highly expressive about faith and that another quarter or so are fairly expressive) is similar to the findings presented in Monsma, *When Sacred and Secular Mix*, where a survey of 113 faith-based providers of services to children and families showed that one-quarter rated high on a religious practices scale.

10. Smith and Sosin, "The Varieties of Faith-Related Agencies."

11. This conclusion is also emphasized in Rock, "Stepping Out on Faith."

12. These and additional numeric summaries of Salvation Army programs can be found at www.salvationarmyusa.org.

13. Ibid.

14. Ibid.

15. Winston, *Red-Hot and Righteous*.

16. Allahyari, *Visions of Charity*, especially chapter 4.

17. Regional variations in Catholic Charities activities are described in Loconte, "Anxious Samaritan."

18. A study of such coalitions in the Houston area is presented in Pipes and Ebaugh, "Faith-Based Coalitions."

19. This is consistent with Pipes and Ebaugh's findings (ibid.) that most coalition directors indicated discomfort in talking about spiritual matters with a client unless the client initiated the discussion.

20. Quoted in DiIulio, "Three Faith Factors," 54.

21. Colson, "Statement on Faith-Based Initiatives," www.breakpoint.org.

22. Batty, "National Institute on Drug Abuse Report," summary available online at www.teenchallenge.com/main/studies.

23. Petersen, "Teen Challenge International: A White Paper."

24. Ibid., 6.

25. Johnson, "Assessing the Impact of Religious Programs and Prison Industry on Recidivism."

26. Sherman, "Implementing 'Charitable Choice,'" online at www.philanthropyroundtable.org.

27. Campbell, "Beyond Charitable Choice," 224.

28. Boston's Ten Point Coalition was established in 1992 as a collaborative partnership between black churches and Boston police. Harvard sociologist Christopher Winship has studied the subsequent trends in youth violence; see Berrien and Winship, "Should We Have Faith in the Churches?"

29. Zald, *Organizational Change;* Chambre, "Changing Nature of 'Faith' in Faith-Based Organizations."

30. Relatively little has been written about the administration of faith-based service agencies, but see Jeavons, *When the Bottom Line Is Faithfulness;* on non-profit management more generally, the issues I emphasize here are similar to those discussed in Young, "Executive Leadership in Nonprofit Organizations."

31. For a discussion of the broader climate urging the increased use of effectiveness measures among nonprofits, see Ryan, "New Landscape for Nonprofits."

32. See Barman, "Asserting Difference"; this case study concludes that competition for financial resources may encourage such differentiation among nonprofits, and that "facing a densely occupied market, nonprofits will claim to be different and distinct from rivals" (p. 1215).

33. This conclusion is consistent with the research presented in Netting, "Church-related Agencies and Social Welfare."

34. Sherman, "Fruitful Collaboration between Government and Christian Social Ministries."

CHAPTER 6. THE RECIPIENTS OF SOCIAL SERVICES

1. The data presented in table 6.3 are based on calculations from the March 2001 Annual Demographic Survey, table 2 (ferret.bls.census.gov/macro/032001/pov/new02_00.htm).

2. Other studies of low-income families, for example, suggest that many depend on friends and family for help with needs such as child care, transportation, home health care, or financial assistance; see Newman, *No Shame in My Game,* and Edin and Lein, *Making Ends Meet.*

3. The figures reported are from my analysis of Wilson's Urban Poverty and Family Life Survey. The data are available from the Interuniversity Consortium for Social and Political Research (ICPSR) at the University of Michigan. The percentages that reported attending religious services once a week or more in Wilson's study varied by gender and race but on the whole were similar to those in national studies; specifically, 27 percent of non-Hispanic white women, 36 percent of African American women, 40 percent of Puerto Rican women, 53 percent of Mexican American women, 20 percent of African American men, 26 percent of Puerto Rican men, 27 percent of non-Hispanic white men, and 42 percent of Mexican American men.

4. Data from the Urban Poverty and Family Life Study is discussed at length in Wilson, *When Work Disappears.*

5. Often referred to as the "deprivation hypothesis" about religion, this argument was emphasized more a generation ago among scholars of religion than it has been recently; see, for example, Glock and Stark, *Religion and Society in Tension,* chapter 13.

6. For example, some research among African Americans suggests that lower-income persons exhibit stronger denominational loyalties and rely more heavily on measures of spiritual comfort; see Chatters, Taylor, and Lincoln, "African American Religious Participation."

7. See, for example, Smith, "Churches and the Urban Poor."

8. I used the "reltrad" classification variable, which is described in Steensland, Park, Regnerus, Robinson, Wilcox, and Woodberry, "Measure of American Religion."

9. In addition, mainline Protestants have lower birthrates and black Protestants higher birthrates; see Park and Reimer, "Revisiting the Social Sources of American Christianity."

10. For a recent review of this literature, see Small and Newman, "Urban Poverty after 'The Truly Disadvantaged.'"

11. Compared to the lowest-income group in the Lehigh Valley Survey, Kathryn Edin and Laura Lein found somewhat similar instances of hardship in

their study of low-income single mothers: Among welfare-reliant and wage-reliant mothers respectively, 31 and 24 percent had run out of food, 7 and 39 percent had been unable to obtain or pay for medical treatment, 34 and 36 percent had gone without a phone or had had phone service disconnected, and 17 and 17 percent had experienced disconnected utilities; see *Making Ends Meet*, p. 113.

12. Results from OLS regression of the total number of serious problems experienced by income (in thousand dollars), education (in years), number of children in household, gender, a dummy variable for female-headed households with children, dummy variables for two categories of age, language, black, Hispanic, average income of census tract, and tract-level unemployment rate. For a more detailed examination of these data, see Wuthnow, Hackett, and Hsu, "Effectiveness and Trustworthiness of Faith-Based and Other Service Organizations."

13. Other research among low-income persons has similarly found education to be positively associated with increased participation in community organizations and social networks in general; see Rankin and Quane, "Neighborhood Poverty and the Social Isolation of Inner-City African American Families."

14. The same variables as in the previous multiple regression model were included in the analysis.

15. See, for example, Breger et al., "In Good Faith," especially pp. 12–15. Available online at www.pewforum.org.

16. This conclusion is emphasized in Wineburg, *A Limited Partnership*. In addition, Edin and Lein found that 31 percent of welfare-reliant mothers in their study had received some form of "agency-based" assistance (from sources such as private charities) including direct financial assistance for rent or utilities, vouchers for food or clothing, and student loans or grants averaging $117 monthly; see *Making Ends Meet*, chapter 6

17. Based on logistic regression analysis of models for selecting each kind of organization as the dependent variable and including the following as independent variables: female, black, Hispanic, age, income, education, kids, number of problems experienced, having received informal support, and church attendance.

18. See Black, "Poverty and Prayer."

CHAPTER 7. PROMOTING SOCIAL TRUST

1. Bies and Tripp, "Beyond Distrust."

2. For instance, see Bahr and Houts, "Can You Trust a Homeless Man?"

3. In the social scientific literature on trust, the inherent complexity of the concept has often been reduced by situating discussions within the hypothetical contexts of game theory; for instance, Bacharach and Gambetta, "Trust in Signs." Organizational theorists, however, have increasingly supplemented rational-choice

theories with discussions of the social and emotional dimensions of trust; see Kramer, "Trust and Distrust in Organizations." For present purposes, I want to consider trust in the real-life contexts in which caregivers and recipients experience it and talk about it.

4. For a recent review, see Levi and Stoker, "Political Trust and Trustworthiness."

5. From quite different perspectives, this argument is made in Coleman, *Foundations of Social Theory,* chapters 5, 8; Putnam, *Making Democracy Work;* Fukuyama, *Trust;* and Seligman, *Problem of Trust.*

6. Lewis and Weigert, "Trust as Social Reality."

7. Chanley, Rudolph, and Rahn, "Origins and Consequences of Public Trust in Government."

8. Putnam, *Bowling Alone,* chapter 8.

9. I have discussed the wider literature on trust and civil society in my book *Loose Connections,* chapter 8.

10. The most comprehensive review and analysis of survey data about trust is Uslaner, *Moral Foundations of Trust.*

11. See Ross, Mirowsky, and Pribesh, "Powerlessness and the Amplification of Threat."

12. See Hardin, *Trust and Trustworthiness,* chapter 4.

13. Similarly, organizational theorists have suggested that trustworthiness is primarily determined by the trusted party's perceived ability, benevolence, and integrity; see Mayer, Davis, and Schoorman, "An Integrative Model of Organizational Trust."

14. For a more detailed examination of these data, see Wuthnow, Hackett, and Hsu, "Effectiveness and Trustworthiness of Faith-Based and Other Service Organizations."

15. Toulmin, *Uses of Argument.*

16. Related arguments about the significance of parenting and family relationships in fostering trust and cooperation have been discussed by Uslaner, *Moral Foundations of Trust,* and Fukuyama, *Great Disruption.*

17. For examples of the effects of bereavement, see Davidman, *Motherloss.*

18. Uslaner, *Moral Foundations of Trust,* chapter 2.

19. Compare the stories here with the accounts for choosing a career that I describe in my book *Poor Richard's Principle,* chapters 4 and 5.

20. Recent research in congregational studies has even identified a "family" congregational model that emphasizes love, support, and close ties among all members; see Becker, "Congregational Models and Conflict."

21. See, for example, Smith, "Factors Relating to Misanthropy in Contemporary American Society."

22. Analysis of these rituals of routine interaction was of course the stock-in-

trade of Erving Goffman's sociology, for instance, *Presentation of Self in Everyday Life.*

23. Examples can be found in my book *Growing Up Religious.*

CHAPTER 8. EXPERIENCING UNLIMITED LOVE?

1. See discussions such as Jencks, "Varieties of Altruism," and Cohen, "Altruism and the Evolution of Civil Society."

2. See Bahr and Bahr, "Families and Self-Sacrifice," and Kagan, "Morality, Altruism, and Love."

3. For a recent overview of the literature, see Post, Underwood, Schloss, and Hurlbut, eds., *Altruism and Altruistic Love;* within social science, one of the first contributions that continues to be heavily referenced is Sorokin, *Ways and Power of Love.*

4. Monroe, *Heart of Altruism,* is an excellent example of research on rescuers that illustrates the paucity of information about the perceptions of those who are rescued.

5. Social scientists, for example, have increasingly rejected a stark dichotomy between self-interest and altruism in favor of a more nuanced continuum of varying degree; see Krebs and Van Hesteren, "Development of Altruistic Personality," Monroe, "A Fat Lady in a Corset."

6. In emphasizing the cultural shaping of love, I follow the important sociological work of Swidler, *Talk of Love.*

7. The significance of sacrificial love in families is evidenced by recent studies inspired by concerns for its perceived decline; see Browning, Miller-McLemore, Couture, Lyon, and Franklin, *From Culture Wars to Common Ground.*

8. The complex origins of altruistic commitments are examined in great depth by Daloz, Keen, Keen, and Parks, *Common Fire.*

9. This meaning of respect is similar to that in Sennett, *Respect in a World of Inequality.*

10. Wolfe, *Moral Freedom.*

11. Bellah, Madsen, Sullivan, Swidler, and Tipton, *Habits of the Heart;* Nolan, *Therapeutic State;* Rieff, *Triumph of the Therapeutic.*

12. Such consequences of professional norms in social services are discussed by Glenn, *Ambiguous Embrace,* chapters 5 and 7, and Cnaan, Wineburg, and Boddie, *Newer Deal,* chapter 4.

13. On the importance of internalized religious narratives, see Post, *Spheres of Love,* especially chapter 7.

14. See also Post, "Tradition of Agape."

15. Geertz, *Interpretation of Cultures,* p. 90.

16. See, for example, Lipset, *American Exceptionalism.*

17. See Cnaan, *Newer Deal,* chapter 4, and Glenn, *Ambiguous Embrace,* chapter 7.

18. Steensland, "Failed Welfare Revolution."

19. Wuthnow, *Acts of Compassion.*

20. Such arguments are discussed in Cnaan, *Newer Deal,* especially chapter 7.

CHAPTER 9. PUBLIC POLICY AND CIVIL SOCIETY

1. Pew Research Center for the People and the Press, *2002 Religion and Public Life Survey* (machine-readable data file), available online at http://people-press.org/dataarchive; see also the Pew Research Center's *Americans Struggle with Religion's Role at Home and Abroad* (March 20, 2002), online at http://people-press.org/reports.

2. My analysis of the *2002 Religion and Public Life Survey,* weighted data.

3. Other research suggests that African American congregations are more likely than white congregations to be engaged in service activities directed at underprivileged members of nearby communities; see Chaves and Higgins, "Comparing the Community Involvement of Black and White Congregations."

4. Similarly, other studies have found a positive relationship between biblical conservatism and support for economic redistribution policies intended to help the poor; see Pyle, "Faith and Commitment to the Poor," and Clydesdale, "Toward Understanding the Role of Bible Beliefs and Higher Education in American Attitudes toward Eradicating Poverty."

5. In the National Congregations Study, African American pastors were significantly more likely than white pastors to say they would consider applying for government funding under the Charitable Choice provision; see Chaves, "Religious Congregations and Welfare Reform."

6. In logistic regression analyses of support for government funding of church-based programs in which all the independent variables shown in table 9.2 are included, the coefficients for favoring the Christian conservative movement are the only ones that are significant for the respondents in all four columns.

7. Emerson and Smith, *Divided by Faith.*

8. Milbank, "Religious Right Finds Its Center in Oval Office"; Will, "African American Inroads for the GOP."

9. Twelve percent of African Americans who were very favorable to the Christian conservative movement said they had voted for Bush in 2000, compared with 3 percent of those who were mildly favorable or opposed to the Christian conservative movement.

10. Among the many sources on the Christian conservative movement, see

especially Martin, *With God on Our Side;* and Green, Rozell, and Wilcox, eds., *Christian Right in American Politics.*

11. Hunter, *Culture Wars,* describes many of the issues that set conservative Christians apart from the rest of the public, but curiously does not discuss social welfare policies.

12. Dionne, "A Shift Looms"

13. Rosin, "Applying Personal Faith to Public Policy."

14. Foer and Lizza, "Holy War."

15. Leonard, "Black Clergy Back Bush Initiative."

16. The items in the table from 2001 are from the 2001 Religion and Politics Survey conducted by the Pew Research Center for the People and the Press; the results are from my own analysis; the data are available from the Pew Research Center's Web site, as is an accompanying report, "Faith-Based Funding Backed, but Church-State Doubts Abound" (April 10, 2001), http://people-press.org/reports.

17. See Regnerus, Smith, and Sikkink, "Who Gives to the Poor?"

18. Cooperman, "Faith-Based Charities May Not Be Better, Study Indicates."

19. For a discussion of the marginalized origins and potential influence of the Christian Right see Hopson and Smith, "Changing Fortunes."

20. This is also emphasized by Steinfels, "Holy Waters."

21. Niebuhr, *Social Sources of Denominationalism.*

22. See, for example, Sider and Unruh, "No Aid to Religion?"

23. Jeavons, "Public Services? Private Faith?"

SELECT BIBLIOGRAPHY

Allahyari, Rebecca Anne. *Visions of Charity: Volunteer Workers and Moral Community*. Berkeley: University of California Press, 2000.

Ammerman, Nancy Tatom. *Congregation and Community*. New Brunswick, NJ: Rutgers University Press, 1997.

———. *Pillars of Faith: American Congregations and Their Partners Serving God and Serving the World*. New Brunswick, NJ: Rutgers University Press, 2004.

Axinn, June, and Mark J. Stern. *Social Welfare: A History of the American Response to Need*. 5th ed. Boston: Allyn and Bacon, 2001.

Bacharach, Michael, and Diego Gambetta. "Trust in Signs." Russell Sage Working Paper, Russell Sage Foundation, New York, 1997.

Bahr, Howard M., and Kathleen S. Bahr. "Families and Self-Sacrifice: Alternative Models and Meanings for Family Theory." *Social Forces* 79, no. 4 (2001): 1231–58.

Bahr, Howard. M., and Kathleen C. Houts. "Can You Trust a Homeless Man? A Comparison of Official Records and Interview Responses by Bowery Men." *Public Opinion Quarterly* 35, no. 3 (1971): 374–82.

Barman, Emily A. "Asserting Difference: The Strategic Response of Nonprofit Organizations to Competition." *Social Forces* 80, no. 4 (2002): 1191–1222.

Barna, George. *Baby Busters: The Disillusioned Generation*. Chicago: Northfield Publishing, 1994.

Bartkowski, John P., and Helen A. Regis. *Charitable Choices: Religion, Race, and Poverty in the Post-Welfare Era*. New York: New York University Press, 2003.

Batty, Dave. "National Institute on Drug Abuse Report." Teen Challenge, Inc., 2000.

Becker, Penny Edgell. "Congregational Models and Conflict: A Study of How Institutions Shape Organizational Process." In *Sacred Companies: Organizational Aspects of Religion and Religious Aspects of Organizations*, edited by N. J. Demerath III, Peter Dobkin Hall, Terry Schmitt, and Rhys H. Williams, pp. 231–55. New York: Oxford University Press, 1998.

Becker, Penney Edgell, and Pawan H. Dhingra. "Religious Involvement and Volunteering: Implications for Civil Society." *Sociology of Religion* 62, no. 3 (2001): 315–35.

Bellah, Robert N., Richard Madsen, William M. Sullivan, Ann Swidler, and Steven M. Tipton. *Habits of the Heart : Individualism and Commitment in American Life*. Rev. ed. Berkeley: University of California Press, 1996.

Bender, Courtney. *Heaven's Kitchen: Living Religion at God's Love We Deliver*. Chicago: University of Chicago Press, 2003.

Berrien, Jenny, and Christopher Winship. "Should We Have Faith in the Churches? The Ten Point Coalition's Effect on Boston's Youth Violence." In *Securing Our Children's Future: New Approaches to Juvenile Justice and Youth Violence*, edited by Gary S. Katzmann, pp. 200–224. Washington, DC: Brookings Institution Press, 2002.

Bies, Robert, and Thomas Tripp. "Beyond Distrust: 'Getting Even' and the Need for Revenge." In *Trust in Organizations: Frontiers of Theory and Research*, edited by Roderick Moreland Kramer and Tom R. Tyler, pp. 246–60. Thousand Oaks, CA: Sage Publications, 1996.

Black, Helen K. "Poverty and Prayer: Spiritual Narratives of Elderly African-American Women." *Review of Religious Research* 40, no. 4 (1999): 359–74.

Breger, Marshall, Stanley Carlson-Thies, Robert A. Destro, Richard T. Foltin, Murray Friedman, Nancy Isserman, John A. Liekweg, Forest D. Montgomery, Melissa Rogers, Duane Shank, Julie Segal, Jeffrey Sinensky, Stephen Steinlight, and Heidi Unruh. "In Good Faith: A Dialogue on Government Funding of Faith-Based Social Services." Pew Charitable Trusts, Washington, DC: 1999.

Browning, Don S., Bonnie J. Miller-McLemore, Pamela D. Couture, K. Brynolf Lyon, and Robert M. Franklin. *From Culture Wars to Common Ground: Religion and the American Family Debate*. Louisville, KY: Westminster John Knox Press, 1997.

Bruce, Steve, ed. *Religion and Modernization: Sociologists and Historians Debate the Secularization Thesis*. New York: Oxford University Press, 1992.

Bush, George W. "Rallying the Armies of Compassion." White House, Washington, DC, January 2001.

Campbell, David. "Beyond Charitable Choice: The Diverse Service Delivery Approaches of Local Faith-Related Organizations." *Nonprofit and Voluntary Sector Quarterly* 31, no. 2 (2002): 207–30.

Carroll, Jackson W., and Wade Clark Roof. *Bridging Divided Worlds: Generational Cultures in Congregations*. San Francisco: Jossey-Bass, 2002.

Casanova, José. *Public Religions in the Modern World*. Chicago: University of Chicago Press, 1994.

Cerulo, Karen A., ed. *Culture in Mind: Toward a Sociology of Culture and Cognition*. New York: Routledge, 2002.

Chambre, Susan M. "The Changing Nature of 'Faith' in Faith-Based Organizations: Secularization and Ecumenicism in Four AIDS Organizations in New York City." *Social Service Review* 75, no. 3 (2001): 435–55.

Chanley, Virginia A., Thomas J. Rudolph, and Wendy M. Rahn. "The Origins and Consequences of Public Trust in Government: A Time Series Analysis." *Public Opinion Quarterly* 64, no. 3 (2000): 239–56.

Chatters, Linda M., Robert Joseph Taylor, and Karen D. Lincoln. "African American Religious Participation: A Multi-Sample Comparison." *Journal for the Scientific Study of Religion* 38, no. 1 (1999): 132–45.

Chaves, Mark. *Congregations in America*. Cambridge, MA: Harvard University Press, 2004.

———. "Religious Congregations and Welfare Reform: Who Will Take Advantage of 'Charitable Choice'?" *American Sociological Review* 64, no. 6 (1999): 836–46.

Chaves, Mark, Helen M. Giesel, and William Tsitsos. "Religious Variations in Public Presence: Evidence from the National Congregations Study." In *The Quiet Hand of God : Faith-Based Activism and the Public Role of Mainline Protestantism*, edited by Robert Wuthnow and John Hyde Evans, pp. 108–28. Berkeley: University of California Press, 2002.

Chaves, Mark, and Lynn M. Higgins. "Comparing the Community Involvement of Black and White Congregations." *Journal for the Scientific Study of Religion* 31, no. 4 (1992): 425–40.

Chaves, Mark, Mary Ellen Konieczny, Kraig Beyerlein, and Emily A. Barman. "The National Congregations Study: Background, Methods, and Selected Results." *Journal for the Scientific Study of Religion* 38, no. 4 (1999): 458–76.

Clydesdale, Timothy T. "Toward Understanding the Role of Bible Beliefs and Higher Education in American Attitudes toward Eradicating Poverty, 1964–1996." *Journal for the Scientific Study of Religion* 38, no. 1 (1999): 103–18.

Cnaan, Ram A., with Stephanie C. Boddie, Femida Handy, Gaynor Yancey, and Richard Schneider. *The Invisible Caring Hand: American Congregations and the Provision of Welfare*. New York: New York University Press, 2002.

Cnaan, Ram A., with Robert J. Wineburg, and Stephanie C. Boddie. *The Newer Deal: Social Work and Religion in Partnership*. New York: Columbia University Press, 1999.

Cohen, Jean L., and Andrew Arato. *Civil Society and Political Theory, Studies in Contemporary German Social Thought*. Cambridge, MA: MIT Press, 1992.

Cohen, Ronald. "Altruism and the Evolution of Civil Society." In *Embracing the Other: Philosophical, Psychological, and Historical Perspectives on Altruism*, edited by Pearl M. Oliner, Samuel P. Oliner, Lawrence Baron, Lawrence A. Blum, Dennis L. Krebbs, and M. Zuzanna Smolenska, pp. 104–29. New York: New York University Press, 1992.

Coleman, James S. *Foundations of Social Theory*. Cambridge, MA: Harvard University Press, 1990.

Colson, Charles. "A Statement on Faith-Based Initiatives." *Breakpoint*, May 22, 2001.

Cooperman, Alan. "Faith-Based Charities May Not Be Better, Study Indicates." *Washington Post*, May 25, 2003, A7.

Daloz, Laurent A. Parks, Cheryl H. Keen, James P. Keen, and Sharon Daloz Parks. *Common Fire: Leading Lives of Commitment in a Complex World*. Boston: Beacon Press, 1996.

Davidman, Lynn. *Motherloss*. Berkeley: University of California Press, 2000.

Davidson, James D., and Jerome R. Koch. "Beyond Mutual and Public Benefits: The Inward and Outward Orientations of Non-Profit Organizations." In *Sacred Companies: Organizational Aspects of Religion and Religious Aspects of Organizations*, edited by N. J. Demerath III, Peter Dobkin Hall, Terry Schmitt, and Rhys H. Williams, pp. 292–306. New York: Oxford University Press, 1998.

Day, Phyllis J. *A New History of Social Welfare*. 4th ed. Boston: Pearson Education, 2003.

DiIulio, John J. Jr., "The Three Faith Factors." *Public Interest* 149 (2002): 50–64.

DiMaggio, Paul J., and Walter W. Powell. "The Iron Cage Revisited—Institutional Isomorphism and Collective Rationality in Organizational Fields." *American Sociological Review* 48, no. 2 (1983): 147–60.

Dionne, E. J. Jr., "A Shift Looms: The President Sees Consensus while Religious Leaders Disagree about the Church-State Divide." *Washington Post*, October 3, 1999, B1.

Djupe, Paul A., and J. Tobin Grant. "Religious Institutions and Political Participation in America." *Journal for the Scientific Study of Religion* 40, no. 2 (2001): 303–14.

Edin, Kathryn, and Laura Lein. *Making Ends Meet: How Single Mothers Survive Welfare and Low-Wage Work*. New York: Russell Sage Foundation, 1997.

Emerson, Michael O. and Christian Smith. *Divided by Faith: Evangelical Religion and the Problem of Race in America*. New York: Oxford University Press, 2000.

Foer, Franklin, and Ryan Lizza. "Holy War." *New Republic*, April 2, 2001, 14–16.

Fukuyama, Francis. *The Great Disruption: Human Nature and the Reconstitution of Social Order*. New York: Free Press, 1999.

———. *Trust: Social Virtues and the Creation of Prosperity*. New York: Free Press, 1995.

Gallup, George Jr., and D. Michael Lindsay. *Surveying the Religious Landscape: Trends in U.S. Beliefs*. Harrisburg, PA: Morehouse Pub., 1999.

Geertz, Clifford. *The Interpretation of Cultures*. New York: Basic Books, 1973.

Gilman, Michele Estrin. "'Charitable Choice' and the Accountability Challenge: Reconciling the Need for Regulation with the First Amendment Religion Clauses." *Vanderbilt Law Review* 55 (April 2002): 799–888.

Glenn, Charles Leslie. *The Ambiguous Embrace: Government and Faith-Based Schools and Social Agencies*. Princeton, NJ: Princeton University Press, 2000.

Glock, Charles Y., and Rodney Stark. *Religion and Society in Tension*. Chicago: Rand McNally, 1965.

Goffman, Erving. *The Presentation of Self in Everyday Life*. Garden City, NY: Doubleday, 1959.

Greeley, Andrew. "The Other Civic America: Religion and Volunteering." *The American Prospect* 32 (1997): 68–73.

Green, John Clifford, Mark J. Rozell, and Clyde Wilcox, eds. *The Christian Right in American Politics: Marching to the Millennium*. Washington, DC: Georgetown University Press, 2003.

Green, John C., and Amy L. Sherman. "Fruitful Collaborations: A Survey of Government-Funded Faith-Based Programs in 15 States." Hudson Institute, Washington, DC, 2002.

Griffith, R. Marie. *God's Daughters: Evangelical Women and the Power of Submission*. Berkeley: University of California Press, 1997.

Gross, Kristin A. "Volunteering and the Long Civic Generation." *Nonprofit and Voluntary Sector Quarterly* 28, no. 4 (1999): 378–415.

Guth, James L., John C. Green, Corwin E. Smidt, Kyman A. Kellstedt, and Margaret M. Poloma. *The Bully Pulpit: The Politics of Protestant Clergy*. Lawrence: University of Kansas Press, 1997.

Hackney, Charles H., and Glenn S. Sanders. "Religiosity and Mental Health: A Meta-Analysis of Recent Studies." *Journal for the Scientific Study of Religion* 42, no. 1 (2003): 43–55.

Hardin, Russell. *Trust and Trustworthiness*. New York: Russell Sage Foundation, 2002.

Hart, Stephen. *What Does the Lord Require? How American Christians Think about Economic Justice*. New York: Oxford University Press, 1992.

Hodgkinson, Virginia Ann, and Murray Weitzman. *Giving and Volunteering in the United States: Findings from a National Survey.* 1996 ed. Washington, DC: Independent Sector, 1996.

Hodgkinson, Virginia Ann, Murray S. Weitzman, and Arthur D. Kirsch. *From Belief to Commitment: The Activities and Finances of Religious Congregations in the United States; Findings from a National Survey.* 1988 ed. Washington, DC: Independent Sector, 1988.

Hoge, Dean R., Charles Zech, Patrick McNamara, and Michael J. Donahue. "The Value of Volunteers as Resources for Congregations." *Journal for the Scientific Study of Religion* 37, no. 3 (1998): 470–80.

Hopson, Ronald E. and Donald R. Smith. "Changing Fortunes: An Analysis of Christian Right Ascendance within American Political Discourse." *Journal for the Scientific Study of Religion* 38, no. 1 (1999): 1–13.

Hunter, James Davison. *Culture Wars: The Struggle to Define America.* New York: Basic Books, 1991.

Inglehart, Ronald and Wayne E. Baker. "Modernization, Cultural Change, and the Persistence of Traditional Values." *American Sociological Review* 65, no. 1 (2000): 19–51.

Jeavons, Thomas H. "Public Services? Private Faith? What Should the Role of Religion Be in the Provision of Social Services?" Paper presented at the Independent Sector Spring Research Forum, Bethesda, Maryland, March 7, 2003.

———. *When the Bottom Line Is Faithfulness: Management of Christian Service Organizations.* Bloomington: Indiana University Press, 1994.

Jencks, Christopher. "Varieties of Altruism." In *Beyond Self-Interest*, edited by Jane J. Mansbridge, pp. 53–67. Chicago: University of Chicago Press, 1990.

Johnson, Byron R. "Assessing the Impact of Religious Programs and Prison Industry on Recidivism: An Exploratory Study." *Texas Journal of Corrections* 28 (2002): 7–11.

Jones-Correa, Michael A., and David Leal. "Political Participation: Does Religion Matter?" *Political Research Quarterly* 54, no. 4 (2001): 751–71.

Kagan, Jerome. "Morality, Altruism, and Love." In *Altruism and Altruistic Love: Science, Philosophy, and Religion in Dialogue*, edited by Stephen Garrard Post, Lynn G. Underwood, Jeffrey P. Schloss, and William B. Hurlbut, pp. 40–50. New York: Oxford University Press, 2002.

Kramer, Roderick M. "Trust and Distrust in Organizations: Emerging Perspectives, Enduring Questions." *Annual Review of Psychology* 50 (1999): 569–98.

Krause, Neal, and Christopher G. Ellison. "Forgiveness by God, Forgiveness of Others, and Psychological Well-Being in Late Life." *Journal for the Scientific Study of Religion* 42, no. 1 (2003): 77–93.

Krause, Neal, Christopher G. Ellison, and Jack P. Marcum. "The Effects of

Church-Based Emotional Support on Health: Do They Vary by Gender?" *Sociology of Religion* 63, no. 1 (2002): 21–47.

Krause, Neal, Christopher G. Ellison, Benjamin A. Shaw, John P. Marcum, and Jason D. Boardman. "Church-Based Social Support and Religious Coping." *Journal for the Scientific Study of Religion* 40, no. 4 (2001): 637–56.

Krause, Neal, Christopher G. Ellison, and Keith M. Wulff. "Church-Based Emotional Support, Negative Interaction, and Psychological Well-Being: Findings from a National Sample of Presbyterians." *Journal for the Scientific Study of Religion* 37, no. 4 (1998): 725–41.

Krebs, Dennis L., and Frank Van Hesteren. "The Development of Altruistic Personality." In *Embracing the Other : Philosophical, Psychological, and Historical Perspectives on Altruism,* edited by Pearl M. Oliner, Samuel P. Oliner, Lawrence Baron, Lawrence A. Blum, Dennis L. Krebbs, and M. Zuzanna Smolenska, pp. 142–69. New York: New York University Press, 1992.

Lam, Pui-Yan. "As the Flocks Gather: How Religion Affects Voluntary Association Participation." *Journal for the Scientific Study of Religion* 41, no. 3 (2002): 405–22.

Leonard, Mary. "Black Clergy Back Bush Initiative." *Boston Globe,* March 20, 2001, A1.

Levi, Margaret, and Laura Stoker. "Political Trust and Trustworthiness." *Annual Review of Political Science* 3 (2000): 475–507.

Lewis, J. David, and Andrew Weigert. "Trust as Social Reality." *Social Forces* 63, no. 4 (1985): 967–85.

Linder, Eileen W., ed. *Yearbook of American and Canadian Churches.* Nashville: Abingdon Press, 2002.

Lipset, Seymour Martin. *American Exceptionalism: A Double-Edged Sword.* New York: W. W. Norton, 1996.

Loconte, Joe. "The Anxious Samaritan: Charitable Choice and the Mission of Catholic Charities." Center for Public Justice, Washington, DC, 2000.

Lupu, Ira C., and Robert W. Tuttle. "Government Partnerships with Faith-Based Service Providers: The State of the Law." Roundtable on Religion and Social Welfare Policy, State University of New York at Albany, 2002.

Lynn, Laurence E. "Social Services and the State: The Public Appropriation of Private Charity." *Social Service Review* 76, no. 1 (2002): 58–82.

Mahedy, William, and Janet Bernardi. *A Generation Alone: Xers Making a Place in the World.* Downers Grove, IL: Intervarsity, 1994.

Martin, William C. *With God on Our Side: The Rise of the Religious Right in America.* New York: Broadway Books, 1996.

Mayer, Roger C., James H. Davis, and F. David Schoorman. "An Integrative

Model of Organizational Trust." *Academy of Management Review* 20, no. 3 (1995): 709–34.

Maynard, Elizabeth A., Richard L. Gorsuch, and Jeffrey P. Bjorck. "Religious Coping Style, Concept of God, and Personal Religious Variables in Threat, Loss, and Challenge Situations." *Journal for the Scientific Study of Religion* 40, no. 1 (2001): 65–74.

Milbank, Dana. "Religious Right Finds Its Center in Oval Office." *Washington Post*, December 24, 2001, A2.

Mitchell, Alison. "Clinton Urges a Jobs Role on Churches." *New York Times*, September 7, 1996, 10.

Monroe, Kristen Renwick. "A Fat Lady in a Corset: Altruism and Social Theory." *American Journal of Political Science* 38, no. 4 (1994): 861–93.

———. *The Heart of Altruism: Perceptions of a Common Humanity*. Princeton, NJ: Princeton University Press, 1996.

Monsma, Stephen V. *When Sacred and Secular Mix: Religious Nonprofit Organizations and Public Money*. Lanham, MD: Rowman & Littlefield, 1996.

Musick, Marc A., John Wilson, and William B. Bynum Jr. "Race and Formal Volunteering: The Differential Effects of Class and Religion." *Social Forces* 78, no. 4 (2000): 1539–70.

Netting, Ellen F. "Church-Related Agencies and Social Welfare." *Social Service Review* 58, no. 3 (1984): 404–20.

Newman, Katherine S. *No Shame in My Game: The Working Poor in the Inner City*. New York: Alfred A. Knopf and the Russell Sage Foundation, 1999.

Niebuhr, H. Richard. *The Social Sources of Denominationalism*. New York: Henry Holt, 1929.

Nolan, James L. *The Therapeutic State: Justifying Government at Century's End*. New York: New York University Press, 1998.

Olasky, Marvin N. *The Tragedy of American Compassion*. Washington, DC: Regnery Gateway, 1992.

O'Neill, June E., and M. Anne Hill. "Gaining Ground? Measuring the Impact of Welfare Reform on Welfare and Work." Manhattan Institute, Center for Civic Innovation, New York, 2001.

Orloff, Ann Shola. *The Politics of Pensions: A Comparative Analysis of Britain, Canada, and the United States, 1880–1940*. Madison: University of Wisconsin Press, 1993.

Park, Jerry Z., and Samuel H. Reimer. "Revisiting the Social Sources of American Christianity, 1972–1998." *Journal for the Scientific Study of Religion* 41, no. 4 (2002): 733–46.

Park, Jerry Z., and Christian Smith. "'To Whom Much Has Been Given . . .':

Religious Capital and Community Voluntarism among Churchgoing Protestants." *Journal for the Scientific Study of Religion* 39, no. 3 (2000): 272–86.

Parsons, Talcott. *Talcott Parsons on Institutions and Social Evolution: Selected Writings*. Edited by Leon H. Mayhew. Chicago: University of Chicago Press, 1982.

Peterson, Douglas. "Teen Challenge International: A White Paper." Teen Challenge International USA, Washington, DC, 2001.

Pew Research Center for the People and the Press. "Faith-Based Funding Backed, but Church-State Doubts Abound." Washington, DC, 2001.

———. "Americans Struggle with Religion's Role at Home and Abroad." Washington, DC, 2002.

———. "Among Wealthy Nations U. S. Stands Alone in Its Embrace of Religion." Washington, DC, December 19, 2002.

Pipes, Paula F., and Helen Rose Ebaugh. "Faith-Based Coalitions, Social Services, and Government Funding." *Sociology of Religion* 64, no. 1 (2002): 29–68.

Pope, Liston. *Millhands and Preachers: A Study of Gastonia*. New Haven, CT: Yale University Press, 1942.

Post, Stephen Garrard. *Spheres of Love: Toward a New Ethics of the Family*. Dallas: Southern Methodist University Press, 1994.

———. "The Tradition of Agape." In *Altruism and Altruistic Love: Science, Philosophy, and Religion in Dialogue*, edited by Stephen Garrard Post, Lynn G. Underwood, Jeffrey P. Schloss, and William B. Hurlbut, pp. 51–71. New York: Oxford University Press, 2002.

Post, Stephen Garrard, Lynn G. Underwood, Jeffrey P. Schloss, and William B. Hurlbut, eds. *Altruism and Altruistic Love: Science, Philosophy, and Religion in Dialogue*. New York: Oxford University Press, 2002.

Putnam, Robert D. *Bowling Alone: The Collapse and Revival of American Community*. New York: Simon & Schuster, 2000.

———. *Making Democracy Work: Civic Traditions in Modern Italy*. Princeton, NJ: Princeton University Press, 1993.

———. "Social Capital Benchmark Survey, 2000." Storrs, CT: Roper Center, 2001.

———, ed. *Democracies in Flux: The Evolution of Social Capital in Contemporary Society*. New York: Oxford University Press, 2002.

Pyle, Ralph E. "Faith and Commitment to the Poor: Theological Orientation and Support for Government Assistance Measures." *Sociology of Religion* 54, no. 4 (1993): 385–401.

Rankin, Bruce H., and James M. Quane. "Neighborhood Poverty and the Social

Isolation of Inner-City African American Families." *Social Forces* 79, no. 1 (2000): 139–64.

Regnerus, Mark D., Christian Smith, and David Sikkink. "Who Gives to the Poor? The Influence of Religious Tradition and Political Location on the Personal Generosity of Americans toward the Poor." *Journal for the Scientific Study of Religion* 37, no. 3 (1998): 481–93.

Rieff, Philip. *The Triumph of the Therapeutic: Uses of Faith after Freud.* Chicago: University of Chicago Press, 1987.

Rimor, Mordechai, and Gary A. Tobin. "Jewish Giving Patterns to Jewish and Non-Jewish Philanthropy." In *Faith and Philanthropy in America: Exploring the Role of Religion in America's Voluntary Sector,* edited by Robert Wuthnow and Virginia A. Hodgkinson, pp. 134–64. San Francisco: Jossey-Bass, 1990.

Rock, JoAnn. "Stepping Out on Faith: New York City's Charitable Choice Demonstration Program." Roundtable on Religion and Social Welfare Policy, State University of New York, Albany, 2002.

Rosin, Hanna. "Applying Personal Faith to Public Policy." *Washington Post,* July 24, 2000, A1.

Ross, Catherine, John Mirowsky, and Shana Pribesh. "Powerlessness and the Amplification of Threat: Neighborhood Disadvantage, Disorder, and Mistrust." *American Sociological Review* 66, no. 4 (2001): 568–91.

Ryan, William P. "The New Landscape for Nonprofits." *Harvard Business Review* 77, no. 1 (1999): 127–36.

Schmidt, Steffen W., Laura Guasti, Carl H. Lande, and James C. Scott, eds. *Friends, Followers, and Factions: A Reader in Political Clientelism.* Berkeley: University of California Press, 1977.

Schwadel, Philip. "Testing the Promise of the Churches: Income Inequality in the Opportunity to Learn Civic Skills in Christian Congregations." *Journal for the Scientific Study of Religion* 41, no. 3 (2002): 565–75.

Scott, James C. *The Moral Economy of the Peasant: Rebellion and Subsistence in Southeast Asia.* New Haven, CT: Yale University Press, 1976.

Scott, Jason D. "The Scope and Scale of Faith-Based Social Services." Rockefeller Institute of Government, State University of New York, Albany, 2002.

Seib, Gerald F. "Bush and Gore Find the Faith in Social Policy." *Wall Street Journal,* July 28, 1999, A24.

Seley, John E., and Julian Wolpert. "Secular and Faith-Based Human Services: Complementarities or Competition." Paper presented at the Spring Research Conference, Independent Sector, Washington, DC, March 6–7, 2003.

Seligman, Adam B. *The Problem of Trust.* Princeton, NJ: Princeton University Press, 1997.

Sennett, Richard. *Respect in a World of Inequality.* New York: Norton, 2003.

Sherman, Amy L. "Fruitful Collaboration between Government and Christian Social Ministries." Center for Public Justice, Washington, DC, 1998.

————. "Implementing "Charitable Choice": Transcending the Separation between Church and State." *Philanthropy* January/February (1999).

Sider, Ronald J., and Heidi Rolland Unruh. "No Aid to Religion? Charitable Choice and the First Amendment." In *What's God Got to Do with the American Experiment?*, edited by E. J. Dionne Jr. and John J. DiIulio Jr., pp. 128–37. Washington, DC: Brookings Institution Press, 2000.

Skocpol, Theda. *Protecting Soldiers and Mothers: The Political Origins of Social Policy in the United States.* Cambridge, MA: Harvard University Press, 1992.

Skocpol, Theda, and Kenneth Finegold. "State Capacity and Economic Intervention in the Early New Deal." *Political Science Quarterly* 97, no. 2 (1982): 255–78.

Skowronek, Stephen. *Building a New American State: The Expansion of National Administrative Capacities, 1877–1920.* Cambridge: Cambridge University Press, 1982.

Small, Mario Luis. "Culture, Cohorts, and Social Organization Theory: Understanding Local Participation in a Latino Housing Project." *American Journal of Sociology* 108, no. 1 (2002): 1–55.

Small, Mario Luis, and Katherine S. Newman. "Urban Poverty after 'The Truly Disadvantaged': The Rediscovery of the Family, the Neighborhood, and Culture." *Annual Review of Sociology* 27 (2001): 23–45.

Smith, Christian. "Theorizing Religious Effects among American Adolescents." *Journal for the Scientific Study of Religion* 42, no. 1 (2003): 17–30.

Smith, Christian, with Michael Emerson, Sally Gallagher, Paul Kennedy, and David Sikkink. *American Evangelicalism: Embattled and Thriving.* Chicago: University of Chicago Press, 1998.

Smith, R. Drew. "Churches and the Urban Poor: Interaction and Social Distance." *Sociology of Religion* 62, no. 3 (2001): 301–13.

Smith, Steven Rathgeb, and Michael R. Sosin. "The Varieties of Faith-Related Agencies." *Public Administration Review* 61, no. 6 (2001): 651–70.

Smith, Tom W. "Factors Relating to Misanthropy in Contemporary American Society." *Social Science Research* 26, no. 2 (1997): 170–96.

Sorokin, Pitirim A. *The Ways and Power of Love: Types, Factors, and Techniques of Moral Transformation.* Boston: Beacon Press, 1954.

Spillman, Lyn, ed. *Cultural Sociology.* Malden, MA: Blackwell Publishers, 2002.

Stack, Carol B. *All Our Kin: Strategies for Survival in a Black Community.* New York: Harper & Row, 1974.

Stark, Rodney. "Physiology and Faith: Addressing the 'Universal' Gender Difference in Religious Commitment." *Journal for the Scientific Study of Religion* 41, no. 3 (2002): 495–507.

Steensland, Brian. "The Failed Welfare Revolution: Policy, Culture, and the Struggle for Guaranteed Income in the U.S." Ph.D. dissertation, Princeton University, 2002.

——. "The Hydra and the Swords: Social Welfare and Mainline Advocacy, 1964–2000." In *The Quiet Hand of God: Faith-Based Activism and the Public Role of Mainline Protestantism*, edited by Robert Wuthnow and John Hyde Evans, pp. 213–36. Berkeley: University of California Press, 2002.

Steensland, Brian, Jerry Z. Park, Mark D. Regnerus, Lynn D. Robinson, W. Bradford Wilcox, and Robert D. Woodberry. "The Measure of American Religion: Toward Improving the State of the Art." *Social Forces* 79, no. 1 (2000): 291–318.

Steinfels, Peter. "Holy Waters: Plunging into the Sea of Faith-Based Initiatives." In *Sacred Places, Civic Purposes: Should Government Help Faith-Based Charity?*, edited by E. J. Dionne and Ming Hsu Chen, pp. 327–35. Washington, DC: Brookings Institution Press, 2001.

Swedberg, Richard. *Principles of Economic Sociology*. Princeton, NJ: Princeton University Press, 2002.

Swidler, Ann. "Culture in Action: Symbols and Strategies." *American Sociological Review* 51, no. 2 (1986): 273–86.

——. *Talk of Love: How Culture Matters*. Chicago: University of Chicago Press, 2001.

Thomas, George M. *Revivalism and Cultural Change: Christianity, Nation Building, and the Market in the Nineteenth-Century United States*. Chicago: University of Chicago Press, 1989.

Tocqueville, Alexis de. *Democracy in America*. Translated by George Lawrence. Edited by J. P. Mayer and Max Lerner. 1st ed. New York,: Harper & Row, 1966.

Toulmin, Stephen Edelston. *The Uses of Argument*. Cambridge: Cambridge University Press, 1964.

Trattner, Walter I. *From Poor Law to Welfare State: A History of Social Welfare in America*. 6th ed. New York: Free Press, 1999.

Unruh, Heidi Rolland, and Ronald J. Sider. "Religious Elements of Faith-Based Social Service Programs: Types and Integrative Strategies." Paper presented at the Annual Meeting of the Society for the Scientific Study of Religion, Columbus, OH, October 2001.

Uslaner, Eric M. *The Moral Foundations of Trust*. Cambridge: Cambridge University Press, 2002.

——. "Religion and Civic Engagement in Canada and the United States." *Journal for the Scientific Study of Religion* 41, no. 2 (2002): 239–54.

Vallet, Ronald E., and Charles E. Zech. *The Mainline Church's Funding Crisis: Issues and Possibilities.* Grand Rapids, MI.: W. B. Eerdmans, 1995.

Verba, Sidney, Kay Lehman Schlozman, and Henry E. Brady. *Voice and Equality: Civic Voluntarism in American Politics.* Cambridge, MA: Harvard University Press, 1995.

Wallace, Anthony F. C. *Rockdale: The Growth of an American Village in the Early Industrial Revolution.* New York: Knopf, 1978.

Warner, R. Stephen. "The Place of the Congregation in the Contemporary American Religious Configuration." In *American Congregations*, edited by James P. Wind and James Welborn Lewis, pp. 54–99. Chicago: University of Chicago Press, 1994.

Will, George F. "African American Inroads for the GOP." *Washington Post*, April 27, 2003, 7B.

Wilson, John. "Volunteering." *Annual Review of Sociology* 26 (2000): 215–40.

Wilson, John, and Marc Musick. "Who Cares? Toward an Integrated Theory of Volunteer Work." *American Sociological Review* 62, no. 5 (1997): 694–713.

Wilson, William Julius. *When Work Disappears: The World of the New Urban Poor.* New York: Alfred A. Knopf, 1997.

Wineburg, Robert J. *A Limited Partnership: The Politics of Religion, Welfare, and Social Service.* New York: Columbia University Press, 2001.

Winston, Diane H. *Red-Hot and Righteous: The Urban Religion of the Salvation Army.* Cambridge, MA: Harvard University Press, 1999.

Wolfe, Alan. *Moral Freedom: The Search for Virtue in a World of Choice.* New York: W. W. Norton, 2001.

Worthington Everett L., Jr., *Dimensions of Forgiveness: Psychological Research and Theological Perspectives.* Philadelphia, PA: Templeton Foundation Press, 1998.

Worthington Everett L., Jr., Steven J. Sandage, and Jack W. Berry. "Group Interventions to Promote Forgiveness: What Researchers and Clinicians Ought to Know." In *Forgiveness: Theory, Research, and Practice*, edited by Michael E. McCullough, Kenneth I. Pargament, and Carl E. Thoresen, pp. 228–53. New York: Guilford Press, 2000.

Wuthnow, Robert. *Acts of Compassion: Caring for Others and Helping Ourselves.* Princeton, NJ: Princeton University Press, 1991.

——. *After Heaven: Spirituality in America since the 1950s.* Berkeley: University of California Press, 1998.

——. *All in Sync: How Music and Art Are Revitalizing American Religion.* Berkeley: University of California Press, 2003.

——. *Christianity and Civil Society: The Contemporary Debate.* Valley Forge, PA: Trinity Press International, 1996.

————. *The Crisis in the Churches: Spiritual Malaise, Fiscal Woe.* New York: Oxford University Press, 1997.

————. *God and Mammon in America.* New York: Free Press, 1994.

————. *Growing up Religious: Christians and Jews and Their Journeys of Faith.* Boston: Beacon Press, 1999.

————. "Learning Forgiveness: The Role of Small Group Ministries, a National Study." Center for the Study of Religion, Princeton University, 2001.

————. *Learning to Care: Elementary Kindness in an Age of Indifference.* New York: Oxford University Press, 1995.

————. *Loose Connections: Joining Together in America's Fragmented Communities.* Cambridge, MA: Harvard University Press, 1998.

————. "Mobilizing Civic Engagement: The Changing Impact of Religious Involvement." In *Civic Engagement in American Democracy,* edited by Theda Skocpol and Morris P. Fiorina, pp. 331–63. Washington, DC: Brookings Institution Press, 1999.

————. *Poor Richard's Principle: Recovering the American Dream through the Moral Dimension of Work, Business, and Money.* Princeton, NJ: Princeton University Press, 1996.

————. "Religious Involvement and Status-Bridging Social Capital." *Journal for the Scientific Study of Religion* 41, no. 4 (2002): 669–84.

————. *Sharing the Journey: Support Groups and America's New Quest for Community.* New York: Free Press, 1994.

————. "United States: Bridging the Privileged and the Marginalized?" In *Democracies in Flux: The Evolution of Social Capital in Contemporary Society,* edited by Robert D. Putnam, pp. 59–102. New York: Oxford University Press, 2002.

————, ed. *Between States and Markets: The Voluntary Sector in Comparative Perspective.* Princeton, NJ: Princeton University Press, 1991.

————, ed. *Vocabularies of Public Life: Empirical Essays in Symbolic Structure.* London: Routledge, 1992.

Wuthnow, Robert, and John Hyde Evans, eds. *The Quiet Hand of God: Faith-Based Activism and the Public Role of Mainline Protestantism.* Berkeley: University of California Press, 2002.

Wuthnow, Robert, Conrad Hackett, and Becky Yang Hsu. "The Effectiveness and Trustworthiness of Faith-Based and Other Service Organizations: A Study of Recipients' Perceptions." *Journal for the Scientific Study of Religion* 43, no. 1 (2004): 1–17.

Wuthnow, Robert, James Davison Hunter, Albert Bergesen, and Edith Kurzweil, eds. *Cultural Analysis: The Work of Peter L. Berger, Mary Douglas, Michel Foucault, and Jürgen Habermas.* London: Routledge & Kegan Paul, 1984.

Young, Dennis R. "Executive Leadership in Nonprofit Organizations." In *The Nonprofit Sector: A Research Handbook*, edited by Walter W. Powell, pp. 167–79. New Haven, CT: Yale University Press, 1987.

Zald, Mayer N. *Organizational Change: The Political Economy of the YMCA*. Chicago: University of Chicago Press, 1970.